THE NURSERY SCHOOL AND KINDERGARTEN

Human Relationships and Learning

Seventh Edition

THE NURSERY SCHOOL AND KINDERGARTEN

Human Relationships and Learning

KATHERINE READ
Formerly of the School of Home Economics
Oregon State University

June Patterson
Child Development Department
Connecticut College

HOLT, RINEHART AND WINSTON
New York   Chicago   San Francisco   Dallas
Montreal   Toronto   London   Sydney

Dedication to:
Maurice Baker
and
Ben F. Patterson

The authors wish to thank the following photographers for their kind permission to reproduce their photographs:

Jean Berlfein: pp. 11, 25, 27, 32, 56, 60, 115, 163, 171, 175, 179, 182, 201, 205, 219, 239, 251, 259, 288, 289, 291, 296 (bottom), 325, 338, 354
Charles Doersan, III: pp. 5, 10, 21, 31, 43, 53A, B, C, 67, 100, 104, 124, 125, 232, 265, 266, 280, 282, 306, 308, 314, 318, 348, 362, 366, 367
Susan Hollander: pp. 149, 351
Marianne Hurlbut: p. 386
Robert Overstreet: pp. 62, 349, 359
Myron Papiz: pp. 133, 342, 346
Santa Monica College: p. 18
Susan Szasz: p. 193

Library of Congress Cataloging in Publication Data

Baker, Katherine Read.
  The nursery school and kindergarten.

  Sixth ed. published in 1976 under title:
The nursery school.
  Includes bibliographies and index.
  1. Nursery schools. I. Patterson, June,
1924–   joint author. II. Title.,
LB1140.B27 1980   372.21   79–25455
ISBN 0–03–055221–4

Preface

The seventh edition of *The Nursery School* has been retitled *The Nursery School and Kindergarten*. The kindergarten age has been included in this edition because of our conviction that there is a need for continuity between a good nursery school and a kindergarten program. Learning is a continuous process. The nursey school program and day-care program should build on the learning and development of the first months and years in the home. The kindergarten program should, in turn, build on the learning and development that has taken place in the nursery school. This relationship between nursery school and kindergarten becomes critical as more and more children attend nursery school and go on to kindergarten.

Children in nursery school and kindergarten tend to approach learning in similar ways. They are both engaged in broadening their horizons, learning most from experiences in which they themselves participate actively. Young children are learning to manage impulsive behavior, to gain skill in living, and to work with others. They thrive on a close personal relationship with the teacher.

In this edition we have enlarged the section on curriculum, adding more detail and including a kindergarten program. Play continues to be emphasized as a most important mode of learning for the young child. We have continued our emphasis on understanding and guiding children's personality development, on helping them to manage their impulses constructively, and on providing opportunities for them to build satisfying social relationships. Basic to this approach is the need to understand ourselves as adults if we are to guide children wisely.

There is a tendency today to try to hasten the children's intellectual development, teaching what is more appropriate for first grade children in kindergarten or even nursery school. Pushing the children in their development may "short change" some children who are left without the background experiences for optimum learning later. The best preparation lies in completing each stage, having had as full and as rich an experience as possible, consistent with each child's own style and pace of learning. To help children develop their optimum potential, the teacher needs to be sensitive to where each child is in the process of learning and to be aware of how to support each child's learning. Every child should feel increased self-confidence because of successful learning.

Young children's needs are the same, whether at home, in day care, nursery school, or kindergarten. Young children are in a critical period of their development, physically, socially, emotionally, and intellectually. Each child is an individual, different from any other. Each child needs understanding guidance which respects the child's own rate and style of growing and learning. Each child needs a rich variety of experiences, opportunities to explore, discover, and try to make sense out of the world.

The emphasis in this book is on personality and intellectual development and on teaching as a creative process. We hope that the book will be useful to parents, students, teachers, and others who come in contact or work with young children.

We wish to express our appreciation to Baxter Venable who, as our editor at W. B. Saunders Company, inspired and generously helped in the preparation of this edition. Special thanks go to Betty Lark-Horovitz, artist and teacher, who has given us the drawings which appear at chapter headings and on the cover. To Bonnie Allison and Reggie Anderson we express our sincere appreciation for their contribution to both substance and style of the text. For thoughtful reading and comments that helped shape this edition, we are grateful to Louise McGarry, Marion Bissell, and Camille Hanlon. We are pleased to acknowledge our debt to Mildred Reardon who typed the manuscript with efficiency and good humor. Finally, we wish to express appreciation to Ruth Stark, senior project editor, Holt, Rinehart and Winston, for her skill, patience, and concern for the quality of the manuscript.

Katherine Read Baker
June Patterson

January 1980

Contents

Part One

THE SETTING

Mommy and Maya
(girl, 4.1)

Introducing the People in the School or Day-Care Center

Education shall be directed to the full development of the human personality and to strengthening of respect for human rights and fundamental freedoms. (DECLARATION OF HUMAN RIGHTS, UNITED NATIONS)

''The single most important thing in human cultural behavior is literally and specifically the way we bring up our children'' (LaBarre, 1949:211). This statement by an anthropologist points to the significance of the task of those responsible for bringing up children, whether they are parents, or teachers, or members of any other group relating to young children.

For many years there has been concern among people about meeting the needs of children. Today this concern is based on more knowledge. However, with more knowledge comes increased responsibility for providing each child with what he or she needs for sound growth. Research findings have emphasized the importance of the first year of life and the necessity of meeting adequately the physical, emotional, social, and intellectual needs of the young child.

The educational programs we shall be considering are ones conducted in nursery schools, kindergartens, and day-care centers. These are places where children learn as they play and share their day-to-day life experiences with other children, guided by adults who have an understanding of child growth and development and of the learning process. These are also places where adults learn more about human behavior and relationships as they observe and participate in the program of the school.

What is a well-conducted program of education for young children? What do teachers need to know about child growth and development and learning? What skills do they need in guiding young children? We shall be looking for answers to these and other questions—even though the answers may often be incomplete.

The material presented here is addressed to those who are beginning to teach in a nursery school, kindergarten, or day-care center, but it can also be of use to those who care for children anywhere. Young children have the same developmental needs whether they are at home or in an educational setting. Anyone working in an educational program for young children, even the most experienced teacher, needs to be learning as well as teaching: The two processes are inseparable.

The order of the material in this book does not indicate the degree of its importance. It reflects the fact that one must begin somewhere. Some matters of immediate importance appear early on and are developed later in more depth. Although one may wish to start out teaching with a great deal of knowledge and understanding, one must be content to learn at each step of the way. If one can allow oneself to learn at his or her own pace, one can be a great deal more accepting of a child learning at his or her own particular pace. The more knowledge we have, the more we realize how much there is to know. We must begin at the bottom and acquire knowledge at each new level. The going demands our best effort: It is never dull; it remains challenging; and it is always rewarding.

THE CHILDREN

A school for young children is a place where people are important. We will start by introducing the people one finds there, beginning with the children.

We Learn from the Children

We add to our knowledge of child development as we observe children. Our observations of a particular child contribute to our understanding of him or her and at the same time contribute to our understanding of children in general. Our knowledge of child development gives us a framework for observing and understanding the behavior of a child. In Chapter 8, Observing Children, we will describe a framework for observation and some ways to observe. At this point, however, we will be introduced to some children who have specific personality characteristics and behaviors, which

Children find friends at school.

will enable us to understand what may lie behind the behavior of other children, like them, whom we may meet in other schools.

Charles, Who Is Fighting To Find His Place

Charles (3.6), a rosy-cheeked, brown-eyed boy, comes running into the school in the morning, greeting the teachers and the children with enthusiasm and plunging into activity. Everything captures his attention: a new book on the table, a bird's nest brought in by one of the children, the pin on the teacher's dress, the garage of blocks that the children are building. Observed over one 50-minute period, he engaged in more than 30 activities with apparent whole-hearted interest.

He is eager to join other children in whatever they are doing and makes many attempts to get others to join him. He directs any play that he is engaged in with a flow of excellent language and a vigor and enthusiasm that overwhelms the opposition. But the other children drift away from him or reject his advances, perhaps because he cannot brook opposition. He hits or bites when blocked or even when there is no apparent provocation. He is impulsive and quick, and thus it is difficult for the teachers to keep him from attacking others. He is constantly taking things from other children. If he sees someone using a tricycle, he immediately wants it. If he sees someone swinging, he wants to use the swing himself.

He has picked up many adult verbalizations which he only partially understands. He knows that words are often used to justify acts. "I want to swing," he cries, when he sees Jill on the swing. "Why?" asks Jill reflectively. "Because I have to learn how," he answers her. He quickly gets on the tricycle that Bruce has left for a minute. When Bruce cries, "I want it," his answer is, "When people get off trikes, I have to get on and ride around."

Usually he does not wait until people get off. When he is absent with one of his rare colds, Mary's comment is, ''I'm glad. Now he won't bite me today.''

His behavior often surprises the teachers as well as the children. One morning as he started to pour a drink, he said to the teacher cheerfully, ''Do you know what I'm going to do?'' To her negative reply, he answered, ''I'm going to pour this water on the floor.'' He did just that before her startled eyes. And then, he immediately mopped it up willingly, and became absorbed in watching the way it ran down the corridor, exclaiming, ''The water doesn't wait for me.''

His observations and his approach to problems reveal an attention to detail. He enjoys stories and listens with sustained attention to an adult reading. He looks thoughtful when adults give explanations and seems to understand the reasons for requests or suggestions. One gets the impression that he can see the value of constructive ways of interacting with people, but that his own feelings get in his way and are often more than he can manage. He is eager for social contacts, but gets carried away by his impulses, and he appears genuinely sorry when he hurts another child.

Typical of Charles's behavior is the following incident. As he came on to the playground one morning he saw Bill on a tricycle. He ran to him, grasping the handlebars firmly and saying in a persuasive voice, ''Give me your trike, Bill. I want to pull you.'' Bill made no move to give up the tricycle and Charles repeated the request several times in the same persuasive tone. Then still talking, he pushed Bill off and rode away, calling back, ''I'll be right back, Bill. I'm only going to take a little ride.'' Bill ran after him and grabbed for the tricycle. Charles hit him, and the teacher had to intervene and help Bill recover his tricycle. Deprived of the tricycle, Charles threw himself on the ground, crying loudly. Suddenly he jumped up and ran to the shed where the toys were kept, calling to Bill to wait for him. He came out with another tricycle and rode after Bill, trying in vain to get Bill to play with him.

The demands for adjustment have been heavy for Charles in his home. The family has moved many times. Charles's parents think he is a difficult child to manage. They seem to expect adultlike behavior from this little boy: He has been spanked, threatened, made to sit on a chair, and reasoned with. They appear to have little understanding about what a load their expectations have been for him or how often he has been confused about what is expected. A new baby at home has complicated the situation further. Again, his parents have not recognized what the addition of the baby to the family has meant to Charles. They have succeeded in making him hide his feelings to such an extent that they report that ''he adores his baby sister and is very sweet to her.'' His biting at school is probably related to this situation at home.

Anxious to conform to adult standards, eager for friendships with children, and having strong drives and confused feelings, Charles is very much in need of guidance and quite able to profit from it. He needs to be with people who will reduce the difficulties he has to face, who will give him suggestions for solving his problems acceptably, and who will interpret the needs of others to him. Because of his intellectual capacity, his strong drives, and his physical vigor, he can be either a damaging influence or an inspiring one, depending on the guidance he is given. With the leadership qualities he possesses, he may go in either of these directions.

Janie, Who Has Had Understanding*

Janie (5.2) is a tall, attractive child with curly brown hair, who has been in the same school for two years. She usually comes to kindergarten with her grandparents who take care of her during the day while her mother works. Janie's parents were divorced four years ago when she was an infant. Her mother returned to work two years later. Janie and her seven-year-old brother visit their father, who lives a three hour's drive away, twice a month.

Janie does many things for herself and takes a great deal of pleasure in her developing independence. She uses mature language which reflects her enthusiasm for pretending and assuming roles in dramatic play, enjoyment in social conversation with her friends, and reflective thinking. She is well coordinated in movement activities and enjoys using her body in a variety of ways. She makes choices easily and selects new as well as a variety of familiar classroom activities on her own and with her friends. She is independent in solving problems with materials and equipment and usually finds solutions. She sustains her work and play over a long period of time.

Janie initiates conversations with familiar adults and asks them for necessary help. She forms relationships with new adults slowly, however, and does not reveal herself easily to adults who are unfamiliar to her. At the beginning of each school year, Janie's teacher has provided many opportunities for Janie to work with her. They have talked together about common interests. Her teacher has observed Janie as she plays and at times has participated in her play. Over time, Janie has come to trust her teacher and seems more able to initiate contacts with her.

Janie approaches other children easily and is accepted enthusiastically by them. She has many interesting ideas for dramatic play which other children find attractive. She takes turns and shares easily with others. Janie is usually able to resolve conflicts in mutually acceptable ways with other children who are also able to do so. Yet, she can assert herself adamantly when other children infringe on her rights. For example, when one particular aggressive boy stepped on her tray of assorted buttons during a classification game, she asked that child with annoyance: "How would you like it if you had a tray of buttons and someone stepped on it?" Disarmed by her comment, the other child immediately withdrew sheepishly.

Janie is well organized in her approach to using materials and equipment, and she enjoys practicing and perfecting her skills. Dramatic play is one of her favorite activities. She participates in rich, complex interactive play with

* Recorded by Reggie Anderson

other children. She enjoys playing a variety of roles which often reflect well-organized ideas about her environment. For example, one day Janie appeared to be playing the role of another child's mother in a housekeeping setting. She was sitting at a table "eating" when she held up a pair of toy handcuffs and started talking to her "child" about them. Her teacher, who had been observing the play off and on, was surprised to see the handcuffs, and she remarked to Janie that she thought she was playing a mommy. Janie turned to her teacher and very matter-of-factly clarified, "Yes, but I'm a *police* girl, too!"

Janie is a resourceful and competent child with much confidence in her own abilities. She is cautious with new adults, but with the assistance of a warm and giving teacher, she has learned to trust familiar adults. Without actively leading, Janie is a strong force in the group.

Juan, Who Watches Others

Juan (4.1) is a beautiful, dark-eyed boy who gravely watches what goes on around him in the day-care center. Juan's mother was very glad when he was ready to enter the center. From the time he was an infant, she had been taking him with her when she went out to do housework in various homes. He had been a good baby and cried very little. Nonetheless, it had not been easy for her to manage, because she was alone and was supporting herself and the child. As Juan grew older, he played quietly or watched her as she worked. He understood that he was not to touch the things around him or to disturb other people. By the time he had reached the age of four, his mother felt that he needed to be with other children and to start learning more than she could teach him. She had already tried to teach him letters, without much success. She was relieved when she found that the center would accept Juan.

When Juan began day care, he was able to let his mother leave after the first day. He made no protest. But now, after several weeks in the center, he is still a "watcher." He seems interested in what the other children do, but when they approach him or make an effort to draw him into play, he smiles shyly and withdraws. He seems bewildered and prefers to play alone.

Juan is skillful in manipulative play with puzzles or in stringing beads. He does not often use the large blocks or engage in any vigorous play. He follows the teacher's directions and fits into the routines of the center. He sits quietly at the table at lunchtime and rests when it is time. He remains rather passive, doing what is suggested, but initiating very little on his own.

What is Juan really like? The teachers feel that they do not know. He presents them with challenges. How can he be helped to do more exploring, discovering, and creating on his own? How can he be helped to develop the language skills for communicating that he needs so much in learning, now as well as in the future? How can he be helped to learn how to play with other children?

The teachers are slowly finding ways to gain his trust. They expect to help him change from being passive into being actively involved in tasks and play. They plan to help him find friends. They will help him discover his own individual patterns, as he learns and grows in the center.

Nettie, Who Wishes She Could Be Important to Someone

Nettie (3.4) is the fourth child in a family of five. Her home is a busy, crowded place where relatives come and go. Nettie is often brought to school by these relatives and never seems to know who may be coming for her at dismissal time. Her mother seldom comes. If her mother does come, she usually waits outside, sending an older sister in to get Nettie.

Nettie has no close friends among the children. She seems to feel that no one likes her. It is easy to see why. When she plays with children, she wants the largest share of materials, or she teases and runs off with some favorite item. The children soon refuse to let her play with them.

She is restless and distractible in her play, going from one piece of equipment to the other. Here is a sample of her behavior during a few minutes of activity. She sees a spoon in the sandbox, jumps in and digs with it, then drops it as her eye falls on a red truck another child has just left. She pulls the truck across the yard, but leaves it to climb on the ladderbars for a few seconds. Then she turns to the workbench where a group is pounding and sawing, but she does not wait for a turn with the tools. She wanders over to the housekeeping corner where she kicks at a doll buggy, bringing an angry response from the child whose "baby" is in the buggy.

Nettie seems to invite rejection from the children, but she continually seeks attention from the adults. When there is a visitor in the school, Nettie will follow the visitor, talking and clinging to him or her. She demands attention. She never seems to be satisfied. With three older sisters and a younger brother at home, one suspects that she has not had much attention. Her contacts with people are on a superficial level. She seems always to be seeking something and never finding it. Learning and achieving do not interest her.

What can the school do for Nettie? Nettie's attendance at school has been rather irregular during the three months she has been enrolled. The staff is not satisfied with the results of their work with her. They believe they must take another look at what is happening to her. They realize that it is not easy to give attention to a child who is always demanding it. Perhaps the best answer may be to let someone volunteer to be Nettie's "special" teacher, one who will devote herself to building a firm relationship with this little girl, who has never felt sure that anyone thinks of her as an important person.

If Nettie can feel valued in a relationship with someone, she may be free to persist in tasks for a sustained period of time and to develop skills in activities and in communicating with others. Nettie needs help from the teachers in seeing herself as a valued person. She needs help in becoming independent and resourceful in making use of the opportunities to learn and grow at school. She needs to feel the satisfactions of achievement and competence.

Ellen, Who Finds It Hard To Trust the World and the People in It

Ellen (4.9) is a child who was born with a physical deformity requiring corrective surgery. She was in the hospital several times as an infant and very young child. When Ellen was in the hospital, her mother was not allowed to stay with her, and could only see her during visiting hours.

Ellen is physically normal now, but she bears both the scars of her operations and the psychological scars left by the hospital experiences she had. Her hospitalizations and surgery came at a critical time in her development, when she should have been learning to trust herself in the world. Instead, she learned to be suspicious and unsure of herself. She is very jealous of a younger brother who was born shortly after her last hospital stay.

Ellen's parents were eager for her to enter school. The bonds of affection between Ellen and her parents were close, but they felt that she would gain a great deal from being in school. They were delighted when she was enrolled.

When Ellen entered school, she moved rather clumsily and often had a pouting expression on her face. She was a heavyset, stolid-looking girl with thick dark hair. Her motor coordination was poor for a child of her age, and she avoided active play. She did not join the children in playing on the jungle gym or the ladderbars. She seemed aware of her lack of skill and was defensive about it.

Ellen needed her mother when she entered school. She did not remain near her mother, but she would protest vigorously if her mother indicated that she

A teacher can provide encouragement.

was going to leave. She seemed to want to be sure that she could control the matter of her mother's leaving. Both the staff and the mother felt that it was important for Ellen to feel that she could keep her mother there. They knew that she would feel sure of herself in time. Meanwhile, the teacher tried to build a good relationship with Ellen. Ellen had accepted help from her teacher from the beginning, but seemed to keep her interaction on an impersonal level. She was suspicious of people.

Over a period of many weeks, her teacher continued trying to maintain a warm, friendly relationship with the child, giving her extra encouragement when she tried something new or was successful in any motor skill. She also let Ellen decide as many things as possible. When she had to refuse to comply with one of Ellen's requests, she did so firmly and matter-of-factly, explaining the reason and adding, "I would like to let you do it, but I can't because. . . ."

In addition, her teacher made a point of including many items for dramatic play of the doctor–nurse–hospital variety. She read stories about children and hospital experiences. It took a long time before Ellen became interested in these books after she had enjoyed a lot of messy play—getting her hands into sticky clay and playing with water. By this time, she viewed her teacher as her special friend, which seemed to make her feel more secure, and she began using the dramatic play materials.

Children enjoy creating shapes in damp sand.

The change in Ellen by the end of the year was rewarding to everyone. She was enjoying active play, using her body freely, and keeping up with the other children in climbing, riding a tricycle, and engaging in other large muscle activities. She sometimes talked with her teacher about what had happened to her in the hospital as though what she experienced there was really a thing of the past for her. She was steadily making progress in learning about the world and the people in it and in finding it rewarding to achieve, to build skills, and to cope with stress. The school had been successful in providing Ellen with some of the support she needed.

THE PARENTS

PARENTS ARE IMPORTANT PEOPLE

Next we will look at some of the parents we may meet. Parents are important people; they are the child's first teachers. They give the child his first experiences with loving relationships; they serve as his first models; and they direct his first learning opportunities.

They are also important because they are people with feelings and needs. They must cope with difficulties and seek personal satisfactions. Their relationships with the child are loaded with some of the deepest human feelings. We need to know something about parents and to respect the part they play in bringing up the children we meet at school.

Parents are all different. What are they like? What does the school or day-care center offer them?

Charles' parents are glad to have him attend school. They are both very busy people. While they are proud of this handsome little boy and love him very much, they often find him difficult and trying. He does not fit easily into the dream they have of a well-behaved child who does them credit. They look forward to the time when it will be easier for him to understand what they want. They are glad to shift the burden of caring for Charles to the school for a time. Charles' father has never come to the school, and his mother seldom has time to visit. She has to get back to the baby or on to some engagement.

*Janie's mother** is an active woman, who enjoys her full-time job as the Director of a Head Start program, and who values the rest of her time which she spends with her young daughter and son. However, she has not always found her life to be so rewarding. Janie's infancy was a stressful period in her life. At the time, her son was a very active two-year-old, and she was unhappy in her marriage. Her decision to divorce her husband was a painful one, and soon after the divorce, she sought the help of a psychiatric social worker. During her two-and-a-half years of therapy, she began to adjust to

---

* Recorded by Reggie Anderson

and accept her new life-style and decided to return to work. Her resourceful-ness, her desire to be a good mother, and her background and training in child development have helped her to anticipate and meet the needs of her children throughout a difficult period in her own life. She feels fortunate that her parents can care for her children during the day so that she can work. She likes Janie's school and her teacher and thinks that it is a good place for her daughter to be. Although she can only visit Janie's school infrequently, she takes her daughter to school and meets her whenever she has a day off. She speaks with Janie's teacher over the telephone from time to time, and attends all the parents' meetings which are scheduled at night.

Juan's mother misses him, but she is relieved that he can be in day care. Having him in the center makes it much easier for her to manage her work, and she feels that he needs school. She hopes he will be a "good" boy. She wants Juan to do well and to have some of the opportunities that were denied her. She sometimes worries about him, but she hesitates to talk with the teachers. She doesn't find it easy to talk with people. Juan and she have been close to one another without using many words. She is not very clear about what schools for young children are like, but she knows that Juan enjoys going there.

Nettie's mother is very relieved to have Nettie in school. Nettie was al-ways a fussy child and often cried. Even a hard slap was not enough to stop her. Nettie's mother does not believe in "babying" children, and she did not "baby" Nettie. She herself had never had much mothering. Her own mother died when she was a child, and she was sent to live with an aunt who never really wanted her, but who tried to do her duty to the child. She had married young, probably to escape from what must have been a loveless home. She was proud and pleased with her first baby, but then things became difficult. Her husband left her. Nettie is the third child of her second marriage. Even though there are many members of her husband's family in and out of the house, she often feels lonely and unwanted, as she did when she was a child. She gets depressed. She is sure that the people who teach at the school must look down on her; however, she is glad to have Nettie there just the same.

Ellen's parents are very grateful to have Ellen in the school. They feel that she is thriving in this situation, so different from her separation experiences when she was hospitalized.

Ellen's mother was glad to stay with Ellen as long as the teacher felt it helped her. Ellen's father willingly carried the extra work at home. The mother observed with interest what the teachers did at school and how they guided the children. She feels that she learned many things that have helped her understand better what Ellen needs and how she and her husband can encourage Ellen's development at home. Both parents feel that the teachers care about Ellen and are watching her development with pleasure. The bur-den of concern they had known earlier has been lifted. They welcome con-ferences with the teacher and are glad of the help they have received.

As we can see, all of these parents have different needs. They look at the school and the teachers in different ways. For all of them the school and the teachers play an important role in their lives.

Charles, Janie, Juan, Nettie, and Ellen are like some of the children whom we will meet in the school. Their parents are like some of the parents there. Who are the other adults in the school, and what are they like?

THE ADULTS IN THE SCHOOL

ADULTS ARE PEOPLE WITH FEELINGS THAT NEED TO BE UNDERSTOOD

Adults are people with the same kinds of feelings as children, but they are likely to express their feelings less directly and openly. Their responses have been modified by many experiences that have taught them to control and often to conceal their feelings even from themselves. An adult who is angry seldom hits or throws, but he or she may do the next task poorly or may be critical of someone else for no apparent reason. Many times the adult's responses are as inappropriate or unacceptable as the child's, but they are harder for us to relate to the cause. The responses of an adult do not change so quickly as a child's, perhaps because they are patterns of behaving that have been in use for a long time.

But there is an important difference between the child and the adult that gives the adult an advantage. The adult has a greater capacity to be objective, that is, to look at his or her own feelings and behavior. Because of this capacity the adult can modify responses and make them more appropriate, as he or she comes to understand them. Understanding ourselves, what we feel and why we respond as we do, is very important to all of us. We need to understand ourselves, for our feelings will influence the relationships we build and maintain with other people.

Self-understanding is especially important for teachers, because children are influenced by the feelings of teachers. It is important for us as teachers to learn to understand our feelings, so we can be honest and realistic and respond in appropriate and constructive ways to people and to situations. We are in a better position to help children understand themselves when we understand ourselves.

WE ARE LIKELY TO FEEL INADEQUATE IN A NEW SITUATION

We will start by looking at how students or beginning teachers* will probably feel as they start working in a school. We will try to understand these feelings, because it may help us understand the feelings of the children as they, too, begin school.

---

* In our general discussions, for convenience and to avoid tedious sentence structure, we will use the pronoun "she" for the teacher and the pronoun "he" for the child. We realize that half of the children in a school are likely to be girls and some of the teachers will be men. No discrimination is intended in either case.

When beginning work with children most students are going into a situation that is new to them. They may not be sure of what to do. They do not know the children or the teachers, and they are unfamiliar with school procedures. They may not know simple things like where the paints or the mops are kept. Even though they have been given directions and have been shown through the school, they are sure to find that they have forgotten or were not told many of the things they need to know. Unexpected things keep happening, things for which they are not prepared.

In these situations a student may try something that does not work out the way she expects. She may greet a child cheerfully only to have the child reply, "I don't like you." She may follow the example of the teacher in approaching a group with the words, "It's time to put things away now," but she may get a different response from the children such as, "We're not going to."

She has many questions. Should she interfere when one child hits another? Should she just watch? Should she ask an experienced teacher for help? What should she do?

It is not comfortable to feel unsure and inadequate. It is easy to blame someone or something as a defense against this feeling. A student may become critical, disapproving of the teachers and the program and what the children are allowed to do. Or she may turn away from the unfamiliar or difficult situations. She may busy herself with familiar things or spend time with the passive, "easy" children. She may do a great deal of needless talking or giving directions as a way of reassuring herself. She may even blame herself for not knowing what to do. Any of these responses may make it harder to become more adequate.

We Need To Feel Comfortable about Being Inadequate in the Beginning

All these responses are natural. In a new situation everyone has feelings of inadequacy. These feelings are not easy to face. The important thing is to realize how we feel and to understand something about why we feel as we do.

First of all, students can expect to feel inadequate when they begin participating in the school and probably for some time after that. They cannot possibly be prepared for all that may happen. No one can give instructions that will cover everything, certainly not in the time there may have been for preparation. Of course, students will not feel sure of what is expected of them or of what they are supposed to do. The teacher who is guiding them may not be sure of these things herself, as she does not know them yet or know what is possible for them.

What we can do about the feeling of inadequacy at this point is to feel comfortable about having it. It is all right to be inadequate when one begins a learning experience. No one should expect to know in the beginning what will be learned in time, and there is a lot to learn at first. Therefore, we might as well try to live as comfortably as we can with this uneasy feeling and enjoy our successes as we begin to have them.

WE HAVE OTHER FEELINGS, TOO

Although the first feelings we usually encounter and deal with are those of inadequacy, there are nonetheless other feelings that encourage us. A child's face lights up when he sees us come into the room, and we know that our relationship with him is a source of strength. He is seeing us as someone who cares, who can be depended on, and who has something significant to give to him. It makes us feel good inside to be this kind of person for a child. It gives us confidence.

Or, a child may bring us a drawing he has made, saying softly, "It's for you." It is the kind of gift that warms the heart. We are rewarded, also, when we watch a child struggle and then succeed in actually cutting through the piece of wood with the saw or spooning pancake batter into a pan, all on his own. The glow of satisfaction on his face or expressed through his body makes all our planning and teaching efforts seem worthwhile. We share in his accomplishment. We can truly feel that we are engaged in "the most important thing in human cultural behavior," as we succeed in helping a child to act and to learn with confidence.

WE WERE ALL CHILDREN ONCE

It is important for us to understand ourselves, if we are to understand others. We are all alike in many respects, and we all have some common experiences that may influence our responses. In the first place, all of us were children once. We can never escape that fact. What happened to us then still influences what we are like now. Some of us may wish that our childhood experiences had been different. Others may feel grateful on the whole for the events of their childhoods. But whatever the case may be, we can still understand ourselves and other adults better by trying to understand what children are like and by observing how things affect them.

The way our needs were met during the period of dependency, when we were tiny and helpless, and dependent on the adults around us, still affects what we do. If we lived with people who met our needs with warmth and love, if we were fed when we felt hungry and played with and cuddled when we wanted attention, then we were *satisfied* during this period. If the adults around us were themselves satisfied people who did not try to prolong needlessly our dependence, then we were free to become independent when we were ready. If we grew up under conditions like these, we are now neither fighting against being dependent nor seeking reassurance by constantly demanding more protection than we need.

Others of us may have lived with people who did not provide pleasant experiences during this period. We were not fed when we felt hungry. We were left to "cry it out" when we felt helpless and alone. There may have been many reasons for such handling by our parents, such as lack of knowledge of the real needs of infants, poor health, too many responsibilities, or the influence of our parents' own childhood experiences. Under these circumstances, we may have fought against being dependent, finding it hard later to accept the necessity of ever being dependent in any situation. Or we may have continued seeking to have our "dependency needs" met by trying to be more dependent than we needed to be, as though to make up for what we did not have earlier.

We Were All Members of Families

Another factor influencing our behavior is the position each one of us held in our families. Some of us were only children; others were oldest, youngest, or any number of middle positions. The position means different things in different families (Koch, 1960). Families are likely to be competitive. Children want and compete for their parents' or each others attention. Some are more successful than others in getting it.

In the school, for example, a teacher who happens to be the youngest in her family may identify with the youngest child in the school and resent seeing him teased. She may want to see the aggressor punished, just as she wanted to see punishment given to those who teased her when she was a child. Under the guise of wanting to be "fair" she may try to impose a "justice" that really belongs to a situation from her own past, from which she has not yet succeeded in untangling herself. Recognizing that patterns of past feelings still exist gives a person a better chance to handle situations in the present with understanding.

We All Met Frustrations in the Growing-Up Process

Let us take one more example of the way our childhood patterns enter into how we feel and behave in the school or anywhere else. As a result of the frustrations that are an inevitable part of the growing-up process, we all have feelings of resentment and hostility, and we handle them better if we can recognize them. It is needless, and may be damaging, to try to deny these feelings. We all have them because as babies we were subjected to many limitations. The baby can't reach the toy he dropped. He trips and falls when he tries to walk. He isn't allowed to touch interesting objects. Frustration rouses resentful and sometimes hostile feelings.

How much hostility a child feels depends somewhat on whether the adults in his world help to minimize the inevitable frustrations, or whether they aggravate and increase frustration by a mistaken idea of "teaching" the child. If the necessary limitations are imposed firmly but with gentleness by a comfortable, confident, loving person, they will not rouse much resentment, but if limitations are imposed by one who is cross, confused, and struggling with his own feelings of hostility, they will rouse a great deal of negative feeling in the child. The child will want to fight and hurt in return, and these feelings will spill out in many situations against anyone who interferes with him.

Few of us are fortunate enough to have been handled all the time by people who tried to decrease the feelings of hostility and resentment that are part of the growing-up process. Most of us feel more resentment than we can manage comfortably on all occasions. Our feelings spill out in inappropriate ways in many situations. When these negative feelings spill out inappropriately, they may make us feel guilty and afraid without knowing what is wrong. They may keep us from learning things that we may really want to learn.

ALL OF US HAVE NEGATIVE FEELINGS THAT NEED TO BE DRAINED

We all have a store of negative feelings. These feelings need to be drained in various ways, such as through vigorous activity, or through some satisfying expression of art or music, or by ''spilling things out'' by talking to a friend, or in doing something that makes us feel more adequate. When we have such outlets, we keep our negative feelings down to manageable proportions.

Helping children be successful can make a student feel adequate.

ALL OF US NEED TO IDENTIFY THE NEGATIVE FEELINGS WE HAVE

If negative feelings are not drained, they may come out later in ways that are difficult to identify. Feeling very strongly about a thing, for example, is an indication that it is serving as an outlet for extra emotion, especially if most people do not seem to feel as strongly as we do about the same thing. It may be good to stop and ask oneself, "Why do I feel so strongly about this?" We can direct strong feeling more safely when we understand why we feel as we do. The likelihood of our meeting the needs of the child is increased if we understand our own needs and feelings.

For example, a teacher finds herself feeling very indignant that a child is allowed to play with his food at the table and even to leave some of it uneaten. She may feel this way because she was not allowed to play with her food when she was a child. Now that she has accepted adult patterns and identified herself with the adults in this situation, all the resentment that she felt at being denied the delightful experience of playing with food, as well as tasting it, is turned into resentment about seeing a child permitted to do what she was not allowed to do and what she was forced to consider "bad." It is not easy to take on values, and we often pay a heavy emotional price when they are forced on us too early. We cannot bear to see others getting by cheaply.

We shall not discuss here whether or not a child should be allowed to play with food. We are only pointing out that it is important to be able to make decisions about the child's behavior on the basis of its meaning for the child, and whether or not it is a good thing for him, instead of on the basis of our own personal conflict. In other words, it is important to be able to identify the emotional forces that lie behind our reasoning.

ALL OF US TEND TO RESIST CHANGE

A characteristic that we all have in common is that of resistance to change. In spite of ourselves we find all kinds of reasons for avoiding real change in our thinking and in our behavior. New ways of behaving, no matter what their merit, are rejected until we manage to handle our resistances. Most resistances are the result of childhood experiences. Recognizing this, a teacher can handle her resistance more appropriately, saying to herself, "I don't have to feel and behave as I did when my mother (or my big sister or my father) was bossing me. I'm no longer a child. I'm grown-up, and I'm free to use a suggestion, if I think it is a good one, or to reject it, if I think it is a poor one." She can free herself from the control that childhood patterns may still be exerting over her in adult life.

The more insecure we are, the less likely we are to feel that we can afford to change, for change involves uncertainties. Even a too-ready acceptance of a new point of view may mean only a superficial acceptance, in itself a defense against any real change. It is important for us to be aware of this universal tendency to resist the new, the different, so that it will not block us when we try to profit from the thinking of others. We must assert our right to use opportunities—whether it is a morning in the school, a discussion period, or the reading of a book—to reach our own conclusions.

WE NEED TO ACCEPT ALL THE FEELINGS WE HAVE

It is essential for all of us in the school not to feel ashamed or guilty about the feelings we have. We have been taught so often that we must be "good" that we may be afraid to face the negative feelings that exist in us. They go unrecognized and thus interfere with our thinking more than they would if we had accepted them.

As adults we can afford to look at our feelings, because we have more capacity for managing them than we had as children. As children, our strong feelings overwhelmed us. Perhaps anger turned into a violent temper tantrum. We may have felt guilty and afraid, and we may not have had much help from the adults around us at this point. Now that we are grown, we have less need to feel so afraid. We have more ability to handle feelings when we know that they exist.

WE NEED TO RECOGNIZE THE AMBIVALENCE OF FEELINGS

It is also essential to be aware of ambivalence in our feelings. Feelings are usually mixed. Feeling comfortable or uncomfortable, enjoying and not enjoying, loving and hating are all mixed together, although we may be aware of only the feeling that is strongest at the moment. We may be surprised at sudden changes in feeling, because we have not been aware that other feelings were present all the time. We may want to learn more about people and yet resist learning. We may like and dislike the same person; he, in turn, may have some of both kinds of feelings about us. We seldom feel all one way or all the other way about a person or an experience.

WE NEED TO TRY TO UNDERSTAND RATHER THAN JUDGE OURSELVES AND OTHERS

We all have many kinds of feelings, pleasant and unpleasant, and most of us want to make changes in some of our feelings and ways of behaving. Real change is not likely to take place as a result of disapproval or blaming ourselves or anyone else. Change more often takes place as a result of being able to consider feelings and circumstances and making an effort to understand them.

It does not help to blame ourselves and feel very discouraged, for example, when we are unsuccessful in dealing with a child's behavior, or when a child or an adult rejects us for some reason. Nevertheless, it does help if we think about how we felt when it happened, what we did, what we might have done instead, and what the situation may have meant to the other person. By reflecting in this way we will gain new insights into the situation. We may find that we have a more successful, satisfying experience the next time. We may gain more confidence in ourselves and our capacity to grow. Passing judgment on others or ourselves does little to bring about improvement.

Some of the things we may discover about ourselves and others when we try to understand rather than judge behavior may be confusing or disturbing to us. Understanding is not a simple task, for human behavior is complex and difficult to understand. It is often helpful to talk over our problems in understanding interpersonal relations with a teacher, director, or principal whose wider experience and knowledge has added to his or her understanding of human relations and behavior.

EACH ADULT SHARES COMMON PROBLEMS

The whole school is thus full of human beings who must understand and accept their feelings and those of others in the school. Each adult shares some common problems.

Students, as they start teaching, have the problem of facing and accepting the almost inevitable feelings of inadequacy that a new situation brings.

Parents whose children are in the school face the problem of being able to leave the child free to take the step toward greater independence that going to school represents. Their confidence in what they themselves are as parents and the degree of security that their past experiences have brought them will play a part in the ease with which they face their new role of parents with children attending school.

Teachers must continue their professional growth and deepen their understanding of the ways to meet the needs of children and parents in the school.

The secretary is an important person in the school.

The *secretary* must share the goals of the school and find satisfaction in his or her contribution toward the well-being of the school.

The *cook* must share in the goals of the school, too. He or she must find satisfaction in what he or she is doing for and with the children, as the food is prepared and served.

The *janitor* must be able to understand and accept the needs of children, if he or she is to see the job as one of making the school a satisfying place for children instead of merely a good place for a janitor.

The *director* or *principal* must continue his or her professional growth and deepen his or her understanding of ways to support children's and teachers' learning. The director or principal must be able to help build a staff relationship that facilitates human relations and supports the educational program.

For everyone, the school can be a human relations laboratory. It can be a place where we learn more about ourselves and about others, as we gain understanding, ability, and skill in guiding children's growth, learning, and development.

PROJECTS

1. Recall and report an incident in your own childhood when you were about the same age as the children you are observing. What significance do you think this incident had for you?

2. List some of the things that children do that you find annoying. List some of the things that you enjoy watching children do. Keep this list and check it later to see whether or not your feelings have changed. If they have, how would you explain the changes?

SUPPLEMENTARY READING

Caruso, J. Phases in student teaching. *Young Children,* 1977, *33* (1):57–63.
Coles, R. *Uprooted Children.* New York: Harper & Row, 1971.
Greenberg, M. The male early childhood teacher. *Young Children,* 1977, *32* (2):34–38.
Rubin, I. *Jordi and Lisa and David.* New York: Ballantine, 1968.
Menninger, W. *Self-Understanding—A First Step in Understanding Children.* Chicago: Science Research, 1951.

2

Scribble
(girl, 3.3)

Programs and Types of Centers

Programs for young children should offer opportunities for learning adapted to what is known about the developmental needs of young children. Adults in the school or day-care center share with parents the responsibility for promoting sound growth and learning at a period when growth and learning are rapid and significant. Respect for the individual child and his needs are the basis for a good school or center program.

DEFINITION OF NURSERY SCHOOL, DAY CARE, AND KINDERGARTEN

A nursery school is a program for the education of late two-, three-, four-, and early five-year-old children. The kindergarten is a program for the education of late four-, five-, and early six-year-old children. Both nursery school and kindergarten are usually half-day programs that are from two to three hours long. Neither is designed for parents who work, but nevertheless, many parents of children who attend nursery school and kindergarten do work. The ages of children in day care range from infants and toddlers through five-year-olds or even school-age children. Day care is designed as a supplement to the family's care for part of a day outside the home. Day care takes place in centers with groups of children or in family-sized groups in family day care.

States set legal minimum standards for kindergarten in public schools. Many communities also have legal minimum standards for day care. In some communities the day-care standards apply to any group of six children meeting on a regular basis and apply to public and nonpublic nursery schools and kindergartens. Some communities have federally funded Headstart and Follow Through programs that enroll four- and five-year-old children. In addition, there is federal and state support for nursery school and kindergarten programs for children with special needs. Programs funded from public monies operate in accordance with guidelines issued by the sponsoring governmental agency.

CHARACTERISTICS OF A SCHOOL FOR CHILDREN AGES THREE THROUGH FIVE

The nursery school, day-care center, and kindergarten are laboratories where children are actively engaged in learning rather than lecture rooms where learners are talked to while they sit quietly. In a program designed for the developmental needs of the three- through five-year-old child, children are seldom all doing the same thing at the same time. They work and play individually or in small groups. An observer looking into such a setting, may see one group of children engaged in dramatic play in a homemaking corner; another group building with blocks; a child or two working independently looking at books or building with a construction game; another group playing a matching game; another group making an aquarium; and a child watching others work and play. The observer visiting in turn, classes of three-, then four-, then five-year-olds will notice increasing independence, as well as increasing complexity in the materials being used and in the work and play in each successive group.

Teachers work as a team planning and carrying out a program based on each child's needs. In a setting where students and aides act as teachers, daily plans which include goals for each child must be communicated to these adults, too. In this way, all adults are enabled to act on behalf of each child's learning. There is structure to the day, and this order is made known to all participants—adults and children. A schedule exists, which may be modified to meet individual children's needs. Teachers have a high regard for individuality; they are ready to be flexible; and they are willing to observe, to reflect, and to plan anew within a day and through the week. The daily and weekly plans depend on the skill and talents of the teachers and other human resources available, as well as on the possibilities and limits of the physical environment of the school itself and the surrounding community.

Ample opportunity for rich play is an essential characteristic of a setting planned to meet the developmental needs of nursery school and kindergarten children. Play is an avenue for learning. Young children need many opportunities for looking, touching, hearing, tasting, and moving, if they are to learn. Three-, four-, and five-year-old children use play as a way to discover

A small group discovers and observes a snail.

and master themselves and their world. They also use play as a way to represent their past and present experiences. Discovery is an active process for them—discovery of liking and not liking things and people, discovery of how to manage feelings, and discovery of ideas.

Each group of three- and four-year-olds will have at least two adults, one of whom will be a trained teacher. Children these ages need a great deal of care to keep them safe and to help them learn to use teachers as resources, to delay gratification, to gain self-control, to cope with feelings, to care for their own personal needs, to use language, to make choices, to solve problems with people and materials, to be skilled with their bodies, to work independently, to work with other children, to share, to take turns, to take care of their own and school property, to participate in snack, lunch, story, music, and movement activities, to use and become skillful with a wide variety of materials and equipment, and to build concepts.

Kindergartens usually have only one teacher; however, a second adult is very important for a group of five-year-olds who enter school for the first time. Children entering school at five will need to gain many of the same skills, abilities, and understandings stated above for younger children. Because the children are five years old they may be learning at a different rate and at a different level of complexity, but they lack experience in a group setting. One teacher, no matter how competent she may be, cannot focus on and respect each child's interest, style, and rate of learning. Working with an entire group, one teacher cannot encourage independence and initative and help each child increase his awareness of the world around him.

THE PROGRAM AS IT FUNCTIONS FOR CHILDREN

To provide the reader with some images of what a school might be like for young children, the activities of two children will be followed through a morning at school. The first description is of a boy in nursery school; the second description is of a girl in kindergarten. Following these two descriptions is a discussion of how a child's experiences in day care, after a morning in kindergarten, will differ from those of his experiences in the school program.

CLARK, A NURSERY SCHOOL CHILD

Clark (3.6) arrives with his mother at 8:45 A.M. They greet his teacher, Miss B, and all stand at the door for a few minutes talking with each other. Clark's mother says good-bye and reminds him that his dad will come for him at noon. He gives her a big hug and runs out to the playground. He plays there for half an hour, riding a tricycle vigorously for a while and then joining a group of children who are hauling the building blocks to a corner of the playground to make a fort. Most of the children on the playground participate in this project for a time. A climb up the agility net and a slide down a fireman's pole complete Clark's cycle of outdoor activity.

He comes inside and takes off his boots and sweater with very little help from his teacher and places them in his locker. Then, he uses the toilet, washes his hands, and plays with the soap and water for a moment or two. He dries his hands, goes into the playroom and talks with a teacher for a few moments. He looks at two girls who are playing in the homemaking corner; the teacher suggests that maybe they need a "father." He is accepted as "father," and he sweeps busily, wheels a doll buggy around, and converses over the telephone about an evening engagement. The group has a conflict about who is going to use the toaster. Clark leaves the situation. He begins to paint at the easel and becomes absorbed in his painting. He paints large areas with vivid color covering the paper. His second painting is quite similar to his first one. In a businesslike way Clark removes his finished paintings and hangs them up to dry. He appears to be relaxed and content as he leaves the easel. He has been at school for about an hour.

Teachers and children are beginning to clean up the room; Clark helps by washing the paint brushes. After clean-up a snack is served. He goes to a table for some juice and an apple. He waits for a teacher to peel his apple, because he does not like the skin. He listens as several children and a teacher talk about the group's visit to a nearby farm to pick the apples. Clark says that he picked up yellow and red apples. He likes the red ones best; they are juicy and sweet. He finishes his snack and puts his cup and napkin in the wastebasket. He joins a group marching to music that the teacher is playing on the piano. He tries the drum and then the bells, while he marches. When the marching stops, Clark stays with the group around the piano where all begin to sing with the teacher. He requests a song. His request is honored, and he sings with gusto.

When the singing is over Clark goes to his locker to put on his sweater and boots to go outside. He needs help with finding the left and right boots, but puts on his sweater without assistance. Outside he joins four children who are involved in digging, each in a separate hole, some filling pans and some transferring the dirt to a big pile. They comment as thoughts occur to them. They have occasional conflicts, most of which are settled without help from the teacher. There is plenty of space and materials. They are all involved in their play and seem to enjoy being together. Clark finds a worm, and the other children crowd around to see how it moves. He announces that the, "worm is fat when short and thin when long." By the time the group begins to grow weary, it is 11 o'clock and almost time to go home. They pick up the shovels and pails and return them to the outdoor shed. The children gather on a bench outside, and their teacher gets a book on insects and worms. She reads the paragraph on earthworms, and the children look at the picture of

Listening to a story is a pleasant way to end the morning.

the earthworm in its habitat. Clark eagerly adds his account of a worm, as others do. They wonder about what it might be like to be a worm. Clark demonstrates the way a worm moves by wiggling on the grass. The teacher recalls an experience she had with worms when she was fishing. Clark says he has gone fishing with his dad. They decide to try fishing at school. The teacher assures them that she will have fishing poles ready for them in the morning. Now, she has a story about an inch worm to read. The children listen and make comments, sometimes relevant to the story and sometimes not. The teacher listens to their spontaneous comments and then refocuses their attention on the story. When the story is over, Clark's dad is standing by the gate. The teacher bids Clark good-bye until tomorrow. The nursery school day is over for him; it is 11:30 A.M.

LOUISE, A KINDERGARTEN CHILD

Louise (5.6) is in her spring semester at kindergarten. She enters the classroom with four classmates who ride on the same bus. It is just 8:30. All of the children are warmly dressed, for it is a cold, crisp March day. Louise greets Miss A, her teacher. Louise, as well as the other children, has a small bag of vegetables in her hand. She puts her bag on the top of her locker, removes her mittens, cap, and coat while chatting with her friends. She puts them away and sits on a low bench to remove her boots. She seems particularly relaxed and sociable this morning. With her boots off and put away, Louise takes her bag of carrots over to the sink and goes over to the assistant teacher to choose her activities for the first part of the morning.

Louise gets her envelope from the file and turns to look at the block area and the model of the school which the children have been working on for the past few days. Miss L, the assistant teacher, is standing near the low bulletin board on which the teacher always places a list of the day's options which are both written and pictured. Louise turns to listen as Miss L reads the list of the day's activities aloud to several children. When it is Louise's turn to make a decision, Miss L looks at Louise's folder and says, ''The story you dictated yesterday is clipped to your envelope. Did you plan to make a book for the 'school' today?'' ''Yes,'' responds Louise, ''and I want to make soup, too.'' ''It will take the soup a long time to cook so you will need to make the soup first. Ask Randy to help you wash the vegetables and by that time Miss A will be ready to help you read the recipe.'' ''Yep,'' says Louise, as she takes the envelope from Miss L and replaces it in the file. She then skips over to the sink where Randy has put the vegetables in a dishpan of water.

For the next few minutes Louise and Randy scrub the vegetables and combine washing vegetables with some water play. Louise stops, dries her hands, and puts on an apron from a basket nearby on the floor. Three other children and Miss A come to help; Louise brings the washed vegetables to a large rectangular table where there is a written and illustrated recipe, six cutting boards, six vegetable peelers, and six paring knives. For the next few minutes they peel and cut the vegetables; there is a great deal of social conversation. Louise reads the pictures on the recipe. The children and teacher read the recipe together to be sure they have everything needed for the soup. Then Louise reads it, and the other children follow the directions, putting all the ingredients into an electric cooker. Each child cleans up his own place. Louise washes the table, while two children take the peels outside to the rabbit, and one child and the teacher wash the knives, peelers, and cutting boards.

Louise pulls off her apron, puts it in the basket, and goes to get her story from her envelope. She stands watching several children making playground equipment from tinker toys. "It's a swing," Albert tells her. "Yes, I know," she responds and looks delighted.

It is now 9:15. Louise goes to a shelf and gets colored pencils, paper, and scissors, and takes them to a table. For the next 40 minutes she carefully makes a tiny book, printing in the story she dictated to a teacher the day before and illustrating it with pictures. It looks so beautiful to her that she places it in her locker, "To take home and show my mother. I'll bring it back to use in the 'school' tomorrow."

Louise goes to the toilet, washes her hands, and returns to the classroom commenting, "The soup smells good!" She helps Miss L wash the tables, so they will be ready for snack. Clean up is in progress, and most children are helping. When Louise finishes cleaning the tables, she counts out five chairs for three tables and six chairs for one table at Miss L's request. She then goes to the rug near the piano to look at a book. Miss A is at this rug and is talking to each child about his choices of the previous period and making plans for tomorrow. Miss A makes notes from these conversations which she will use to plan the options for tomorrow. It is 10:10.

As the children finish looking at their books, they replace them in the bookrack. Some children talk with each other; Louise and several others lie down and close their eyes looking very relaxed. Two children are helping Miss L serve the soup. As children and snack are ready, Miss A dismisses children to go to snack. Each teacher joins a table for snack. There is social conversation at the tables, although some children just eat and relax. As children finish eating, they clean up their places and return to the rug for a story. Louise is one of the last to finish. She liked the soup.

Miss A and the children sing until all return to the rug and then she reads a story. Louise, as the other children do, listens, chuckles, and makes spontaneous comments about the story.

After the story, the outdoor options, which are written and pictured, are read to the children. They are asked to think about what they would like to do outside and to make their choices, as they put on their outdoor clothing. They go to their lockers, dress, and go outside. It is 10:45.

Louise chooses to play in the tree house with four other children. This play has been going on for several weeks. Although each day the theme is the same—they are super heros—the content has developed and grown more complicated. They require a space, but no properties are needed for their imaginations to soar. They stay within the sight of a teacher, but require no help in solving problems that occur in the play, for all participants are strongly motivated to continue. Compromise, restructuring, and give-and-take are all accomplished without a break in the continuity of the play.

At 11:10, Miss L tells the children that it is almost time to go home. "Play five more minutes, and then I'll call you to get your belongings from your locker to take home." Five minutes later she says, "Time to get your things from your lockers and go to the bus." Louise is the first to come; she wants to take her "book" home. At 11:20 five of the group go out to wait for the bus with Miss A. Louise and her four friends get on the bus and wave good-bye to their classmates and teachers.

HOW DAY CARE DIFFERS FROM NURSERY SCHOOL AND KINDERGARTEN

Because it must fit the working hours of parents, day-care center hours will be longer than those of the nursery school or kindergarten. In addition to a planned educational program, the day will include many of the kinds of opportunities that parents, home, and neighborhood provide. Day care will meet more of the child's needs for physical care, for rest, and for nutrition than will the nursery school or kindergarten programs. It may include opportunities to garden, to help with food preparation, to shop in a grocery store, to visit repair shops, and to visit parks, libraries, and museums. Based on the teacher's knowledge of individual children's home and neighborhood settings, day care will provide many opportunities to supplement the home. A part of the planned program will be time to talk with and work alongside an adult and only one or two other children. There will be time for the child to be alone to pursue an interest and time for him to play with a few children away from a large group. The program will endeavor to offer many of the advantages of an extended family.

The children will probably arrive from about 7:30 to 8:30. This long interval for arrivals allows a teacher not only to talk with parents for a few minutes, but also to help each child make the transition from home to school. The teacher may put her arm around one child, give another child a pat or a hug, listen to a child tell about what happened at home, or remind another child that today is the day for the chickens to hatch. A snack may be ready, or a teacher and child may prepare a snack to supplement a hurried breakfast. As more children and teachers arrive, they will separate and go to their different groups.

The morning program for the three- and four-year-old children will be much like the regular nursery school morning. Kindergarten children who come to day care may leave the center and go to a class in a nearby school or stay in the center for their educational program. In either case, their time in kindergarten will be much like the morning for the kindergarten child described above. If children do leave the center for a part of their day, they will need to be welcomed back and helped with the transition from their other school to day care.

Before lunch, at about 11:45, all children will need time to relax by singing with a group, listening to records, or having a time alone with a book or favorite building set. They will need time to wash their hands before they eat. Children will eat in a "family group" with three or four children and a teacher who is familiar with their eating patterns. As they finish lunch, they may go to the bathroom to brush their teeth; wash their faces; pull off their shoes, socks, and tight clothing; and use the toilet. There will be some carefully selected materials for children to use, as they wait their turn in the bathroom or while their cots are being put into place for naps. Some children may help clean the tables and floor, and others may help put out the cots. There will be a floor plan for the cots. A regular place to rest or sleep facilitates the transition from activity to rest. Shades drawn and lights off help to promote sleeping.

Children wash before eating and enjoy the process.

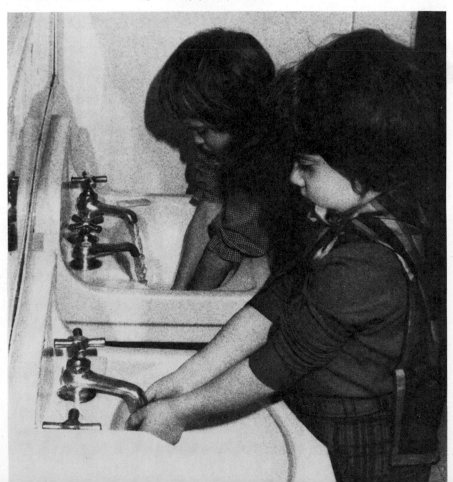

Lunch is served in the full-day program.

Most three-, four-, and five-year-old children will sleep after a vigorous morning. The sleep period may last from an hour-and-a-half to two hours. Some children, however, will only need to rest. Rest time should be no more than an hour. An adult familiar with each child's ritual for sleep or rest will be with the children at the transition time from lunch to sleep or rest. Children who only rest, may be provided with materials to use during resting. These materials will be selected so that the child may play quietly on his cot without disturbing others. It is helpful to those who sleep if the children who rest are in a separate room.

At about 1:30, as the first children get up from rest or wake from sleep, teachers are there to help them with the transition to wakefulness and activity. This is a time when the adult can give care to individual children, such as hairbrushing, changing a Band-aid, or, perhaps, helping with a change of clothing. Because all children will not wake at the same time, it will also be a time for conversation, planning for or anticipating the events of the afternoon. A piece of fruit or a cup of juice is a welcome refreshment, as well as providing needed nutrients.

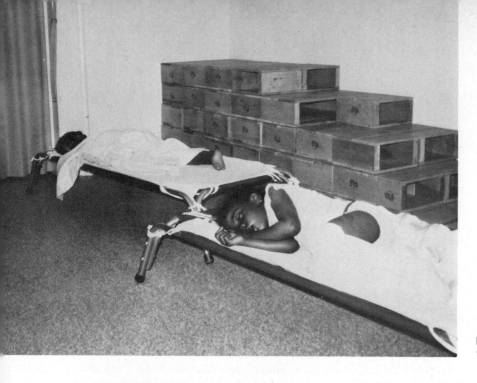

Nap may last from an hour to
two hours.

After nap is a good time to
share a book with a friend.

PATTERNS IN ALL GOOD PROGRAMS

From these descriptions of the morning and full-day programs we can see that a homelike atmosphere prevails in the school. There is a free flow of activity, indoors and out, with very little regimentation. There is companionship among children and adults. The adults give security and order to the day and extend opportunities for children. A child fits easily into this world. It is equipped to suit his needs. It offers wider opportunities and more freedom than most homes can. The teachers are burdened with fewer other responsibilities than most parents are.

TYPES OF PROGRAMS

Head Start, Follow Through, and *Title I* are federally and state funded programs designed for children from low-income families. Parents and members of the community have been expected to become involved in these programs as volunteers or paid assistants under the supervision of a trained teacher. For all these programs, the law mandates a local advisory committee, composed of parents, that is to be directly consulted for all program decisions.

The atmosphere in day care is homelike.

Home-based programs are being tried in which a trained teacher visits the child at home and instructs the parent in good guidance practices. These practices include ways of stimulating intellectual development. An interesting recent addition to these programs is the toy lending library. The toys from these libraries may be loaned to the home-based teacher or directly to parents.

The majority of children in *day-care centers* are children whose parents are working outside the home. The cost of good day care is high. Budgets in most centers are inadequate. Support comes mainly from philanthropic or governmental agencies, although there are also centers run privately for profit. Some churches operate day-care centers. Most groups charge a fee on a sliding scale, according to family ability to pay, with the agency making up the balance.

Licensed centers are required to meet state and local health and safety regulations, but enforcement is often inadequate. Few states have regulations relating to educational standards, and many centers still remain unlicensed.

Colleges or universities may have *laboratory schools* for the purpose of teacher training and research. These activities add to our knowledge of young children. Teachers in laboratory schools are not only teachers of children, but also supervise college students who are gaining practical experience. Although these schools are usually financed by the institution itself, parents often pay a tuition fee.

There are programs designed for young children with *special needs*. Some of these schools serve children with a variety of developmental problems. Other settings may specialize in particular developmental problems, such as cerebral palsy or mental retardation. A few schools are designed as therapeutic schools for seriously disturbed children. All these schools are staffed with specially trained teachers who may work with other professionals, such as psychiatrists, social workers, and speech therapists. In many of these schools parents receive counseling as a part of the total treatment.

In some cases it is considered desirable to have the child with a developmental problem in a regular school group, if this group is staffed in such a way that his needs and those of the other children in the group can be met. For example, a blind child may be enrolled in a group of sighted children, or a child with cerebral palsy may be enrolled in a group of normal children. With a trained person, who understands the handicap and can help the parents and the other children in the group to deal constructively with the questions and anxieties a normal person inevitably feels, the experience may be a rewarding one for the group as well as for the handicapped child. Head Start and laboratory schools may include children with mental or physical handicaps.

The number of *private schools* has grown rapidly in the last few years. Because of their cost, these schools usually serve children from wealthier families. When private schools are staffed by competent, trained people, they provide good education and care for a limited group of children. Very few states, however, set adequate standards or give educational supervision to private schools. The result is that there is little assurance for parents and children that such schools are always good schools. Parents themselves must depend on becoming qualified to judge whether or not a school offers a constructive experience, if they wish to protect their children.

Schools that emphasize one aspect, such as music, or one method of teaching, often make less use of the knowledge and insights available today and tend to be less valuable in promoting all aspects of development. But in any particular school it is likely to be the teacher as a person who is most important to the child attending the school.

Another type of program is the *cooperative school,* organized by parents who employ a trained teacher and assist her in carrying out a school program. With good professional leadership and a seriously interested group of parents, these schools have often developed sound programs at somewhat less cost than the private school. Many of these groups have found adequate quarters in churches. Some well-established groups have constructed their own buildings.

Parents who participate in the cooperative school face special problems in their relationships with their own children because of the dual role they play as assistant teachers and parents. Careful attention needs to be given to working through the conflict which this dual role may present to both child and parent. When these roles are defined, parents and children both gain from the school experience. The close contacts with other parents who have children at the same stage of development, the sharing of responsibilities, and the need to face and talk through problems as they arise in the school mean a great deal to parents, especially parents of only children or parents with their first child. Because of the complexity of relationships in the setup, cooperative schools often benefit from using the help of a psychiatrically trained consultant.

Many churches have schools run by a trained staff as a service to young children and their parents, or they may provide quarters for a parent-cooperative school, as we have mentioned.

Parents have also arranged informal neighborhood play groups which run for a short time and meet the needs of the neighborhood group at the time.

SELECTING A SCHOOL OR CENTER

There are many different types of programs today giving care to young children. No one type of program meets the needs of all children or their parents. All programs should meet the universal needs of children for good physical care with ample opportunity to develop their potentials socially, intellectually, and emotionally, and to overcome as far as possible any handicaps that may exist. Different programs offer somewhat different methods of trying to reach these goals.

Because there are many types of schools, it is important to be informed about what good early childhood education is in order to select a program. Every parent planning to enroll a child in a group must visit the program first and decide whether it provides the climate in which his child can grow best. One of the purposes of this book is to help the reader learn to identify good programs in early education. Publications that may be helpful in selecting a school or center are listed in the bibliography at the end of this chapter.

HOME–SCHOOL CONTACTS

There should be close contacts between the home and the program after the child enters. Exchange of information and frequent discussions are especially necessary if there are differences in expectations for the child. Consistency and compatibility are important, as home and school work for the sake of the children. Both teachers and parents need to be sympathetic to each other's problems as well as to respect each other's values and methods.

Parents as well as children need to feel at home in the school or center. Parents should be welcomed and encouraged to stay to observe whenever they wish. The teachers should consult often with the parents, sometimes by telephone and often in the daily contacts they have, as parents bring or call for children. They need to share accounts of incidents that seem important, so that each may understand the child better. The parents should feel free to consult the teacher. Parents and teachers may plan and make decisions together about what the child may need. The home and the school are working toward the same goals.

The value of a parent's visit to the school is increased when someone on the staff takes time to interpret to the mother or father something about what is taking place, explaining the purpose of an activity or of the method used in meeting a situation. Misunderstanding is prevented by such discussion, and the parent may thus be enabled to better support and extend the work of the school for the child when he is at home.

PARENTS OFTEN FEEL INADEQUATE

Parents often feel inadequate and defensive as they try to meet the new demands made of them. The gap between what they have experienced as children and what their children may experience is a large one and not easily bridged. Yet it is more important than ever that parents be able to maintain their values and behave responsibly toward their children. If teachers are understanding and sympathetic, the school can be a support to parents, as they carry out their task. Both parents and children should find satisfaction in the "growing-up" process, and for this reason parents need encouragement, positive guidance, and an environment that makes possible constructive solutions to problems. Teachers can meet some of these needs for parents, just as they do for children.

TEACHERS OFTEN FEEL INADEQUATE

Teachers, too, often feel inadequate and defensive, as they try to meet the new demands being made of them. They need the support of the parents, if they are to plan and carry out sound programs. A teacher needs to learn from the parent more about what the child is like, the kinds of opportunities he has had, what his interests are, and how he responds at home, if she is to understand him well at school. With the help of the parents, she can plan more wisely for this child. The parents need the teacher's help in keeping in touch with their child. They need to know what he is like at school and what the school is offering him, if they are to understand his growth and to give him the help he needs at home.

CONTACTS BETWEEN PARENTS AND TEACHERS

The school offers parents an opportunity to learn more about child growth, development, learning, and ways of guiding children's growth through observations in the classrooms. There are many opportunities for contact even when parents do not participate in the program directly. There will be *informal conversations* daily, as parents come and go. These contacts may be short, but they are often significant to both parent and teacher, because of the information exchanged and the friendly climate created. Car pools or group arrangements for transportation are a handicap, because they cut down on the number of such contacts. In settings where children ride to school by bus or in a car pool, teachers can keep in touch with parents by telephone. There are also *conferences* that the teacher and parents arrange together, outside of school hours, when there is a chance for uninterrupted conversation. *Group meetings* of parents and staff members can be held regularly. They offer opportunities for bringing up questions and for talking over subjects of general interest. Usually these meetings are discussion meetings. Occasionally there may be a speaker who answers questions after giving a talk of interest to both parents and teachers.

Participating in the school program offers parents an opportunity to learn more about children and about guidance. Parents may take part as volunteers, paid workers, paraprofessionals, or aides. By participating they may help broaden the program or meet the needs of individual children.

Besides its educational value for parents, the school can be of value because it offers parents and children an opportunity for some time apart from each other. There is a real need for some time apart when families live in small homes or apartments under crowded conditions. When there is little

A parent's special skill may help broaden opportunities for children.

outdoor play space available and no help from relatives, parents and children need some separation. With a child literally underfoot almost constantly, a parent is likely to find it difficult to be loving and patient or to keep from overwhelming the child with too close or too anxious attention. The child in a small family may carry a heavy burden when the anxiety, irritation, or attention centered on him is undiluted and undivided. Schools give both parents and child the opportunity to have some freedom from contacts that may be limiting because they are constant and close.

Community understanding and support are important for every school or center. The school is of value to the community and needs support from it. Teachers need to help citizens become acquainted with the school and with its purposes.

PROJECTS

1. Make a survey of the community, and report on the number and types of schools or centers that serve the needs of young children. What are the provisions for the care of young children whose mothers are working?

2. Visit a day-care center and a Head Start program. What are the goals of these groups and how well are these goals being met?

SUPPLEMENTARY READING

Fein, G., and A. Clarke-Stewart. *Day Care in Context*. New York: Wiley, 1973.

Klein, J. Mainstreaming the preschooler. *Young Children,* 1975, *30* (5):317–326.

Landreth, C. *Preschool Learning and Teaching*. New York: Harper & Row, 1972.

Moore, S. The effects of head start programs with different curricula and teaching strategies. *Young Children,* 1977, *32* (6):54–61.

Robinson, H., and B. Spodek. *New Directions in the Kindergarten*. New York: Teachers College, 1965.

National Association for Young Children. *Some Ways of Distinguishing a Good Early Childhood Program*. Washington, D.C.: NAEYC, 1975.

3

Flowers
(girl, 4.7)

History and Theories Influencing Contemporary Ideas in Early Education

To understand contemporary programs for young children, we must view how they evolved through the nineteenth and twentieth centuries. We offer this historical perspective in brief summaries of the histories of nursery school, kindergarten, and day care. The structure and organization of current programs reflect modern views and theories, as well as historical influences. As an introduction to the modern ideas, we have selected three theories of development that have been particularly influential in recent programs for young children. Finally, we present twelve tenets in a philosophy of early education that we believe offer a valid rationale for contemporary programs.

HISTORY

The discussion of the history of programs for young children will be organized by the type of programs: nursery school, day care, and kindergarten.

THE NURSERY SCHOOL

The first nursery school was established in 1911 in England by Rachel and Margaret Macmillan. The Macmillans had worked with children in health clinics in the London slums and wanted to prevent the physical and mental illness they found so prevalent among the children in these slums. Much of their work was based on the ideas of a French educator, Edward Sèguin, who had worked with mentally retarded children. Sèquin had devised methods that focused on teaching sensory development. The Macmillan sisters thought of the nursery school as a place where children were to be nurtured. The nursery school program they planned included opportunities for children to learn to take care of themselves, to assume responsibility for some ''housekeeping'' chores, as well as activities in learning language, colors and forms, reading, writing, arithmetic, and science. Grace Owens, a contemporary of the Macmillans, believed that the needs of three- and four-year-old children could be met best by programs that provided large blocks of time for play and other unstructured activities such as art, woodworking, water and sand play. She thought that reading, writing, and arithmetic should not be introduced to three- and four-year-old children.

About the same time as the Macmillans and Grace Owens were beginning nursery schools in England, Dr. Maria Montessori was working with retarded children in Italy. Montessori, like the Macmillans, was influenced by the work of Sèguin. After working with mentally retarded children she began to teach normal children in the slums of Rome. She was convinced that children learned best by being active, by doing rather than by sitting and being talked to. In this regard her ideas were similar to those of John Dewey in the United States. She developed sets of materials that were self-correcting, needing little supervision, and that could be used in a sequence from simple to complex. Montessori was interested in children's intellectual development and in their development of good work habits. She was less concerned with the social, emotional, and creative development of children.

In the 1920's Susan Isaacs directed a small school in England, for economically advantaged children, which also followed an activity-centered program. Isaacs had an interest in research and kept full notes of her observations of children's responses. She was interested in studying social, emotional, and intellectual aspects of development and interpreted her observations with insights from Freud's and Piaget's theories. Her goal was the development of the whole child. Isaacs provided the children with a rich variety of practical materials and encouraged children to explore these in their play.

Rachel and Margaret Macmillan, Grace Owens, Susan Isaacs, and Maria Montessori all had an impact on nursery schools in the United States. In the 1920's a number of teachers who had worked with the Macmillans and Grace Owens came to this country to demonstrate the English nursery school in New York, Boston, and Detroit. Susan Isaacs influenced thinking about the nursery school in the United States through her published observations and

Unit floor blocks are used widely today in nursery schools and kindergarten.

reports on children's learning and social development. Her use of the theoretical frameworks of Freud and Piaget represents groundbreaking work. Most schools continue to use Montessori's idea of a step-by-step progression in children's learning. These women's ideas about the child as an active learner continue to be implemented in programs today.

One of the first nursery schools which opened in the United States was the Play School, founded by Caroline Pratt, in 1913. It was later called the City and Country School and was directed by Harriet Johnson with the assistance of Lucy Sprague Mitchell. This school was the laboratory for the Bureau of Educational Experiments, which later became the present Bank Street College of Education. It was Caroline Pratt who designed the unit floor blocks used widely today in nursery schools and kindergartens.

Hull House, founded by Jane Adams in Chicago, opened a nursery school in the 1920's to serve children of the large immigrant population in the area. This school was used for the purpose of teacher education by students from the National College of Education. Although there was very little interest in nursery education during the twenties, the Chicago area had two nursery schools in public schools. One was the Franklin School in the lower north side of the city, a poor socioeconomic area; the second nursery school was the Winnetka School located in a well-to-do suburb. These two public schools existed in part because of Rose Alschuler's interest in children and their welfare. She gave generously of her time and money to help maintain the best possible educational programs in both of these settings.

In 1922, the Merrill Palmer School of Motherhood and Home Training, later the Merrill Palmer Institute, opened a nursery school in Detroit with Edna Noble White, a home economist, as the director. This laboratory nursery school was used for training young women from different colleges and universities throughout the country in the field of child development. Also in 1922, a day nursery on Ruggles Street opened in Boston and became the

Ruggles Street Nursery School, headed by Abigail Eliot. The programs of both of these schools were modeled after the school run by the Macmillan sisters in London.

A 1931 study surveyed 203 nursery schools in the United States (Davis, 1932). About half of these first schools were opened in colleges and universities as a result of the child-study movement. Some were financed by grants from foundations, such as the programs in institutes at the University of Minnesota, the University of Iowa, and the University of California at Berkeley. Others were financed by the institutions themselves, usually in women's colleges or home economics departments of land-grant colleges or universities. About one-third of these schools were privately controlled and about one-fifth were sponsored by child-welfare agencies. One particularly influential school, administered by Dorothy Baruch in Pasadena, California, was used as a laboratory for teacher education by college students. This school was later incorporated into what is now Pacific Oaks College of Education.

Lawrence K. Frank was one of the organizing forces behind the institutes in the universities mentioned above and the grants to women's colleges. He saw the need for systematic, intensive research in child development and parent education. He was able to translate many of his ideas into action first through the Laura Spelman Rockefeller Fund and later through the Josiah Macy Foundation. He thought of child development as multidisciplinary and believed it should draw from anthropology, biology, sociology, medicine, psychology, and psychiatry in order to understand the development of the individual (Senn, 1975).

In October 1933, during the economic depression, the Federal Relief Emergency Administration authorized the establishment of nursery schools to provide unemployed people with work. By 1938, these Works Progress Administration schools (WPA) had provided valuable opportunities for the care of 200,000 needy children. The program continued through 1942 with about 37,000 children attending WPA nursery schools each year (Bremner, 1974). These schools were free and provided well-balanced meals; rest; good physical, medical, and health care; and an educational program appropriate for the age groups. Teachers from primary and high-school levels, social workers, and others who were unemployed were given short courses at universities and colleges that had laboratory schools. In-service training was also provided by professionals who advised teachers in their own schools. The establishment of free nursery schools was seen as a pioneer movement in the United States and raised hope that nursery schools would become a permanent institution in this country. Yet, the funding for the WPA free nursery schools came abruptly to an end in 1943.

With the outbreak of World War II the Federal government passed the Community Facilities Act, popularly known as the Lanham Act, which provided funds for child care for children whose mothers were engaged in war-related industries. Some centers were sponsored by industry, some by community agencies. The centers that were established varied in their standards, depending on the training of the staff who was available. Many centers endeavored under difficult circumstances to carry on a nursery school program in the day-care setting.

One of the most successful of these centers was in the Kaiser Shipyards in Portland, Oregon. Two well-planned buildings were constructed at the entrances to each of the two shipyards. This program met the child-care needs of mothers who worked in the shipyards. At the peak of the war, as many as 500 children a day were cared for in a twenty-four hour program, six days a week. The centers had well-planned meals and health care to meet the needs of infants and children up to school age. Hot meals to be taken home were available at a modest cost.

The programs at the Kaiser Centers, under directors Lois Meek Stoltz and James Hymes, represented a synthesis of ideas and philosophies, because the teaching staff had been trained in colleges and universities from all over the country. When these two centers closed abruptly at the end of the war, some of the nursery school trained teachers remained in day-care work while others went into nursery school teaching. This dispersion of professional staff was typical in many Lanham Act schools. The mix of nursery school teachers with day-care experience and day-care teachers with nursery school experience has resulted in a relationship which has continued to the present time.

The growth of the nursery school during the 1950's was attributed to the increase in the number of parent cooperatives. A common characteristic of cooperatives was that parents often served as assistant teachers and provided a trained teacher, space, equipment, and materials. Another focus of the cooperative school was parent education—initiated by the parents themselves.

There was concern during the 1950's that the United States was falling behind other nations in preparing its young people to deal with the rapidly changing technological world. Programs of research in child growth and development multiplied in the 1950's and 1960's. Evidence continued to support the significance of early childhood experiences for later school performance.

Head Start, a federally funded project for four- and five-year-old children from families of low income, began in the summer of 1965. It has been estimated that approximately 11,000 centers served 561,360 children that summer (Steiner, 1976:30). Project Head Start evolved from the 1964 Economic Opportunity Act's provisions that were designed to attack poverty through community action programs. Head Start had five components: (1) medical and dental services for children; (2) social services and parent education; (3) use of volunteers; (4) services directed toward children's psychological development; and (5) school readiness (Bremner, 1974:1820). In 1970, when most of the community action programs were on the wane, Head Start maintained its political popularity and survived the dissolution of the Office of Economic Opportunity.

The professional organization, The National Association for Nursery Education, founded in 1929, with only a few hundred members, has now grown to over 10,000 members. In 1964, that original organization was renamed The National Association for the Education of Young Children or NAEYC. This group now spans the nursery, kindergarten, and primary years. It meets annually and has state associations affiliated with it in most states. The NAEYC journal, *Young Children,* is published bimonthly.

DAY CARE

Day care was first established in large cities by social reformers and welfare groups for the physical care of infants whose mothers worked. Three factors seemed to influence the need for these day nurseries: (1) the Industrial Revolution, which provided opportunities for mothers to earn money outside the home; (2) the medical discoveries that related sanitary conditions to health; and (3) the finding that working mothers' infants had a higher death rate than that of infants whose mothers who did not work (Fein and Clarke-Stewart, 1973). Taken together, these factors directed attention to the need for infant day care that focused on infant health.

In 1844, the first crèche was opened in Paris to provide physical care and prevent the death of infants (Forest, 1927). Ten years later, in 1854, the first day nursery in the United States was opened at the Nursery and Child's Hospital in New York City. Mothers who worked and had been patients at this hospital left their children each day to be cared for by the nurses. In 1858, in Troy, New York, and in 1868, in Philadelphia, similar nurseries for infants were opened. By 1897, there were approximately 175 such nurseries for children of immigrant and poor working mothers. Almost all of these nurseries were located in settlement houses (Bremner, 1974). Many nurseries expanded to include facilities for toddlers and preschool-age children. With this expansion and the need for care by large numbers of children, overcrowding occurred, and it became difficult to provide good physical care. In 1898, the National Federation of Day Nurseries was founded to raise the standards of care.

By the turn of the century at least two programs were sponsored by public schools. One was located in Los Angeles, California (Whipple, 1929), and another in Gary, Indiana (Dewey and Dewey, 1919). In these centers, as well as in those located in settlement houses, the child's physical health and well-being were still primary goals. Thought was being given to teaching children orderliness, good manners, and other social values. A few centers reflected the influence of Froebel and the kindergarten movement in the United States and added "gifts," "occupations," songs, games, and stories as a part of the child's day.

In the 1920's, as nursery schools were introduced to the United States in private schools, colleges, and universities and influenced by the child-study movement, day care was influenced by the educational programs of the nursery school. At that time day care and nursery schools were similar in structure and program. For example, although day care was a longer day, both were full-day programs; health, nutrition, and social and emotional development were primary goals of the programs; and nursery school trained teachers worked in both settings.

Perhaps more striking than these similarities was the difference in the populations served by day care and nursery school. Although day care had been seen as a necessary service to immigrants and poor working mothers, it was beginning to be viewed as a service that should be provided only when the need could be justified. Whereas, nursery school was seen as a supplement to the upper-middle- and upper-class home, it was viewed as one of many options available to such families.

During the 1920's and 1930's the number of day-care centers had diminished. In the 1940's, after the outbreak of World War II, women were again needed as part of the labor force for war industries. The passage of the Lanham Act in 1941 provided federal money to support new group services for families in war impact areas. These services were clustered in day-care centers in which the directors and head teachers were professionally trained in nursery school education.

Currently, there is a renewed interest in public funded day care for the children of working parents. This interest is shown not only by parents who must work because of economic necessity, but also by men and women who believe such services should be available to any person responsible for children and who chooses to work.

KINDERGARTEN

Friedrich Froebel opened the first kindergarten in Brackenburg, Germany, in 1837. The curriculum, based on a mystical religious philosophy, included moral, intellectual, and physical education for children three through seven years of age. Froebel developed a precise system of "gifts" or "playthings," occupations or handiwork activities, songs, games, stories, and gardening. All of these activities were symbolic and designed to teach the unity of the individual with God, the unity of the individual with nature, and the unity of the individual with other people. Froebel valued the child as a child and saw play as serious and significant. He viewed the child as a unique, creative, and productive person who learned through activity. Froebel laid an important foundation for what would be a later conception: the child-centered school.

In 1856 Margaretha Meyer Schurz, who had studied with Froebel, opened the first kindergarten in the United States in the parlor and front porch of her own home (Weber, 1969). This was a German-speaking kindergarten for the two Schurz children and their four cousins.

On a visit to Boston, Margaretha Schurz met Elizabeth Peabody and introduced her to Froebel's ideas about kindergarten. In 1860, after reading

Froebel's work, Elizabeth Peabody opened a private kindergarten based on her conception of Froebel's ideas. Later she and her sister, Mary Mann, published a book entitled *Kindergarten Guide*. By 1867, although the kindergarten idea and her school had flourished, Elizabeth Peabody doubted that she understood Froebel's intent well enough, and she closed her school and went to Germany to learn more about the kindergarten. On her return from Germany she continued to be influential in the kindergarten movement through writing and publishing the *Kindergarten Messenger* and later writing in the *New England Journal of Education* (Ross, 1976).

The first public school kindergarten was established in 1873, in St. Louis, Missouri. The Superintendent of Schools in St. Louis, William T. Harris, had met Elizabeth Peabody who had tried to convince him to make kindergarten a part of the public school. Nevertheless, it was Susan Blow, who had observed kindergartens in Germany, who convinced him to let her teach one kindergarten class as a demonstration project. The success of this project is evidenced by the fact that by 1879 there were 53 kindergartens in the St. Louis public schools. It is interesting to note that in these first kindergartens there was one teacher, an assistant teacher, and often volunteers. Susan Blow's project in St. Louis provided a model for other public schools that later would establish kindergartens.

By the turn of the century, kindergartens were established in 30 states with two-thirds of the 4500 programs sponsored by private, humanitarian organizations, such as churches, missions, and philanthropic agencies (Butts, 1955). This growth of kindergartens in the private sector accompanied two views popular in society during the end of the nineteenth century: (1) that children needed and deserved loving and kind nuturance; and (2) that the poor should be prepared for vocations. Kindergarten was seen as a program that could implement these ideas. The kindergartener, as the teacher was called then, after teaching all morning, worked in social services in the afternoons to help unemployed parents seek jobs and to get free medical and dental care for children and their families (Hill, 1941).

At the turn of the century there were two distinct points of view about the conduct of kindergarten education. One group continued to follow Froebel and argued against the revision of his ideas. The other group was influenced by G. Stanley Hall and John Dewey. The International Kindergarten Union, formed in 1892, became a forum for the debate.

Hall was the President of Clark University and Chairman of the Department of Psychology. Through his efforts Clark became the center for the new child-study movement. Hall believed that children's interests, feelings, and their play were important factors in planning a curriculum. He also believed that educational theory and practice could advance only when the nature of childhood and the stages of development were clearly understood.

In order to test his educational ideas, John Dewey established a laboratory school at the University of Chicago in 1896. Dewey believed that the child learned as he used real objects for real purposes, as he coped with real situations, as he managed and understood his own experience, and as he judged his own work. He also believed that real objects and real situations within the child's own social setting could be used for problem solving and learning.

The impact of Hall's and Dewey's ideas on their own students, as well as on teacher education, accounts in part for the development of the unique character of the kindergarten in the United States.

About 1912, there was a flurry of excitement in educational circles over a new system of education developed by Maria Montessori in Italy. A number of people visited Rome to observe her system. In general, they concluded that her system did not allow the child to be spontaneous, that the goals of the program were too narrow, and that it was a formal, mechanical system not compatible with current knowledge about learning. Some private Montessori schools were established in the United States in the mid-1920's, but most were discontinued or changed their form in the 30's and 40's. However, they were revived again in the 1960's. Some have followed the original Montessori ideas quite closely, while others are variations of the system.

From 1900 to 1925, kindergarten education was characterized by debate, experimentation, and curriculum development. Across the country there were people deeply involved in planning and revising kindergarten programs in light of new knowledge. Patty Hill Smith, Caroline Pratt, Jessie Stanton, and Margaret Naumberg in New York City; Alice Temple in Chicago; Lucy Gage in Nashville; Frederick Burk and Barbara Greenwood in California, and many others were devoted to improving the quality of life for children through programs in early education.

The diversity of school systems and the large number of institutions providing teacher education seem to make impossible any single, precise description of early or contemporary kindergartens. At the same time, we believe it is important for students to understand that current programs do reflect their historical origins as well as more modern perspectives. Throughout the twentieth century kindergarten curriculum and its rationale have been influenced by political, economic, and social events, as well as by the accumulation of information from studies in psychology, sociology, anthropology, and child development. For example, in the 1920's programs were likely to reflect "habit training" based on Edward L. Thorndike's and John B. Watson's ideas. Expansion of kindergarten programs were curtailed during the depression. In the 1930's Arnold Gesell's studies, based on his views of maturation, were interpreted as "age norms" for many kindergarten children. In the 1940's and 50's the influence of the mental health movement appeared in programs, which emphasized social–emotional adjustment. In the 1960's emphasis on intellectual and language development may be seen as a response to the need for sophisticated competencies in adults in an industrial, technological society.

The professional organization, The International Kindergarten Union

A few kindergarten children may be interested in writing books for their library.

(IKU), was founded in 1882 with its first members being kindergarten teachers. In 1924, the IKU and The National Council of Primary Teachers joined together and founded the *Journal of Childhood Education*. Six years later, in 1930, they merged into The Association for Childhood Education which is now the international organization, The Association for Childhood Education International (ACEI). It meets annually, has affiliations in all states, and publishes a journal during the months of October through May.

THREE THEORIES THAT HAVE INFLUENCED PROGRAMS IN NURSERY SCHOOL, DAY CARE, AND KINDERGARTEN

Among the many investigators in the area of child growth and development we have selected three whose thinking has contributed most significantly to our understanding of human behavior: Sigmund Freud, Erik Erikson, and Jean Piaget. Many other investigators have made important contributions, but they have not developed such comprehensive theories. The theories of these three men were based on careful observations of human behavior, much of which were done under natural rather than laboratory conditions.

CONTRIBUTION OF SIGMUND FREUD

The theories of Sigmund Freud (1957, 1960) have greatly influenced our understanding of personality development. His work in the late nineteenth and early twentieth centuries has been carried forward by many others and has become part of our thinking about personality. It includes the concept of the unconscious, that great reservoir of universal feeling within us, which we can never be directly aware of, but which influences what we do. It also includes an emphasis on the significance of the individual's earliest experience in determining attitudes and patterns of behavior and the existence of infant sexuality.

Freud described the early stages in development as the *oral,* the *anal,* and the *phallic,* with their respective sources of excitement and satisfaction, followed by a latency period lasting until adolescence. He pointed to the male and female components in the personality of every individual and the process a child goes through in establishing his or her sex identification.

Freud developed the method known as "psychoanalysis" for gaining insights into the defenses built up by an individual that block the creative use of energies. Psychoanalysts working with disturbed young children have used "play therapy" as a method of treating children's emotional disturbances. Play therapy is based on the principle that in play children often reveal indirectly or symbolically the conflicts they are feeling. Among these therapists is Anna Freud, the daughter of Sigmund Freud, who has made important contributions to our understanding of children.

The process of discovering and accepting one's sex, according to Freudian theory, takes place in the first years of life and becomes the basis for normal sexual adjustment later in life. In the beginning, all infants relate closely to the primary care-giver. Later, the infant moves toward identification with the parent of his or her own sex, male or female. The struggle of the male child to shift identification from the mother to the father is known as the "oedipal conflict" and is most acute in the third, fourth, and fifth years. We see boys of this age asserting themselves in vigorous, aggressive ways, imitating males and needing to have their father's attention and approval.

Young boys in families in which the father is absent may have a serious problem; they have a real need for contact with a man from whom they can learn male attitudes and behavior. Schools should have men as teachers and care-givers to meet this need, either as regular staff members or as volunteers. The staff in schools for young children may be predominantly female, but it should not be exclusively so. Girls, also, need contacts with males in order to develop their femininity. Girls shift to a new relationship with their mothers, that is, identifying with the mother as a female. The shift to identifying with the same-sex parent is more gradual for girls than for boys.

In the school we observe the interest that children have in each other, as they use the toilets together and observe differences in the sexes. A girl may be interested in the boy's penis and wonder why she lacks one. All children are interested in the subject of babies and where they come from. They have many misconceptions, which can slowly be cleared up by offering the correct information, as it is wanted. Both boys and girls try out male and female roles in their sociodramatic play, as they seek to discover more about what these roles are like in the grown-up world.

CONTRIBUTION OF ERIK ERIKSON

Erikson's (1950, 1959) interest in personality development led him to observe people in different cultures. From his studies he formulated a theory of stages in personality growth, with each stage having a major "task." He presented an outline of these stages at the 1950 White House Conference in Washington. According to Erikson, a "task" consists in resolving the conflicting impulses that characterize the stage in a favorable direction. We will consider the crises and tasks of the preschool years, as Erikson has outlined them.

The first and most basic task in healthy personality development is achieving a *sense of trust outweighing the sense of mistrust.* In the first year or more of life the infant needs to feel that the world is a trustworthy place and that he himself is trustworthy. This sense of trust will grow out of the experiences the infant has with his primary care-giver and later with other significant people in his world. Out of many experiences of having his needs met, being fed when hungry, being kept warm and safe, and being handled with loving care, he begins to trust the world. This feeling enables him to meet the new, the unexpected, and the frustrating situations that come later. Because of these positive interactions, the individual learns to trust his own capacity to meet what comes.

D. W. Winnicott, an English pediatrician and psychoanalyst, has also contributed to our understanding of the importance of early mothering and its influence on personality development. Winnicott (1957) pointed to the importance of a mother's adaptation to her infant in the first weeks and months when, by her sensitive management, she adapts completely to the infant at first and then gradually withdraws this complete adaptation, as she senses that the infant is ready to tolerate delays and frustrations—in other words, when he has developed sufficient trust. By presenting the world to him "in small enough doses," she enables the infant to build a sense of trust over mistrust, which is the cornerstone of a healthy personality.

All through life we continue to need experiences that contribute to our feeling that the world is a place where we can feel comfortable and trust ourselves. The most critical point, the crisis point, for the development of this trait occurs in the earliest months of life. The infant needs protection then from experiences that produce mistrust which may overpower him. For example, separation from the care-giving person, even when it is brief, may be overwhelming to an infant. It may seem an eternity to him because of his undeveloped sense of time.

Mutual adaptation is an important element here. As the weeks and months go by, under favorable conditions the infant builds up a large "bank account" of trust from which he can draw. His care-giver can then expect him to make adaptations to her needs and the needs of others. By her expectations his care-giver shows her trust in him and in his growing capacity to delay satisfaction.

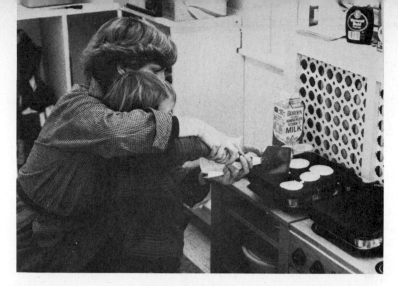

A trustworthy teacher can help a child learn to trust himself.

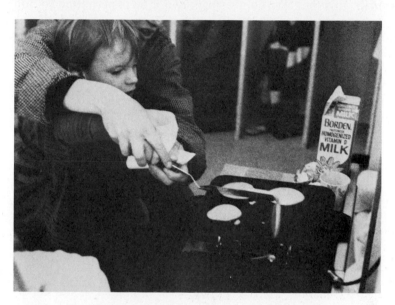

Infants differ in their responses. Some seem to grow to trust easily, and others find it more difficult. It is the care-giver's sensitive management that enables an infant to succeed in developing a healthy balance of trust over mistrust. The task of continuing to build trust remains important throughout the early childhood period. In fact, throughout life, as one suffers disillusionment, one needs to restore one's faith in oneself and in the trustworthiness of others.

The second task in healthy personality growth is that of developing a *sense of autonomy outweighing the sense of shame or doubt.* Already toward the end of the first year we can see evidence of the child working on this task. It becomes the major task of the second and third years. The primary care-giver must be sensitive to the great need of the child to assert his independence at this time. It is the "Me do it" stage, and if he is permitted to "do it," the child has the chance to begin to take steps in organizing himself as a learner. It is the age of "No" and frequent "contrariness." Out of being allowed to be autonomous is born an independent individual capable of feeling "I *am* someone."

Mutual adaptation between the child and his primary care-giver is again important here. If this task is to be accomplished there must be sufficient autonomy to balance the necessary dependence the child has on his care-giver and the doubt he feels about his ability to be autonomous. It is a period when discipline should be mild and reserved for the most necessary points. If we can accept his self-assertion, we find the child usually does what we want, because he can feel that *he* is deciding to do what we have asked. Giving him choices, avoiding confrontations, and introducing a play element all are helpful to the child at this stage. In this way we are protecting him in his task of beginning to feel himself autonomous, "I *am* and I am important and powerful," in his own small world. Feeling autonomous is far superior to feeling helpless and doubtful as one faces life.

The third task in personality growth as outlined by Erikson is that of developing a *sense of initiative outweighing the sense of guilt.* It is the important personality task of the child of three, four, and five years, although we see many signs of initiative earlier. In this stage the child is more actively exploring and investigating, he is beginning to ask questions to think new thoughts, to try himself out in all kinds of ways, as he takes the initiative. He is also developing a conscience, a sense of being responsible for actions as an autonomous person. A conscience is necessary and valuable, but it should not carry too heavy a load at this point in healthy personality growth. A four-year-old can easily feel *too* guilty for some transgression or guilty for the wrong things. It is important that his sense of initiative, of being able to forge ahead and try, should outweigh his fear of wrongdoing. Understanding guidance is needed in this period, if the child is to emerge with a large measure of initiative outweighing, but still maintaining, his capacity for guilt.

In this stage the child has an urge to make and to do things. It is a creative period in personality growth. A four-year-old who may be helping to carry the blocks back to the shelves where they belong may suddenly discover the interesting patterns they make as they tumble from his wagon or the way in which they can be stuffed into the holes in the fence. He begins a new and imaginative form of play. He will need a reminder about the job at hand and perhaps some help in getting on with the task, but we can do this with an appreciation for what he has discovered and for the excitement he feels for his discovery. When one is four or five years old, life should be made up of such experiences.

This period is an important one for intellectual development. The groundwork is being laid for the child's current and future learning in school. With a firm foundation of trust and a sense of being an autonomous person, he exercises his initiative, taking hold of opportunities, as offered, and making something out of them. This is the period in which most young children are when we first meet them in schools. We should consider this task, as we guide them. There will be unfinished business, however, left over from the earlier stages for almost all children. We need to give help with all these tasks, if sound personality growth is to continue, but the major task for a care-giver of a child in this period is to encourage and support the child's sense of initiative.

The next stage, the development of a *sense of industry outweighing the sense of inadequacy or inferiority* is the important task of the school-age child and continues through to adolescence. At this stage the healthy child sees himself as a "worker" and a "learner." Games with rules, skill in sports, and group activities become important. He is a school child ready to accomplish in learning under favorable circumstances. In Piaget's terms, he is in the intellectual stage of "concrete operations."

As we work with young children, we will keep in mind these personality tasks and the help we may be able to give children in order that the crises may be resolved in ways favorable to healthy development. We will adapt our ways of working with children, so we can support the balance of trust over mistrust, the balance of autonomous feeling over doubt, and the balance of initiative over guilt; we will value the child's developing sense of industry over inferiority, as he becomes a learner and worker.

CONTRIBUTION OF JEAN PIAGET

Piaget, a Swiss psychologist, became interested in observing the development of his own children and devoted himself to studying their behavior, especially the evidences of reasoning and judgment. He continued to observe and interview many children and he developed a theory of how children think and learn. His work has greatly influenced the program of the British Infant Schools. He was well known in Europe before he was "discovered" by American educators in the late 1950's.

Piaget (1954) has sought to trace how motor skills, perceptions, and cognitive abilities are acquired in a process of assimilating new experience to

Sensorimotor learning: a child explores clay.

preexisting structures. He calls these structures schemata and proposes that the schemata are changed by what has been assimilated. This change is called accommodation. He seeks to understand how the infant and child become capable of assimilating new experiences and carrying out increasingly complex activities through changes of schemata. He theorizes that development takes place as a series of stages, each being an advance from the last one, with reorganization and adaptation going on continuously.

The first stage, from birth to about two years, Piaget calls the *sensorimotor stage*. The infant has the ability to act and the ability to organize his perceptions. The normal infant is capable of looking, listening, feeling, tasting, smelling, and moving. It is through his ability to act and to organize his perceptions that the infant begins to know his physical and social world. Through time, with experiences and maturation, the child's behavior becomes intentional. He comes to know people and objects exist even when he cannot see them and that people and objects move when he is not looking. He begins to anticipate events; he finds that he can make things happen; he begins to imitate sounds and use language. Piaget calls this *sensorimotor* learning, for it takes place through using the senses and movement.

The second of Piaget's stages, from about the age of two years to six or seven years, is *preoperational thought*. This stage is further divided into two substages: *preconceptual* and *intuitive thought*. During the preconceptual substage, which extends from about two to four years of age, the child develops "symbolic function" or imagery. What was known in a sensorimotor way is now beginning to be known by signs and symbols. That is, the child is beginning to use mental representation of people, objects, and

In play children form mental symbols as they enact adult roles.

events not present in his immediate environment. Ginsberg and Opper (1969) say:

> In order to deal with things, he no longer requires that they be immediately present; instead, he is able to create a mental substitute for the real thing. This ability frees the child from the immediate here and now. Instead of having to manipulate things, he works with their substitutes. The child forms mental symbols through imitation. The child looks at things, handles them, and acts like them, and in these ways incorporates a great deal of information about them. . . . In fact, imitation may be considered to bridge the gap between sensorimotor and later intelligence. (p. 84)

The child continues to use the sensorimotor mode, although his intellectual development from this time onward gradually moves toward conceptual thinking.

During the second substage, *intuitive thought,* which appears at approximately four years and extends to about seven years, Piaget emphasizes that the child's thought is characterized by more complex representation, although judgments continue to be made on the basis of perceptions. For example, Steven (5.3) was reminded to wash his hands after toileting. "But my hands aren't dirty," he responded plaintively. True from his point of view, there was no dirt to be seen on his hands.

Children in this substage can put like things together to form groups or classes of objects. Their criterion for class inclusion is based on functional, formal, and physical properties. The limitation at this stage is not understanding the hierarchy of classes, the relationship between "all and some." For example, children were harvesting radishes and peas from the school garden. Eric (4.8) quickly sorted the peas into one basket and radishes into another. He knew the names, peas and radishes; he called them both vegetables, knowing some were peas and some were radishes: he knew by looking that there were more radishes than peas. When asked if there were more vegetables or more radishes, he answered, "Radishes." His response demonstrates the limitation of thinking in this substage; that is, not being able to deal with the relationship between the subclasses and the superordinate class.

The third stage of Piaget's theory is *concrete operations*. This stage begins at about seven years of age and continues to eleven or twelve years. It is characterized as consisting of an internalized or mental action that enables the child to reverse his thinking and to return to his starting point. These actions are called concrete operations, because the starting point is always with real objects and relations that the child perceives. When a child understands the relationship between classes and subclasses and between the whole and its parts, when he can order objects in terms of size, shape, weight, age, or some other criterion, when he knows that certain properties of objects remain constant, even though the objects change in position and arrangements, he is said to be in the stage of concrete operations.

Teaching Strategies Are Based on Theory

Our observations of children hold more meaning for us when we can relate child behavior to stages in growth. We become aware that a two-year-old who refuses a proferred hand on a steep slope is exercising his urge to be autonomous. When he stops to poke his finger into a hole or to touch every object he sees, he is learning about the world through all his senses. A three-year-old's questions are evidences of intellectual growth and the desire to understand what he is observing. The group of four-year-olds arguing in the homemaking corner have reached a stage of competency in language and can communicate and work out compromises. A year or more earlier the same children would have been pursuing their own purposes in parallel play.

TENETS IN A PHILOSOPHY OF EARLY CHILDHOOD EDUCATION

A philosophy is based on beliefs and on knowledge. The way we undertake to educate children will depend on what we believe to be most essential or important for an effectively functioning human being in a democratic society. It will also depend on what is known about the growth and development of young children.

The *overall goal* of early childhood education is to provide a child with an environment that will promote his optimum development at a period when growth is rapid and the child is vulnerable to deprivation of appropriate opportunities, new knowledge, and new relationships.

All aspects of growth are considered in the program, *physical* development, the *social* development, the capacity to enjoy relationships and get along with other people, *emotional* development, including growth in confidence and understanding of oneself as a person and growth in ability to express thoughts and feelings and to manage impulses, and *intellectual* or cognitive development, including language competency, nourished through guidance in a stimulating environment.

The following assumptions are common to most early childhood education programs. They embody principles we will be using, as we work with children individually or in groups. They are tenets in a philosophy of early childhood education which underlie a program.

1. *Every child is an individual with his own rate and style of learning and growing, his own unique patterns of approach to situations, and his own innate capacities.* His genes and his experiences as a family member have made him different from any other individual. He has his own strengths and vulnerabilities. Some of these differences may seem to be "deficiencies," if his behavior fails to fit the expectations of a particular situation. A child from a Spanish-speaking home, for example, may seem "backward" when compared with children in an English-speaking group. We need to accept each child as an individual within his own "frame of reference" and values, without employing any limited or preconceived standards. A child skillful in cooperation with others may not be successful in competitively motivated situations; for example, a child with manual skills may be considered "deficient" in an academic setting. To do justice to individuals, we need to broaden our horizons to include respect for the strengths of individuals.

Every child needs opportunities adapted to his individual needs, with respect for his individuality. For example, Juan, described earlier, waits and watches before entering an activity; while Janie approaches and enters new situations without waiting to watch what others are doing. Guidance for individual children takes into account each child's style of approaching new situations.

2. *The genetic constitution and the environment together determine the course of development of an individual.* We may say that the genes determine the limits of development, and the environment determines how much of what is possible will be achieved. A normal person is born with the capacity for developing speech, for example, but he does not learn to talk unless he is with people who use speech. The kind of language he learns and how well he uses the language will depend on his environment.

A normal person is also born with an ability to experience a range of feelings. What he will feel, his biases and prejudices, his loves and hates, will grow out of his experiences. We influence the direction and the extent of development in the children we teach in school.

3. *Intelligence develops as it is nurtured.* Cognitive development depends on adequate and appropriate physical, mental, and social stimulation supplied by the home, the school, and the community. The "critical period" for nurturing intelligence seems to occur early in the life of individuals. The

This girl understands the
meaning of the word
"heavy."

individual needs a range of suitable experiences and opportunities to act on
these. He needs to feel secure and valued by people who also value learning.

4. *All aspects of development are interrelated: physical, social, emotional,
and intellectual.* The child develops as a whole, with each area influencing
and being influenced by what takes place in other areas. In planning a program, we consider the child as a whole, not just one aspect of his development. For example, in planning opportunities for developing physical skills,
we are also interested in how these skills build self-confidence, increase
opportunities for contacts with other children, and add to the child's knowledge of the physical world.

5. *Growth means change.* Changes take place not only in a child's height
and weight, but also in his capacities and characteristics. Changes are often
accompanied by conflicts or disturbances, until a new equilibrium is
reached. During these periods of change the child is likely to respond well to
appropriate guidance or help. Our role is to influence growth changes in
positive, healthy directions, physically and psychologically.

Children's behavior changes, as circumstances change. When a child is
tired or ill, for example, he behaves differently from when he is rested or
well. When we say that a child is "dull" or "lazy" or "selfish," we are
reporting *only* an inference based on what we see at the moment. In time, or

under different circumstances, or in someone else's view, the child might be described differently. We change, too. With more experience and more understanding, we perceive different meanings in children's behavior.

6. *Growth takes place in orderly sequences or stages, with each successive stage depending on the outcome of previous stages.* No stage can be skipped without handicapping the child. Rates of growth and development differ within an individual child, as well as among children, but the sequence of stages is uniform. A child sits up before he walks; he laces his shoes before he can tie his laces. Age gives only a general indication of what to expect because children differ in the time they take to complete a stage, but not in the order in which the change takes place. For example, most six-year-olds and some five-year-olds can tie shoe laces, but very few four-year-olds can.

Having time to complete each stage, with a variety of opportunities for learning appropriate to the stage, enables the child to leave one stage behind and move on, fully prepared for the next. Pressure or "nudging" to move on before a stage is completed inhibits sound growth and development, just as blocking the forward movement does.

In every stage there are certain aspects of development that are "critical," most vulnerable to deprivation and most likely to benefit from optimum conditions. Severe protein deficiency in the diet of the twelve- to twenty-four-month-old child, for example, will impair physical and intellectual development, but the same deficiency may have only a temporary effect on an adult. Between six months and twelve months, for example, the infant is at a critical stage in his development of a feeling of trust. He is more disturbed by an extended separation from his mother, at this point, than he will be later.

7. *Play is an important avenue for learning and for enjoyment.* Children learn through active involvement in play, using all their senses; through doing things to and with materials; through representing concepts in play, rehearsing roles, and thus clarifying them. Children test out, explore, discover, adapt, classify, organize, and reorganize their experiences as they play.

Exploration, mastery, sustained attention, and effort are a part of play; they also characterize learning. Play calls for initiative, imagination, and purposefulness. It calls for motor skills and for social skills. Beginnings of symbolic thinking occur in play. Play with other children is considered essential for healthy personality development. The values of play are increased by informed guidance and a wide variety of appropriate materials and equipment, as well as by a provision for space and uninterrupted time.

8. *Attitudes and feelings are important in learning and in healthy personality growth.* The attitude of the child toward himself, the way he feels about himself, is an important factor in his learning and in his mental health. If he is to develop well, a child needs to feel that the significant people around him like him and feel that he is an able person. A positive self-concept or self-image enables the child to use his capacities well.

Becoming aware of one's own feelings and those of others and finding avenues for expressing feelings in constructive and creative ways are other

Woodworking requires
planning, motor skills, effort, concentration—and
facing consequences.

important aspects of learning. They can be fostered by understanding guidance. Self-control results from being aware of one's impulses and having
avenues into which negative impulses can be channeled. Imagination and its
expression in art and language and its use in problem solving can also be
stimulated through a favorable environment.

9. *Behavior is motivated by extrinsic and intrinsic factors.* Extrinsic forms of
motivation consist in giving attention, approval, or reward for a specific
behavior; in withholding attention; in disapproval; in punishment to reinforce behavior; or in making it more likely that the child will repeat or desist
behaving in some way. The effectiveness of the reinforcement will depend in
part on the relationship existing between the child and the one who reinforces. Personal relationships play a large part in motivation.

Intrinsic motivation comes from inside the child, arising out of his curiosity, his drive toward competence, and his past experiences in finding satisfactions or in not finding them. In using a hammer or a saw, for example, the
child may persist, because he has an end in mind or because he finds satisfaction out of the increasing competency he feels in doing the job. Intrinsic
motivation tends to be more effective and to lead to more lasting change in
behavior.

Timing of reinforcement and type of reinforcement used at any point are
important. The child who is doing something because he wants to do it may
not need reinforcement, as does a child who is doubtful about himself and his
ability. The first child may want to be sure of the teacher's interest, but he is
not dependent on her for external reinforcement.

10. *Understanding, responsible guidance is necessary, if the child is to develop
his potential.* In his early years the child needs care-givers who like him, who
are generous and warm in feeling, who can assume responsibility for setting
limits, who are informed and resourceful in providing him with a favorable

environment, who enjoy learning themselves, who can feel respect for the child as well as for themselves, and who can communicate with children. Learning is personal for the child and is influenced by his relationships with those who provide for him and guide him. Personality development depends, too, on personal relationships with care-givers who serve as adequate "models" for the child.

Parents are the child's most important teachers. Teachers need to work with parents. Teachers and parents can learn from each other. Early childhood education programs should respect the parent–child relationship. Teachers have responsibility for interpreting programs to parents, as well as understanding the expectations of the parents about the education of their own child.

11. *The development of a young child suffers, if there are deficiencies in nutrition and health care; in attention and loving care; in opportunities to play and have relationships which nourish social, emotional, and intellectual growth.* Some apparent "deficiencies" are only differences in experience, such as those in language competency where English is not the first language. When real deficiencies do occur, they can best be compensated for by going back and supplying what was lacking in earlier stages, giving sound growth the opportunity to take place, rather than pushing a child on to the next stage.

12. *A healthy environment is the right of every child and the first responsibility of the community, the state, and the nation.* A healthy environment provides adequate health care, food, shelter, and community services including schools and services that offer support to families. It includes a family life free from excessive burdens of economic insecurity, deprivation, and discrimination, with adequate provision for satisfaction and stimulation for all members of the family. A child-development center is one of these community services. It contributes to the child and the family at a critical point in their lives.

Throughout the rest of our discussion, we will try to apply and make explicit the application of these assumptions, or tenets, to programs that meet the developmental needs of young children.

SUPPLEMENTARY READING

Erikson, E. *Childhood and Society*. New York: Norton, 1950.

Erikson, E. *Identity and the Life Cycle,* Vol. 1, New York: International Universities Press, 1959.

Freud, A. *Psychoanalysis for Teachers and Parents*. New York: Emerson, 1935.

Kesson, W. *The Child*. New York: Wiley, 1965.

Moore, S. Old and new approaches to preschool education. *Young Children,* 1977, *33* (1):69–72.

Piaget, J. *The Language and Thought of the Child*. New York: Basic Books, 1954. (Originally published, 1924.)

Weber, E. *The Kindergarten: Its Encounter with Educational Thought in America.* New York: Teachers College, 1969.

4

Man with Guitar
(boy, 4.0)

The Children and the Teaching Staff

We have described the characteristics of our conception of a good nursery school, kindergarten, and day-care program; we have followed a child through each program; we have listed types of centers serving young children; we have outlined the basic beliefs and tenets in a philosophy of education for young children. We will look now at factors to be considered in the more detailed planning for a program.

Attending school may supplement the child's home and neighborhood life, supplying a variety of opportunities not possible to the same extent at home, such as companionship with other children and guidance by trained adults who care about children. For children in a full-day program, the school not only supplements the home, it also contributes some of what the home is unable to provide because of limitations in time, space, or opportunity.

THE CHILDREN

Part of the answer to questions about *selection of children* attending the school or center will lie in the type of school and the needs it serves in the community. The population of the public school kindergarten is usually drawn from the particular district that school serves. A Head Start school, a school for physically or mentally handicapped children, or a laboratory school is planned to meet special purposes. The children are selected with these particular purposes in mind. Many schools, on the other hand, will decide to meet a variety of needs, enrolling some handicapped children, for example, or children from diverse cultural backgrounds.

Schools are fortunate if they include children of different races and socio-economic backgrounds. Under the guidance of understanding teachers, such diversity brings significant enrichment in the opportunities for all children. Children are sensitive to the feelings and attitudes of others. Under favorable conditions they develop constructive and realistic attitudes which can lead to better human relationships and perhaps to less complacency about discrimination on the part of society. Positive attitudes about a wide variety of other people begin in early schooling.

In any particular school, decisions will need to be made as to the number of children to enroll, the ages and the ranges in age, the length of the school day, and the number of teachers and aides.

NUMBER OF CHILDREN IN A GROUP

In a school planned to meet the needs of children, there will not be a large number of children in any one group. Space arrangements, the ages of the children, the length of the school day, the purposes of the program, and the experience of the staff will be among the factors which determine the exact number. Large groups create strain and reduce the contribution that a school can make to individuals.

To meet individual needs in an optimum way there should be no more than 20 children in a kindergarten group. The numbers in a nursery school group will be smaller. If some of the children are late two-year-olds and young threes the numbers will be much less. In a group set up to meet special needs, such as those of handicapped children, the numbers will be still smaller. The numbers of children in full-day group day care should also be very small because their teachers must meet many more of the child's physical and emotional needs.

AGES OF CHILDREN

The nursery school serves the needs of late two-, three-, four-, and sometimes five-year-old children. Most fives are ready for kindergarten, one which builds on the child's home and nursery school experiences.

The best evidence that we have at present indicates that most children are ready for group experience when they are about three years of age. Unless they can enter programs especially adapted for infants and toddlers, children seem to need three years in which to "live out" the period of dependency on parents, to achieve sufficient security in the home and with their parents to be ready to belong to a school group, and to identify with adults outside the home (Keister, 1970; Provence, Naylor, Patterson, 1974). Taking this step too soon in a group not adapted to the child's needs may distort growth as much as failing to take the step when the time is right.

Every parent will recognize in her child an eagerness to be with other children long before he is three. This readiness can be met by informal interactions with other children. Such opportunities help prepare the child for regular, sustained group participation later.

Many two-year-olds gain from a program planned especially for their needs. The program will probably be one or two hours, or less, a day, perhaps only two or three days a week, with care-givers present most of the time when the child first starts school. The real satisfaction that children of this age have in playing beside other children and the benefits they gain from play in an environment rich in opportunities for explorations and communication make such programs well worthwhile.

AGE RANGE IN A GROUP

Most schools are flexible in the range of ages, the age span depending on the goals of the school, the needs of the community, and the children served. There is evidence that a narrow age range in a group may increase competitiveness among children and offer less chance for the learnings that come from being with children who are both younger and older. Some teachers find it easier to provide opportunities adapted to each child's needs when the age range is within a year. Chronological age is not, however, the only measure of maturity. The range in levels of development is large in any group, whatever the range in age.

In a "family type" or "mixed age" group, the younger children have the opportunity to learn through watching and playing with older children. The older children, in turn, may gain from helping and playing with the younger ones. Cooperative play seems to occur more easily. The mixed age group at times takes skillful teacher guidance to prevent the younger children from continually taking passive roles or to prevent the older child from interfering in the play of younger children. Patterns of relating to siblings at home may be repeated and can then be worked through in the school.

We can only conclude on the evidence we have at present that the optimum range in age may depend on the preferences of the teachers or on the needs of particular situations.

LENGTH OF THE SCHOOL DAY

The length of the school day varies in different schools. The nursery or kindergarten age child gains from school attendance that supplements his home experience. Two-and-a half to three hours a day spent away from home with other children in school serves this purpose for most children. In day care, where the needs of the family make a longer school day necessary, the program will adapt its pace to meet the demands the longer day makes on the child. The child will have a nap at school or at least a period for rest. More of his nutritional needs, more of his dependency needs, and more of his learning needs will be met at school.

THE STAFF

NUMBER OF STAFF

The number and type of staff members in a school will depend on the size and purposes of the school. In a large school there will be a variety of staff members—a principal or director, teachers, assistant teachers, aides, perhaps students in training, and volunteers who may or may not be parents. There may also be a secretary, a cook, a person responsible for the cleaning and maintenance of the building, and possibly a "handy man." There may be people from other professions, such as a social worker, a speech pathologist, a nurse or doctor, and perhaps a psychologist or psychiatrist who act as consultants.

In a school program planned to meet the needs of young children, there will always be *more* than one adult with each group of children, regardless of the size of the group. There will be one trained teacher to every eight or ten children. The ratio will be lower for children with special needs or very young children.

Additional staff is needed when two-year-olds are enrolled in the group, since they need attention and individual care from a teacher, such as help in dressing, in using the toilet, and, at times, even in eating. The two-year-old also needs to have someone to turn to for encouragement or comfort—the

Two year old children enjoy playing alongside each other.

teacher must be there when he needs her, and she must be a person who enjoys, but does not foster, the dependency of a young child.

When children with physical or emotional handicaps are enrolled, the school needs additional staff. A blind or partially sighted child, a deaf, spastic, emotionally disturbed, or mentally retarded child requires more help from a teacher than does a child without a handicap. All these children may gain from being in a group of normal children and may contribute to the experiences of the other children when the situation is well planned and well staffed. A balance must be maintained between meeting the needs of special children and the needs of the rest of the group. For the good of all, the group should not be overweighted with handicapped children; otherwise the gains will be less for everyone.

The number of staff needed is also influenced by the physical arrangement of the classroom and the playground. Teachers can direct all their energy to meeting the needs of children, and the staff can be at a minimum, if the toilets and the playground are right next to the classroom, if there is ample storage space adjacent to where materials will be used, if children can move freely from one area or room to another without needing adult help, and if there are no "blind spots" in the rooms or yard.

PERSONAL CHARACTERISTICS OF TEACHERS

There is ample evidence that the teacher as a person is the most important single factor in determining what a school experience will be like for children. Not only a teacher's skill but also her attitudes and feelings will influence what she does for and with the children.

A teacher needs to be in good physical health and to get adequate rest if she is to meet the daily demands of a group of active young children. A teacher also needs to be emotionally stable and able to manage her moods so that they do not interfere with her responses in the teaching situation. She needs to have confidence in herself and in others, a capacity for warm personal relationships, and a zest for living and learning. A sense of humor and a "light touch" will help her keep a perspective, as she meets the daily crises in work.

A good teacher is flexible, resourceful, independent in her thinking, realistic, and capable of sustained effort. She is sensitive and responsive, but able to use authority in constructive ways. She trusts herself enough to experiment and to act with spontaneity. She is not immobilized by her own errors, but learns from them. In addition, she has a sense of order, an appreciation for beauty and the wonder of life, and a belief that each child can learn.

It takes time for a teacher to grow in understanding and skill, just as it takes time for a child to grow. We will find that becoming a competent teacher is a process that continues throughout one's teaching career. There will be teachers in different stages of "becoming" in any group. Learning to become a teacher involves developing an awareness of what is significant to

learn, as well as gaining skills in teaching. One cannot skip any stages in growth. The attempt to take shortcuts may preclude the possibilities of growth in later stages.

QUALIFICATIONS OF TEACHERS

The *teacher* in charge of the group should be well trained, with previous experience in nursery or kindergarten teaching. Her training will include a college or university degree with a major in early childhood education or its equivalent. Her degree will include courses in mathematics, history, science, social science, music, art, and the humanities, with special emphasis in the fields of child development, psychology, and education. Her preparation will also include laboratory participation and student teaching with groups of young children. The more extensive her training and experience, the better she should be able to do her job and make good use of her staff.

The *assistant teacher* should also have training in child development and in nursery school or kindergarten methods. She should have an understanding of personality development and the learning process in young children. As part of her training, she should have worked with a group of young children under the supervision of a trained and experienced teacher.

In nursery schools or day-care programs assistant teachers may be persons trained as Child Development Associates under a program funded by the federal government in which academic work is coordinated with field experience. Credit is given for previous practical experience. A minimum of 50 percent of the training time is spent in supervised experience.

AIDES

Some schools use aides as assistants to supplement the professionally trained staff members. These aides may work on a full- or part-time basis. They may be young men or women interested in children, or older men or women whose children are grown.

Aides contribute to the program in many ways. They may assist with housekeeping duties, keeping things in order, helping clean up after messy play, helping prepare paints or clay, or repairing equipment. They may supervise to make sure children are safe and may assist teachers by reading or telling stories, by singing or playing an instrument in a music period, and above all, by spending time with individual children who need special attention.

The contribution an aide makes can have special value in a school where there are underprivileged children. Every child needs to feel that there is a special place for him. He needs to feel that he is valued by someone. Some children have had little attention, because their parents were ill or are burdened with work or the demands of a busy life. An aide may be able to help these children by attending to their special needs. For example, she can help a child play, talk with him, or enjoy books with him.

When there are assistants or aides working in a school, it is important that

they understand clearly what is expected of them. They need to know such things as where materials are kept, how they are to be prepared, and what rules about their use are to be enforced. Aides need to be given enough support to be successful for the sake of both the children and themselves.

The successful use of aides will depend on the care taken in their selection, which should consider the fitness of their personalities and their motivations. It will also depend on the opportunities they have for "in-service" training. After they begin work, as with all staff members, aides or assistants must have opportunities to talk over situations that concern them, voice their uncertainties, and ask questions. They need to see the relationship between what they are doing and the whole and to feel that their contribution has significance. They need to discover the intrinsic satisfactions in developing competence.

VOLUNTEERS

Volunteers may be helpful in enriching the program of the school. They may come regularly, carrying out duties similar to those of an aide, or they may come for special purposes. One may come in occasionally to play a musical instrument, such as a violin, flute, or horn. There might be a volunteer who loves animals and can bring a pet to school or invite the children to visit and get acquainted with the animal at home. Someone who has a collection of interests, such as a shell collection, may bring some bits to share with the children.

Volunteers can contribute needed services, too, helping with transporta-

A volunteer helps the children explore the properties of clay.

tion on excurions or coming into the school to prepare snacks or to work with children on special days. Parents may welcome the opportunity to participate in such ways. They gain from taking part in the program.

Assistants, either aides or volunteers, whatever their age, bring their individual capacities for human relationships. When they are able to offer a warm, loving, "caring" type of relationship to a child, they bring him something of great importance. If they are to be successful, there must be someone responsible for giving them adequate directions and a background for understanding individual children, as well as some knowledge about how a child learns and what a child needs to learn. This guidance must be given without diminishing their spontaneity or interfering with their own "style" of relating to children. Success with even one child opens up the possibilities for success with other, different children. For teenagers it may open up new possibilities for success with their own children some day.

Professional Growth Experiences for Staff Members

All teachers need continuing opportunities for professional growth. Some of these opportunities will occur within the school setting itself. There will be regular staff meetings for planning and for discussing questions that arise about the program, about individual children, about the philosophy of the school, and about planning curriculum. These meetings make possible a pooling of experiences and an exchange of viewpoints. They can help build understanding and improve relationships within the staff. Some staff meetings will include all those who work in the school, others will include only the regular staff members who are working with the children. Sometimes parents may participate in meetings.

In a school there will be individual conferences between the principal or director and the teachers. The school may bring in consultants, preferably on a regular basis, to discuss aspects of growth and development, or to focus on the problems of individual children. Principals or directors will observe individual classrooms and get to know the children well in order to be helpful to teachers as they plan for children.

Other professional opportunities may come through membership in professional organizations such as The Association for Childhood Education International and the National Association for the Education of Young Children, as well as through attendance at lectures, discussion groups, seminars, and other meetings. The teacher should also have time for leisure activities unrelated to teaching—such as attending a concert, taking an art class, dancing, skiing, or traveling—which help her return to the job relaxed and renewed.

Staff Discussions

The staff discussions that are held regularly as part of the program in every school will center around planning, evaluating, and increasing insights.

Staff discussions center around planning, evaluation, and increasing insights.

Planning

In group discussions staff members may spend time planning for future activities, such as cooking with the children, deciding what supplies may be needed, how they will share the responsibilities, what the goals may be, and how teaching and learning will be evaluated. They may discuss how the budget will be allocated to meet the needs of the school. If a trip is planned, arrangements will have to be made. What and how will these be done? They may evaluate the day's learning opportunities and decide on a change in the arrangement of the housekeeping corner or the placement of the easels.

Improving Insights

Staff members will also raise questions. One may ask, "I wonder what happened today when the boys were fighting over the wagon outside?" In describing the incident, another member may suddenly realize more clearly just what did happen, and the part she may have played in it. Insights into situations and into the needs of individual children grow as a result of such thoughtful consideration.

As they recall a number of incidents about a particular child, the staff members may begin to understand more clearly the meaning of his behavior. They may develop a more consistent and constructive plan for helping the child learn, or they may realize that they need to understand much more about the child. They may decide to observe and make notes about this child and to discuss his behavior again at the next staff meeting.

Another staff member may comment, "I realized today that I have never given much attention to Jane. She doesn't seem to need it. Now I'm beginning to wonder if she is missing out somehow. She hasn't changed much since she entered school.'' The staff can then pool their feelings and observations of Jane, trying to assess her behavior to see whether her patterns are those of independent competence or of passive avoidance of difficulty.

Then someone may comment, "I really felt angry when Jim kicked me today and told me to go away when I was trying to help him." Others assure her that Jim has made them angry, too, and they have felt frustrated and uneasy about their responses to him. In talking about the situation, they feel some relief and can begin to smile at themselves. He is such a little boy, rejecting these big grown-ups. They begin to wonder what the world must be like for Jim, if he sees everybody in it as an enemy. Why does he feel and act this way? What can they do to help him change his perceptions of people and of himself? How is one friendly and firm with such a child?

Staff discussions are one of the ways in which teachers evaluate what is taking place in the school and plan the next steps.

Maintaining Relationships

Staff members become better teachers through such discussions, but discussions like this depend on good staff relationships. The development of good relations may be helped by drawing up some "ground rules" for conducting a discussion such as the following.

It is understood that all members agree to:

1. Respect individual differences in feeling and in "styles" of working and accept the fact that there are many possible ways of reaching a goal.
2. Refrain from passing judgment on what another person does. Instead, they join in looking at questions and in thinking about them, rather than condemning or criticizing. One may ask, "I wonder why you did that?" attempting to understand; or "I wonder what else could have been done?" attempting to seek alternative solutions.
3. Respect, as a matter of "professional ethics," the confidentiality of personal things that are discussed in the staff meeting and not to repeat these outside the professional setting.

In the climate of acceptance set up by such agreement, staff members are better able to be honest and objective in looking at their own as well as at children's behavior. They are better able to function with competence, channeling their energies into common goals, less entangled by the universal problems of jealousy and rivalry. They are better able to work out ways of facing the problems of authority which everyone must face. They are freer to grow in their insights into human relationships, just as they hope to help the children grow in understanding their relationships with others.

PROJECTS

1. In the school where you are observing or participating, check these points:
   a. The number of children in each group.
   b. The ratio of boys and girls in each group.

c. The ratio of children and adults in each group.

d. The training and the experience of the staff members.

What factors are considered in selecting the children?

2. Arrange to observe in a "family type" group, where ages are mixed; also observe in a group where the ages of the children are within about a year of each other. What differences are there between the two groups? What differences might be due to the difference in age range? What are the advantages and disadvantages?

SUPPLEMENTARY READING

Association for Childhood Education, International. *Aides to Teachers and Children.* Washington, D.C.: ACEI, Bulletin 24, 1968.

Cohen, D. Continuity from prekindergarten to kindergarten. *Young Children,* 1971, *26* (5):282–286.

Cohen, D., and Brandegee, A. *Day Care, 3, Serving Preschool Children.* Washington, D.C.: Department of Health, Education, and Welfare, Publication, No. (OCD) 74-1057, Government Printing Office, 1974.

Provence, S., Naylor, A., and Patterson, J. *The Challenge of Daycare.* New Haven: Yale University Press, 1977, Chapters 3 and 11.

5

Houses
(boy, 3.0)

The Building; the Equipment and Materials; the Use of Space and Time

The essence of any school program is to be found in what the children who attend actually do: in the pattern of activities in which they engage from day to day, and the equipment and the people involved in these patterns of activity. (PATTERSON, 1971:802)

We consider the playrooms and playground as the centers for the child's daily life in school. This point of view places a great emphasis on the plan of the building, the selection and use of the equipment and materials, and the use of space and time.

The physical layout and its boundaries are important considerations in planning a program for young children. The space should be ordered so that a child can move from one room or place to another without help. The room and yard should include places for privacy as well as for company. Materials, equipment, and space should be simply and functionally organized in

75

order that the children may use them without unnecessary help from an adult.

When one school experimented with space arrangements, the teachers found that the children seemed to value roominess and openness most. When the children were given the opportunity to change the arrangement of the furniture in the room, they dispensed with the tables, preferring to work on the floor. They left the room rather bare and open. The teachers reported that the children seemed more constructively occupied with materials in the room they had arranged themselves and they needed less teacher help in solving conflicts (Pfluger and Zola, 1969).

Kritchevsky, Prescott, and Walling (1969) present a useful analysis of play space, based on a three-year study made in day-care centers. According to their analysis, quality depends on the content and the organization of the space. They classify contents into the following three groups: simple units, which can be used in one way, such as a swing or a wagon; complex units, which can be used in two ways, such as a sand table with digging equipment; and super units, consisting of three or more play materials combined, such as a sandbox with play materials and water. Complex and super units allow for more types of activities and for use by more children at one time.

Using such a classification, the teacher can check the play areas to see whether or not there is a wide variety of activities and enough choices for each child. For example, is there a sufficiently wide variety of materials in the units available, or is there a narrow range, such as a lot of tricycles and no wheelbarrows or wagons? Are the number of play spaces sufficient to provide a place for every child and also to permit a change of activity?

THE BUILDING

In a building specially planned for young children a southern exposure is desirable for both rooms and playgrounds. Rooms for young children should be and are required by law in most states to be located on the first floor. If there is an elementary school located in the same building, it is wise to place the younger children adjacent to the primary grade children.

PARKING SPACE AND PROTECTED ENTRANCE

Parking space near the children's entrance reduces the traffic hazards for children and is convenient for parents' cars and for buses. Covered entrances adjacent to hard surface driveways enable children brought by car or bus to enter school without undue exposure to bad weather.

If a main entrance is planned, it should be spacious enough to accommodate parents and children as they come and go. It should be attractive and lead directly to classrooms. Outside doors that lead to the street should have child-proof latches.

AMOUNT OF SPACE INSIDE AND OUTSIDE

The National Association for the Education of Young Children recommends at least 35 square feet of free floor space per child indoors and 75 square feet of space per child outdoors for nursery school and day-care programs. Although the recommended amount of space in public school kindergartens varies somewhat from state to state, in general, the recommendation is a minimum of 40 square feet of indoor space per child.

CLASSROOMS

A rectangular or irregularly shaped room is preferable to a square one because the organization of space in the room can be more attractive and flexible. In the selection of color schemes, careful consideration should be given to the amount of natural light available. Wall colors should make the room cheerful, but not confusing. We recommend pastel shades for walls, perhaps accented by the use of deeper color on the woodwork.

Ceilings and *walls* in the classrooms should be acoustically treated, so that children will not be overstimulated by the voices and noise produced by the groups as they work and play. In cold or damp climates, where children spend a great deal of time inside, acoustical treatment of ceilings and walls is essential to decreasing the stress created by noise.

Floors should be covered with linoleum or vinyl tile, so they will be easy to

Careful attention should be given to the amount of natural light available in a classroom.

clean. They should be thoroughly washed each day. Area rugs with a low pile can be used in the block corner to muffle noise and to provide a comfortable, warm place for children to sit on the floor. A rug is useful in a section of the classroom where children gather as a group throughout the day.

Doors should open out and be easy for children to open. Many state laws require panic bolts low enough for children to use and two exits for each room. Large glass sliding doors make an attractive, light room; they should be made of safety glass and have wire mesh in the lower half to protect children. Because a large expanse of glass can cause heat and glare on sunny days, these doors should have a wide overhanging roof or be placed on a side of the building that the sun does not reach directly. If the room needs to be darkened for sleep, shades or blinds are necessary to cover the glass.

Windows should be low enough for children to see outside with sills no more than two feet from the floor. Shades or blinds may be needed on windows.

Heat vents, radiators, and *pipes* should be free of hazards. Radiators should be screened, and pipes should be covered to protect children. If the furnace is in the building, it must be enclosed in a fireproof room with a metal self-closing door. This area must be free of inflammable materials. Fire extinguishers should be provided for each room or as recommended by the local fire department.

Toilet facilities should adjoin the classroom and be easy to reach from the playground. Two low toilets and three wash basins with low mirrors are needed. A mixing faucet or a separate hot water heater that can be set at a low temperature is recommended to protect children from hot water burns. An exhaust fan in the toilet room is recommended.

Low room dividers such as open and closed shelves that can be easily moved by adults are recommended, because they facilitate supervision, protect children's work and play from interference, and make rearrangement of space possible.

Two sinks in the classroom are desirable, one at adult height and a low one for children. Children will use the sink in some of the same ways adults do, and also for painting, water play, cooking, and other activities. A paper cup dispenser should be located adjacent to the children's sink at a level low enough for children to reach.

Lockers for children's clothing and personal property should be located in the room or in an alcove adjacent to a door to the playground. Lockers should have three compartments—a top shelf for caps, mittens, gloves, and personal belongings; a middle section with hooks for sweaters and coats; and a bottom shelf for boots or rubbers. It is helpful, particularly in cold climates, if all of the lockers are not located in the same area. This will avoid overcrowding when children are all dressing at the same time.

One *bulletin board* near the entrance for parents and several large bulletin boards located at the eye level of children are recommended.

Indoor storage space is needed for a variety of materials and equipment. In

A low sink for children is desirable in a classroom.

full-day programs cots should be stored on dollies in a well-ventilated closet. Blankets can be stored with the cots or in a separate place.

Orderly storage, necessary for quick and efficient retrieval of materials and equipment, can be accomplished with several walk-in storage closets where materials are organized by function—for example, art materials; dramatic play materials and block accessories; musical instruments; woodworking supplies; and games, puzzles, and manipulative toys. Clearly labeled boxes, shelves, and bins facilitate the orderly arrangement of materials and equipment. When the entire staff uses these supply closets, it takes careful planning of the space and considerable effort on the part of all to maintain the order.

CONFERENCE ROOM

A room that can be used for parent meetings, staff meetings, and parent conferences facilitates a school program.

STAFF ROOM

There should be a staff room with a toilet and wash basin nearby. The staff room may be used for an additional parent conference room. This room should have a telephone, a locked file for children's records, and shelves for books and pamphlets.

KITCHEN

A day-care center will have a kitchen which is often a center for activity in the program. Nursery school and kindergarten programs can be enhanced considerably through the use of a kitchen. If there is no access to a kitchen in a program there are many safe, small appliances that can be used in classrooms to provide cooking opportunities for children.

A washer and a dryer are an asset to a nursery school and kindergarten. They are useful to dry wet snow suits as well as keeping many things children and teachers use each day clean. In day care the washer and dryer are necessary equipment for washing and drying sheets, blankets, and children's clothing.

STAIRS

When it is necessary for children to use stairs, there should be a low railing on each side. We suggest treads be ten inches deep and risers six and one-half inches high. Different levels, with two or three stairs, can provide an interesting area in a classroom, as can a platform with a railing around the top that children can walk on and below.

CUSTODIAN'S CLOSET

A large well-ventilated closet with a hopper sink is needed to store cleaning equipment and supplies. It is important that this closet be used solely for this purpose. It should have a door knob five feet from the floor, so that children cannot open the door.

COAT CLOSET

There should be a place for teachers, visitors, parents, and others to hang their outdoor wraps and a place to put extra shoes and boots. The closet or coat rack is best located close to the classroom or playground. A shelf above the coat rack to put other personal belongings is a useful addition.

PLAYGROUND

The playground should be adjacent to the classroom. It should contain sunny and shady areas and have a variety of surfaces, such as grass, dirt, sidewalks for wheel toys, and a hard surface area for play when the ground is wet. Drainage in the yard should be adequate, so that the playground can be used almost every day of the year.

A covered outdoor shelter adjacent to the building is desirable, so that children can play outdoors on rainy and cold days.

An outdoor sink in places where weather permits facilitates flexibility in planning. A faucet with a water hose is a must.

There should be a child-proof *fence* around the playground with adequate fastenings on the gates.

Esthetic landscaping will add variety, contrasts, and interest for children and adults. Nut and fruit-bearing trees and bushes provide interesting learning opportunities. Different kinds of areas, such as a hill and a slope, a digging area, sand pits, and a garden area make different kinds of play and learning possible.

Outdoor storage space that is adequate to store a wide variety of play equipment and materials is essential. A shed for wheel toys can be incorporated into climbing equipment with a "garage" below. A large shed for planks, tents, sawhorses, garden equipment, portable climbing equipment, sleds, and a variety of other equipment used outside is necessary. If there is a covered play area, outside storage for hollow blocks can be adjacent to the area where they are likely to be used. A small shed located near the sandbox where materials and equipment that are often used in sand play can be stored makes it easier for children and teachers to set up for play and replace materials and equipment when play is over.

SAFETY AND HEALTH

A teacher must be able to estimate quickly what may be a hazard and must take steps to remove these dangers. The health and safety of the children are a first responsibility of the teacher. It is wise for every school to carry accident insurance to cover children and staff.

When children are ill, there must be a place where they can be cared for and rest comfortably. Such a room should be located where someone known to the child will be present or can see the child, as through a doorway or a glass partition.

BEAUTY

In addition to being safe and functional, a school should be an esthetic place where attention is given to color, pleasing lines, texture, and shapes—a graceful arrangement of flowers in a bowl; a picture on the wall; an interesting mobile; the pile of a rug; a woven wall hanging; and children's work displayed attractively. Children are learning about esthetics and respond to beauty in their surroundings.

Many schools for young children must use space in existing buildings that do not have many desirable features. There are advantages and disadvantages in every building whether it is planned for children or adapted for children's use. Much can be done in remodeling; in thoughtful organization of available space; and in providing functional, esthetic materials, equipment, and decorations to make the facilities serve the needs of children.

EQUIPMENT AND MATERIALS

Equipment is durable classroom and playground furnishings. In contrast, materials are supplies or stocks of provisions that are expendable and used at different times throughout the year. For suggestions of the selection of equipment and materials, we are guided by the young child's developmental needs, a point of view about learning, and respect for individual differences. We favor equipment and materials that encourage children to explore, to discover, to create, and to invent, such as hand lenses, clay, pulleys with ropes, and inclined planes. There should be equipment and materials to help children organize their ideas about the world, such as a treehouse with steps or rope ladder to climb, a slide and a fireman's pole to slide down, and several levels that provide places to see the playground from a variety of perspectives. Many furnishings and provisions will lend themselves to use with a minimum of adult help, such as sand, colored pencils, and books. At the same time, there will be equipment that requires more extensive help for children to learn to use independently, for example, a record player for three-year-old children or a typewriter for the kindergarten.

EQUIPMENT

Equipment should be sturdy, safe, and capable of serving a wide variety of purposes. No one list is ever complete, nor should it be, because the inventiveness of parents, teachers, and children can make a school's equipment unique. Yet, there will be some equipment common to all schools.

Chairs should be sturdy and some should stack easily. They should differ in height, from 9 to 14 inches, to fit the varying heights of children. Variety and interest may be added to the room by including low arm chairs and a variety of cushions for children to use in various ways. Several 16-inch chairs, a rocker, and a comfortable arm chair should be provided for adults to sit in alone or with children.

Low *tables* that differ in height, from 12 to 20 inches, should be available. Some of these will be used with chairs, others will be low enough for children to sit on cushions and use them. Round tables (42″), small tables (30″ × 22″), and large tables (60″ × 30″), some of which can be fitted together to make larger units, will allow flexibility in the classroom arrangement.

A *piano,* a *record player,* and a *listening center with earphones* is desirable in each classroom. A *tape recorder* and a primary *typewriter* are needed in the kindergarten.

A large set of *unit floor blocks* should be a part of every classroom's basic equipment. If properly cared for, they will last for years. There should be *shelves* for the storage of the blocks, so that they can be organized and stored by shape and size. The youngest children will not need every shape and size, but these blocks can be added to the kindergarten collection. *Large hollow blocks* that are multiples of each other should be available to all groups, but need not be purchased for each classroom.

Several levels provide places to see the playground from a variety of perspectives.

The homemaking corner should include the following: *stove, sink, cupboard* for dishes, *small table* and *chairs,* a *small rocking chair, small chest* with several drawers, a *rack* for hanging clothes, and *doll buggies.*

Easels which are available in single, double, and triple sizes, should be found in each classroom. *Racks* for hanging paintings to dry will be needed. Clay may be stored in a large *crock* or small trash can with a tight fitting lid.

A *book rack* that can be attached to the wall or a portable one, if space allows, is another valuable piece of equipment.

A heavy *workbench,* several *sawhorses,* and tools such as a *vise, hammers,* and *saws* are also important pieces of equipment. The tools should be real and functional.

Climbing equipment of all kinds should be provided, such as a jungle gym, ladder boxes, ladders, large crates, commando or agility nets, rope ladders, sewer pipes, and tree trunks. Stable and unstable bases of support provide challenging learning opportunities for children.

Building equipment such as large hollow blocks, boards of different lengths, sawhorses, packing boxes, used tires, and canvas or nylon sail fabric to use as a tent or a roof allow children to construct their own play space.

Imaginative play and motor skill development will be encouraged by having places to crawl through, places to look down from, places to slide, places to swing, and vehicles to ride and pull.

A *sand area* in which to dig roads and waterways, to make mountains and tunnels, to find bits of iron, to discover the properties of sand and water, for dramatic play and for making pies, cakes, and cookies is an indispensable place.

Gardening and *dirt digging areas* offer opportunities for dramatic play, to explore the properties of dirt and water, to plant a garden, and to find earthworms and insects. They are easy areas to provide.

Cages for pets that live at school or visit will provide proper housing and will allow for their adequate and convenient care.

SAFETY CONCERNS

Sometimes equipment seems dangerous at first glance, especially real tools and outdoor climbing apparatus. It must be remembered that children want to gain mastery and need adventure in play. Every child should have the pleasure of using a *real* workbench and hammer or digging with a small, real spade. He should have the opportunity to experience the thrill of climbing up high and sliding down a firepole. A child only learns to use equipment by using it again and again. Our concern is with the *safe use* of equipment. Giving a child too much help may result in his doing something that is beyond his ability or level of skill. It is at such times that he is likely to have an accident. Safe use means maintaining certain rules about the use of equipment, such as permitting only one child at a time on a ladder. Safe use means showing a child how to use a piece of equipment safely—placing a ladder in a secure way or carrying a sharp implement with the point downward. Helping children learn to use equipment safely allows them to become competent and to move freely. Learning about safety is an important aspect of learning to use equipment.

MATERIALS

A list of materials could be endless. In general, materials should be selected that directly relate to the program's objectives and to the particular children in the program. The chapters on curriculum areas will give the reader specific examples of materials related to objectives and to planned learning opportunities.

SPACE

Arrangements of space make a statement to children and adults about what is to take place in it. A broad walk that circles a playground like a road will handle tricycle traffic in a way that an unbroken block of hard surfacing will never do. A deep pile carpet, pillows, and books in a low rack, all within an enclosed area, invite leisurely, relaxed looking and reading, while a table and chairs with books on a shelf may not.

The expected kinds of relationships among adults, among adults and children, and among children are reflected by the space arrangements. For example, if a principal's office has child-size chairs and objects of interest to children, it probably means that she expects children to visit and has provided for their comfort and interests. A social, cooperative relationship between children can be facilitated by supplying two or more items of a kind. For example, two telephones make it possible for the children to use them in a cooperative fashion, such as talking to each other.

The way space is structured implies a relationship between children and the available materials and equipment. For example, a table arranged with four chairs, four clay boards, a tray of tools in the center of the table, with a crock of clay on the floor nearby, and a basket of aprons indicate that four children may work at the table, and that the children can put on their own aprons, help themselves to clay, and choose their own tools.

The ways that the teacher expects children to engage in learning are evident in the continuity and change of the space and materials through time. *A room is not arranged at the beginning of the year for the entire year.* The block area may take only one-fourth of the floor space at the beginning of the year in a kindergarten, but by the end of the year about one-third of the space may be used for blocks. Only a few materials are put out for use at any one time. In the first few weeks of school it is probably wise to put out materials and equipment known to be familiar to the children. Materials that are easily identified with the cultural patterns of the community are important. Materials and equipment are added, as children become more familiar with the school, and as they gain competence and mastery in using them. For example, at the beginning of school simple, one-piece cut-out puzzles with familiar content may be placed on a table for children to use with a teacher. As the children learn to use these puzzles, four- to six-piece jigsaw puzzles may be added. Later, puzzles with increased complexity are added to the simpler ones already on the shelf for the children.

A recent investigation of preschool programs concluded that there are three main factors that seem to be related to the quality of the programs observed (Day and Sheehan, 1974). These are: (1) the organization and utilization of physical space; (2) the child's access to materials and the way in which these could be used; and (3) the amount and type of adult–child interaction. With two of these three factors relating to space and equipment, we can see how important these aspects of the environment are.

According to Kritchevsky, Prescott, and Walling (1969), when space is well organized, it will have sufficient empty space, a broad, easily visible path through it, ease of supervision, and efficient placement of storage units. Based on their observations, the authors concluded that not less than one-third and not more than one-half of the play space should be empty. The empty space should be capable of being used in different ways, such as for setting up a store or for building with blocks. It should be easy for a child to see how to get from one place to another without interfering with any activities. It should also be easy for the teacher to see what is going on in the room without having to walk through the room. Low room dividers that separate play centers make this possible.

The authors point out that the advantage of well-organized space is that the teacher has more "discretionary time" or "time to act out of her own choices made in terms of her knowledge, experience and sensitivities, just as the children are acting out of theirs. . . . It is not necessary for the staff to provide directed activities as a compensation for spatial inadequacy . . ." (Kritchevsky, Prescott, and Walling, 1969:25).

By proper organization of space, the teacher can make the available space serve the needs of the group most effectively. She can eliminate points where activity is likely to be unproductive or full of conflict. She will give herself more time to observe and to work with individuals or small groups. Using space well is an important aspect of good teaching.

TIME

Decisions about the length of the day or year are usually made on the basis of money, facilities, precedent, and how long parents are at work. For example, a day-care center that serves the needs of children of working parents may be open from 7:30 in the morning until 6:30 at night each working day in the year; whereas, a college or university laboratory nursery school may follow the institution's calendar and have morning sessions only. Most nursery and kindergarten children attend school two-and-a-half to three hours a day. Head Start and public school kindergarten will depend on the particular state's legal definition of "school day" and "school year." Day-care children may attend on a full- or part-time basis, depending on their parents' schedules.

The time within a day and for a school year is a "given." Teachers endeavor to plan for and use time in ways most productive for children's developmental needs and learning. It is useful and compatible with the way children learn to think of time in blocks of a week or month, rather than one day at a time. For example, a teacher planning for language arts, science, math, social studies, art, music, and dance all in one day will surely find that children will be *busy* every minute and will not have time to think and choose. Having time to wander, to look, and to be reflective is valuable to children's learning. When plans are made for a week, then each area of the curriculum may have its rightful place in that week. Children can be introduced to a wide variety of opportunities that will broaden and deepen their interests, understandings, skills, and abilities.

Within the given time of each day, teachers will work out a schedule for the day that meets the needs of the particular children in a particular group. Schedules will consider the children's interests and involvement and will revolve around such "givens" as arrival, snack, and dismissal in a part-day program or arrival, snack, lunch, sleep or rest, and dismissal in a long-day program. The availability of special staff or facilities may also determine a daily schedule. Large blocks of time between these "givens" should be planned, so that children have freedom and learn to use it to make choices within the structure.

There are some generalizations that can be made about a schedule, because all children have some needs in common. Any program for young children should provide for the following:

1. active involvement in work and play outdoors
2. quiet involvement in work and play indoors
3. opportunities for not being involved and for rest and relaxation
4. toileting and washing
5. nourishment of some kind

Children, also, need an order in the events of the day. Those children who have known little order in their lives at home may be especially in need of order in their school day. A fixed sequence to parts of the program gives a child confidence in himself, because he knows what to expect. He can predict the order of the day. The order need not be rigid; it should be flexible. It should also be modified, from time to time, for a trip or a special event. Flexibility can be predictable, too. Children should be a part of this planning for flexibility. The following are suggestions for events and a sequence in a schedule.

ARRIVAL

A child likes to know what to expect when he arrives at school. He likes to know that the teacher will be there to greet him, that she is waiting for him to arrive, and that she expects him to greet her, too. It is a time to tell him about the options for the first part of the day and something she has planned with him in mind. It is likely to be a time when children share information with their teacher about what has happened to them outside of school.

WORK OR PLAY INDOORS OR OUTDOORS

The planned options for this part of the day are arranged or the "stage is set" before the children arrive. This planned arrangement allows the children to think about the options and make their choices.

CLEAN-UP

Clean-up goes on throughout the morning, as a child finishes using materials. For example, before leaving his work with clay, the child rolls the clay into a ball and puts it back in the crock. Prior to snack, materials that will not be used later are reordered or put away.

SNACK TIME

A mid-morning snack provides a time for food, rest, relaxation, and social conversation. The snack should be nutritious. Some suggestions are fruit, fruit juice, milk, raw vegetables, cheese, yogurt.

GROUP TIME

The size of the group will depend on the children's ability to attend to the activity taking place during group time. The activity may be a music period with singing or rhythmic activities; a story period with reading, or storytelling, or creative dramatics; a discussion time for making plans or talking over past experiences; or a special event such as someone playing a musical instrument or demonstrating how adults use a potter's wheel.

WORK OR PLAY INDOORS OR OUTDOORS

Different options are presented at this second indoor or outdoor period. There may be several learning opportunities planned for children to practice specific skills, such as tumbling on a mat, walking a balance beam, climbing a ladder bar, and throwing and catching balls.

CLEAN-UP

At the end of the morning, all the children may participate in putting away materials.

DEPARTURE

After preparations for ending the day, the time comes to say "good-bye" to classmates and to the teacher. Something needs to be planned that will give a sense of ending before welcoming the arrival of parents or getting on the bus to go home, such as sitting with a group listening to music.

In a day-care center, kindergarten age children might leave the center to attend kindergarten in a school nearby. If so, the work or play period before departure to kindergarten will be planned with their needs in mind. Other children may return to the center just before lunch and need time to talk with the day-care teacher about what happened at kindergarten or just time to make the adaptation back to the center before preparation for lunch.

Preparation for Lunch

After preparations for the end of the morning, children may toilet and wash, relax with some quiet activity or group singing, listen to recorded music, or help with setting the tables.

Lunch

This meal is usually served at a fixed time, family style, to small groups of children.

Rest or Nap

A rest period on cots for children who do not sleep should not be more than one hour. Children who do sleep may sleep as long as two hours. Longer sleep periods may indicate illness or some problems in adjustment.

Afternoon Play

Children will wake one or two at a time, and juice or milk may be served at this time. The afternoon play time will be planned for small groups of children. For some, it may include a trip to the grocery store, a bus ride, or a tricycle trip around the block. Other children may do some cooking, help with laundry, or play indoors or outdoors in small groups. This time of day will not be planned as school time, but rather designed to approximate activities that could take place in a home and neighborhood.

Late Afternoon Snack

This may be a snack that small groups or individual children plan and prepare for themselves from food on the shelf or in the refrigerator for this purpose.

Late Afternoon

This time of day will be designed for individual children to make choices or for children to be directed into activities that require little or no interaction with others. Reading, listening to records, building with building game sets, playing with miniature toys, or working on a project that the child defines are examples of such activities.

A Flexible Schedule

A flexible schedule for activities throughout the day encourages *initiative* on the part of children and teachers. It sustains interest. It permits the individual child and groups of children to develop projects over a period of time. A schedule exists as a framework; it gives a sense of sureness and order to the day.

Scheduling includes attention to the needs of teachers, too, if they are to meet the children's needs. Opportunity for rest; provision of efficient, convenient work areas; sufficient help with materials and equipment, and assistance with cleaning are important so that teachers may have time and energy to meet the children's needs. Professional recognition as well as stimulation is needed, also, so that there is a feeling of worth and sense of learning and growing as teachers work. Regular staff meetings are part of the week's schedule, as is time for conferences with parents.

HOUSEKEEPING

Just as parents at home know that order reduces needless frustration, the teacher in the school finds that having a place for materials and equipment and keeping things in their place make for a smoother program. Students, assistants, or volunteer workers in the school find it easier when they know where materials are kept. A neat label on a shelf indicating what is kept there helps those working in a school to be clear about what to replace there. Children, too, gain from knowing that things have a place. They can expect to find them in this place and to take responsibility for putting them back in the place where they can find them again.

When teachers find material scattered during the day, they will take time to restore order, not in such a way that it interferes with children's activity, but in a way that it adds to the activity by giving a sense of new opportunities. They will also be alert to wiping up spilled water or paint or washing a table that may need to be cleaned. It will be important to have mops, cleaning cloths, a broom, and a dustpan conveniently near for both children and adults to use.

Another important aspect of housekeeping with which even the beginning student in the school can assist is in making sure that materials are available and that equipment is in working order. If the easel is set up, it needs to be checked to be sure that the paint jars still have plenty of paint in them. A piece of broken equipment should always be removed, or repaired, if possible. It is discouraging to a child to struggle with a toy which is supposed to stand upright, but does not because a part is missing. He may feel that something is wrong with him, and thus he fails to learn what he might have learned through using the equipment. As a result, he may carry the frustration he feels into his next encounter with things or people where it may again interfere with his learning. Difficulties may be avoided by keeping materials and equipment in good condition. Keeping equipment in good condition, for example, means keeping surfaces smooth to prevent splinters, or renewing the paint on painted surfaces as it wears off. Children will be encouraged to treat equipment with care when teachers keep it in good order and respect its upkeep themselves. Teachers set a pattern for children to follow even in housekeeping tasks.

PROJECTS

1. Draw a diagram of the indoor space and a diagram of the outdoor space in the school where you are. Indicate where a teacher is needed if the areas are to be adequately supervised.

2. Considering the units of equipment as simple, complex, and super, check to see if the number of play units or "spaces" is adequate for the number of children who may be using them.

3. Comment on the variety in play materials available.

4. Comment on the organization of the play space. Are the pathways clearly visible? Does supervision appear to be easily given? Is there enough but not too much empty space?

SUPPLEMENTARY READING

Association for Childhood Education, International. *Housing for Early Childhood Education*. Washington, D.C.: ACEI, Bulletin 22A, 1968.

Association for Childhood Education, International. *Play—Children's Business: A Guide to the Selection of Toys and Games*. Washington, D.C.: ACEI, Bulletin No. 7A, 1968.

Butler, A. *Early Childhood Education: Planning and Administering a Program*. New York: Van Nostrand, 1974.

Ellison, G. *Play Structures*. Pasadena, Calif.: Pacific Oaks College, 1974.

Part Two

BASIC TEACHING SKILLS

6

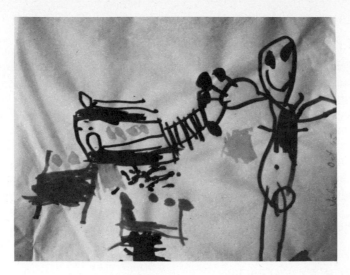

No Title Given
(*boy, 4.7*)

Initial Support through Guides to Speech and Action

We have described the school itself. Now we turn to the question of how we will fit into a school as students. How can we best meet the demands made on us by the school situation while we are learning about children and teaching?

Each of us will respond somewhat differently to the beginning of work with children. Some of these responses may interfere with what we do, while others may be helpful. We discussed in an earlier chapter the necessity of accepting the fact that we may feel uncertain and uncomfortable in the school initially. Too frequently we only increase these feelings by struggling against them, making it more difficult to develop constructive ways of acting.

In any new situation we begin to have confidence as we gain understanding and competence, when we learn ways of behaving that are useful and build a framework in which to function. In the school setting we can ask ourselves, "What help can I get from the experienced teacher? What help can I find in my own past experience in related situations, or in books or in discussions that will help me to function?" In this chapter we will list some guides to speech and action that may be useful and give support as one begins teaching. These supports or simple guides can be applied in an increasingly individual way with added practice.

The success of some of these guides depends in part on the relationship built up with individual children. Time is required to build, as well as to understand relationships, but during the process these rules can give cues to appropriate action. In time, with increasing insight, each one of us will make her own generalizations and add new interpretations. Each of us will find the way that is right for us. There are many right ways.

In written form, these statements may seem like letters in an alphabet. Only when they are combined by thoughtful practice into larger units, will they have much meaning. At this point they must be accepted as part of the alphabet that goes to make a "language" used in guiding behavior.

The 15 points which follow can serve as guides to speech and action in the beginning when the school situation is an unfamiliar one.

GUIDES TO SPEECH AND ACTION

STATE SUGGESTIONS OR DIRECTIONS IN A POSITIVE FORM

A positive suggestion is one which tells a child what to do instead of pointing out what he should *not* do. If a child has already done something he should not have done, or if we think that he is about to err, he needs help in getting another, better idea. We give him this kind of help when we direct his attention to what we want him to do.

It has been demonstrated experimentally that directions stated positively are more effective than the same directions given negatively. This generalization can be proved informally in many situations. For example, a teacher in school was finding it difficult to weigh the children, because almost every child reached for support, when he felt the unsteadiness of the scale platform. When the teacher asked them not to touch anything, she had very little success. She then changed her negative direction to a positive one, "Keep your hands down at your sides," and the children did just that. Telling them what to do, instead of what not to do, brought results.

A question is *not* a statement. We may find ourselves phrasing something in the form of a question instead of a statement because of our own uncertainty. For example, we may say, "Don't you want to pull the plug?" when what we mean is that we want the child to pull the plug, but we are not at all certain that we can persuade him to do it. What we should say, "It's time to pull the plug now and dry your hands. It's time for a story."

A positive direction is less likely to rouse resistance than a negative one. It makes help seem constructive rather than limiting and interfering. Perhaps the child is acting in a particular way because he thinks it annoys us. By emphasizing the positive, we reduce the attention and the importance of the negative aspect of his behavior. We usually help rather than hinder when we make a positive suggestion.

In addition, when we make suggestions in a positive way we are giving the child a sound pattern to imitate, when he himself directs his friends. He is likely to be more successful, to meet with less resistance, if he puts his suggestions in a positive form. We model a social tool for him to use. One can tell something about the kind of direction that a child has received, as one listens to the kind of direction that he gives in play.

Having clearly in mind what we want the child to do, we can steer him toward this behavior with more confidence and assurance and with more chance of success. Our goal is clear to us and to him. We are more likely to feel adequate and to act effectively when we put a statement positively.

To put directions positively represents a step in developing a more positive attitude toward children's behavior inside ourselves. Our annoyance often increases, as we dwell on what the child should not be doing, but our feelings may be different when we turn our attention to what the child should be doing in the situation. We may have more sympathy for the child's problem as we try to figure out just what he could do under the circumstances. It helps us to appreciate the difficulties he may be having in figuring out a better solution.

An experienced teacher might say, "Keep the book on the table, not on the floor." With these words she lets the child know what he should avoid, while at the same time she emphasizes the appropriate behavior. There are some situations in which it is helpful to state the negative behaviors *after* the positive behavior, especially if the negative action would bring about undesirable consequences. For example, if a child is about to pick up a hot pan, one might say, "Hold the pan by the handle, not the sides," adding, "The sides are too hot to hold."

As a new teacher, it is wise to use only positive statements to guide children. It is worth correcting oneself, when one gives a negative direction. The following are examples of directions stated positively:

1. "Ride your tricycle around the bench," instead of, "Don't bump the bench."
2. "Throw your ball over here," instead of, "Don't hit the window."
3. "Leave the heavy blocks on the ground," instead of, "Don't put the heavy blocks on that high board."
4. "Give me the ball to hold while you're climbing," instead of, "Don't climb with that ball in your hand."
5. "Take a bite of your dinner now," instead of, "Don't play at the table."
6. "Take little bites, and then it will all go in your mouth," instead of, "Don't take such big bites, and then you won't spill."
7. "Play softly on the piano," instead of "Don't bang on the piano."

GIVE THE CHILD A CHOICE ONLY WHEN YOU INTEND TO LEAVE THE SITUATION UP TO HIM

Choices are legitimate. With increasing maturity one makes an increasing number of choices. Although we accept the fact that being able to make decisions helps to develop maturity, there are some decisions that a child is not ready to make because of his limited capacities and experience. We must be careful to avoid offering him a choice when we are not really willing to let him decide the question. Sometimes one hears a mother say to her child, "Do you want to go home now?" When he replies, "No," she acts as though he were being disobedient, because he did not answer the question in the way she wanted him to answer it. What she really meant to say was, "It's time to go home now."

Questions such as the one above are more likely to be used when a person feels uncertain or wishes to avoid raising an issue that he is not sure he can handle. Sometimes using a question is only a habit of speaking. It is confusing to the child to be asked a question, when what is wanted is not information, but only confirmation. It is important to guard against the tendency to use a question, unless the circumstances make a question legitimate.

Circumstances differ, but usually the young child is not free to choose such things as the time to go home or the time to eat or rest. He is not free to hurt others or to damage property. In some circumstances, he is free to decide such things as with whom he wants to play, what materials he will use in play, or whether he needs to use the toilet (except in the case of a very young child).

Sometimes a child may be offered a choice to clarify a situation for him. For example, he may be interfering with someone's sand pies, and the teacher may ask, "Do you want to stay in the sandbox?" A response of "Yes" is defined further as, "Then you will need to play at this end of the box out of Bobby's way."

It is important to be sure that your questions are legitimate ones.

Use Your Voice as a Teaching Tool

A quiet, firm manner of speaking conveys confidence and reassures the child. All of us have known parents and teachers who seem to feel that the louder they speak, the greater their chances of controlling behavior. We may also have observed that these same people often have more problems than the parents and teachers who speak more quietly, but are listened to.

It may be necessary to speak firmly, but it is never necessary to raise one's voice. The most effective speech is simple, direct, and slow. Decreasing speed is more effective than raising pitch.

It is a good rule never to call or shout across any play area, inside or outside. It is always better to move nearer the person to whom you are speaking. Children, as well as adults, grow irritated when shouted at. Your words will get a better reception if they are spoken quietly, face to face.

Speech conveys feelings, as well as ideas. Children are sensitive to the tone quality, the tightness in a voice, which reveals annoyance, unfriendliness, or fear—no matter what the words may be. The teacher should try to use a pleasant tone of voice, and she may find her feelings improving along with her voice.

The teacher sets a pattern, too, in her speech, as she does in other ways.

Children are more likely to use their voices in loud harsh ways if the teacher uses her voice in these ways. Voice quality can be improved with training, and every one of us could probably profit from speech work to improve our voice. A well-modulated voice is an asset worth cultivating.

USE METHODS OF GUIDANCE THAT BUILD THE CHILD'S CONFIDENCE AND SELF-RESPECT

We need to learn constructive ways of influencing behavior if we are to promote healthy personality growth. Neither children nor adults are likely to develop desirable behavior patterns as a result of fear or shame or guilt. It is not constructive to label a child's behavior "naughty" or "selfish" or any other such label. This kind of labeling only lowers the child's self-esteem, who may even begin to see himself as a person with these qualities, a person of very little worth. Improvement will be more apparent than real, and any change is likely to be accompanied by resentment and an underlying rejection of the desired behavior.

It takes time to learn constructive ways of guiding behavior. The first step is to eliminate the destructive patterns we use. We must discard the gestures, the expressions, the tones of voice, as well as the words that convey the impression that the other person should feel ashamed of himself. In passing judgment on another, we make the other person feel that we do not respect him. It is hard for a person to change his behavior, unless he feels some respect for himself. The young child is especially dependent on feeling that others respect him.

If we believe that there are reasons that a person behaves as he does, reasons that patterns of reacting are established, we will not blame the individual for his behavior. We may see it as undesirable or unacceptable, and we may try to change it, but we accept and respect him. We will not add to his burden by passing judgment on him. Labeling behavior means we are passing a judgment that is undiscriminating and fails to take circumstances into account. It often prevents us from observing closely.

A child will be helped if we accept him as he is and try to make it possible for him to find some success, rather than reprove him because he does not meet our standards. Here is an example.

Mark (5.5), an active child with a short attention span, who often acts destructively, sits down and starts to put a puzzle together. He whines when a piece does not fit in the first place he tries, and throws the piece on the floor. The teacher says, "Does it make you angry when it doesn't fit right away?" She puts the feeling he appears to have into words, thus indicating her acceptance of it and him. This comment gives him the attention he needs in a positive way and conveys to him the feeling that his teacher cares about him and his feelings. She reaches down, gets the piece and passes it to him. He completes the puzzle successfully. She says, "That's fine. You did it." She does not reprove him for throwing a piece on the floor or expect him to pick it up. He is not ready to meet such an expectation. It is more important for him to have some success. She helps him be successful and respects him for what he can do.

HELP A CHILD SET STANDARDS BASED ON HIS OWN PAST PERFORMANCE, RATHER THAN ON COMPARISON WITH PEERS

Comparing one child to another is a dangerous way to try to influence behavior. We may get results in changed behavior, but these changes may not all be improvements. Some of these results will be damaging to the child's feeling of adequacy and his friendliness.

Competitive schemes for getting children to dress more quickly or to eat more of something may have some negative side effects. Children who are encouraged to be competitive are very likely to quarrel more with one another. In any competition someone always loses, and the loser is likely to feel hurt and resentful. Even the winner may be afraid of failing next time, or he may feel an unjustified superiority if the contest was an unequal one. Competition does not build friendly, social feelings.

Competition not only handicaps smooth social relationships, but it also creates problems within the child himself. We live in a highly competitive society, but the young child is not ready to enter into much competition until his concept of himself as an adequate person has developed enough so that

Children should feel sure of acceptance, whether they succeed or fail.

he can stand the strains and the inevitable failures that are part of competition. Constant success is not a realistic expectation and does not prepare a child well for what he will meet later. On the other hand, too many failures may make him feel weak and helpless. Both extremes are poor preparation for a competitive world. For sound growth it is important to avoid competitive kinds of motivation, until children have developed ego strength and can balance off failures with successes.

This discussion raises a question about what is sound motivation. Do we really get dressed in order to set a speed record or to surpass someone else? Or rather, is it not true that we dress ourselves because there is satisfaction in being independent and that we complete dressing quickly in order to go on to another activity? There may be a point in spending time enjoying the process of dressing if there happens to be nothing of any greater importance coming next. We may be better off when we get pleasure out of doing a thing, not just in getting the thing done. It is wise to be certain that we are movitating children in a sound way, even though the progress may seem slow. We ensure a sounder growth for them, and give them a better preparation for the years ahead.

Children should not feel that their only chances for getting attention and approval depend on being "first," "beating" someone else, or being the "best." They should feel sure of acceptance whether they succeed or fail. One has only to listen to children on a playground to realize how disturbing highly competitive feelings are to them. Statements like: "You can't beat me," or "I'm bigger than you," or "Mine is better than yours" increase friction and prevent children from getting along well together.

REDIRECT THE CHILD IN WAYS CONSISTENT WITH HIS PURPOSE AND INTEREST

A teacher will be more successful in changing the child's behavior if she attempts to turn his attention to an act that has equal value as an interest or outlet for him. If he is throwing a ball dangerously near a window, for example, she can suggest a safer place to throw it. If he's throwing something dangerous, because he's angry, she can suggest an acceptable way of draining off angry feelings—like throwing against a backstop, using a punching bag, or hammering at the workbench. In the first case his interest is in throwing, and in the second case it is in expressing his anger. A teacher's suggestions for acting differently will take into account the different meaning in his behavior. She will always try to suggest an alternative that meets the needs he is expressing in his behavior.

Danny (4.6), for example, stands up in the sand and throws a pan at Susan (4.5), who is startled and begins to cry. Danny has been playing in the sandbox for some time. The teacher assumes that he has lost interest and needs a suggestion for doing something more active. She says, "Danny, Susan didn't like being hit with a pan. If you want to throw something, there's a ball over there. Let's fix a place to throw." She turns a barrel on its side and suggests to Danny that he try throwing the ball through the barrel.

He tries it and is successful. They throw it back and forth. Another child joins and takes the teacher's place in the game. It involves a great deal of running and chasing, which both children enjoy.

If a group is disorganized, that is, running around after a long period of quiet play, its members may need a suggestion about engaging in some vigorous and constructive play such as raking leaves outside. Their needs will not be met by a suggestion about sitting quietly and listening to a story. The meaning of their behavior lies in a need for activity. The teacher's part is to help them find some acceptable expression for this need. If they are running and out of control, because they are fatigued by too much activity and stimulation, a suggestion about listening to a story meets their need for rest.

Effective redirection often requires imagination, as we will show in the following example, where the teacher gave a suggestion which captured the interest of these particular children.

Donnie (4.4) and Michael (4.8) are at the top of the jungle gym and notice a teacher nearby, who is busy writing. They shout at her, "We're going to tie you up and put you in jail." They have a rope with a heavy hook on it. Donnie climbs down with it saying, "I'm going to tie you up!" He flings it toward the teacher and stands looking at her. She says, "I think you don't know what I'm doing here, Donnie, do you? I'm writing down some things I want to remember." She continues, "I wonder if you could use the hook to catch a fish from the jungle gym. It would take a strong man to catch a big fish from the top of that jungle gym." He picks up the rope and climbs up the jungle gym, and the teacher ties a "fish" on to the hook. The boys have fun pulling it up and lowering it for a fresh catch.

Effective redirection faces the situation and does not avoid or divert. The teacher who sees a child going outdoors on a cold day without his coat does not help him when she stops him by saying, "Stay inside and listen to the story now." She is avoiding the question of the need for a coat. She helps him by saying, "You'll need a coat on before you go outside." In another situation, a suggestion of a substitute activity may help the child, as in the case of two children wanting the same piece of equipment. The teacher helps when she says to one, "No, it's Bill's turn now. You might rake these leaves while you're waiting for your turn." Redirection should help the child face his problem by showing him how it can be met, not by diverting him.

TIME DIRECTIONS AND SUGGESTIONS FOR MAXIMUM EFFECTIVENESS

The timing of a suggestion may be as important as the suggestion itself. Through thoughtful practice and insight one can increase one's skill in giving a suggestion at the moment it will do the most good. When a suggestion fails to bring the desired response, it may be due to the timing.

Advice given too soon deprives the child of a chance to try to work things out for himself. It deprives him of the satisfaction of solving his own problem. It may very well be resented. A suggestion made too late may have lost any opportunity for success. The child may be too discouraged or too irritated to be able to act on it.

Help at the right moment may mean a supporting hand *before* the child loses his balance. It may mean arbitration *before* two boys come to blows over a wagon, or it may mean the suggestion of a new activity *before* the group grows tired and disorganized. Effective guidance depends on knowing how to prevent trouble.

Douglas (3.9) says to Robert (3.11), "There's Pam. Let's hit her." They run over and hit Pamela and run away. The teacher comforts Pamela and then goes after the two boys. They are already interested in digging and appear resentful of her interfering with their digging. If the teacher could have stopped them firmly and quickly, as they started toward Pamela, she might have made it clear to them that she expected them to control their impulse and that she was there to help them control it. She might have asked them what other possibilities there were for action. They were more ready to learn the lesson before they hit rather than afterward.

Observe the Individual Ways Children Use Art Media, Explore the Materials Yourself, but Avoid Making Models for Children To Copy

When an adult models or draws a house, a horse, a snowman, or shapes a pot children may watch and then often ask, "Make one for me." It isn't of much use to say, "You make one for yourself." They cannot do it as well and may feel that the adult is uncooperative. Most children will drift away from the activity. With standards set so high, there is little use to try using the materials.

Some children will not touch paint or clay, because they can't "make something." They may envy the joy of the child who is free to explore the material. A child who is free to splash color on the easel, and delight in its lines and masses, takes pleasure in what he can do. He has no patterns to follow, but enjoys the texture, color, line, or combinations he can make and is content with what he has done.

The skillful teacher will avoid getting entangled in making models. She will sit at a table feeling the clay, taking it apart, putting it back together, and rolling it in the palms of her hands, bending and stretching it. She can invest the material with value by exploring it and enjoying it as the children do. She will be careful not to make an object or work at her level, no matter how inexperienced she is with these materials.

The need for help with techniques will come later, after the child has explored many media thoroughly and knows what he wants to achieve and asks for help. Then the child is ready for learning how to use the material to express better what *he* wants to express, but not to imitate better.

GIVE THE CHILD THE MINIMUM OF HELP IN ORDER THAT HE MAY HAVE THE
MAXIMUM CHANCE TO GROW IN INDEPENDENCE

There are all kinds of ways to help a child help himself, if we take time to think about them. For example, we can let him help to turn the door knob with us, so that he will get the feel of how to handle a door knob and may be able to do it alone someday. We can suggest that he put on his rubbers while he sits beside us instead of our picking him up and holding him on our laps, a position which will make it hard for him ever to do the job himself. Too many times the child has to climb down from the adult's lap, when he might have started in a more advantageous position in the first place.

Giving the minimum of help may mean showing a child how to get a block or box to climb on, when he wants to reach something rather than reaching it for him. It may mean giving him time enough to work out a problem rather than stepping in and solving it for him. Children like to solve problems, and it is hard to estimate how much their self-confidence is increased by independent problem solving. To go out and gather a child into one's arms to bring him in for lunch may be an effective way of seeing that he gets there, but it deprives him of the opportunity to take any responsibility for getting himself inside. It is important to give a child the minimum of help in order to allow

A little help at the right time allows the child to be successful.

him to learn himself as much as possible. In leaving the child free to satisfy his strong impulse to be independent, we support his feeling of confidence in himself. "I can do this all by myself," or "Look what I can do," he says.

We must remember, however, that looking for opportunities to let the child do things for himself does not mean denying his requests for help. When a child says, "Help me," as he starts to take off his coat, he may be testing out the adult's willingness to help. The adult does not meet the test if she replies, "You can do it yourself." She reassures him if she gives help freely, with a full measure of willingness. If she cannot, for some reason, she answers like this, "I'd like to help you, but I'm busy just now," giving whatever real reason she has for not being in a position to help. A child may say, "Swing me," and he may be wanting assurance that the teacher really values him enough to do extra, unnecessary things for him. He seeks a relationship with the teacher. It is important to offer him a friendly, giving type of relationship.

Confidence in self is based on a foundation of trust in others and a feeling of being valued by others. When a child *asks* for help, we listen to his request and answer it in a way that will make him less afraid of being helpless and dependent on us. Giving help when it is needed in no way interferes with our efforts to avoid giving unwanted help, with our efforts to leave the child free to act independently. We will give only the help that the child feels he needs.

Make Your Directions Effective by Reinforcing Them When Necessary

Sometimes it is necessary to combine several techniques in order to be effective. A verbal suggestion, even though given positively, may not be enough in itself. "It's time to come in for lunch," may need to be reinforced by another suggestion such as, "I'll help you park your wagon," if the child is reluctant to leave his play, and then reinforced by actual help in parking. A glance at the right moment, moving nearer a child, a verbal suggestion, and actual physical help are all techniques, and one must decide when they are to be used. Give only the minimum help necessary, but give as much help as may be necessary.

One teacher says quietly, "It's time to go inside now," and moves toward the house. The child moves with her. Another teacher says, "It's time to go inside," and stands as though waiting to see what the child will do. He stays where he is, for her behavior does not reinforce her words. Her behavior suggests something different.

When several children are playing together, for various reasons some will accept suggestion more readily than others. Success with one child will reinforce one's chances of success with others. It is wise to consider which child to approach first, when one wishes to influence a group.

One of the most common faults of parents and teachers is that of using too many words, and of giving two or three directions when one would have been sufficient. Anxiety and insecurity often take the form of oververbalizing, showering the child with directions. Children willl develop a protective "deafness" to too many words. It is important to have confidence in the child's ability to hear and respond to one suggestion, given only once. It is better to combine different techniques until one is successful rather than to depend solely on words.

Learn To Foresee and Prevent Rather than Mop Up after a Difficulty

Forestalling is the most effective way of handling problems. We are all aware that "an ounce of prevention is worth a pound of cure." This is true in working with children. The best strategy depends on foreseeing and forestalling rather than mopping up after a difficulty. It takes time to learn what to expect in certain types of situations with particular children or particular combinations of children in order to be successful in forestalling problems.

Learning to prevent problems is important because, in many cases, children do not profit from making mistakes. The child who approaches others by doing something annoying may only learn that people don't like him, and this feeling may become a reality. He may learn acceptable ways of approaching others if the teacher, observing that he is about to go up to a group and knowing what he did previously in a similar situation, says to him, "If you'd like to play with them, you might knock first or ask Michael if he needs another block," or makes some other suitable suggestion. She may move into the situation with him to give him more support by interpreting to the group what his intentions are, or even to help him accept his failure and find another place where he might have a better chance of success. If she waits until he fails, he may be unable to learn anything constructive; he may only run away.

Learning from doing may not be possible for the child, because the consequences may be too serious. In some cases, even if the child does suffer consequences, he may interpret them incorrectly. He may not really understand what is involved. This is often true where responses of others or their values and standards are concerned.

Sometimes children tell us what they are going to do. In these cases we need to listen and prevent what may be undesirable, not wait until the damage is done, when there is little chance to learn from the situation.

Clearly Define and Consistently Maintain Limits When They Are Necessary

There are some things which must not be done. There are limits beyond which a child cannot be allowed to go. Much of the difficulty between adults and children that is labeled "discipline" exists because of confusion about what the limits are. In a well-planned environment there will not be many "no's." The necessary "no's" will be clearly defined; the child will understand them, and the adult will maintain them.

We are very likely to overestimate the child's capacity to grasp the point of what we say. Our experience is much more extensive than his. Without realizing it we take many things for granted. If he is to understand what the limits are, these limits must be clearly and simply defined for him.

When we are sure that a limit is necessary and that the child understands it, we can maintain it with confidence. It is easy to feel unsure or even guilty about maintaining limits. We may not like to face a child's unhappiness or his anger. Our own feelings may bother us. We may be afraid to maintain limits because we were overcontrolled, and we turn away from the resentment and hostility that limits arouse in us. Because of our past experiences, we may not want to take any responsibility for controlling behavior. Gradually we should learn to untangle our feelings and handle situations on their own merits with confidence and without hesitation.

The adult must be the one who is responsible for limiting children, so that they do not come to harm, do not harm others, or destroy property. Children will feel more secure with adults who can take this responsibility. They will feel free, because they can depend on the adult to stop them before they do things that they would be sorry about later.

Use the Most Strategic Positions for Supervising

Sometimes one will observe a beginning teacher with her back to most of the children as she watches one child. On the other hand, the experienced teacher, even when she is working with one child, will be in a position to observe at a glance what the other children are doing. She is always alert to the total situation.

Turning one's back on the group may represent, consciously or unconsciously, an attempt to limit one's attention to a simple situation. It is quite natural that one should feel like withdrawing from the more complex situations at first, or that one should take an interest in one particular child, because other children seem more difficult to understand. These are normal tendencies, but one should guard against them. It is important to develop skill and extend one's horizons. Observation of the total situation is essential to effective guidance. It is essential if the children are to be safe.

Safety requires teachers who are alert to see that all areas are supervised, not just one area. A teacher can be most helpful to the group when she is observing all the children and their interests. The teacher who is reading to children, for example, may encourage, with a smile, a shy child to join the reading group or she may forestall trouble by noticing a child who is ready for a change in activity and encouraging him to join the group, before his lack of interest disrupts the play of others.

Sitting rather than standing is another technique for improving the effectiveness of supervision. The teacher is often in a better position to help a child when she is at the child's level, and children may feel freer to approach the adult who is sitting. It also makes possible more unobtrusive observation.

In a school where there may be several adults, it is important that the adults avoid gathering in groups, such as near the entrance, in the locker room, or around the sandbox. It may limit the children's feelings of freedom and may increase any tendency they have to feel self-conscious or to play for attention. Too many adults in one place may also mean that other areas are being left unsupervised.

Where one stands or sits is important in forestalling or preventing difficulties. A teacher standing between two groups engaged in different activities can make sure that one group does not interfere with the other.

"Remote control" is ineffective control in the nursery school, in day care, and in the kindergarten. Stepping between two children who are growing irritated with each other may prevent an attack, but it cannot be done if the teacher is on the other side of the room. Trouble in the homemaking corner, for example, may be avoided by a teacher moving quietly near as tension mounts in the "family," and suggesting some solution. Her suggestion is more likely to be acceptable if her presence reinforces it. Trouble is seldom avoided by a suggestion given at a distance.

Depending on the physical plan of the school, certain spots will be more strategic for supervision than others. If the teacher is standing near the entrance to the coat room, it will be easy for her to help a child stop and hang up his coat before he goes on to play. If she is standing on the far side of the room, she is not in a position to act effectively, if he chooses to disregard her reminder. Some places are favorable because it is possible to observe many corners from these positions. Other areas may be "blind spots" for observing.

Choose the position for standing or sitting that will best serve your purposes. Study a floor plan of the school where you are teaching and check the spots that are strategically good for supervision. List places where close supervision is needed for safety, such as the workbench.

Make Health and Safety of the Children a Primary Concern

The good teacher must be constantly alert to the things that affect health, such as seeing that drinking cups are not used in common, that towels are kept separate, that toys that have been in a child's mouth are washed, that the window is closed if there is a draft, and that wraps are adjusted to changes in temperature or activity.

The good teacher must also be alert to things which concern the safety of children. Being alert to safety means observing and removing sources of danger such as protruding nails, unsteady ladders, or boards not properly supported. It means giving close supervision to children who are playing together on high places or to children who are using such potentially dangerous tools as hammers, saws, and shovels. This guide is familiar, clear-cut, and important. The skillful teacher never relaxes her watchfulness.

INCREASE YOUR OWN AWARENESS BY OBSERVING AND TAKING NOTES

Underlying all these guides is the assumption that teaching is based on the ability to observe behavior objectively and to evaluate its meaning. As in any science, conclusions are based on accurate observations. Jot down notes frequently, statements of what happens, the exact words that a child uses, and the exact sequence of events. Make the note at the time or as soon after the event as possible, always dating each note. Reread these notes later and add your interpretations. Skill in observing and recording is essential in building understanding. Improve your ability to select significant incidents and make meaningful records.

PROJECTS

1. Observe and record ten directions stated positively which you heard a teacher use in the nursery school. Contrast each with the corresponding negative statement. Indicate the effectiveness of each statement you recorded, giving the reasons that the statement did or did not seem effective.

2. Observe and record five questions asked by the teacher. Classify the reason for asking a question such as: (1) to get information about a fact; (2) to discover an opinion or preference; (3) to suggest a possibility; (4) to clarify a situation; or (5) another purpose. How effective was the question in each case?

3. Report a situation in which the suggestion or help given was well timed. Why? Report a situation in which the suggestion or help given failed, apparently because of poor timing. Why?

4. List ways in which you have observed a teacher protecting the health and safety of the children in the nursery school.

SUPPLEMENTARY READING

Pratt, C. *I Learn from Children.* New York: Simon & Schuster, 1948.

Rowen, B. *The Children We See: An Observational Approach to Child Study.* New York: Holt, Rinehart and Winston, 1973.

Veach, D. Choice with responsibility. *Young Children,* 1977, *32*(4):22–25.

Car, Policeman, Stop Light (boy, 4.4)

7 Discipline, Setting of Limits, and Using Authority

Be firm and tolerant with the child . . . and he will be firm and tolerant with himself. He will feel pride in being an autonomous person. He will grant autonomy to others; and now and again he may even let himself get away with something. (ERIKSON, 1959:70)

No subject is likely to be of more concern to a parent or to a teacher than that of discipline. Healthy, well-functioning children will misbehave at times. Their behavior must be controlled for their own good as well as for the good of those around them. Adults must make decisions about the actions to take when a child's behavior is unacceptable or unsafe for himself or others. Discipline is a necessary part of guidance.

Some adults think of discipline as synonymous with punishment. What is discipline? What is punishment? What is permissiveness? What are some essentials for sound discipline?

DISCIPLINE

Discipline refers to actions taken by adults to help a child change his behavior by identifying for him what kinds of behavior are acceptable to the people whose approval he wants, and by helping him to understand the possible consequences of his behavior. Discipline may involve stopping a child and taking responsibility for helping him change his behavior.

With the toddler, discipline may mean a firm "No" and the substitution of an acceptable object for a forbidden one, or it may mean redirection into an acceptable activity. A toddler may begin to understand a simple statement of *why* he is not allowed to touch or do something. Giving a child the reason lays a foundation for the management of his own behavior in the future. The child is beginning the process of learning self-control. He is helped in developing his capacity for self-control when he is with adults whose behavior is consistent and predictable and who "model" desirable behavior.

PUNISHMENT

Punishment refers to the actions taken by an adult to change a child's behavior by making him suffer physically or emotionally. The young child is often unclear about why he is being punished; he may be confused about the kind of behavior that the punishing adult finds acceptable. As a result, punishment may leave the child feeling angry, resentful, and guilty. He may only learn that he is "bad." Such feelings contribute to a child's sense of self-doubt, and the child who lacks confidence is less ready to assume responsibility for self-control.

PERMISSIVENESS

The word "permissive" is interpreted differently by different people. It is sometimes used to describe a kind of nonguidance that permits a child to do anything he wants to do. Allowing a child to act impulsively without guidance is neither realistic nor helpful to his self-regulation. This kind of caregiving does not help the child to control his impulses. Such behavior on the part of an adult can be a sign of irresponsibility or ignorance.

We will use the word permissiveness to refer to an attitude of permitting, freely and generously, all legitimate activity for a child in his particular stage of development. It reflects, on the part of the adult, a "giving" quality and a feeling of happiness that a child is competent to do the things he wishes to do. A child wants to be an acceptable person, but he is in the process of learning, and needs the assistance of an older, wiser person to help him learn to act in acceptable ways. A child, whether a toddler or a school child, profits from living in an environment that is permissive, but where limits, when needed, are clear and enforced firmly by someone who cares about him. The way a child is stopped or the way a limit is set for his behavior is important.

DISCIPLINE THAT BENEFITS THE CHILD

As adults who work with young children, we are responsible for helping the child learn about living safely and with satisfaction in the world with others. Our relations with all children should be based on an attitude of respect for each child as an important person. Adults should be guided by accurate knowledge and understanding of child growth and development and of this child in particular.

Growing up is a long, complicated process. It takes a long time to internalize standards for behavior. Young children do not always act in ways which adults find acceptable. They must sometimes learn by testing out the limits set by adults. A child needs and has a right to a certain degree of freedom to explore, discover, and create his own standards for behavior. He can only develop a personal sense of autonomy and initiative when the adults around him are loving and firm. Such adults permit only what does no real harm and produces no real anxiety in, or rejection of, the child. We can have confidence in the child and in ourselves, knowing that in time, with support and help, he will learn to master his impulses and aggressive urges without losing the ability to be aggressive at appropriate moments, whether in loving or hating (Winnicott, 1957). Unless we have this confidence, we may respond to the child's misbehavior in punishing ways which can be damaging to him.

There is evidence that the kindergarten child may profit from firmer discipline, as he tests out limits and tries to discover for himself what is safe and what is acceptable. He has more knowledge and more experience. If he is developing well, he feels more confidence in himself than he did just a year before. Greater permissiveness with the two- and three-year-old child, on the other hand, gives him time to extend his horizons and gain self-confidence, while being protected by a responsible adult. Too much ''disciplining'' too early, or too little too late, can interfere with a healthy solution to the problems of coping with authority, which face every individual in maturity.

In middle childhood and adolescence other factors enter into questions of discipline. Sensible discipline in early childhood tends to reduce the strains of adolescence and lays the foundation for self-control during this stage of development, as well as later (Winnicott, 1972).

WAYS IN WHICH THE ADULTS HELP THE CHILD DEVELOP SELF-CONTROL

There are many ways in which adults help the child develop self-control. Some of the ones most relevant to school are explored in the following discussions.

Accept the Child's Need To Assert Himself

The young child is in the process of becoming an independent person. He has the urge to assert himself and thus prove that he is independent. In *not* doing what he is told, he asserts his independence at times. He is testing out what it is like to be an autonomous person, a person in his own right. The urge to assert oneself is important and necessary to healthy development. A child needs to feel that it is possible to assert himself safely, just as he also needs to find that he can live with restrictions and limitations. The kind of discipline that he receives will determine how well he learns to be assertive, as well as how he learns to limit his own behavior. For example, as an infant, the child may have closed his mouth tightly, refusing the food his parent offered. Instead of interpreting this behavior as defiance, the wise parent waited, giving him time to assert his independence, knowing that he would soon be ready to continue with the feeding.

Most healthy children will still test some limits in their environment as they enter each new school setting. A few may test limits more frequently because of "unfinished business" left over from their past. In each successive setting a child needs to have teachers who are responsible, patient, and confident, who display sympathetic firmness, and who convey a caring attitude toward him.

Our feelings probably matter more than the methods we use in discipline. If we expect that a child will misbehave at times (destroy, or defy, disrupt a story group or the play of other children) we will not be disturbed by this behavior. We may find it easier to respond in ways which will help the child to assert himself without being intrusive or disruptive. We may be helped, too, if we realize that it is not necessarily our failure that brought about this behavior, but perhaps it is only the result of the ordinary conflicts encountered in growing.

Take Action When Action Is Needed

We may have to *restrain* a child who is about to hurt another, for example, by holding him with firmness. In taking action we respond as a confident authority. Although the child may be very angry with us at the time, he will ultimately feel safer and less anxious. We can acknowledge his feelings by saying something like, "I know you are angry with me, but I cannot let you hurt John." Understanding and sympathy can accompany firmness. We should never act aggressively toward the child or try to lower his self-esteem by calling him "not nice," "bad," or "naughty." When he can listen, we explain why the behavior is not permitted and what other action he might take to channel his feelings more constructively and competently. We act as responsible adults, who can help him learn to control his impulses.

We may need to *remove* a child from a situation that is too difficult for him to manage acceptably on his own. The child who keeps disturbing the play of other children in the sandbox must play somewhere else. We should isolate a child only when he cannot control his own behavior. Such behavior may be due to fatigue or overexcitement. We should be honest with the child about the reasons for his separation from the group. We want him to view the time away from the group as a relief, rather than as a punishment. He can have an opportunity to play alone quietly with something he enjoys until *he* feels ready to be with others.

We may need to *deprive* a child of an object or from participating in an activity as a consequence of his behavior. A child who knowingly uses a hammer in the wrong place should be deprived of the hammer for a time. The child who disregards the teacher's instructions on a walk outside the school grounds should not be allowed to accompany the group on a trip the next time. For the deprivation to have meaning to the child it must be related to the unacceptable behavior and occur within a time span understandable to the particular child.

Set Reasonable Limits

There are not many prohibitions in a favorable school environment for young children. The important limits relate to safety, general welfare, and the protection of the rights of others. These limits must be clearly defined and consistently maintained for each child.

For example, a child is not permitted to leave the school premises on his own. Teachers usually put this in a positive way to children, saying, for example, "Stay where the teacher can see you, so she can keep you safe." If a child does go beyond the limits of the school yard, he meets with disapproval and suffers some consequence such as being restricted to a specific area in the yard. We explain the reasons that his behavior must be limited; however, we know that he does not fully understand why the act is dangerous. We also know that his control over his impulses is too weak to be reliable at all times. We must be responsible to watch and take care of him. He usually obeys us, because he trusts that we care about him and set limits for his protection. He needs the support of our limits.

Children often need help in respecting the rights of others, such as the right to keep possession of an object while using it or the right to be free of disturbance in carrying out an activity. For example, two young three-year-olds playing together in the sand may come to blows over the possession of a spoon. The teacher steps in, putting her arm around the one who has taken the spoon by force and saying, "No, Bill was using the spoon. Please give it back to him. I will help you find another one." She may add, "Hitting hurts. Next time, ask him to give you the spoon when he finishes using it." If there are tears, she comforts the one who is crying and says, "I'm sorry you were hit. It hurts, I know." As a teacher is observing the children, she may be able to step in with a suggestion before the hitting occurs and prevent the struggle. The most effective guidance is helping the child find a solution at the point where he faces a conflict.

Learning to control impulses is difficult for the child. Time and experience with both freedom and control are necessary if the child is to learn self-control. On the part of the teacher it requires knowledge about children's thinking, learning, and development, as well as insight and understanding about the individual child. Such understanding and insight will grow out of many careful observations of a child and of children, as they work and play together.

Use Timing and Time Effectively

There is a right moment for stepping into a situation if guidance and redirection are to be most effective. The new teacher will find it helpful to observe experienced teachers, making notes when possible, and thinking over what she observes as well as relating her observations to her own experience. The impulsive child, for example, will need help more quickly than the placid or slow-moving child.

Every child needs to have the opportunity to help himself as much as he can, even in settling disputes. The teacher must study each child until she can decide the timing of assistance and what help will be most useful to him. Children's temperaments and styles differ and so do the kinds of help they require and can accept. The guidance given must fit the child at a specific moment. The teacher's relationship with a child will be a factor in determining when to step in to prevent a conflict that is beyond a child's ability to manage. Success in timing of help comes with experience and reflection. New teachers will make mistakes in judging when to step into situations. Risking errors is a part of learning to teach as well as learning to learn.

A child sometimes just needs to be given time to accept directions. When we say to a child, "You will need to put your boots on before you go out. The grass is wet outdoors this morning," we do not have to see that he marches right over to his locker to put on his boots. He may have to protest a bit until

There is a conflict of interests over possession of a cap.

he convinces himself that here is a demand with which he must comply. We may have to stop him if he starts to go outdoors without his boots, but we give him time to accept the limit and then comply or stay inside.

Here is another example. Eric (4.0) is outside playing in the sand and has pulled off his shoes and socks. The teacher thinks it is too cold outdoors for bare feet. She goes over to Eric, and sits on the side of the sandbox quietly. Then she says, "It feels good, doesn't it, Eric," and smiles, enjoying it with him. She continues, "I wish I could let you play in your bare feet in the sandbox, but I think it is too cold to be outdoors without your shoes on. You'll have to put them back on this time. When the weather is warmer, you can take them off outside." She adds, "I used to like to be barefoot when I was a little girl. Now I'll help you put your shoes on." Together they get the shoes back on while Eric tells her about what he was doing. Eric is a very independent child who has often resisted directions. Because his teacher knows his temperament, she takes time to enjoy the moment with him and let him know she understands. Eric is then able to accept the necessary limit and cooperate. There was no need for the teacher or for Eric to act quickly in this situation.

Develop Skill in Defining and Explaining Limits

Every teacher needs to give attention to developing skill in using language that the child can understand, as she defines and explains the behavior expected of him. Too many words confuse a young child. It is as though he cannot process so many words in a relatively short time. He stops listening. Limits should be stated clearly, in a precise, specific, and concrete way. It takes practice to use language effectively with young children, as well as an understanding of each individual child's stage of development. A quick appraisal of the child's emotional state helps in choosing the right words for a particular situation.

When a child hits another child, for example, the teacher must stop him, and she must also help him to understand the reasons for her actions. She must explain how the other child feels (hurt and unhappy) and how she feels (disapproves) about this behavior. She should also try to make a positive suggestion about what can be done in the situation. "Next time *tell* him what you want," or "Next time tell him you want him to move his truck." In some situations the teacher may state the consequences if the child does not change his behavior. To a child who is throwing sand, she may say, "You will have to leave the sandbox unless you can stop throwing sand."

The teacher may help two children who are in conflict by interpreting the actions of each, thus helping them begin to think about behavior rather than to act on impulse. Children can begin early to understand that there are reasons why people behave as they do. Guided by a teacher, four- and five-year-old children often benefit from discussing the reasons why a conflict occurred, and what might be done at another time. Talking over problems is an important step in learning about social relations for four-, five-, and six-year-old children.

Thoughtful Planning of the Environment and the Schedule

Thoughtful planning of the environment and the schedule will often prevent the occurrence of conflicts or issues and reduce the need for discipline. Adequate and well-arranged space, where supervision is easily managed, will help promote positive relationships among children and enable them to work and play together with a minimum of conflict. Making available a wide variety of carefully selected materials will also help to reduce conflict, because the teacher has planned something to interest each child. When conflicts are frequent in any particular area, the teacher should observe carefully and try to determine if a different arrangement of space or equipment might create a more favorable situation.

Keeping the subgroups small is also a preventive measure. A rule of thumb for a teacher is that the number of children in a subgroup should be about the same as the age of the child, that is, three three-year-olds, four four-year-olds, and so on. When planning options or choices for children in a period of the day, there should be about twice the number of work and play spaces as children (Kritchevsky, Prescott, and Walling, 1969). For example, there might be seven options for a group of sixteen four-year-olds with spaces for four children at each option. This would make a total of 28 play spaces. Small groups give each child an opportunity to participate and receive needed help from a teacher or another child. Such planning minimizes the potential for conflict.

A flexible schedule meets the needs of children, but requires more skill on the part of a kindergarten teacher and more skill and cooperative effort on the part of teachers of three- and four-year-olds. When the schedule is flexible, individual interests and needs are more likely to be met.

A schedule that calls for little waiting on the part of children reduces the need for discipline. Frequent conflicts between a child and an adult do not produce sound learning. Teachers should seek to understand why issues are arising and remedy the cause or causes. Sometimes moving snack to an earlier time or making group times shorter can reduce stress. Children can take much more responsibility for their behavior if the environment and events are well planned to meet the changing needs of individuals and the group.

Model Acceptable Behavior

The word "discipline" derives from the word disciple or follower. It suggests an important element in self-control, that of following an example. The child wants to be like the adults who are important to him. Teachers are important people to children. If the teacher is calm, speaks quietly, and manages her own feelings acceptably when she encounters difficult situations, she gives the child a positive example to follow. If she can meet frustrations without piling up feelings of irritation and if she can respond to defiant behavior without anger, she gives the child a model for dealing with his own feelings and with similar situations he will face.

Children in a group are aware of how the teacher responds to a child who is disruptive. If that child is handled with firmness and understanding, other children are reassured that the teacher is trustworthy. They learn about limits for behavior, and they see a demonstration of an appropriate response. Anger does not need to be met with anger in return, but it can be coped with reasonably and channeled in constructive ways.

Even the most competent teachers are not always successful models. Everyone has stress and strain to cope with at times. We can try to understand our own needs and meet them. For example, we can try to avoid fatigue. Rested, satisfied people are more likely to model acceptable behavior. Yet, there will be times when stress will cause us to be less sensitive to and thoughtful of others or to respond with irritation in a situation we would have handled better at another time. This is a time to model ways to accept the responsibility for our behavior and ways to apologize. Children are remarkably resilient and forgiving when one gives them the opportunity.

USING AUTHORITY

"You're the boss of the whole school," remarked Susan (4.4) to the teacher as they sat eating lunch together, and she added with deliberation, "Last year the school was all the bosses itself." Susan had evidently been trying for some time to figure out who was "boss" at the school. She had been raised on "issues" at home, and her parents were still trying to show her who was "boss" in their house. She must have been puzzled about the school situation at first, until she selected the teacher as the source of authority.

For many people, as for Susan, the problem of authority is a confusing one and remains so all through their lives. As children these people have been made to feel that the role of boss is the most important one. When they are grown, they struggle to do some bossing themselves or to resist being bossed by others. This struggle interferes with their solutions to other problems: They hurt themselves and often the people they love in their efforts either to boss or to resist bossing.

Discipline that leads to a struggle over who is going to be "boss" is damaging to a child. It does not help children respect themselves or others. Like Susan, people who have met this kind of discipline have little concept of what it means to be a responsible member of a group. They are not ready for the self-discipline that democratic living demands.

Authority takes many forms. Some people have experienced authority mostly as a succession of commands or "don'ts." They associate authority with punishment. All of us at some time have met with authority that was needlessly harsh, restrictive, and not based on respect for individuals. Fortunately, most of us have most often experienced authority based on love and a caring attitude. Limits are essential if the young child, or any of us, is to be safe. The problems of authority or the setting of limits can be worked out in a way that has positive values for the individual.

Our Own Feelings Are Important When We Use Authority

If the authority we experienced as children was mainly reasonable and sympathetic, we will be able to exercise authority ourselves with more confidence and with more respect for individual needs. Our goal is to help children to take more and more responsibility for their own behavior, that is, to be their own authority. To prepare them adequately for this role we must be clear about our feelings on the subject. We must be aware of the adaptations we have made. Our feelings about these adaptations will facilitate or interfere with the exercise of discipline that benefits the child.

When a child defies us, for example, how much threat do we feel because of his behavior? Are we secure enough to see the child's defiance in the light of what it represents to the child rather than what it means to us? Do we face this behavior by overreacting, because we identify with the rebellious child or because we feel a threat to our own autonomy? Can we be responsible adults, no longer little and helpless, who can support a child in his struggle for independence while maintaining necessary limits for his behavior? Can we be confident, responsible authorities capable of acting with respect and understanding? Let us look at two teachers whose feelings made it difficult for them to exercise authority.

Miss X was a teacher who had difficulty in helping the children in her class control their behavior. The children often lost their control and engaged in a great deal of destructive behavior. She was a sympathetic person with insight and at times was skillful in turning the group's energies back into constructive activities. After they had overturned the furniture, for example, the children usually did complex block building. They were often creative and played well together, but some of the timid children in the group suffered. They were frightened by their own anxieties after participating in or watching an episode of uncontrolled behavior.

Miss X was a person who had never been able to accept discipline herself. She had grown up as an only child in a strict household. She conformed outwardly but expressed her resistance in indirect ways. She was never on time; she never quite finished a task; she was absentminded. As soon as she was grown, she had left her home. In her work with children she was determined that they should not suffer from the "boss" type of authority, as she had. Because she had not experienced authority as a help, she found it difficult to use it constructively with her group. A sensitive, creative person herself, she gave her group freedom, but was not able to meet their needs for the support of limits in their out-of-bounds or destructive behavior.

Miss S was another teacher who bitterly resented the way in which she had been treated at home as a child. As a child she had too often experienced a form of discipline that served only as an outlet for hostility and aggressive feelings. Her feelings against authority were very strong. She could not limit the children in her group because she would have disliked herself too much for doing it, or she might even have disliked the children for "making" her act that way. She was thus unable to discipline in a constructive way.

It is true that aggressive feelings may come out in the use of authority. People may punish, because they wish to hurt; in punishing they may pour out their aggressive, hostile feelings. At times all of us drain off feelings in inappropriate ways and with the wrong person. If we face the hostile, aggressive feelings we inevitably have, we are better able to cope with them and find appropriate and constructive avenues for their expression. We can keep or direct them where they belong, and they need not spill out in inappropriate places. We can act with confidence when the limits we impose are meeting the child's needs rather than serving as an outlet for our own feelings.

When we enforce a standard of behavior that interferes with a child's impulse to act as he wishes, we may expect the child to be angry with us or at least to feel resistant or resentful. He has every right to feel this way, but he does not have the right to act out these feelings if the action is destructive to himself or others. We are acting responsibly when we stop this type of behavior. It is important that we accept and not deny his feelings, and help him express his feelings in words. He may be able to reflect on what happened, with the teacher's help, after he has "ventilated" his feelings. With his feelings identified and "off his chest," the child is ready to channel his energies more constructively. Having a sense of humor and imagination helps in these situations.

We have a right to our feelings, too. We sometimes get angry or annoyed, and we must face and acknowledge these negative feelings in ourselves and cope with them. It will help to talk over the kinds of feelings we have with other people, such as our colleagues, who can reflect on them with us. We may share our feelings, and when we accept them, we discover new aspects of ourselves as teachers. We may feel more self-respect. And perhaps we can manage our feelings in more mature ways as we work with children.

In the school a teacher may say to a child, for example, "You make me very cross when you do. . . ." Her words help the child to perceive her feelings and to understand the impact of his behavior on another person. The child is less bewildered when the feelings he arouses in others are identified directly. Putting feelings into words makes them more manageable. If we as teachers face and manage our own feelings, we help create the kind of climate in which a child can learn to recognize feelings in himself and others, and learn to cope with them in ways that are constructive and even creative. He will then be less afraid of his own feelings and those of others.

THE ROLE OF GUILT

Some feelings of guilt are probably necessary in learning to change behavior. We must feel truly sorry about our behavior if we are to change. And we can only be sorry because we *care*. A measure of guilt may be a first step in changing behavior, but a heavy load of guilt does not lead to desirable changes. The result of a heavy load of guilt may be that the child's controls break down. He may no longer care. Then he is in a position where he may destroy himself or others. We as adults should be careful to avoid adding to the burden of guilt children carry, just as we do not interfere when they must face feelings of guilt that are reasonable and within their capacity to bear.

THE IMPORTANCE OF DECISION MAKING FOR THE CHILD

Making decisions for oneself is a part of taking responsibility for one's behavior. In guiding children we look for situations in which they can make their own decisions. We give a child a choice whenever choices are possible. We look for alternatives in action where a child can select what he prefers to do. There are many matters about which the child is not yet ready to make judgments, but there are other situations in which he can make decisions. These opportunities are important for his growth in autonomy. If we give the child a choice or ask for an opinion, we must be sure that it is a legitimate choice or question. If we ask the child, "Are you ready to go now?" or "Are you through painting?" we must be in a position to accept his answer. Here are two examples of a situation which often occurs in school. Note the different ways in which two parents manage the same situation: Henry (3.9) is a roly-poly, somewhat immature little boy. His father comes in and says to him, "Are you ready to go?" "No," says Henry sturdily. His father answers, "Well, even if you're not, you're going anyway. Put your things away and come along." His smile relieves his words, but the words suggest a reason that Henry remains immature. He is treated as a much younger child. One senses that he feels helpless. Dick (3.8) says to his mother when he sees her, "I don't want to go home." His mother answers with a smile, "I know you like it here and you want to stay, but we have to go now. We'll be back in the morning." Her words show that she accepts his feeling. It isn't difficult for Dick to leave.

There is, of course, a danger in giving the child responsibility or authority for which he is not ready. Winnicott (1957) points out:

> It is the task of parents and teachers to see that children never meet so weak an authority that they run amok, or that they must, from fear, take over the authority themselves. Anxiety-driven assumption of authority is dictatorship . . . the calm adult is less cruel as a manager than a child quickly becomes when he is responsible for too much. (p. 174)

We must remain the confident authority, while we present the child with reasonable alternatives from which he can make his own choices.

CHANGING PATTERNS OR STANDARDS

We live in a society that is not, on the whole, a "giving" one with children. The emphasis in childrearing is on restriction, on not touching, on staying dry and clean, and on being quiet. Relationships are often given less consideration than objects. The needs of the child to assert himself and to find avenues of autonomy, initiative, and self-expression are often not accepted. The child may suffer a handicapping loss of self-confidence as a result of such patterns. As we shift to a more giving or permissive attitude, we should not bear a burden of guilt when we sometimes act in a way that is *not* giving. In changing our patterns of discipline it becomes all the more important to remember that limits have a positive value if they are appropriate for the child and are wisely maintained. Limits do give support to children. We must be ready to use them with confidence. We must feel sure that sound discipline promotes healthy social, emotional, and cognitive growth.

Our world is constantly changing and so are many of our standards. What was once unacceptable may now be acceptable. Matters related to behavior are relative. In different cultures there are different standards for behavior. In our society individuals must be prepared to make their own decisions about how to behave. The final stage in personality growth according to Erikson is that of resolving the conflict between a sense of ego integrity and that of despair. Supporting the child's sense of being a worthwhile person and giving him opportunities to make decisions appropriate to his level of development help lay the foundation for this final stage in maturity, that of an individual with a sense of integrity, confident in doing what he feels is right.

PROJECTS

1. Observe and report a situation in which a limit was set for a child's behavior. How did the adult define the limit? How did the adult maintain it? What was the child's response? What were the values for the child in the situation? How do you think he felt about himself in the end?

2. Report a situation in which the statement of a limit was well timed. Why did you feel the timing was good? What was the result? Report a situation in which the timing was poor or the teacher failed to maintain the limit set. What was the result?

SUPPLEMENTARY READING

Anthony, E., and Gilpin, D. *Three Clinical Faces of Childhood.* New York: Spectrum, 1976.

Caldwell, B. Aggression and hostility in young children. *Young Children,* 1977, *32*(2):4–13.

Fraiberg, S. *The Magic Years.* New York: Scribner's, 1959. Chaps. 5 and 8.

Redl, F., and Wineman, D. *Controls from Within.* Glencoe, Ill.: Free Press, 1952.

Stone, J. *Discipline.* Washington, D.C.: National Association for the Education of Young Children, 1978.

Zigler, E., and Hunsinger, S. Supreme court on spanking. *Young Children,* 1977, *32*(6):14–15.

8

Bird
(*girl, 3.9*)

Observing Children

All teachers need to develop skill as observers. They need to see and record as accurately and as objectively as possible what is happening in situations. Teachers learn most about children by studying their behavior directly. By learning to observe with objectivity, to make careful notes, and to go over these thoughtfully, a teacher increases her understanding of a child's behavior.

The teacher as an observer is someone who is, herself, part of the situation. She is an "involved observer" or "participant observer." Hers is not an easy task. She is interested in the meaning behind the behavior. To achieve even a measure of objectivity takes practice and self-discipline. The teacher's accurate observation record can make a valuable contribution toward understanding a child's behavior and planning for his learning.

Objectivity means seeing what is actually taking place. It means observing without being influenced by value judgments like "bad," "good," "right," or "wrong." It means trying to reduce the distortions that are the result of biases, defenses, or preconceptions.

Students need to develop their skills in making observations before they undertake the role of "participant observer." As a part of their training for teaching, they need to spend a great deal of time observing and recording their observations of young children.

Teachers need to continue making observations as a part of their teaching. The teacher can carry a pad and pencil with her in a pocket to make notes and keep records describing behavior as it occurs. She will jot down the words said by the child, for the exact words are hard to recall later, and she will note the date and add a word or two about the circumstances. Such notes are valuable. They are the "raw material" out of which understanding grows. When written up more completely later, and filed, notes make up a record about a child. This record should be reviewed and summarized at intervals. It can be used in evaluating a child's progress, in making plans for him, and in preparing for a conference with his parents.

Every teacher should try to manage time during the week when she can step aside and do more sustained observing. She may have a special purpose in mind, such as trying to discover how a certain child approaches other children, or why there is trouble so frequently in the block-building corner, or how the setup for finger painting might be improved. If the staff feels that a particular child is having difficulty, they may all try to observe him throughout a week, making notes on what they observe. One of them may take time to do a longer observation in order to add still more information. Pooling these records, they can discuss his behaviors in a staff meeting. They will have more accurate information about his strengths and vulnerabilities and be better able to plan for him.

TYPES OF RECORDS

There are many types of observational records. The *informal, random notes* that a teacher makes are of value in understanding a child's behavior. They usually record characteristic behavior, or significant behavior, or examples

The quality of a child's involvement is an important part of an observation record.

A teacher may plan a particular task in order to observe a specific ability.

of a particular type of behavior. The *diary record* or *running record* is an observational record covering a period of time, including all that can be recorded in that time interval. *Sampling records* are observational records repeated at intervals. *Selected observations* may be made of certain types of activity, such as observations of a rest period or of children's skill in making parquetry designs or a child's behavior on the first day at school.

A useful reference on the subject is the monograph by Cohen and Stern (1978), *Observing and Recording the Behavior of Young Children*. Two books by Susan Isaacs, *Intellectual Growth in Young Children* (1966) and *Social Development in Young Children* (1972) contain a wealth of examples of situations involving children individually and in groups, recorded with interpretive comments.

A good teacher will spend time observing, making records, and using these to increase her understanding of young children and their behavior. Here are some examples of different kinds of records.

INFORMAL NOTES

5/12 Bruce (5.6), constructing a building, tried to enlist the help of Marvin, saying, "You can be a roof helper," and then turned to me, "You are so tall you can help with the roof." Example of Reasoning and Social Skill,—K.R.

REPORT OF A SINGLE INCIDENT

10/6 As I came out onto the playground, Joe (5.1) ran up and asked me to tie his shoe. I bent over and did it for him. Off he ran, and then Betsy (4.2), who had been sitting on the step, said, "Wait." She reached down, carefully untied her shoelace, and stuck her foot out, asking me to tie her shoelace. I smiled at her, tied it, and patted her; off she went.—K.H.

Comment and Interpretation

In this record one is struck by the *un*self-conscious way in which Betsy asked for a share of the teacher's attention. The teacher seemed willing to accept her request and give her an extra bit of attention. It appeared to satisfy Betsy, and she moved away into activity rather than just sitting. It would be worth observing Betsy further to see whether she may be an "easy" child, who is not getting much attention, or whether she has a real problem with jealousy or with finding her place in the group. At least she is showing that she has ways of coping with the situation.

TEN-MINUTE RUNNING RECORD

10:30 Billy (4.4) is kneeling in front of a low blackboard, carefully drawing diagonal lines of scallops across the board, pursing his lips as he draws. Kim (4.1) comes up, kneels beside him, and draws a heavy dark line through his scallops; and then she sits back with a pleased expression. Billy looks at her in surprise and then back at the board. He picks up the eraser and carefully erases both lines. He appears to ignore Kim and begins to draw scallops again, tracing the lines of the previous scallops, which are still faintly visible. As he draws the fourth scallop, Kim reaches out and draws another dark line intersecting the scallops. Billy sits back on his heels and looks at the board, but not at Kim, frowning slightly. Then he reaches forward and erases the board, glancing at Kim. He begins to draw the scallops again, this time looking at Kim each time he makes a scallop. Just as he begins the fourth one, again Kim reaches out and scribbles over his drawing. Billy turns to her, raises his hand with the eraser over his head, and then lets it fall. He turns back and uses the eraser to erase the board very thoroughly.

10:35 Billy draws a line down the center of the blackboard, saying as he finishes, "There," and pointing to the side nearest Kim, "Use your own spot." He sits quietly back on his heels and says with determination, "I'm going to be a good boy." Kim, bringing her eraser across the entire board, says, "Now we got to race." Billy says, as though to himself, "I don't care." Then he says to Kim, "Do you want to erase your name?" "OK," Kim answers. Billy draws a "B" on the board.

10:39 Just then a teacher calls to Kim to tell her that it is her turn to have the swing. She jumps up and runs off. Billy goes back to work on his scallops. When he finishes he leans back on his heels and, with apparent satisfaction, says, "There's my monster."

Comment and Interpretation

The observation seems complete, giving details that enable us to reconstruct what has taken place. The descriptive phrases that are used, such as "looks at the board, but not at Kim" and "diagonal lines of scallops," are clear. It is objective, free of interpretation. The impressions are clearly labeled as "with determination" or "with apparent satisfaction." We have an objective picture of Kim's and Billy's behavior, relatively unclouded by what the observer thought.

Billy seems wholeheartedly involved in his own purpose. He copes with the problem of Kim's interference in an unusual way. First, he tries to ignore it. He almost seems to want to pretend she isn't there. As she persists, he repeats his attempt until it obviously is unsuccessful. He feels like hitting her with the eraser, but he controls the impulse. Perhaps he feels better after he drains off some of this feeling by erasing the board vigorously (as he would like to have wiped her out).

Then Billy moves on to another level of coping. He divides the space, one side for Kim and one for himself; he probably hopes he will be undisturbed. His internalized adult conscience comes out in the words, "I'm going to be a good boy." He is trying to exorcise the monster with these often heard words. Kim, however, is operating on a different level. She feels aggressive and competitive, and she suggests a race. At this point Billy tries to persuade himself that he doesn't care. This device doesn't seem to work, and he then comes up with a remarkable solution. He decides to give her something to erase, her own name, a wonderfully positive suggestion with significant overtones. It is in line with her interests at the moment, and the "B" he draws is the first letter of his own name, probably the only name he knows how to write. As she has been intent on destroying his product, erasing the "B" seems significant. When Kim leaves at this point and Billy is able to finish his drawing, it becomes a "monster," probably carrying the load of frustration and resentment that he feels. It seems to satisfy him.

Billy's control over his impulses seems to be very strong. His strengths lie in his ability to put his feelings into words and finally to express them in his drawing. One might wonder whether or not this control is almost too great for a four-year-old boy and may interfere with his standing up for himself with other four-year-olds. "I'm going to be a good boy" is not an easy thing when one is with others who have not "internalized" this concept. It leads him into some unusual problem-solving actions: dividing the board with Kim and giving her something to erase. These actions demonstrate his capacity to cope with a situation on a high level and, later, his capacity to use drawing as an avenue for finally expressing the feeling that he has not allowed to come out more directly.

How effective his defenses are, where they will lead him, and what they really mean to him can only be understood after further observations of Billy. Billy is the third child in a family of four children. One suspects that Billy has had a lot of help in coping with the interferences of a younger sibling in a family where standards are high and relationships are good. What help does he need in the school?

We also meet Kim in this record, the minor character in the drama, at a moment when she has been thwarted in carrying out a purpose. She wants to swing, and she has had to wait for a turn. She begins to frustrate someone else, teasing and annoying Billy, but not in an unfriendly way. She is apparently an active child; she does something rather than wait. She is also sociable, and she turns to another child rather than to an object. She tries actively to get Billy's attention. In making a line through his drawing, she is also probably draining off some of *her* frustration. She is persistent, but she is not concerned with trying to be a "good girl." She, too, can make a suggestion. Her suggestion, "We got to race" is a vigorous, competitive one, but she is flexible. She accepts Billy's different suggestion about erasing her name instead. She quickly returns to carry out her original purpose when the teacher calls her. She seems to be a normal, healthy four-year-old.

Kim's behavior is a reminder to us that any child who has to "wait" may need some teacher help. To be left at loose ends, frustrated in the immediate carrying out of a purpose, is not easy for a child. As teachers, we need to be alert to the child's need for a suggestion about what to do while waiting. Perhaps the waiting time can be used for a conversation with the child. At least we need to keep an eye on what the child does in the waiting period. Kim needed some help in coping with her problem. She put a burden on Billy in this case.

SITUATION FOR DISCUSSION

An Incident in the Homemaking Area in a Play Group*

Background Information

Alicia (3.2) is the youngest of ten children in a warm, loving Mexican-American family. Her mother takes care of Davie and Donald during the day, so the three children are well acquainted.

Davie (3.0) is also Mexican-American. He lives with his mother, who works outside the home, and with his grandparents.

Donald (3.0) has parents who are in the process of getting a divorce.

Situation

Davie walks into the homemaking corner where Alicia is sitting at the table pretending to eat eggs. She scrapes her spoon across the plate, puts it into her mouth, smacking her lips. With her eyes sparkling, she says, "Davie, have some eggs!" Davie pulls a chair away from the table and sits down.

---

* Recorded by Jane Martin.

Alicia, pushing her plate toward him, says, "Come closer to the table, Davie, and eat your breakfast." Davie pulls his chair nearer to the table and very seriously begins to "eat."

Donald, who has been curled up in the cradle in the corner, gets out and comes to the table. He starts picking up the dishes. With two already in his hands, he grabs for Davie's plate. Davie frowns and in a positive tone says, "No, you have two plates. This is mine." He grabs his plate and holds it firmly, raising his hand to hit Donald. Alicia immediately says, "Don't hit Donald, Davie." Without a word Donald turns and walks out of the homemaking corner. Alicia starts clearing the table and putting the dishes in the sink. Davie remains at the table, a frown on his face, his lips set tight, still holding his plate.

Comment

What may the behavior of these children suggest to an observer? Alicia is revealed as a friendly, secure child, with imagination. She enjoys pretending and takes the maternal role in this sociodramatic play. She appears to identify with her mother. She seems to have good patterns in family relationships to imitate. She uses positive statements, "Come closer to the table, Davie." She defines limits, "Don't hit Donald, Davie." She seems social, alert, and practical.

Donald is in a "baby" role in the cradle when the incident begins, but he changes this role, apparently somewhat jealous of the role Davie is taking with Alicia. He acts aggressively toward Davie, but Davie defends himself. Alicia is looking out for Donald and forestalls Davie's retaliation. Donald, apparently sure that Alicia is not neglecting him, leaves the situation. He has not spoken a word. He seems less free to be creative in his play than the others and less sure about relationships. Curling up in the cradle may signify his wish for greater security and more babying than he has known.

Davie appears friendly and social. He enters easily into the imaginative play suggested by Alicia. When Donald interferes, Davie stands up for himself. He makes an excellent positive statement, "No, you have two plates. This is mine." He is ready to be aggressive, but does not hit Donald when Alicia warns him not to. He has control over his impulses, but he seems puzzled in the end, holding firm when it is no longer necessary. Is he more upset than we might think?

Individual differences are evident in these three children. They will need guidance of different types from the teacher.

What help could these children use? Davie may need to have an adult clarify or explain to him by commenting quietly, "You wanted to keep your plate. That was right. Donald didn't need it. It was good to tell him, and I think he understood." The adult might then have continued, "I wonder if Alicia would like someone to help her with the dishes," thus suggesting another step in the play to help Davie get started again. He may need help in recovering from situations, leaving them behind, and becoming less concerned with the "right" and "wrong" of behavior. As a little boy, he may be finding it difficult to try to live up to the standards and expectations of three older people.

PROJECTS

1. Observe one child for a ten-minute period, keeping a record of what the child does and says in this time. Comment on what you have learned about the child or what questions the observation has raised.

2. Select a piece of equipment and observe and record which children make use of it through a period of 20 minutes. Summarize your observations. Of what value is this equipment?

SUPPLEMENTARY READING

Almy, M. *Ways of Studying Children*. New York: Teachers College, 1959.

Cohen, D., and V. Stern. *Observing and Recording the Behavior of Young Children*, 2d ed. New York: Teachers College, 1978.

Issacs, S. *Social Development in Young Children*. New York: Schocken Books, 1972. (Originally published, 1933.)

Roskin, L., N. Taylor, and F. Kerckhoff. The teacher as observer for assessment: A guideline. *Young Children*, 1975, *30* (5):339–344.

Boy in Boat
(*boy, 3.11*)

Helping Children Adjust to New Situations

We all know what it is like to be in a new situation. We suggested earlier that one of the first steps for us to take in the school was to accept the feelings that we had because we were new and strange to the situation. We probably felt that we had to defend ourselves against feelings of inadequacy. We had to learn to feel comfortable.

EACH CHILD HAS CHARACTERISTIC PATTERNS OF RESPONSE TO NEWNESS

The child faces feelings similar to those of the adult when he meets new situations, such as entering school or accepting the approaches of unknown people. He may defend himself against the uncertainty and inadequacy he feels by inappropriate behavior or by rejecting the new people, places, or events. Because we know what it is like to feel strange and inadequate, we will find it easier to understand the child's behavior. We may be able to recognize the meaning behind what the child does. We may be better able to help him meet new situations. What the child or the adult will do depends on his individual makeup and his past experiences.

What is considered a "good adjustment" to a new situation? Obviously fear is very limiting, and uncritical acceptance sometimes reveals a lack of awareness that may lead to undesirable consequences. What we might consider most desirable is a readiness to accept differences, and an ability to pick out familiar elements and relate the unknown to the known.

THERE ARE REASONS FOR DIFFERENCES IN ADJUSTMENT

What lies behind differences in children's responses to the same situation? We can be certain that the same situation does not seem the same to all children. Demonstrable differences in responsiveness to stimulation are present at birth or soon after. One child, for example, will be more disturbed than another by a sudden, loud noise or a difference in the intensity of light. New people, places, and events will have different meanings for each child, depending on the sensitivity that is part of his constitutional difference.

Each child also brings his own past experiences to a new situation. These experiences have prepared him differently. It does not matter if we do not know specifically what these past experiences have been as long as *we accept the child's present behavior as having some meaning.* Being taken to a new place may mean pleasant possibilities to one child and disturbing possibilities to another. We can expect and accept different behavior from different children.

The many daily experiences which a child has are probably of more importance in influencing his adjustments than any single disturbing event. In other words, the sum total of the child's experience is usually of greatest importance. It is desirable, therefore, for the child's daily life to contribute to making him feel more secure and more adequate. We are not likely to gain strength by being hurt; we are certain to acquire scars.

A child who is forced into making adjustments for which he is not ready is less prepared for further adjustment. He may try to conceal his feeling, as is sometimes the case with the child whose mother declares, "He doesn't mind being left anywhere." The strain this child suffers may be evident only in indirect ways, as in a loss of creativity, an inability to play, greater dependence, or increased irritability. Nevertheless, many occurrences of feeling strange or frightened, however small and seemingly insignificant, add up to a total that may be disastrous for sound adaptation and adjustment.

ENTERING SCHOOL IS AN IMPORTANT STEP

Entering school offers important new experiences to the child. It means leaving his familiar home and depending on adults other than his parents. It means finding a place for himself in a group of other children about his own age. There are new toys, different toilet arrangements, and a strange play area. He meets a variety of responses from the other children, some of them

A separation experience: saying good-bye at school.

apparently unreasonable responses. He must trust the teachers to understand him and keep him safe in these new situations.

The child's feeling of confidence in himself will be strengthened if he can make these adaptations successfully. For many children, attending school can confirm their sense of trust already fostered in the home and neighborhood. For other children there are valuable opportunities at this point to "work through" previous problems and take steps in rebuilding a shaken sense of trust.

Readiness for School

What makes a child ready for school? Why do some children enter eagerly and others hold back from the new experience? What can we do to reduce the difficulties to manageable proportions for all children?

Here we will refer to the concept of developmental tasks as outlined by Erikson. According to this concept, the development of a sense of trust is the first and basic task for a healthy personality. The sense of trust grows out of feeling cared for by loving parents. The child who feels safe with his parents can proceed to feel safe with other people. There are many reasons why one child may not feel as safe or secure as another. Many moves, leaving little in the way of familiar physical surroundings to tie to, frequent separations from parents, or separations coming at critical times in development may make it harder for a child to develop a sense of trust.

Because feeling secure contributes significantly to healthy personality development, it is important to reduce the stress of entering a school, so that this experience may add to, rather than threaten, the child's feeling of being safe. Safeguards include avoiding starting a child in school shortly after a new baby has arrived, after the family has just moved, or after there has been some upsetting change in the family such as his mother starting to work outside the home. If it is necessary for the child to start school under circumstances like these, he should be given much more time and support to make the adjustment.

The Significance of Entering School for the Child

Entering school may contribute to growth in important ways; let us try to understand the significance of entering school for the child and his parents. Then we will outline some possible steps to follow, which can help promote healthy growth.

The tasks facing the child in entering school are twofold. First, he must feel free enough to come to school, relate to the people there, and use the materials. Secondly, he must resolve the conflict inevitably felt in leaving something behind in order to go on to something else.

The conflict to be resolved in this case is lessening the close dependency on his parents or other care-giver in order to live in the world the school offers and to find new satisfactions that it makes possible for him. In going forward, he must leave behind a measure of dependency in order to take a step in the direction of independence. He must resist his desire to cling to the relationship with his care-giver, which has been the main source of his satisfaction and security up until now. He must act on the wish to separate himself from her and be ready to explore new relationships which may also prove to be sources of satisfaction.

For some children who may have found their sources of satisfaction in a number of other people, as with children from large families, there may be less conflict. These children have already found security in a variety of relationships and have less need to hold on to dependency. There are children, too, who have not known closeness to any one person and who do not appear to need any support. They have other needs which are likely to come out later in other ways. For the child from a small family with mainly positive relationships, there will still be some degree of conflict to resolve, a step to take in growing up, as he enters school and leaves his family for even a short time.

Each Child Comes with Different Strengths and Vulnerabilities

In meeting these tasks each child brings different strengths and vulnerabilities with him. His own constitutional endowment will differ, his sensitivity, his tempo of living, and the intensity of his response. One child may delight in sounds, another in color, another in movement. One child may respond quickly, reacting to a variety of stimuli; another may respond slowly. Some children will come to school having known much uncertainty and fear. Others will have known more of the familiarity and the safety. In addition, each child comes with his own set of expectations about school and with his own interests.

Relationships with His Care-giver and His Teacher Are Important

The quality and variety of relationships with people which each child has known will also differ. Of these relationships, the one with his primary care-giver will probably have the most effect on the way the child proceeds toward independence. If his care-giver has been able to help him develop a sense of trust, she will have satisfied in large measure his pressing infantile dependency needs. He is now free to move on to develop new relationships which will meet new needs. The conflict he feels in separating himself from her is more easily resolved when he does not carry a heavy burden of "unfinished business" in the way of infantile dependency.

The teacher plays a significant role because of the help she gives the parent as well as the child. They both face a new kind of separation. The teacher can give support to the parent's desire to leave the child free to separate as well as support the child's desire to move toward independence. The teacher will do this best when she sees clearly what the significance of entering school may be for both child and parent.

It is not simple for a teacher to move with certainty, for each child and each parent differ in what he or she brings to the situation and in what he or she needs to find in it. In addition, the teacher herself may be handicapped by set patterns of the way school entrance is handled, or by her own fears, her own need to control, or the way her own dependency needs have been met. As she develops sensitivity and skill, she will find satisfaction in helping the child work out the problems involved in school entrance. If the teacher can help the child and the parent with separation at this time, she has given them help which will be of value now and in future separation.

The Process of Helping the Child and His Parents

How does the teacher proceed in helping the child and his parents? How may the philosophy of early education be translated into action in this particular experience? We will suggest a series of steps that may be taken to help a child enter school.

In outlining these steps we need to recognize that, in many situations, the steps will necessarily have to be condensed, as in the case of a parent who is employed. Attending school for an hour with his mother, father, other relative, or care-giver may be all that can be managed as a first step for the child. It should be emphasized that *no* young child should *ever* be left at a school without any preparation. He should have someone staying with him on his first day, and the first day should never be a long one. The mental health of a child is too important to put at risk in this way. Attending for only part of the time for the first week saves time in the end because the child is less likely to be overtired and to succumb to an infection.

Step One: A Parent-Teacher Conference

The first step is a conference between the teacher and one or both parents. In this conference the teacher explains the policies of the school to the parents, makes clear the matter of fees, health regulations, hours, and steps in admission. She tells them something of the program, of their part in it, and tries to answer the questions they have. She learns something of the child's interests and skills and some of the parents' expectations for this child. She may ask the parents to fill out a developmental history and home information form to be kept in the school.

One of the important parts of the conference will be a discussion of the steps to be taken in enrolling the child in the school. These steps will need to be clarified in subsequent conferences, but it is essential for the parents to understand that someone well known to the child must be there for the child to turn to in the first days of school.

In discussing the kind of help the child will need from the parents, the teacher will point out that the child needs to feel that his parents are glad to have him go to school and that school is a good place to be. The child also needs to feel, not that a parent is leaving him, but that the parent is letting him do the leaving and will always be glad when he returns.

Step Two: Parent and Child Visit the School

The next step is to give the child some concept of what school is like through a visit to the school. The child needs a picture in his mind when he hears the word "school," "kindergarten," or "center." He needs to be anticipating what lies ahead in as realistic a way as possible.

Visiting the school when other children are not present keeps the situation simple and manageable for him. There are not so many new and unknown factors. He can become familiar with aspects of the physical setup, discovering areas where he feels secure. He is protected against what may seem to him as unpredictable behavior in other children. He has an opportunity to enter into a relationship with his teacher without competition from other children dividing her attention. She has an opportunity to become acquainted with him and to take a step in understanding what his needs and interests are likely to be and what role she may play as his teacher.

Step Three: Parent and Child Attend a Short Session

The third step, following the initial visit, is for the child to visit with his parent at the school when school is in session. School as a place where children are present is thus added to the concept he is forming about a school. He can watch, make the contacts he wishes, and participate only as he is ready.

Children will differ in the way they use this visit. Some will make many contacts with children. Others will follow, watching from a distance. Still others will return to the play materials which they enjoyed on the earlier visit, seeming to pay little attention to the other children around them.

The teacher will add to her understanding of a particular child by observing him in this new situation. She also has many opportunities to help him. Seeing his interest in something, she may place this material near him, bringing it easily within his reach. If he looks at a child painting at the easel, she may walk nearer with him and say a few words about the paint, the colors, and so forth. She does not push him into activity. She only moves with him, if she feels this action makes him feel more secure. He may find the piano, and together they may share some music, with other children joining them. If he is most interested in watching what other children are doing, she may comment on what is going on, mentioning the children's names. Some children may be made anxious by much attention from the teacher until they feel more at home. The teacher can limit her help to a reassuring smile when such a child looks in her direction, and be ready with more active help later.

When a new child enters a group, he holds a special place as a visitor. Other children have a chance to become aware of him as a "new" child. They may become aware of "newness" and the fact that there are steps in proceeding from being "new" to feeling familiar and at home in a group. A wise teacher may use the opportunity to support growth in individual children already in the group. She may say, "Remember when you were new and visited?" She may recall some special incident and add, "Now you know where things go and what we do. You have friends." In this way she points out and strengthens the movement this child has made toward independence and greater security.

There must be opportunities to develop a relationship with the teacher. Through observations of and interactions with the child during his visits, the teacher makes an effort to establish a relationship with the new child. Her task is to help him discover a teacher as a person who is there to be depended on, and who cares for and about him, before he can let his parent go with confidence. For this reason it is important for the teacher to have time to spend with the child or to be available to him. He may need the same person on each visit to whom he can turn if he is to make the separation in a constructive way.

In order to make the best use developmentally of the experience for the child, the teacher will bring only *one* new child at a time into the group. It is difficult to be able to give the needed reassurance to more than one new child at a time. We are speaking here of bringing children into a group. If a group is just forming, it represents a different situation. The teacher may then plan to bring perhaps four children together for an hour with their parents. Four new children are not likely to enter into sustained relationships with each other or to demand a great deal from the adult immediately. She can be available to them all, as she introduces the possibilities of the school environment to them. Another group can come at another hour to go through the same process, and in a few days several such groups may come together to become a larger group entering school. In this way, each child begins in a small group first, and he is with children he knows when he enters the larger group.

A clear understanding about the length of time the child is to stay helps in the adjustment. The wise teacher will have a clear understanding with the parent as to the length of time the child will be staying on his first day at the school. More than an hour spent in an environment that demands as much responsiveness as the school is fatiguing for most children. The child needs to be protected from fatigue. Some children can, of course, stay longer, and many children will wish to do so, but there are advantages in setting a definite length of time for the first visit and maintaining it.

The teacher will decide with the parent on the best time in the day for the child to come. It is important to give consideration to the family schedule in planning. The child is not helped if the running of the home is disrupted by the demands made by the school. The needs of other members in the family must be considered.

During these first days it is usually important for the child that his parent come without bringing other children in the family, if possible. Entering school is a significant event in the life of the child and his parents. If the parent is free to give him all her attention, she may reaffirm for him his sense of being valued by her. This attention may be especially important to him if there is a baby at home who has necessarily been taking much of the parent's time. It may help the child to realize that his parent cares for him at this moment of approaching separation.

One of the reasons for a clear understanding about the length of time for staying is that it helps the parent to feel sure about what is expected. If she knows that she is to bring the child, stay with him for an hour, and then leave, it reduces her uncertainty. She may be better able to relax and use the time to add to *her* picture of what school is like.

The teacher has an opportunity to gain some understanding through the way the parent reacts to this time limit. Does she find it difficult to accept? Does she try to change it, saying as the time for departure approaches, "He's getting along so well. I think he might as well stay on, don't you?" Is she afraid she may not be able to get the child to leave? Does she comment anxiously, "I'm afraid he won't want to go. What do you do about that?" Does she needlessly disturb the child with warnings, "You haven't much time left. It's almost time to go." Is she comfortable with the time limit set?

The parent's feelings influence the child's adjustment. The way the parent feels about sending the child to school will have a profound effect on the way the child adjusts. If she feels reluctant, unsure, or overanxious, she hinders his ability to meet the new situation and grow more independent. It is sometimes hard for both parent and teacher to realize how completely a child senses what the adults who are close to him may be feeling.

There are many reasons why a parent may feel uncertain. She inevitably feels some conflict between wanting to hold on to the child, to prolong his dependence, and wanting the child to be strong and independent. The teacher needs to stand ready with reassurance. She needs to strengthen the parent's acceptance of the reality of what school is and the parent's confidence in her child's readiness for it. A parent may both want very much to have a child in school and yet still not want him there. She may be afraid of the disapproval of people, or of her own feeling of not wanting him home all the time. It is for the teacher to encourage those feelings in the parent which will support the growth of the child toward independence and to reduce the conflict for them both.

The parent helps a timid child by saying, "I will be right here. I am staying with you. I won't leave." She may find a chair where she can see and be seen easily by the child and stay there. She does not push him away from her with words like, "Why don't you go play with the blocks or with that little boy over there."

It is the teacher's, and not the parent's, responsibility to encourage the child to move away from his parent. The parent may show the child by a smile that she is glad to see him when he returns to her side, but she indicates her pleasure in what he has done on his own. If he is hurt or is rebuffed by another child, she gives him the comfort he seeks, but she accepts the incident as part of the reality of existence with others, trying to look at it in the way she hopes that he will. She shows confidence in his ability not to be upset just as she will not be unnecessarily upset.

The teacher finds ways to help both the child and the parent. The teacher is also the one to take the responsibility for helping the child to participate when he is ready. She is always alert to the need to give him support in the efforts he makes to move toward greater independence. When he does leave his parent, the teacher stays near him to give him the protection he needs at first. By staying near him the teacher is also demonstrating to both him and his parent that she is there, looking after him. She makes it easier for the parent to leave the child free to participate.

Some children are helped to make the adjustment if they bring something from home to keep with them at first. While it may not be the usual practice of the school to encourage children to bring their own toys, it may be desirable during the initial adjustment period. It is unlikely that the child will be able to "share" this possession if he is depending on it for support, and he should be protected against having to do so. A simple explanation by the teacher such as, "Mary is new at school and needs to keep her doll. Later, when she knows us better, she may let you play with it, too," will serve to deepen understanding.

Some parents find the time spent at school interesting; others are restless, finding little to interest them. If a parent is interested, she will find it easy to respond to the child's request to come and look at things, but she also needs to make him feel that it is *his* school. She looks at what he shows her, but she will avoid trying to point out many things to him. The teacher, for her part, will look for ways to help the parent appreciate the significance of what is occurring. As she has time, she can sit with the parent, pointing out and explaining what is happening. Some people have had little background for understanding the development of children. They lack interest in it because they know little about it. Parents are almost sure to be interested if they are helped to see the significance of the children's play. The teacher and the school may open up possibilities to parents for growth in understanding which will be valuable through the years.

Step Four: Regular Attendance for Part of the Session without His Parent

The next step for the child in entering school is to attend regularly for part of the session and to begin the process of having his parent leave him at school. The point to keep in mind is that a relationship of trust in the teacher and interest in the school program itself are the sources of support which will enable the child to be successful in staying at school by himself with confidence and a sense of achievement. The first visits have been steps in preparing him for the separation. Most children will need their parent with them for a few days until they feel at home in the school and with the teacher.

One mother reported to the teacher on the second day that her three-year-old son had told her on the way to school, "I want you to go home today, Mummy." Wisely, they decided to follow his request. She went home for a short time and then returned. He was telling them clearly that he felt ready to be left for awhile, and they showed him that they had confidence in him. He did not need her the next day. He was ready to stay at school without his parent.

It is interesting to note that most parents overestimate their children's capacity to adjust. One cannot depend on a parent's assurance that "He'll be all right without me; I've left him lots of times." He may be a child who stands quietly and withdrawn, the very child who needs his parent most because he cannot express his insecurities. He may have had too many experiences of being left! Entering school with his parent may mean the chance to overcome some of the past, to reassure himself by this present situation that his parent really will stay with him when he needs her. This may be the feeling that he needs if he is to be free to explore and enjoy the new setting.

The tendency on the part of most parents to expect too much of their children in the way of adjustment probably indicates how universally adults fail to realize what is involved in learning and growing. We are not accustomed to observing behavior for cues to feelings. We look for what we want to see and not for what is really there.

The teacher plays an active part in helping the child separate from his parent. It is usually necessary for the teacher to take an active part in the process of separation. The teacher is the one who must actively support the child when he shows signs of readiness to leave his parent. If the teacher plays a passive role and leaves the responsibility up to him by saying, "Do you want your mother to go now?'' or ''Is it all right for her to leave?'' she may be asking for an answer that in most cases he is not ready to give.

Some sensitive teachers, concerned about the danger of forcing a separation, lose sight of the growth potentials in the child. They fail to pick up the cues he offers for his readiness to move toward independence provided he can get help. Prolonging his dependency in the new situation may interfere with his growth toward independence, which is the task at hand developmentally. The skillful teacher will help the child reach this goal in the shortest time possible.

During this fourth step in the process of entering school, the child will come for only part of the session. Until he has successfully completed the stage of separating from his parent, it is better for him not to stay for the full program. It is most helpful to the child to leave school when he still finds pleasure in being there. In this way he may look forward to returning another day.

The parent helps with her understanding. As soon as the parent and teacher agree that the child is feeling comfortable at school and is able to accept help from the teacher, they will plan for the parent to leave for a short time. The parent will prepare the child for her leaving, saying perhaps, ''Today, I am going to do some errands while you are at school. I will be gone a little while, and when I get back, I'll see what you are doing.'' If his response is, ''I don't want you to go,'' she may answer, ''I won't go for a while after we get to school, not until I know you are ready. I will tell you and I'll only be gone a very little while.''

The teacher can prepare the child for what he already expects by saying quietly, ''Your mother is going now, John. She will be back very soon.'' With the teacher there, the parent can say good-bye to the child and leave for a short time. If they have estimated the child's readiness correctly, the teacher will be able to help the child handle the anxiety he feels until his parent returns. The teacher will be careful to stay near him.

The first separation should be a very short one if the child is finding it difficult to let his parent leave. Even 15 minutes may seem a long time when one feels unsure of oneself and under some strain. When the parent returns, she will speak to him and then stay for a while, giving the child time to enjoy his play, before they go home together. In this way his parent is showing him the pattern that she will follow. She goes, but she comes back. He is discovering the satisfaction of feeling more and more comfortable about being able to stay at school on his own.

Step Five: Full-Time Attendance

When a parent is able to leave the child almost as soon as they arrive at school and stay away for as long as two hours without his becoming uneasy, the child is ready for the fifth and last step—that of full-time attendance by himself.

Few three-year-old children reach this step in less than a week. Some take much longer. Sleep disturbances, toilet accidents, and increased irritability may be the result of trying to move faster than the child is ready. Good adjustment requires time, and there are less likely to be relapses if the adjustment has not been either hurried or prolonged unduly.

The four- or five-year-old child will probably be able to feel safe at school more quickly than the three-year-old. He has had more experience and more time to develop confidence in his own resources. Sometimes the struggle to make the separation may be unduly prolonged, often because the parent finds it hard to leave the child. The parent may lack confidence in herself, the child, or the school. It is important that the teacher be aware of the point at which the separating has ''bogged down'' and the child wants to stay, but cannot, for some reason, manage it without more help. The teacher needs to take positive steps in this case to resolve the conflict. She will talk with the parent, indicating her feeling that the child is ready to stay by himself, and they will plan together how this step may be accomplished. The teacher will act with firmness and confidence in carrying through the plan. She may some time need to hold the child in her arms when the mother goes, giving him time to cry, putting into words the fact that she knows he wants his parent, that his parent will be back. Then the teacher will help him find his place in the school, sitting with him, watching with him, finding him a familiar toy, or perhaps taking him to visit the homelike kitchen which he enjoyed seeing earlier. While his parent is gone, the teacher will make sure that she is always available if he needs her. She will try to see that the first separation is a successful one. Through it, the child gains confidence to continue separating himself from his dependency on his parents.

It often happens that a child who is disturbed by some event at home or at school will revert to an earlier level of dependency, wanting his parent again. It is important that his real needs be accepted and met. If his adjustment is sound, he is usually quickly reassured by his parent's willingness to stay with him for a time, and it does not take long for him to become independent. Again, the teacher helps him by accepting him and by giving all the support she can to his desire to be more self-sufficient.

TO SUMMARIZE

We may summarize the steps in entering school in this way:

1. The teacher has a conference with the parents in which, among other things, the procedures to be followed as the child enters school are defined.
2. The child and his parent or parents visit the school when it is not in session to become acquainted with the physical setup and to establish a relationship with the teacher.
3. The child and his parent visit during the regular session of the school for a limited, specified time.
4. The child begins attending school regularly for part of the session and begins the

process of separating himself from his parent as soon as he feels comfortable there. The teacher takes the responsibility for planning with the parent the time and method of separation. She may visit in the child's home so that he and she can become better acquainted.

5. The child attends school without his parent for increasingly longer periods until he is coming for the full session.

If the step of moving toward independence and away from the dependency on his parent is taken so that it does not produce more anxiety than the child can manage easily, he is free to enjoy and profit from the school. He gains in self-confidence. We may wonder whether children who have had this kind of help in separation will be as likely later to suffer from panic in strange situations or to be disorganized by feelings of homesickness.

Here are some examples of the ways in which different children make the adjustment to entering school.

Mikey, Who Was Ready To Stay by Himself

Mikey (3.0) was brought to school by his grandmother on the first day. He was the next to the youngest in a family of six children and one of the youngest children in the group. His reaction that day seemed to be one of complete amazement. He darted from area to area and toy to toy, touching everything and exclaiming, "Oh, no! Oh, no! Look at all these toys. All kinds of toys. So many toys!" He could hardly bear to leave when the time came, but wanted to touch everything all over again even though the teacher explained that he could come back the next day. Finally he was persuaded to go and he left saying, "Goodbye, I hope I can come back some day."

On arriving with his grandmother the second day, he made a check to see if everything was still there. He spent most of the time dashing from place to place and exclaiming with wonder at all the things for children. He commented on the fact that there were "little tables and little chairs just for children." When his grandmother tried to leave for a short time, Mikey stated emphatically that she was to stay at nursery school. On Mikey's third day he asked why he had to go while some of the other children could stay. The teacher explained that when he could let his grandmother go and stay at school by himself, he could stay with the others for lunch. The next day he told his grandmother that he was ready to stay with "his teacher" now and she was to go home and come back after lunch. He showed the same pattern of amazement and delight at his first lunch period. He seemed entirely comfortable with the teacher. At the end of the day he said, "I hope I can stay for lunch again someday."

Here we see a child who manages his dependency needs easily but who is almost overwhelmed by the stimulation of an environment new to him. Mikey made an excellent adjustment very quickly. His friendliness, lack of defensiveness, and his delight in the new were a source of help to many children less sure of themselves.

RALPH, WHOSE MOTHER COULD GIVE HIM TIME TO GROW IN FEELING SECURE

Ralph (3.1) was an only child, with a father and mother who were very fond of him. Although they were gentle and kind, they were very anxious to have Ralph meet all their expectations, perhaps because they were not too secure themselves.

On his visit to the school before he entered, Ralph enjoyed playing with the cars and blocks, but he called his mother's attention to everything and referred to her constantly. It was apparent that he depended on her and would not be ready to have her leave for some time, even though he was eager for school and friendly with the teacher.

When he came on the first day of school, he held his mother's hand tightly. She went into the playroom with him and sat down near the block corner. Ralph immediately began playing. When other children approached, he seemed pleased and made attempts to join their play. One of the boys took a block from him in spite of his mild protest. Tears came into his eyes as he relinquished his hold on the block. He turned toward his mother but did not go to her. She smiled sympathetically and encouragingly, not quite sure what to do. The teacher quietly reassured him, "That was your block, wasn't it? I'll ask Bill to give it back. There are other blocks for him. There are plenty for both of you to build with." It was easy to get Bill to return the block, and under the teacher's watchful eye the two played satisfactorily side by side. Ralph returned to his mother's side finally, flushed and happy.

Ralph was inclined to stutter when he became excited. This disfluency showed that he was sensitive to strain and was further evidence that it was especially important to proceed slowly in introducing him to newness. It was also apparent that there would be some strain for him in adjusting to the realities of three-year-old behavior because of the somewhat "adult" standards to which he had been accustomed. He had shown some strengths on that first day in his ability to enjoy not only the play materials, but also the other children, and to accept help from someone other than his mother.

Ralph and his mother went home at the end of an hour, and returned the next day, both eager to be back at school. Ralph's mother watched the things that went on in school with interest. After Ralph and his mother had been coming to school for a week for two hours each day, both his mother and teacher agreed that Ralph no longer needed his mother, but that he still needed a short day at school. He came happily the next morning, knowing that his mother was not staying. When she started to leave, however, he asked her to go to the store and not to go home without him. Apparently he could not quite bear to think of his mother at home without him. She went shopping, and he had a good morning at school. It was nearly a week later that he decided he would like to stay for lunch, like the other children, and did. His adjustment had proceeded smoothly. His mother smilingly remarked one day that she missed being at school, adding, "It was such fun and I learned so much. They're all different, aren't they?" The days had been worth almost as much to Ralph's mother as to Ralph. She had gained confidence in the school, too.

Not long after Ralph entered school, he ran back as he was leaving one day and threw his arms around the teacher's neck and gave her a kiss. It probably showed that he felt he belonged to the school and to the adults who helped him feel comfortable there, as his mother did at home. As the result of his success in adapting to school he had probably grown less tense and felt himself to be a more adequate person, more secure because he now knew he could proceed at his own pace.

SALLIE, A KINDERGARTNER WHO HAD BEEN TO THE SAME SCHOOL BEFORE*

Sallie (5.0) had attended a nursery class when she was four, and as a five-year-old she entered a kindergarten in the same school. Three of the children who had attended school with her the previous year also were enrolled in her kindergarten class.

Sallie's kindergarten teacher, who was new to the school, learned a lot about Sallie, before meeting her, through her former teacher's report, written at the end of the previous year. Her former teacher described Sallie as a friendly, alert, and competent child whose language skills were extremely advanced for her age. She was further described as curious and "full of spunk." She was said to make choices easily, to persist in tasks, and to be a reflective thinker and a good problem solver. Throughout her nursery school year she had made many friends; her relationships with both children and adults were described as warm and giving. Sallie was a well-nurtured child and a good learner.

From the director of the school, Sallie's kindergarten teacher learned that Sallie's parents were warm, supportive, and secure people who loved children. Sallie was their first of two girls. They were very proud of both children. They liked the school, appeared comfortable visiting, and were always interested in the classroom activities.

Sallie came to meet her teacher and inspect her kindergarten classroom with her mother the Friday before she entered school. Her mother reported that Sallie was excited about returning to school and had been talking about "going to be in *kindergarten*" for several weeks. Her mother also mentioned that Sallie had asked her father and herself many questions about what kindergarten and her new teacher would be like. She also said that Sallie had been very fond of her nursery school teacher, who had moved quite a distance away to attend graduate school.

During her initial visit, Sallie spoke freely with her new teacher, her mother, and another child who was also visiting. She seemed especially interested when her new teacher said that she was a friend of her nursery school teacher and that they had attended college together. Sallie first

* Recorded by Reggie Anderson

explored each area of the room and then sat down and assembled a 25-piece jigsaw puzzle easily. After drawing a picture with flopens, she asked her new teacher if she could go outdoors to swing. She left easily with her mother when it was time to go, looking forward to returning at the start of classes. Her kindergarten teacher's observations of Sallie during this initial visit seemed to confirm her former teacher's description of her as a well functioning child—a child free to profit from this new opportunity.

Sallie was the first child to arrive at school on the first day of class. In fact, she even came a few minutes early. She greeted her teacher with a friendly hello, as she put her sweater in her locker. Her father reported that Sallie had awakened an hour earlier than usual, dressed herself, and was ready to come to school before breakfast. Sallie hugged her father good-bye at her locker, then as he started to walk out the door, she ran to give him another hug. She told her teacher right away that she wanted to draw. Sallie stayed at the table and drew several very complex pictures during her first 30 minutes at school.

In contrast to her behavior on her initial visit, Sallie responded minimally in conversation with her teacher and other children, initiating few comments herself. She followed the teacher's directions and made transitions easily at cleanup, and before and after story and snack times. Outdoors, her teacher observed her wandering around the playground and then sitting down on the school steps with her knees drawn up and her chin resting on her hand.

Sallie had been sitting on the steps in this position for several minutes when her teacher went over to her. She suggested some activities to Sallie, but Sallie said that she was tired and just wanted to wait there until her daddy came to meet her. Her teacher sat down beside her and said, ''I can sit with you for a while and keep you company.'' She waited a few minutes more before saying, ''It takes a lot of energy to start in a new class. I feel a little tired myself. I've been waiting to meet the children in my new class all summer, and now I have!'' Sallie sat quietly and glanced at her teacher with a sober look.

After a few moments her teacher continued, ''Sometimes children and grownups feel a little strange and anxious when they start something new.'' Sallie nodded slightly, and her teacher said, ''I'm new here, too. I feel a little strange, but there are a lot of people to help me, and so I know I won't feel strange or anxious for long.'' Sallie turned and looked directly at her teacher without taking her hand from her chin. Her teacher continued, ''There must be a lot that's new to you, too. Let's see, you have a new teacher, there are some children new to the school, and you have a classroom new to you. That's a lot of newness!'' Sallie nodded.

Both sat thoughtfully for a few seconds, and her teacher said, ''I bet Miss C misses you and the other children who were in her class. She likes you and this school. She left here so she could go back to school and learn more things about children, because she likes them.—(pause)—Last year, you got to know Miss C and be her friend. This year, now that I'm your teacher, I hope you and I can be friends. You can have me for a friend and teacher, and Miss C will still be your friend. Maybe she will come visit us sometime and tell us about what she's doing, and you can tell her about what you're doing.'' Sallie listened intently as her teacher spoke to her, her hand dropping from her chin as she turned her face to look directly at her teacher. By this time her father had arrived at the gate. Sallie ran up to hug him and then turned to her teacher and smiled intently at her as she said good-bye.

ALL NEW SITUATIONS NEED TO BE HANDLED THOUGHTFULLY IN ORDER TO BUILD A CHILD'S CONFIDENCE

Entering school is a big adjustment, but it is not the only new situation which the child may face. Any moment during the day may bring something new. When the children go on walks, for example, they may see unfamiliar or even frightening things. New people, places, and events, wherever they are encountered, need to be handled thoughtfully. A child's confidence can be built up or he can doubt his ability to adapt. A visit to the fire station may mean strange noises, unfamiliar people, as well as the sight of the huge fire engine itself. Some children will need to proceed slowly. One child may be able to watch the fire engine comfortably, if he holds the hand of the adult; another may need the safety of being held in the adult's arms. Others may need the reassurance of knowing that they can leave the situation whenever they want.

The necessity of keeping each opportunity within the level of the child's ability to participate in it without anxiety means that at least two adults must go with any group from school to all but the most familiar places. On a walk to the barns, for example, a child may show signs of fear about going inside. An adult will need to stay outside with him, accepting the fact that for some reason he is not ready to go inside. They both can have a pleasant time together outside a barn. Later the child may want to go inside, or he may be willing to return at another time. With his fear accepted and with time to proceed at his own rate, a child will gain confidence in himself as he succeeds in handling the fear. If he is pushed into entering the barn when he is still afraid, he may only learn to conceal his fear or to depend on adult support. In such a case if anything happens which startles him while he is in the barn, such as a cow mooing, he may be thrown into a panic because of the feelings of fear inside him which are released by the sudden noise. He may become more afraid and lose confidence.

A trip to a fire station or a barn is only one example of a new situation. Children are continually meeting new situations. For one child it could be a piece of climbing equipment on the playground; for another child an encounter with a small furry animal; or for another it could be seeing a worm. It is important that teachers respect children's reluctance and fears and help children to cope with these gradually.

A new place for a routine can enhance adaptive behavior.

THE ADULT'S FEELINGS INFLUENCE THE CHILD'S

The attitude of the adult influences the child, and in any emergency it is imperative that the adult meet the situation calmly for the sake of the child. A group of four-year-olds were visiting the fire station one day when the fire alarm sounded. One of the firefighters directed them calmly, "You all stand right against the wall and watch this fire engine go out." His composure steadied the teachers; in a matter of seconds everyone was against the wall, and the fire engine pulled out before the eyes of the thrilled line of children. It was the best trip to the fire station they had ever had. The reports of bombings in World War II showed that children reacted in the way the adults whom they were with reacted. If they were with calm people, they were not likely to be upset even when the situations were terrifying, and they grew hysterical for much less cause when they were with hysterical people.

In planning any opportunity for the children, the teacher must always be familiar with it herself. She must have made the trip so that she can prepare the children for what they may expect. What will it be like? What will they do? What will they see? Will they hear a noise? If there is much that is unfamiliar, it helps to go over it in words so that the children have some framework into which to fit the situation. Often a lively review of what each child saw will help to place the experiences among the "known" things. The review can take place on the way back to school and again later at an appropriate time.

It is usually important to talk to the volunteers and parents about what will help the children enjoy the trip more. Not all adults understand the needs of young children. For example, on a trip to a fire station, a fireman may think it is fun to startle children by blowing a whistle unexpectedly or ringing a bell. If the adults are not helpful, it may be better not to visit the fire station, or at least to be very careful to take only the children for whom such possibilities will not be frightening. People who work with animals can usually be counted on to be gentle and quiet and to help rather than hinder the children's pleasure in the experience they are having.

OBSERVING A CHILD MEET NEWNESS GIVES ONE INSIGHT INTO THE WAY A CHILD FEELS

Observing the way children explore the world outside school is one way to become aware of the different patterns of behavior that children already have. Some children go out to meet the new with confidence. There are others whose areas of confidence are limited, and there are those who are disturbed by the smallest departure from the familiar. Opportunities offered to children must be adapted to what they are ready to accept.

When a child stops to watch something, the wise adult will wait. It is a sign that the child is absorbed in the new, attempting to relate it to what he can understand. He may or may not ask questions. Moving on before he is ready

Getting acquainted with a guinea pig.

will only mean leaving behind unresolved ideas. The habit of exploring the new fully is a sound one and builds feelings of adequacy.

In the first few months at school most children need to be limited to the school itself, before going on any trips. There are many new people, objects, places, and events in the school. By watching, questioning, and participating, the child becomes familiar with the new, whether it be a wasp's nest brought in by the teacher, a visitor in a foreign costume, or just a new toy. When he repeats an activity over and over, he is assimilating it, making it his own. He is adding to his feeling of being an adequate person as he masters the activity.

CHILDREN HAVE DEFENSES WHEN THEY FEEL UNCERTAIN

Children, like adults, have defenses that they are likely to use when they feel uncertain because the situation they are in is new and strange. When children feel unsure of themselves, they may withdraw or retreat from any action and play safe by doing nothing, thus running no risk of doing the wrong thing. This behavior is a type of denial of the situation—like turning one's back on something.

For example, Helen (5.3) came to school and made no protest at her mother's leaving her. She simply stood immobile on the spot where she had been left. If an adult took her hand and led her somewhere, as to the piano, she went passively. She had had many new situations to meet in her short life and much unfriendliness. A frail child, she had protected herself in the only way she could—by being passive. The teachers made no attempt to push her into any activity but gave her friendly smiles, often sat near her, and sometimes took her to the piano or the finger-painting table. Very slowly she began to show some responsiveness.

It was interesting to observe that it was only after Helen had been in school for some months that she began to make a fuss over her mother's leaving and to beg her to stay. It seemed likely that she was just beginning to feel free enough to dare to make some demands on her mother—to indicate how she really felt. Unfortunately, her mother could not accept her demands and refused to "baby" her. Helen stopped this behavior, but she continued to progress at school, making some demands on the teachers and occasionally joining another child in play. When the situation changed in any way, as when there were visitors, she became quite passive. One wonders whether Helen would have been less passive if her mother could have accepted the child's demand that she stay. Would she have felt less helpless? Would she have been less likely to retreat into passive behavior?

Sometimes a child who feels strange and uncomfortable will suddenly begin to play for a lot of attention or act "silly" as though seeking reassurance by surrounding himself with attentive adults. Another child will be aggressive. He may bully others as though to prove to himself that he is big and strong and not as weak and helpless as he fears. These children are doing something active about their problem. They give us an opportunity to help them with it.

Steven (3.6), on the second day of school, appeared disturbed by all the strange children and teachers. He suddenly picked up a toy horse and said, "This horse is going to kill all these many bad people around here." His teacher replied quietly, "I think you don't like finding so many people here. They will be your friends someday." Because they were strange to him, they seemed bad. He was actively trying to cope with his anxiety through projecting onto the horse the wish that he could dispose of them all. He was also communicating to an understanding teacher his need for reassurance.

CHILDREN NEED HELP WHEN THEY ACT DEFENSIVELY

It is not uncommon to see a child, who has been frightened by something startling or unusual, turn and hit a companion with almost no provocation. In this way he drains off the feeling of fear which is uncomfortable. The adult's role is to help him face the feeling and find some acceptable outlet for it. Fear is a less uncomfortable feeling when one is not ashamed of it. It may help if the teacher can say, for example, "Lots of people feel afraid when they hear a big noise like that. It's all right to be afraid. Take hold of my hand and let's walk farther away, then it won't sound so loud. There's no need to hit Billy. He may be afraid, too." The other child will need some explanation such as, "I think he hit you because he felt afraid. I'm sorry." This kind of handling will help each child to understand why people behave as they do.

Often children will actively reject a situation or some part of it because they feel strange and insecure. In the laboratory school the number of adults present may increase any difficulty a child has in accepting adults. Frequently he will meet a friendly advance with the words, "Go 'way, I don't like you." It's like getting in the first blow when you're expecting the worst. For the child's sake, it's important to recognize the real feeling behind these words, to understand its meaning as "Go 'way. I'm afraid of you." It usually *is* better to go away until the child has had more time to make an adjustment. It is sometimes possible for a teacher whom the child does know to interpret his feelings to him in such a case, saying, for example, "I think that you don't like her and want her to go away because you don't know her yet. When you know her, you may like her. Her name is ＿＿＿＿＿＿＿. She might help you find a shovel for digging."

It is important to be able to identify children's defenses and to help them make adjustments that are really appropriate to the situation or to help them discover how to drain off their disturbed feelings in acceptable ways. It is equally important to see that children have experiences in which they feel adequate, so that they will have less need for defenses. When adults can do these things, they offer real help to the child.

PROJECTS

1. Record a situation in which a child was faced with a new experience in the school. Summarize your observation, noting the child's significant reactions and the help given by the adult (if any). Estimate what the experience may have meant to the child.

2. Observe two children of different ages in a grocery store or on a playground, and note the degree to which they seem to feel safe and comfortable in the situation. How do they show their feelings? What defenses do they seem to use against the feeling of being strange and unsure? Is the experience building up or breaking down the degree of confidence the children feel?

SUPPLEMENTARY READING

Bowlby, J. *Separation Anxiety: A Critical Review of the Literature*. New York: Child Welfare League of America, 1975.

Furman, R. Experiences in nursery school consultation. *Young Children,* 1966, *22* (2):84–95.

Gross, D. On separation and school entrance. *Childhood Education,* 1970, *46* (5):250–253.

Warren, R. *Caring: Supporting Children's Growth*. Washington, D.C.: National Association for the Education of Young Children, 1977.

Yarrow, L., and F. Pederson. Attachment: Its Origin and Course. In W. Hartup, ed., *The Young Child,* Vol. 1. Washington, D.C.: National Association for the Education of Young Children, 1972.

Post Office
(girl, 4.9)

10

Helping Children in Routine Situations

We have seen how new situations can contribute to building confidence and security in a child if we accept and respect the child's level of readiness for each situation. If we fail to understand the child's needs, we may find that such experiences only increase his feelings of being little and helpless.

The need to *understand* and *accept* the child's readiness for an experience is as important in everyday events as in new or unusual ones. Events which occur daily may pile up feelings and set patterns in a way that influences growth even more significantly than do the unusual or the new. Teaching that includes an awareness of the child's degree of readiness is needed here, too. If we are to achieve the goal of developing secure people, free to make use of all their capacities, we will do this kind of teaching throughout a child's daily life in all situations.

Routines such as toileting, resting, and eating are everyday events. They serve as a framework around which the child's day is organized. It probably gives the child assurance to know that there are familiar aspects of the day that he can anticipate and understand. It enables him to get a sense of the passage of time and to order his life.

It is not unusual for teachers of four- and five-year-olds to consider children's behavior during toileting, eating, and resting to be issues of importance only to teachers of younger children. What a mistaken idea that is!

153

It is true, however, that most four- and five-year-olds are capable of going to the bathroom independently and of managing themselves appropriately at meal and rest times. Nevertheless, it is important for the kindergarten teacher to recall that toileting, eating, and resting are all very personal tasks in that all of them are associated with procedures and rituals learned within a particular cultural and family setting. Whether a child has attended a nursery school or day-care center before entering kindergarten will not lessen the personal and individual aspects of these activities. In addition, it is well to remember that in any new situation a child may regress, and at such times the child, regardless of age, needs thoughtful and sensitive adult support.

TOILETING

Some of the best opportunities for teaching young children occur in the toileting situation, for toileting is a significant part of the young child's life. It is one about which his feelings are sure to be strong. It offers the possibility for a great deal of growth.

For the child, toileting is associated with many intimate experiences with his parents or primary care-giver, with her care of him, with his efforts to please her, and perhaps with conflicts over her attempts to train him. Toileting may even be related to his ideas about "good" and "bad" behavior. One parent used to leave her child at school with the admonition, "Be a good girl today." What she really meant by these words was, "Stay dry today." Morality such as this is confusing.

When the child is ready for school, at about the age of three years, he has probably only recently been through a period of toilet training. He is not likely to have emerged from this training period completely unscathed. His behavior will tell us something about how he experienced this training.

TRAINING FOR TOILET CONTROL HAS AN EFFECT ON MANY AREAS OF BEHAVIOR

Excessive negativism is perhaps the most common result of toilet training that is not based on a child's readiness. The child who says "no" to everything, who looks on any contacts with adults as a possible source of interference and restriction, may have acquired this attitude during his toilet training period. One of the most resistant, hostile children in one school had been subjected to an early, rigid period of toilet training. She defied adult suggestions and could not share with children. The quality of the relationship she had with her earnest parents can be pictured in the note which her mother sent to school one day, "Pearl has *refused* to have a bowel movement for four days."

Inhibitions of many types may stem from the same source. If the child has been forced to achieve bowel and bladder control before he is ready, his "control" may include the inhibition of spontaneity and creativity in many areas. We see children who were trained early to stay "dry and clean" who are unable to use play materials in creative ways. They cannot get dirty in situations, play in mud, use finger paint, or savor the ordinary joys of childhood and the social contacts that occur in the society of children.

Loss of self-confidence may also characterize the child who has been subjected to early and rigid toilet training. In his experience the products of his body have been rejected and his natural impulses denied expression. He loses confidence in his impulses in other directions. Because he has had to give up too early the pleasure of eliminating when he wants, he is likely to "give up" easily in other ways, unless he goes to the other extreme of asserting himself to compensate for his loss.

The child whose parents have treated his acquiring toilet control in the same manner as any other developmental step is likely to be a more comfortable child. The child who is left free to proceed at his own rate is likely to acquire control rather easily at some time after he has started walking. He will show an interest in the toilet and in imitating the behavior of the people he observes. Parents can make it easy for him to do as they do, and can show the same satisfactions in his successes here as they do in his other developmental accomplishments.

A wise adult accepts resistance as a sign that the child has lost interest and is not ready, and discontinues the efforts she has been making to train him. It is wise not to make an issue out of learning toilet control any more than one would of learning to walk or talk. When there is no pressure, the child himself usually begins to take on the patterns of the adult in regard to toileting sometime between the ages of fifteen and thirty months.

Adult Attitudes and Standards May Complicate the Toilet Problem

Toileting is sometimes complicated for the child by parental anxieties. A parent may give a great deal of anxious attention to the child's elimination. It then becomes unduly important to the child and even disturbs him. He feels anxious, and this anxiety interferes with his behavior.

A parent may express her anxiety by too much attention if she is not sure of her ability to be a "good" parent. She tries to reassure herself by seeing that her child eliminates properly. Or she may be having some difficulty in accepting the changes she has had to make in her life because of the child. She may wish that she could do the things she used to do, but she tries to hide her feelings, even from herself, by concern over the child's elimination. Parents who have these feelings are likely, also, to undertake training early, in a determined way, as part of their efforts to prove themselves "good" parents. Thus they complicate further the problem for the child. The child, in turn, may use the withholding of his stools as an unconscious means of "punishing" his parents for withholding acceptance from him. It becomes hard for healthy attitudes to develop under these circumstances.

Standards about toilet behavior that adults sometimes impose before the child can understand them may confuse the child. Separation of the sexes, demands for privacy, disapproval of many kinds of behavior in relation to the toilet situation can have little meaning for the child. These standards may add feelings of uncertainty, fear, or guilt to the situation. Today standards are becoming more relaxed and better adapted to the child's level of readiness.

Children Gain from Informed Handling of Toileting at School

The important thing for us to remember as teachers in the school or day-care center is that children come from many different backgrounds. Some will have healthy, matter-of-fact attitudes, with no doubts about their ability to handle the toileting situation. They will expect to meet friendly, accepting adults, and they will not be disturbed about toilet accidents. Other children will be confused and insecure. They will resent attempts by the adult to help them and will be upset by any failures to control their elimination. Some will use the toilet situation to express their anxieties, their resentments, or their defiance. Some will not be able to use the toilet at school until they feel comfortable there. They must be helped according to their different needs. All of them, no matter what their background, will gain from informed handling of toileting at the school.

If the handling is to be sound, the children must meet adults in the school who are themselves comfortable in the situation. To feel comfortable is not always easy, for many of us have had experiences in our past that have included being ashamed or confused about the subject of toileting. Being with children and adults who have matter-of-fact attitudes will often help us to free ourselves from the conflicts generated by our own past experiences.

The interest that children show in the subject of toileting can be seen in the frequency with which it appears in their dramatic play. Again and again they will act out with their dolls what is for them the drama of the toilet. This play is a desirable way of expressing any conflicts they may feel and making these conflicts seem more manageable. The school designed to meet children's needs will supply equipment in the homemaking corner that can be used to represent the toilet.

What the Child Does at Toilet Time Is Significant

Toilet accidents, for example, are likely to be common in the first weeks at school and may be indications of the strain that the child is feeling in the new situation. They should be treated as important, and the strains should be identified and reduced for the child in every way possible. The child will be reassured when he realizes that he does not need to be afraid of having a toilet accident. This action on the part of the teacher removes one possible strain. He will gain confidence if he finds friendly, accepting adults to help him when he is wet.

Some children, on the other hand, will react to the new situation of being in school by holding their urine and feces. They will be unable to use the toilet. This behavior will be one indication of the way they feel. It is hardly necessary to say that no pressure should be put on a child to use the toilet until he is ready. He may need to go home after a short stay, or he may be more comfortable after he has wet or soiled himself.

Sometimes a child who has been attending school will suddenly have a series of toilet accidents. These accidents may be a sign of emotional strain or of impending illness and should be regarded thoughtfully. It is our responsibility to talk with his parents and try to discover the sources of the strain. We should not increase the strain by disapproval.

A Child Is Reassured by the Realistic Attitude of the Adult

It cannot be emphasized too strongly that a matter-of-fact attitude about toilet accidents on the part of adults is exceedingly important. If a child knows that toilet accidents are not condemned, he feels much freer and safer. He can proceed to acquire control at his own rate, and toilet accidents do not lessen his confidence in himself.

While we can show pleasure in his successes, we must not value success too highly. An undue emphasis on success may rouse anxiety in the child. If success is valued too highly, the child may find it hard to meet the inevitable failures. We can help him succeed without feeling anxiety. Under no condition should a child ever be made to feel disapproval or be shamed for his failure to stay dry and clean. Shame is not a healthy feeling; it does not contribute to the development of the confidence we all need.

Acceptance of Children's Interest in Each Other at Toilet Time Promotes Healthy Adjustment

Sound handling of toileting also includes a matter-of-fact attitude in meeting situations in which the children show an interest in each other in the toilet. Children need a chance to satisfy their curiosity without becoming confused. Girls will be interested in the fact that boys have a penis and stand when they urinate. The way this interest is received by the adult will influence children's attitudes toward sex later in their development. At this early stage their interest is not very different from their interest in anything else new in the school. A girl who has no brothers at home may not notice sex differences the first time that she uses a toilet beside a boy, but when she does, she will usually want to watch boys frequently as they urinate until her interest is satisfied. She may comment and ask questions. It may help her to have the teacher verbalize in some way, such as, "Bill has a penis. He stands up at the toilet. Boys stand up, and girls sit down."

Psychiatrists tell us that an important factor in sex adjustment is the acceptance of one's sex. In the toileting situation it is usually easier for the boys to feel acceptance because they possess a penis. Many times a girl will try to imitate the boy by attempting to stand—with not very satisfactory results! She learns from her own actions, and no particular comment is needed. Some girls may need help in feeling that being a girl is desirable. The teacher may remark, "Mothers sit down, too," or "Boys have a penis, and girls have a vulva."

PROCEDURES THAT ARE CONSTRUCTIVE

What specific procedures are helpful to children in toileting at school?

The physical setup plays a part in building positive feelings. If the toilet room is a pleasant place, light and attractive, the child is more likely to feel that it is a safe room in which to be. Ordinary, pleasant conversation on any topic will help make a child more relaxed and comfortable. Some children who already possess a comfortable feeling, will not need such distraction, but conversation may help some other children whose feelings may be mixed.

Interest in the plumbing usually rises to a peak around the age of four, and observation of the inside of the toilet while it is being flushed and discussions about water pipes and sewer systems are of absorbing interest. These interests have value. Any attempt to hurry the child out of the situation or to discourage his curiosity will make it harder for him to develop and maintain a healthy attitude. The wise adult will be prepared to spend time and feel comfortable in the toilet with the child.

Small-size toilets are desirable, for the easier it is for the child to manage independently, the more he will gain. If they cannot be obtained, a step can be made to fit in front of the toilet seat. A hinged seat to make the opening smaller may be helpful, too. A door to the room can be a handicap; it may interfere with the ease of supervision. By kindergarten many children will prefer privacy in the bathroom.

Children at the nursery school and kindergarten level can be expected to be independent about their clothing at toilet time if they are properly dressed. Girls can pull down their underpants, and boys can use a fly. There are well-designed pants with elastic tops for both boys and girls. Boys can be reminded to raise the toilet seat before urinating. Both boys and girls can be reminded to flush the toilet after they have used it. When an occasional child refuses to flush the toilet, we can safely assume, as we can with any refusal, that there is some meaning behind it. Children are sometimes frightened by the noise and movement of water in a flushing toilet. They will be reassured in time as they watch others and as they gain more confidence in other places. Their refusal should be respected.

Handwashing should be encouraged after toileting. It is a desirable habit, and a child usually enjoys the washing process. Handwashing is necessary before eating. Children make their judgments on what they see; often their hands look clean to them. If the teacher washes her hands and tells the children it is important to wash one's hands after going to the toilet as well as before eating, they usually accept the idea.

In the school, boys and girls may use the toilets freely together while adults are present. Occasionally a child may find this arrangement difficult and the teacher can explain, "Here at school all children use the toilet together." Standards differ in different places. Adults sometimes ask, "But won't this practice make it harder for a child when he has to learn a different custom?" We must remember that the important thing is to be able to accept the customs that are in use. Toileting on a picnic differs from that done at home. Boys accompany their mothers into public restrooms when they are young, but learn to make a distinction when they are older. Patterns of behavior differ with age, place, and society. The child learns to accept differences, and he begins to understand the reasons for them.

ESTABLISHING A SCHEDULE FOR TOILETING

When a very young child starts school, his teacher can soon discover how frequently he needs to go to the toilet by talking with his mother and by observing his behavior in school.

For the younger child she can establish a schedule to fit his rhythm. She will take most of the responsibility herself, saying to him, "Time to go to the toilet now," and attempting to time her interruptions to a shift in his activity. In this way she will avoid building resistances in him. If she is pleasant and friendly, he will welcome this opportunity for adult contact and attention. Going to the toilet will bring him satisfactions. A new child usually adjusts more easily if he has the same adult helping him each time. He feels secure more quickly and may begin to come to her when he needs to go to the toilet.

As a next step the teacher may ask the child, "Do you need to go to the toilet now?" rather than simply telling him that it is time to go. This question begins to shift the responsibility onto him. If the number of toilet accidents shows that the child is not ready to take this much responsibility, the teacher can drop back to the earlier stage. Many factors change a child's rhythm, such as cold weather, excitement, or drinking more liquids than usual. Even older children will not always remain dry under unusual conditions.

A set schedule for going to the toilet has the disadvantage of not meeting individual needs or not meeting changing needs in the same individual. Nevertheless, as children's needs are likely to follow a similar pattern, it is possible to have a framework within which to expect toileting, and this routine simplifies management. If we remember that the goal of any schedule is to help the child go to the toilet when he needs to go, and not more often, we can work out a schedule that will be flexible. For example, some children may need to use the toilet when they first come to school, depending on their last toilet period at home. The next logical time for an interruption is around snack time, which is usually in the middle of the morning. A toilet period before lunch ensures a lunch period less likely to be interrupted by a trip to the toilet. The more mature children, those who have taken over responsibility for their toileting, will follow their own schedule, but the teacher will find it wise to suggest toileting before lunch or before a trip for them all.

EXAMPLES OF PROBLEMS IN THE TOILET SITUATION

Let us consider some specific problems which may arise.

Mary (4.6) was a delightfully imaginative child with a fine sense of rhythm. She loved music and often played and sang at the piano or danced when music was played. She was friendly with other children and enjoyed "homemaking" play in the dramatic play area. She was curious about many things, played actively outdoors, and enjoyed expeditions outside the school. Toward adults she responded in a very negative way. She resisted suggestions and was likely to become self-conscious and "show-off." She found rest difficult and at the table seemed to concentrate on behavior that she felt might not be acceptable, putting her fingers in the food, throwing it, or running away from the table. She was wet several times a day and consistently refused to go to the toilet. She always changed her underpants immediately, leaving the wet ones on the floor in the toilet room. Her mother reported that she had been toilet trained early and then suddenly began wetting again within the last year. They had "tried everything" to make her stop, even to shaming her and making her wear diapers. At first she would stay wet, but they had succeeded in impressing on her how "dirty" that was, and now she wouldn't stay wet a minute.

It was easy to see where Mary's negativisim came from. It seemed likely that here was an able little girl trying to assert herself. The methods of training and disciplining that her parents had used with her more docile older brother had only increased her resistance. She was defiantly insisting on being independent.

Since she was out to defeat "bossing," it was evident that pressure for conforming to standards, no matter how desirable the standards, needed to be reduced before she could be expected to change her behavior. The whole matter of toileting was dropped in school, and no comment was made on her wetting. There was no insistence put on her to use the toilet. It was hard for her parents to understand that before she could accept adult standards she must be convinced that she was a "free agent," and that they could convince her of this only by accepting her right to wet as she pleased. They themselves valued conformity. They were friendly, intelligent people, however, and very fond of their small daughter. Somewhat reluctantly they followed the suggestion of saying nothing, perhaps because they had tried everything else. It was several months before Mary began using the toilet at school. It might have happened sooner if her parents could have been more wholehearted in turning the responsibility completely over to her. Whenever she was subjected to domination, Mary would revert to a series of wet pants. It was the area in which she felt she could win in the battle to assert her independence. When left to accept things at her own rate, she was an unusually social and capable child who wholeheartedly enjoyed the activities available.

A child does not always express his resistance to pressure as directly as Mary. In a less friendly and understanding home a child may have to conceal his feelings of resistance and resentment.

Jethro (4.4) was a child whose mother reported that she had felt that "the sooner I started him on regular toilet habits the better." She began when he was six months old, and he responded "perfectly." He now says to his younger brother, "I never got my pants wet when I was little." Jethro, however, often sits passively instead of playing. He chews on his blanket, sucks his finger, and is very inactive. His mother reports, "He doesn't enjoy anything that I can see." This child, with perhaps more against him, has not felt strong enough to protest in a direct way as Mary has been able to do. With many other strains added to the pressure to be clean, his position is far less favorable. He is dry, but not free! Spontaneity and creativity have been sacrificed to conformity.

Rita (4.5) was a child whose toilet training had begun at six months and had proceeded smoothly and quickly. Her mother felt that the early training was successful, and it certainly had made matters easier for her. Rita had no toilet accidents at the school, and she was not a resistant child. In fact she was anxious to please. She was lacking in confidence in herself and somewhat tense and easily disturbed by new experiences. She needed reassurance and support from the teachers.

Rita enjoyed school and was friendly with both adults and children—that is, with children who did not get wet. If a child had a toilet accident, Rita avoided him or even actively rejected him in play. One day, for example, Rita was in the bathroom when Gary (3.5) happened to come in. Gary was thoroughly wet, having had one of his not infrequent toilet accidents. Gary was one of the youngest children in the group, but he managed well in spite of the short time he had been in school. He was friendly and eager to play with the other children. Rita watched the teacher help Gary get into dry clothes, but she kept as far away as possible and made her disapproval evident. "He's a bad boy," she remarked to the other children. Throughout the rest of the morning she refused to play with Gary. When he approached her, she would say, "We don't like you," although usually she found it easy to include other children in her play.

Rita had succeeded in staying dry herself because of the way her mother felt about wetting, but she was not able to accept people who failed to keep dry. How will she feel about her own children someday? Will she impose dryness on them, together with tenseness and fear and a rejection of those who do not meet her standards?

MEALTIME

Eating is another area that is important in the development of feelings and behavior. When children enter school, they come with a long past as far as eating goes. They have had many previous experiences with food. These experiences have been satisfying or unsatisfying in varying degrees. The child's attitude may consequently be favorable or unfavorable toward the meal situation.

Like the toileting situation, the meal situation may be highly charged with feeling. "The way to a man's heart is through his stomach" is true in more ways than one. The child's earliest feelings of comfort or discomfort, satisfaction or deprivation, helplessness or adequacy have come from what happened to him when he felt hungry.

ADULT BEHAVIOR AND ATTITUDES INFLUENCE THE CHILD

From the very beginning the child is affected by the way the adults act and feel about his eating. If his first days are spent in a hospital nursery, the infant is probably fed on a schedule because this schedule is part of the routine in most hospitals, not because he necessarily feels hungry then. He is expected to adapt himself to the hospital schedule even though he is adapting himself at the same time to the extreme changes that birth itself has brought. The generations of babies who were fed when they were hungry and cried, and who were kept close to their mothers, probably had an easier time developing positive feelings of trust than babies under modern conditions. The infant's hunger pangs are an individual matter and usually do not fit into a regular schedule. They are acute and distressing to him. If they are not relieved by food, he is miserable, and he is helpless to meet his own needs.

Some hospitals have a "rooming-in" plan whereby mother and baby are together, and shortly after his birth the mother can begin taking some care of her baby and can feed him according to his needs. She can thus not only meet the baby's needs for food, comfort, and reassurance, but also satisfy her own need to be close to and to care for him. The enthusiastic reports of parents who have been able to follow this plan, especially parents of first babies, make us hope that someday more children will receive this kind of start in life.

The more experienced in caring for children a parent is, the more likely she is to trust her child and feed him when he indicates he is hungry. This fact may account in part for the easier adjustment that is frequently seen in later children in families. Even being awakened to be fed constitutes an intrusion which may be annoying to a baby.

BASIC ATTITUDES APPEAR IN THE EATING SITUATION

From the child's behavior in the meal situation at school we can get cues to his feelings and to the kind of adjustment he is making. Appetite is a sensitive index to emotional adjustment. Mary, mentioned earlier, who resisted efforts at toileting, also defied every convention at the table. This behavior was part of her effort to assert her right to be an independent person. When Rita made progress toward becoming a freer, less inhibited individual, her behavior at mealtime changed: She used her fingers more as she ate. She began to dabble them in her melting ice cream in a relaxed way at about the same time that she began playing more freely with the other children. It is important not only from the standpoint of nutrition, but also from that of personality development, that the child's behavior at mealtime be managed with understanding.

EATING WITH OTHERS AT SCHOOL

The ordinary, healthy child enjoys eating. Unless he has had unpleasant experiences in connection with food, he enters school ready to enjoy the mealtime there. He usually has a conservative attitude about food and prefers those foods he already knows. He has his likes and dislikes, and probably he has not done much eating with groups outside his family. At first he may be distracted from eating by having other children around him. The implements, the dishes, even the chairs are likely to be different from those he has used at home. He will probably meet quite a few unfamiliar foods. The expectations of the adults may be different, too. There is a great deal for him to adapt to in the new situation.

Special friends enjoy each other's company at the table.

Goals for Mealtime and Some Ways To Support the Child's Learning

Just as there are goals for learning in other opportunities provided at school, there are goals for mealtime. We want the child to continue to enjoy his food, to learn to like a variety of nutritionally desirable foods, and to practice acceptable ways of eating and behaving at the table. Achieving these goals will take time. Pushing or forcing him will not help and is almost sure to lead to problems.

The teacher should start by making sure that the child can enjoy his meal at school. She can find out from his parents what the child likes and dislikes, and she will try to make sure that some of his familiar well-liked foods are served. She may suggest that he taste all the foods, but she will not insist. She will also consult his parents about the mealtime arrangements at home, so that she can help the child understand the differences at school. She may invite his parent to have a meal at school, so that his parent is in a better position to help the child understand the differences and similarities between mealtimes at home and at school.

The teacher will expect the child to stay at the table at school until he has finished all that he wants to eat that day. She will try to make it easy for him to stay at the table to eat, talking with him and feeding him a bite if he wishes. She acts responsibly, but she avoids issues. She does not insist on a "clean plate."

A child should not be expected to sit at the table until everyone is finished. He should be able to leave when he has finished his meal. There are slow eaters and fast eaters. No one should be hurried. It is another example of how individual differences can be accepted and provided for. Sitting at the table when one has finished eating is a difficult and unreasonable task for children of nursery and kindergarten age.

In addition to staying at the table during the meal, children of three, four, and five can be expected to pour their own milk or juice if it is in small pitchers on the table. They can use a fork as well as a spoon and later a knife. They can serve themselves "seconds" in most cases, sometimes with the teacher's help. They can be expected to wipe up any spilled milk or food if a cloth or sponge is readily available. They may need a little help, but all these tasks promote their growth in independence and responsibility. They are ready and able to learn these skills.

There are *individual differences,* too, *in the amount of food that children eat.* Some children eat much more than others. The same child will eat different amounts on different days, or he may eat a great deal of one food and very little of another. It is a good thing if we avoid any preconceived notions about what or how much a child needs; then we will find it easier to accept the fluctuations in appetite, which are common to all children.

The best practice is to serve very *small* helpings and leave the child free to take as much more as he wants. A child is likely to eat more when he is served small helpings rather than large ones.

Children should have the right to refuse a food and to make choices, but the main meal should precede dessert, and at least some of the main meal should be eaten before the dessert. Drinking milk should be encouraged. With a good mealtime atmosphere, a skillful teacher helps the child live up to her expectations most of the time.

Finger foods, such as toast sticks, carrot sticks, and so on should be served often. Green beans, for example, are often more popular than peas because of the ease with which they can be eaten as finger food. We are primarily interested in nutrition and only secondarily interested in table manners at this point, although table manners are not neglected. The teacher "models" good manners and gives approval to the child who says, "Please," or uses his utensils properly.

A child will usually continue to use his fingers at times long after he has begun to use a spoon. He may revert to an earlier level when he is tired or not feeling well. If we believe that it is important for him to enjoy his food, we will not interfere. Gradually he will depend more and more on a spoon and fork. The kind of manners he will acquire in the end will depend on the example set by the adults around him and not on how much pressure they have exerted on him to meet their standards. On the other hand, his interest in food will be adversely affected by their pressure. We need confidence that the child will acquire the eating patterns of those around him *as he is ready,* just as he acquires their language.

If we move too fast in teaching manners, we may interfere with the child's appetite. Being "messy" with food normally precedes being neat in eating. We remember a three-year-old who ate like an adult, but who ate practically nothing at the table. She did eat between meals when she did not have to conform to the very high standards expected of her at home and the pressures to eat more than she wanted.

Introduce new foods gradually and do not expect the child to learn to like too many foods at one time. Extending food horizons too rapidly does not bring good results in most cases. As he watches others enjoy different kinds of foods the child will be ready to try them himself. Giving him an opportunity to help with the preparation of food in the kitchen may help the child to take more interest in the food at the table.

A child often tends to reject a food because it is new. He may spit it out or make a face. This act, however, may be his first step in learning to eat it. This kind of behavior does not constitute a real rejection. The child will gradually overcome his initial resistance to the food if his behavior does not receive a lot of attention. He will try the food again and, as he acquires familiarity with it, he will probably learn to like it.

How a child feels influences his appetite. There are important emotional factors and emotional consequences to what we do in the eating situation. A secure child, for example, may be able to accept a variety of new foods more easily than a less secure child who may need to cling longer to familiar foods, as in other things, to gain reassurance. The emotional balance of the insecure child may be threatened if he is pushed into eating too many new foods. Feelings of security and confidence will influence the child's ability to accept new foods.

What the child eats will often depend on who is offering him the food. Infants seem to be sensitive to the likes and dislikes of the person feeding them. They are also sensitive to other feelings in the person feeding them. A baby may take his bottle well or accept his cereal when the person who gives it to him is relaxed and enjoys feeding him. He may refuse the same food if it is offered by someone who dislikes the "messiness" of his eating and is tense and uncertain in her relationship with him. Some children eat very little when there is a new teacher at the table, for example, but will taste new foods or eat everything on their plates when the familiar teacher is there with whom they feel safe.

Because feelings and appetite are so closely related, we must recognize that any emotional disturbance will affect the appetite. We all probably have had the experience of losing interest in food for a time because of upset emotional balance. The child who is suffering from anxiety or some other emotion may have little appetite even though he may be physically well. When the emotional problem is solved, his appetite will respond to the normal demands of a growing organism.

Attacking the loss of appetite directly may do a great deal of harm. The immediate effect on the child may be vomiting or storing food in his mouth. The more serious and lasting result may be a strong aversion to food. Being made to eat when one is not hungry is a very unpleasant thing. If eating is to be a pleasant experience for the child, we will avoid forcing him in any way.

Frequent demands to be fed may be regarded as part of a pattern of dependence. Perhaps the standards for eating behavior have been set too high. Often a child will ask to be fed when he grows tired because of the demand on his coordination that eating makes. As his motor skill improves, he will need less help. Sometimes a child asks to be fed because he wants to find out if the adult is willing to help, to be reassured about his ability to get help when he wants it.

There are many direct and indirect ways to help a child enjoy eating. An attractive-looking table appeals to children. Bright-colored dishes, flowers, a neatly laid table, all add to the child's pleasure and interest in food. Food that "looks good," with a contrast in color, is important. Chocolate or lemon pudding, for example, usually disappears faster than plain pudding.

Children's tastes differ from adults' in that children usually do not care for very hot or very cold foods. They do not like mixed flavors, either. A casserole or loaf may be unpopular even though each individual flavor in it may be relished separately. They care less for creamed foods or sauces over foods than adults do, which can be a welcome advantage to a busy cook. Strong flavors or unusual textures in a food are usually less acceptable to a child.

A child will enjoy eating more if he is comfortable at the table. He needs a chair that will permit his feet to rest on the floor and a table that is the right height for him. He needs utensils that are easy to grasp. A salad fork rather than a large fork, a spoon with a round bowl, and a small glass add to his comfort and his pleasure. He is more comfortable if he is not crowded too close to others at the table.

If there is a marker at his place at the table so that he feels no uncertainty about where he is going to sit, he may feel surer of himself. The child will also enjoy getting up and down without help, clearing away his own dishes, and getting his dessert. If he can wait on himself, he may be less restless, too.

Companions can be distracting at times. Eating with other children is fun, and one good eater will influence others, but sociability may need to be kept within bounds by thoughtful spacing and placement of the children. The main business at the table is eating, although conversation has its place.

The teacher may need to help children by influencing the amount of conversation taking place. Conversation sometimes interferes with eating, for children have not mastered the art of talking and eating. In his enthusiasm for communicating with others, a child may forget about eating. If he is a child for whom the teacher estimates that talking to others has more value at the moment than eating, she may give him time to finish later, as in the case of a shy, withdrawn child who is just "blossoming out" and needs to be encouraged to continue. A different child or a five-year-old who is already socially skilled may need to be remainded at some point to "eat now and talk later."

There may be *practical time limitations* inherent in the situation that determine how much time a child can be permitted to spend at the table. Eating should not proceed by a clock. Just as a "set" toilet schedule does not meet the needs of children, so a "set" length of time to eat cannot mean the same thing to all children. Some are deliberate, and some are quick. These differences are reflected in the time they take for their meals. Meals are served because we need food, and we enjoy eating. There is no special virtue in eating to get through a meal.

REST AND SLEEP

Rest is something children need, but often resist, both at home and at school. Many children find it hard to settle down for a rest or nap because it comes as an interruption to play. It may hold special difficulties when children are in a group and distract each other. The teacher herself must feel very sure that rest and sleep are important if she wishes to communicate this conviction to the children.

In the full-day program a nap period will follow the lunch period. The children may be expected to leave the table, go to the toilet, brush their teeth, and go directly to rest, or they may have a period of quiet play until the whole group is ready for rest. The schedule will depend on the physical arrangements of space and on the number of staff available. It is desirable, but not always possible, for children to rest in a room other than the room where they have played actively. Whatever the arrangements, the children should sleep or rest on comfortable cots with a fitted undersheet and with adequate covers over them.

The teacher can set the stage for naps by seeing that the room is in order and everything is ready for rest, with shades pulled down. She will create an atmosphere which suggests rest. She will move quietly herself and speak in a low voice. She will make her expectations clear—that is, she will *expect* the children to come in quietly, remove their shoes and perhaps other garments, and settle down without disturbing others. Her expectations will be reasonable ones. She will give each child time to settle down, with perhaps a whispered word to his neighbor. A child may bring a favorite toy, perhaps, or a picture book to help him relax. The children who do not fall asleep can rest quietly before getting up. It is helpful if they can rest in a place separated from the others.

A rest period usually proceeds most smoothly when the children know the teacher well and have confidence in her. The children are more likely to be restless if the adult is new and strange to them or if there are too many adults present. A new teacher must accept the children's restlessness and not let it make her feel inadequate. The teacher who is more confident will give the children time to settle down in their own ways. Teachers are often tired by the time a rest period comes and are eager to get the children settled. They may find themselves pushing the children into resting. A more relaxed teacher will be able to help children make the transition from wakefulness to sleep.

Dependency Needs Are Greater at Rest Time

One can expect the child to make demands on the teacher at rest time because resting is closely associated with experiences with his parents and their care. His need for them may come closer to the conscious level. He reverts to earlier dependencies. He may want the teacher's attention; he may want to have a blanket straightened just to have some contact with her. Failing to get attention, he may be noisy, which is another way of getting attention. He may be less able to bear the teacher's disapproval at rest time than at other times.

At rest time children are likely to be jealous when the teacher's attention goes to other children. The teacher must be able to make each of them feel that there is enough attention for all. If an individual child needs an extra amount of attention, she will make it clear to other children that this child needs particular help today. Children can accept the fact that at some times a child *needs* particular help. Each child has needed special help at some time. The confident, nurturing person will be most successful in helping the children relax and perhaps sleep.

INDIVIDUAL NEEDS DIFFER

There are individual differences in the amount of rest childlren need, and these differences should be respected. Children who fall asleep will probably sleep for varying lengths of time. As each one awakes, he can get up quietly and put on the clothing he removed. Here is an opportunity for children to grow in independence, with the teacher giving only the help that is needed.

After resting, some of the older children who do not take naps have an opportunity for play in small groups before the younger children are up. The teacher may use the period to provide these children with individual learning opportunities and individual attention. There may be opportunities for trips that are not appropriate to younger children or for games and "work" periods that challenge these children.

The teacher will want to consult with the parents about the child's patterns for resting and for naps at home. Knowing what is customary for him at home will help her adapt the schedule at school to his needs or to allow him the ritual that helps him rest, as she tries to help him develop good patterns for rest and relaxation in his school.

THE RELATION OF ROUTINES AND THE DEVELOPMENT OF INDEPENDENCE

We have discussed some of the meanings which toileting, eating, and rest may have for childlren. We have indicated some of the problems that arise in connection with these routine activities, and we have suggested some ways teachers may facilitate children's learning during these activities.

PROBLEMS OCCUR AT "TRANSITION POINTS"

From the standpoint of the teacher, many of the difficulties she faces in managing these routines exist at transition points, or the points at which she interrupts the child's own activity to direct him into the routine. He may delay, resist, defy, or try to assert himself at these times. Such behavior is appropriate to his developmental level. He needs and wants to direct his own activities or to assert himself against others in order to test himself. Is he really an independent person? How much independence does he have?

If the teacher keeps the child's needs in mind, she will find it easier to meet his resistance without adding to it. For example, if the child is refusing to accede to a necessary request such as, "It is time to come in and get ready for lunch," the teacher may agree to wait until some part is completed rather than insisting on his coming immediately. She may ask the child to tell her when he will be finished and ready. They may compromise and thus cooperate. He will be party to the bargain. She will need to see that the child carries out his agreement, although she can express sympathy for his wishing that he did not need to do so, by saying, ''I know you would like to stay, but it really is time now. You remember we agreed.'' Then she may be able to suggest an important job he can carry out in helping with the serving. She tries, in other words, to help him move toward accepting the necessity of meeting reasonable demands without feeling a loss of self-esteem.

The teacher can value the fact that he is working at growing into a more autonomous, independent person. She can respect his right to assert himself and his desire to do it, but she should also recognize her responsibility to maintain certain reasonable demands. The child cannot do just as he wants to all the time, even though he grows best if he can do what he wishes a good deal of the time when he is young.

The child needs the opportunity of finding that he does not lose his independence just because he accepts some restrictions and meets some demands. It is important for the child to know that his teacher feels clear about what she expects him to do and sure about her right to expect this of him. If she acts with confidence, she makes it easier for him. By actions *confidently,* she is likely to give him more definite and specific directions, to show less impatience, and to be more imaginative in the kind of help she gives him in making the transition. He may be able, in the end, to turn his desire to be independent into satisfaction in being able to work with an adult in a cooperative way. We all must do necessary things that, at the moment, we may not really want to do. Transition points from play to routine activities can be growth points, but this learning takes time.

Clean up time is another transition point that often presents difficulty. Children do not always feel ready to put materials away and help with straightening the playroom. It is a challenge to the teacher to devise ways of helping them feel and act like independent, responsible people at this point. The teacher sets an example with her own actions. She reinforces whatever steps they take in helping by her attention and approval. They can talk as they work together about what they are doing or about the day's events. Sometimes singing together or making up games will help lighten the task. Some children will give more help than others, but the teacher makes no comparisons.

Some of the problems that arise in connection with routines may be related to the physical setup of the school. A crowded locker area creates problems when children are putting on their outdoor clothing. Cots set up in the playroom may make resting more difficult. A change in the situation may be possible. Sometimes making a change in the schedule itself, the time or the sequence, as well as in the physical arrangements may reduce the difficulties which have been arising.

Our Own Need to Help May Interfere with the Child's Need
To Be Independent

Children find great satisfaction in doing a task unaided. Shoes laced in irregular ways, a shirt on backwards, hands only partly clean may be sources of pride to a child because these accomplishments were achieved independently.

The drive to be independent, which every healthy child feels, may come up against one of our own needs, the need to help. This need is especially strong when we feel least sure that we can help. By helping, by doing things for a child, we try to prove to ourselves that we are in fact competent and able. The child's dependency on us reassures us that we have a place in the school.

This is the way a zipper works.

Watch what happens in the locker area. The teacher who is unaware of the situation's potential for a child to learn is the one who steps in and expertly buttons the button which the child has been fumbling with intently. She takes the child's coat from its low hook and holds it for him. Then she may be surprised that he runs away instead of putting it on. She puts in the plug when he is ready to wash his hands, pushes up his sleeves, and hands him the soap. She deprives him of many opportunities to perform tasks that he can do for himself. She herself needs to help, and she acts out of her own need. If she is to handle her strong feeling about wanting to help, she must be aware of this feeling as well as of the values for the child in being independent. Keeping his need in mind, she will plan the situation so that he has a maximum opportunity to do things for himself. She will keep from helping him needlessly.

THE CHILD REVERTS TO DEPENDENCY AT TIMES

When we have recognized the importance of the child's need to be autonomous, as well as the likelihood that we will feel a need to offer help unnecessarily at times, we must still be ready to accept the fact that there are times when the child does need to be dependent on us. Erikson makes it clear that no development is completed at any one stage; we carry on to the next stage the uncompleted tasks of earlier stages. A child may ask for unnecessary help because he wants reassurance that he can still be dependent if he wishes. It may be important to help him with his coat if he asks us, or to tie his shoe when we know he can. In routines we must be certain only that we do not deprive the child of the opportunity to be independent when he is ready.

PROJECTS

1. Observe for 10 minutes in the toiletroom, noting the different responses shown by the children to the situations there. Discuss the possible meanings of the responses you observed.

2. Observe during a meal period, recording the behavior of the children at one table during the mealtime. What differences in individual needs did you observe? What help did the teacher give? What goals did she seem to have in mind?

SUPPLEMENTARY READING

Arnstein, H., and others. *Your Growing Child and Sex: A Parent's Guide.* Indianapolis: Bobbs-Merrill, 1967.

Association for Childhood Education International. *Nutrition and Intellectual Growth in Children,* Bulletin No. 25A. Washington, D.C.: ACEI, 1969.

Fraiberg, S. *The Magic Years.* New York: Scribner, 1959, Chapter 7.

Mugge, D. Taking the routine out of routines. *Young Children,* 1976, *31* (3):209–217.

No Title Given
(girl, 3.6)

The Role of the Teacher

The role of the teacher in a nursery school or kindergarten is a stimulating and challenging one. No two days are ever the same. Each child is unique and has his own individual needs. It is a period when learning is more rapid than it ever will be again. Basic personality patterns are being established. Children are working out strategies for solving problems and developing individual ways of meeting situations. Their concepts are constantly being modified. There is an excitement about learning, and the environment is one in which everyone is learning, both teachers and children. The teacher may sometimes be tired or discouraged but she never need be uninterested. She can use all her skills and find herself growing in the process. She is rewarded by the growth and changes she observes in the children.

In this chapter we will look at the teacher as a person, her skills, and the quality of the relationships she has with a child as she guides him in the school. In the section on Curriculum, we will consider ways in which the teacher may facilitate learning opportunities.

THE TEACHER PLAYS AN IMPORTANT ROLE IN THE CHILD'S PERSONALITY DEVELOPMENT

The teacher is an important person to the young child. Her relationships with the child will influence his learning and his development as a person. The first task of the teacher with the child entering a new group is to build a relationship of trust.

173

Learning is a personal experience for the young child. He learns through relationships with the people who are significant to him. His first attachment bonds are with his parents—his first, and probably his most important, teachers. From them he has learned a great many things among which are patterns of behavior and language. Most children entering school have learned to feel some trust in adults and are ready to relate to the teacher in a trusting way. For her part the teacher needs to show them that she is a trustworthy, reliable person. In some cases the teacher will need to help restore a sense of trust in a child who has not succeeded earlier in achieving a sufficient measure of trust. Every child will have his own pace and style of building a relationship, and the attentive teacher will watch for the nonverbal and verbal cues he gives her to indicate when he feels comfortable. She will accept him as he is and let him show her what he is ready to do. When she has achieved a relationship of trust, she will be careful to let nothing destroy it. In helping a child relate to her in a positive way, the teacher is helping him with his first and most basic task in personality growth which, according to Erikson, is the development of a sense of trust to outweigh the sense of mistrust.

The second task in the development of a healthy personality is the achievement of a sense of autonomy or independence outweighing the sense of dependency. To help the child to achieve this task the teacher will give him many opportunities to be independent, to do things his way, and to make choices when possible. She will encourage him to master skills like climbing, riding a tricycle, fitting puzzles together, or building with blocks. By her approval and encouragement she helps him see himself as someone able to do or make things independently while still using the help that may be needed for success. The teacher is in a position to add to the child's confidence and respect for himself as an independent person because of the relationship of trust they have built together.

The teacher also has an important role to play in helping the child with the third task in personality growth, that of increasing his sense of initiative, his daring to explore, discover, create, and imagine. These feelings should outweigh the sense of guilt or the fear of disapproval or of being wrong. This task is foremost for the healthy three-, four-, or five-year-old. The child's emerging conscience may inhibit him from using initiative because it operates in ways that are too strict or too confused. The child needs a teacher who will help him make distinctions in situations about what is acceptable and what is not, and who does not add to his burden of guilt feelings. The teacher provides many opportunities for a child to explore his interests, enlarging and enriching them. She makes sure he has opportunities to interact with his peers. She takes pleasure in his growing capacity to make discoveries, to reflect on them, to create with a variety of materials, and to give rein to his imagination as he comes to differentiate between fantasy and reality. At the same time, the teacher makes sure that throughout the explorations she keeps the child safe, so that trust and confidence are not damaged.

The teacher helps the child repair his rake.

THE TEACHER ACCEPTS AND RESPECTS EACH INDIVIDUAL CHILD

A good relationship between a teacher and child will make it easier to find constructive ways to discipline and easier for the child to respond in desirable ways. The teacher can be firm in setting realistic expectations for behavior, but still be friendly. She can help the child face the consequences of his behavior, without resorting to punishment that stirs resentment but not repentance.

The significance for the child in having a teacher whom he likes and whom he feels likes him is tremendous. Every child, regardless of family background, will learn and develop best if he has the feeling that he is liked and valued. Young children see the world very subjectively and are influenced by their relationships with people even more than adults are.

The child is also influenced by his teacher's expectations about his abilities. He tends to behave and achieve accordingly. He needs to have a teacher who knows his strengths and vulnerabilities, and who helps him utilize his strengths or capabilities.

We must remind ourselves that the environment from which a child comes has both favorable and unfavorable factors in it. Deprivation of some kind exists in every background. While one child may have experienced poverty in material things, he may be rich in the quality of personal relationships he has known. Another child may have only poor personal relationships, even though he has always lived with material abundance. Each child has had some favorable experience from which he draws strength. It is important that a teacher respect and make use of the strengths that each child has in helping him develop his individual capacities.

We are responsible as teachers for accepting and respecting each individual child as another important human being who is trying to cope with difficulties, to find satisfactions, and to learn. Every child is worthy of the best we have to give him.

THE TEACHER SERVES AS A MODEL FOR CHILDREN

Every teacher serves as a model for the children in her group in many ways. The children are influenced by her. They imitate not only her actions and moods, but also her attitudes. Teachers' attitudes are important to the young child, not only because they influence the way she works with him, but also because they become a part of what the child learns in school. The following are important characteristics of teachers that reflect attitudes, which may influence children's learning positively.

Sensitive and Responsive to Each Child's Feelings and Ways of Behaving
The teacher will observe her own behavior and feelings when interacting with the child so that she can become aware of what behavior affects him. She will observe the child in interactions with others in order to become aware of his impact on others and of their responses to him. She will try to understand the child's thinking, feeling, and behavior from a minimum of nonverbal and verbal cues. She will help the child to observe himself and others, and she will gradually learn to express these observations in a constructive way.

Interested in Understanding People, Experience, and Events without Prejudging Them

The teacher will be engaged in the process of understanding her own cultural–social blind spots. She will increase her awareness of the effects of discrimination on people. The old inequalities of sex, class, and economic condition are no longer acceptable. It is important that we ourselves look at the world around us as free from bias and prejudice as possible. It is in this way that we can help children to take on an accepting and appreciative attitude.

We are a multiracial culture rather than a homogeneous one, and we can profit from our mixture of peoples. Diversity becomes a strength if we use the opportunities it offers. Some nursery schools, kindergartens, and day-care centers consist largely of minority culture children. As teachers we must be aware of the particular strengths these children have. We must value and use their contributions, which will make life richer for everyone. Diversity, when it is accepted and acceptable, enriches the teacher, the children, and the parents.

The teacher must accept and respect the cultural differences of parents as well as children and understand what parents expect of their children. One of her important tasks will be to help all parents understand what sound early childhood education is. On many occasions the teacher will need to explain her program and what she hopes to achieve. She must also listen to parents' ideas and make modifications to accommodate their expectations, without sacrificing the fundamental principles in which she believes. Good education can and will take many forms if the feeling of respect for individuals is present.

There are many kinds of bias that affect the child. A teacher may find herself responding negatively or expecting poorer achievement from a child because he does not, by her standards, speak correct English or does not show the responsiveness she expects. It may not be easy to accept the fact that these differences do not reflect a child's innate capacities. Many so-called deficiencies in children are simply differences in background or experience. The teacher may find herself misunderstanding the meaning of the child's behavior just as the child does hers.

The child can hardly be expected to adjust easily when the values in the classroom are dramatically different from those in the home. It is the obligation of the teacher to understand as much as possible about the child's cultural-social background and to accept him in this context. In accepting a child with understanding, a teacher models accepting behavior. In addition, such acceptance enhances the possibility of the child making use of his school experience to make his own choice, when he is ready, as to where he will find his place in society.

Our traditional sex-role stereotypes are fast disappearing. It has become acceptable for young adults to choose from a wide range of job possibilities. When our present kindergarten children are ready to make vocational choices these possibilities will no doubt be still greater. Many teachers have grown up with biases, based on sex differences, about what adults and children should do. Gender assignment is an important part of a child's self-concept. By the time he or she is two or three years old, perhaps earlier for some, the child can say, ''I am a girl'' or ''I am a boy.'' Gender is important to parents and teachers, too. Whether a child is a girl or boy, however, must not determine, any more than any other individual difference, his opportunity to use an array of materials, to try out a variety of roles, and to express feelings in a variety of appropriate ways. Teachers will enable each child to become an autonomous person who takes initiative, who speaks well, who can be assertive, who is task-oriented, who is capable of solving a variety of problems, who feels competent, and who does well in school. If parents express concern about their child trying out traditionally sex-typed roles or using particular materials, teachers should accept their questions and concerns seriously, and help them understand the values of these opportunities for their young children.

The Teacher Provides an Environment for Exploration

The teacher creates a physical, social, and emotional environment that invites learning through exploration and discovery. She encourages children in their efforts by the questions she asks and by her own zest for finding out about things. The preschool period is the time for encouraging individual initiative and supporting the excitement of discovery, excitement that begins in early childhood and should be preserved through life.

Here is an example of learning by discovery in a group of four-year-olds, which would not have taken place without guidance from the teacher. A potential conflict, with the teacher's help, became a social studies investigation.

> In a block scheme, a boy had built a fish store. . . . Every time [a girl] went to his store to buy fish, he closed it. Finally, in great irritation she yelled at him, "You can't do that. A store has to sell—that's what it's for, stupid." The teacher approached the children and entered the conversation, first by listening, and then by asking, "Can you go shopping in a store anytime you feel like it?" Discussion led to the following conclusions: (1) you do not shop late at night because you have to sleep; (2) stores do have hours for shopping to which people must pay attention. . . . It was decided that the boy and the girl plus two other children who had joined the discussion would take a walk around the block with the teacher in order to find the answer to her question, "How do you know when a store opens and when it closes?"
> They returned from their trip and as they entered the classroom, their newly gained information exploded; "It's on the door," "It's not the same for all the days," "They have a sign." Information was explored and shared. Signs went up on several buildings posting store hours. One child posted times for visits to her house, fixing the hours around the baby's sleeping schedule. (Cuffaro, 1974, p. 28)

It is worth noting the way in which the teacher guided this opportunity. She "entered the conversation, first by listening and then by asking." She took time to find out what the argument was about and then asked the right question. She guided the discussion and supplied information that the chil-

This child knows the excitement of discovery.

dren did not have by making a suggestion about how to find out. The children returned from their trip, excited by their discovery. The results of what they learned appeared in many forms, even the imaginative one of posting a schedule for visiting. It was a social studies and language arts opportunity with meaning for the children. They gained information and, more importantly, they had models for problem solving and answering questions. One talks over the solutions to a problem; one investigates; one reorganizes his ideas. Learning can be exciting!

THE TEACHER PROVIDES OPPORTUNITIES FOR SELF-EXPRESSION

An important part of teaching young children is helping them become competent in expressing thoughts and feelings. Language is an important means of expression. A child needs to be able to put his thoughts and his feelings into words if he is to have satisfying social relationships. Teachers need to be aware of the ways in which this competency can be developed.

There are other avenues of expression. For the young child, art media offer important avenues for expressing feelings and for communicating. He uses art media such as paint, clay, pencils, and flopens freely when they are available. Construction with blocks, manipulative toys, and wood are other ways of expressing ideas and concepts. Body movements and dance are also forms of expression that children enjoy: For example, they like to march when the situation calls for this kind of movement. They also enjoy music; singing is a natural form of expression of feeling for young children.

All of these avenues of expression should be developed in a program for young children. We will discuss the skills needed by the teacher to encourage expression of thought and feeling in Part Four.

PROVIDING OPPORTUNITIES TO COMPLETE ACTIVITIES—USE OF TIME

It is important for the child to have many opportunities to complete a task, whether it is in his work or play. He needs to feel that he has played or done all he wants; he needs to bring an activity to completion himself. This sense of completion may be accomplished in one session or after several weeks of persistent repetition of the same theme. By completing activities a child learns that events have a beginning and an end and that he has some control over how he uses his time. Successful completion of a task or a successful "working through" of an idea helps the child learn to "let go." He can be through with an activity because he is satisfied or "feels full" from it. He can look forward to moving on to new endeavors. We may hear an adult say to a child, "You have painted enough pictures today," or "You have played with the blocks long enough," instead of saying, "There is no more time today for painting." In the first case, the child is being deprived of the opportunity to learn the true meaning of "enough." In some situations there may not realistically be enough time for a child to finish a task or play. That the child is left unsatisfied can be acknowledged, and he can be helped to look forward to tomorrow. Large blocks of time for work and play and flexible schedules are more likely to allow children to complete tasks and pursue interests.

If the teacher is to make the most of children's spontaneous interests, she needs to allow long blocks of uninterrupted time in the schedule for the children to develop and carry through projects while she takes the time to observe their play. She will become more aware of when and how to make suggestions when she has observed and made notes.

THE TEACHER IS AWARE OF THE TIME TO END AN ACTIVITY

Group activities that are teacher-directed should be of short duration. In one school, a young man (a volunteer) brought his guitar along for a song period with the children. They were delighted and almost all of them gathered around him. The opportunity to have a man in the teaching role was new to them. He adapted his songs to their level, and they participated eagerly as he taught them the words. He continued with song after song, enjoying their eager attention. By the time he stopped singing, many of the children were very tired, although only a few had left the group. The children could not settle down for a while after he left. Several children cried and others were disorganized before they became involved in other activities. Several shorter sessions would have benefited the children much more than the one long session had.

THE TEACHER GIVES DIRECTIONS IN A POSITIVE WAY

The competent teacher trains herself to give suggestions and directions in a positive way. She tells the child what he can do and emphasizes how he can be successful—whether climbing a ladder, putting a piece of paper in a typewriter, or solving an interpersonal problem.

An important reason for stating directions and suggestions in a positive way is that they tell the child what he can do. A negative statement almost always has to be followed by a positive one. Too many words only confuse a nursery or kindergarten child. With his self-confidence shaken, he musters his defenses and may be unable to comprehend the second, and positive statement. Affirmative statements about what he may do will not impair self-esteem. They help him build a positive self-concept and make it easier for him to learn and grow in healthy ways.

Everyone working with children, at home or at school, needs to practice giving directions or suggestions in a positive way. Adults and children both will like themselves better when comments are made positively.

HELPING CHILDREN FACE FAILURE IN A POSITIVE WAY

The teacher gives approval and attention to the child when he achieves or behaves acceptably, but she also can accept his failures and try to turn these to constructive use. She may say to the child at the work bench, "Next time hold the hammer this way, and it may be easier to make the nail go in straight." In saying this the teacher helps the child look for causes, consider what has happened, and improve his performance. His errors become a means of learning and not just a failure. He gains a new perspective and approaches situations more positively.

Sometimes the teacher will say, "I wonder why that happened," if she thinks the child is ready to discover by himself the remedy or reason. In doing this she is helping him take a "problem-solving" attitude, one which is very necessary in learning. If he is successful in finding the reason, he gains new confidence in his own capacities. The tower he built may fall down because the base was not broad enough, or because it was not on level ground. It is easy for a child to want to blame someone or to blame himself when something will not work. He can learn to take a less personal way of viewing situations.

THE TEACHER SERVES AS A MODEL IN THE WAY SHE MEETS FRUSTRATION

In the way the teacher meets the frustrations which are an inevitable part of teaching, she sets an example for the children to follow in facing their own frustrations. The teacher is not always successful. Her best efforts are rejected at times. If she can accept this state of affairs, she helps children build a concept of how to live with frustration: One does not need to lose faith in oneself or in others, but can have patience and confidence that the next time will be better.

If the teacher can leave the children free to doubt and question, and to sometimes *not* respond to her suggestions, she is helping them, too. There is uncertainty and there is flexibility. Both serve purposes which can be constructive. The children can build more trust in themselves as well as in the teacher in such a favorable climate.

THE TEACHER IS A SENSITIVE PERSON

The teacher gives support to the child by showing an interest in what the child does, by treating the child's questions with respect, by giving more attention to the positive than to the negative aspects of his performance, and by generous giving of approval for his real accomplishments.

The teacher of young children needs to be interested in *understanding* people, experiences, and events, rather than passing judgment on them. The

Sometimes the teacher helps by participating in play.

teacher also needs to be *sensitive* and *responsive,* able to "listen with the third ear" to what the child may be trying to say through his behavior. The teacher should know the satisfactions of learning and be able to *appreciate the child's accomplishments* as he masters each stage in development. With the help of such a person the child can grow comfortably as a whole person.

The child also needs a teacher who can *communicate* with him, both in language (with an approving word) and in expression and gesture (with a smile or a nod). He needs a teacher who is aware of her own feelings and is able to *express feelings* as well as ideas in constructive and clear ways. The child needs a teacher who *values spontaneity* and yet is able to maintain an *orderliness* in activities and in the setting. In addition, the child needs a teacher who is *imaginative* and *resourceful* and who has a *sense of humor.* These qualities will reassure him and stimulate him. Few of us show all of these qualities in all situations. We have our weaknesses as well as our strengths, but, like the child, we can grow and change with experience.

PROJECTS

1. Observe the teacher in a nursery school, day-care center, or kindergarten and record incidents in which she did any of the following:
   a. created a climate for discovery
   b. extended and enriched an interest or purpose initiated by a child
   c. allowed time for a child to complete a task
   d. played a supportive role in building a child's self-confidence
   e. helped a child to solve a problem for himself
   f. helped two or more children to cooperate

SUPPLEMENTARY READING

Almy, M. *The Work of the Early Childhood Educator.* New York: McGraw-Hill, 1975.

Ekstein, R. The child, the teacher and the learning. *Young Children,* 1967, *32* (2): 195–209.

Katz, L., and E. Ward. *Ethical Behavior: In Early Childhood Education.* Washington, D.C.: National Association for the Education of Young Children, 1978.

Landreth, C. *Preschool Learning and Teaching.* New York: Harper & Row, 1972.

Jones, E. Teacher education: Entertainment or interaction? *Young Children,* 1978, *33* (3):15–23.

Omwake, E. What children and parents are expecting from teacher education. In B. Spodek, ed., *Teacher Education.* Washington, D.C.: National Association for the Education of Young Children, 1974.

Part Three

UNDERSTANDING BEHAVIOR

12

Hospital
(*girl, 4.3*)

Feelings of Security and Confidence

"Look here, teacher, I'm bigger than you think. I'm going to have a birthday soon. Let me do this by myself," said Katherine to a well-meaning adult who was trying to help her.

Katherine's words remind us of how often adults handicap children by acting as though children were unable to meet situations. A child has a difficult time developing confidence when he is surrounded by people who "help" him all the time. Children are often more competent than we think! Katherine was able to express her confidence in herself as a person able to do things, but few children are able to do this because they lack not only the verbal ability but the feeling itself.

As adults, most of us probably wish that we had more self-confidence. We realize that we are likely to do a thing better when we feel confident than when we are afraid of failing. We realize, too, that we get more pleasure out of doing something when we feel adequate and are free from anxiety. For all of us, feelings of insecurity and a lack of confidence are handicapping. The person who has confidence in himself may enjoy undertaking something entirely new in which he lacks any skill, but many people are not free enough of self-doubts to feel that the unfamiliar is a challenge to them.

Security refers to the feelings that come with having had many experiences of being accepted rather than rejected, of feeling safe rather than threatened. Security results from a person's having had positive relationships with people. Confidence refers to the feelings that an individual has about himself, and his concept of the kind of person he is. This concept, too, grows out of the responses other people make to him. Security and confidence are closely related. The secure child trusts himself and others. He dares to be himself and to discover more about himself. As we work with children, we will seek ways of strengthening their feelings of confidence and security.

FOUNDATIONS FOR FEELING SECURE AND CONFIDENT

Feelings of security and confidence develop out of the way the infant's basic needs are met, his experiences with feeding and, later, with toileting, the kinds of responses he gets from other people, and the satisfaction he finds in exploring the world. Out of these early experiences the child builds a feeling of trust in the world, his first task developmentally. Having learned that he can trust others he is ready to trust and have confidence in himself. The attitudes and feelings of his parents are the most important factors in building confidence because he depends largely on his parents for the satisfaction of his basic needs.

If the child's first experiences have made him feel secure and confident because his needs were satisfied, if he has obtained response from people, and if he has had satisfying sensory experiences, he has laid a firm foundation for confidence and security. If, on the other hand, his needs have not been met and if he has failed to get response when he needed it, he has already experienced insecurity and felt inadequate. If he constantly heard the words "no" and "don't" when he reached out for experience, he has already grown to distrust his own impulses. The world does not seem to him a place where he can feel safe, and he builds a picture of himself as a person who is not very adequate to cope with the problems it presents. He may begin to think of himself as a person who is likely to do the wrong thing.

CHILDREN ARE INFLUENCED IN THEIR FEELINGS BY THE ATTITUDES OF ADULTS

Children tend to behave as they feel they are expected to behave, or according to the concept of self they have built up out of the responses of other people to them. Paul (5.6), for example, thinks of himself as a boy who gets into trouble. As he and his father came into school one morning, his father remarked, "See how nice and quiet this place is until you get here!" What is a boy like who hears words like these? He is a boy who is noisy, defiant, and "difficult." He lives up to the picture his father paints.

When Stanley's (5.2) mother brought him to school, she explained to the teacher as Stanley stood beside her, "Perhaps he'll learn things. He just tries for a minute and then gives right up." It was not surprising that Stanley lacked confidence, did not persist, and was unfriendly with both children and teachers.

Ella (3.6) was timid. She didn't join other children in play, but she did like to paint. She was at the easel painting carefully around the edges of the paper when her mother came for her one day. Her mother saw the picture, and she said half scornfully, "Nobody paints like that!" How can one have much confidence if one is considered a "nobody"? Ella didn't expect to have an important place in the group.

In contrast, we see Michele (4.1). Michele was new in the school, eager to be at school, but lacking in skills. Climbing fascinated her. One day she tried very hard to climb a tree even though she was afraid. With some help from the teacher, she finally managed to reach a high limb. Delighted, she called out to everyone, "Look, I'm up here as brave as ever." We see in this incident the elements of healthy personality development. Michele sees herself as "brave." She has made an effort and mastered a difficult feat. She wants to share her delight. She is sure that there will be someone who cares.

Leighton and Kluckholn (1947) in *Children of the People* make an interesting comment on the attitudes that appear in another culture. They describe the way the Navaho treat young children in these words, ". . . the Navaho toddler is given self-confidence by being made to feel that he is constantly loved and valued" (p. 33). Would Ella and Stanley have behaved differently if they had lived under conditions in which they were "constantly loved and valued"? There are many children in our culture who are "constantly loved and valued," but there are many others who are treated as "nobodies," like Ella and Stanley, even though there is no conscious intent on the part of parents to treat them this way.

We live in such a highly competitive society that it is often hard for us to recognize the values that may exist outside of achievement. Parents feel the pressure for accomplishment. They want children who will learn to write their names or who paint good pictures. They push their children, even their toddlers. They do not accept them as they are.

Adults Tend To "Nudge" Children

Dr. James Plant (1937) described this tendency of parents to push their children as quickly as possible from one stage to the next as "nudging" the child in his growth. We are likely to "nudge" children rather than allow them to take time to satisfy their needs in each stage. We do this even though it has been demonstrated that growth proceeds in certain sequences, one stage following another, and that the soundest growth occurs when the child is given time in each stage, "living it out completely" before going on to the next. Dependency, for example, precedes independence; the child who is most independent in the end will be the one whose dependency needs have been most completely met, not the one who was pushed the soonest into being independent. "Nudging" a child from one stage to the next serves to make him feel less secure and more defensive. Children who have been pushed through a stage frequently have to go back and experience it again before they are free enough to go on or secure enough to develop further.

Adults May Make Children Feel Guilty

Children sometimes find it hard to develop confidence in themselves because they feel they are to blame for things that happen. A child may enjoy an activity, such as playing in the mud or exploring a bureau drawer, only to find that what he has done is considered very naughty by the adult. With little basis for real understanding of adult values, and with a great need to please adults because of his dependency on them, he comes to feel uncertain about himself and his behavior. Many times he thinks that his mistakes are much more serious than we really consider them and he suffers from a heavy load of guilt. When we blame him for what he does not understand or understands only in part, we damage his feelings of confidence and trust in himself.

By making events conditional on a child's good or bad behavior, we may increase his sense of uncertainty and lack of confidence. He may feel responsible for events that have no connection. Betty said, "Next week if I'm a real good girl, know where we're going? To the beach!" Let's hope that her parents were not too busy or tired that week or that nothing interfered with their plan. If a child can bring about a trip to the beach by being good, he can cause a calamity by being bad.

Pam (4.2) arrived at nursery school one morning and didn't see the ducks. She was very interested in them and inquired anxiously, "I can't see the ducks." Then she added, "I made a noise. Do ducks get headaches?" She has evidently had to bear a feeling of guilt for causing headaches. Without enough experience to correct his concepts, the child is the victim of his misapprehensions. We may not suspect a child's real feelings or the heavy load of guilt he may feel for events.

Adults May Be Afraid of Spoiling Children

Sometimes adults are afraid to accept children as they are and to meet their needs because they are afraid of "spoiling" them if they do. They needlessly deny and interfere with children because of ignorance of the growth process. They make it hard for the child to think of himself as an adequate person. "Spoiled" children are, in fact, those who get attention *when the adult wants to give it* rather than when the child himself needs it. They are those children who are subject to inconsistent interferences rather than given the support of consistent limits by parents who are willing to take responsibility for limits. Flexible handling that allows the child to live on his own level tends to build secure feelings in the young child rather than to "spoil" him. It reduces to the minimum the denials and interferences that are likely to shake a child's confidence in himself. It accepts him as he is. It helps him feel adequate.

Adults Can Be Permissive without Spoiling

Children need limits set for them from acting in ways that will have damaging consequences or frighten them. The adult who lets a child do anything he wants is an adult who is avoiding her own responsibilities. These limits sometimes can be set at quite different points. One person *will not* interfere with a child or stop him in what he does unless she feels sure the child's action will result in undesirable consequences. The child is thus free to explore and experiment with materials, to act in all kinds of childish ways, and to learn for himself. Another person *will* interfere or stop a child unless she feels sure that what the child is doing is desirable. There is much less room for the child to discover and to try out ways of acting under this latter method. The first person's attitude is a "permissive" one in contrast to the restrictive attitude of the second person.

By permissiveness we do not mean indulgence. Instead, we mean leaving children free to explore, to discover, to create, and to find their own way insofar as possible within acceptable limits. We also mean a generous quality in giving to the child, not a meager giving. "Of course you can," rather than, "I guess you can, but I wish you wouldn't"; or, "Take all you need," rather than, "Don't take much"; or, "There's plenty for everyone," rather than, "No one can have more than one piece." When we give generously, children grow less anxious. They need less. They are more secure. By "permissiveness" we refer to a "giving" attitude, but one with no lack of firmness when firmness is needed.

Children are not helped to build confidence by parents who are indulgent, who give in to them rather than face the unpleasant behavior of a thwarted child. Both parents and child need to learn to face unpleasant realities in constructive ways, rather than avoid facing them.

Adults Need To Be Secure People

Accepting the child as he is and meeting his needs freely are easier for people who are themselves secure. A secure person is relaxed, comfortable, permissive, and giving. He or she does not feel so much need to make demands on others. Secure people are likely to create the kind of environment in which it is easy for the child to think of himself as an adequate person. Mike (5.11), for example, has lived with comfortable parents. He is free of defenses. He looks at the puzzle he worked on the day before and says, "That one was hard for me." He is a secure child. Secure people are usually able to accept the child as he is, inexperienced but eager to learn, growing and changing. They leave the child free to explore and create within acceptable limits.

Insecure people are often defensive and demanding. They are likely to set standards which the child can meet only with difficulty, if at all. They are likely to be very concerned with what other people say about them as parents. If they are to accept children, parents need to be secure people; yet there are many reasons that parents have a hard time feeling secure today. They are handicapped not only by economic insecurities, tensions, and conflicts in the world, by inadequate housing and limited community resources in health and recreation, but also by an education that offers little guidance in understanding parent-child relationships. Paul's father, who spoke in such a belittling way to his son, is typical of many parents. He wants to be a successful parent, but he is without experience or preparation for his role. Like most people, he values success highly and is striving for it in a professional field. His concept of a successful parent is one whose child behaves like an adult. He feels his own failure to achieve this goal with Paul. His love for the child is hidden under his constant criticism. He is not a secure adult. He makes Paul an insecure child.

By the time the child reaches the school, his feelings regarding his security and confidence are well developed. He may have come from a home where he has been accepted by secure parents, or he may have come from a home where his parents are too insecure themselves to be able to accept his immaturity. There is clear evidence (Stevens and Mathews, 1978) showing that the quality of the experience a young child has with his parents is far more important than the quantity or the amount of time spent together. A secure parent, mother or father, who enjoys spending time with the child can contribute greatly to the enrichment of his development even though the time they have to spend with each other is limited. Both boys and girls profit when a father enjoys being with his young children. He brings a different quality to the care-giving. It also seems true that the parent who is finding satisfactions in his own life, at work and at home, is likely to give a child the freedom and the encouragement he needs to develop his own interests. The satisfied parent is likely to provide opportunities outside the home for the child that enrich his intellectual life and increase his confidence.

RECOGNIZING THE CHILD'S FEELINGS

We will raise the question in this section of how we may recognize a child's feelings. How do we identify feelings so that we may be of help to a child?

Children reveal their feelings through behavior. Sometimes they do it openly and directly, and they act as they feel. Sometimes their feelings come out in ways that are more difficult to identify. We must learn to understand; then, we can recognize how plainly they speak to us through behavior.

Perhaps the first step in understanding the meaning of behavior is to be able to look at the way a child behaves without feeling a necessity to change his behavior. We must learn to look at behavior as it is rather than in terms of what we want it to be. We are likely to confuse the meaning of a child's behavior with our own feelings if we try to judge it, if we decide that the child should or should not be behaving as he is.

Security comes from having a
teacher who cares.

THERE ARE CUES TO A CHILD'S FEELING IN NONVERBAL BEHAVIOR

We have already pointed out how children differ in the kinds of adjustments that they make to new situations. These differences have meaning. The adult who wishes to understand a child will observe carefully how he responds in a new situation. She will not decide how the child should respond and try to force this pattern of response on him. If she does, she may damage the child and his development.

Children reveal characteristic attitudes in everyday, familiar situations, too. These cues may be seen in such things as in the way the child walks, runs, holds his hands, in his posture, and so forth. Posture is, of course, influenced by constitutional and environmental factors, but over and above these, reflections of the child's emotional patterns can be seen in his muscle tensions. One child's hands are relaxed, and another's are tense and constantly moving. One child clutches our finger tightly as we walk along with him, a sign of his need for support and the intensity of his feelings. Another lets his hand lie limply in ours, suggesting perhaps the nongiving quality of his relationships with others, in contrast to the warm, responsive grip of still another child who welcomes closeness without clinging to it. These bits of behavior are all cues that help us understand the child's feelings.

Sometimes a conflict the child is feeling is expressed in the movements of his hands, as in the case of the child who is watching finger painting. He may stand at a distance, wiping his clean hands on his shirt or wringing them together, showing us the conflict he feels between his wish to put his hands into the paint and the force of the restriction not to get dirty.

THERE ARE CUES IN A CHILD'S LANGUAGE

Voice quality and language offer cues to feelings. The quality of a child's voice may be strained and tight, or relaxed and easy. It may be loud and harsh, or soft and faint, or it may be confident and well modulated. Even the amount of speech may give some indications of the extent of the child's assurance or of his hesitation. One child talks very little; another chatters almost constantly. These extremes may be reactions to strains and pressures that are making them feel less confident and less secure than they should feel. Many insistent, needless questions are sometimes a symptom of insecurity, a seeking for reassurance more than for any specific answer. Too often these questions meet an impatient rebuff, not calculated to satisfy the need they express.

Spontaneous singing usually indicates confidence and contentment. The child who sings at play is probably comfortable, and it is worth noting the times and places when singing occurs spontaneously. We can learn from this behavior in what areas or on what occasions a child feels secure.

The child who asks the teacher, "Do you want to go outdoors with me?" may really be saying, "I'm afraid to go out by myself. It would help if you wanted to go with me." The teacher needs to understand the meaning behind what he actually says.

The child who says happily, "Isn't this going to be a good gate? I'm building it all myself," is telling us something about what comfortable feelings he has about himself. This same boy's father once remarked about him, "I think he's one of those fortunate people who like themselves." The child liked himself—and everyone else; he was one of the most likable children one could meet. He had been "loved and valued" in his family.

There is a real consciousness of an emerging self in these words of Katherine—the same Katherine who is "bigger than you think"—when she says, "I'm different from all the other people. When other people laugh, I don't, even if it's silly." Katherine feels secure enough to be different.

Through his manner of speech, a child tells us something about himself, too. In the school we are likely to hear children whose words tumble out in broken rhythms or with many repetitions. Young children are just learning to talk, and they often cannot form or recall the words as fast as they wish to get their ideas across.

Because children's language is in its formative stage, it is especially important for us to handle its development with understanding. The repetition and broken rhythm that sounds like what some people call stuttering or stammering is a sign of strain and tension in the child. These strains may be temporary ones such as the piling up of unusual stress that has fatigued the child or too much excitement just at the point in his growth when he is making rapid progress in learning to talk. Language may be the most vulnerable area of development at the moment, and it breaks down under the strains. Or the strains may be of long standing, such as conflicts over relationships in the family or the piling up of hostilities that are allowed no avenue for expression.

If the emphasis is put on the symptom, the imperfect speech, the result may be a serious and lasting speech disorder. It is important to avoid asking him to "stop and say it more slowly" as many people will do. We should simply accept his language and attack the conditions that are causing it. We can make it a point to stop and give the child our full attention when he is speaking, so that he will not feel the need to hurry. We can speak slowly ourselves, so that we will set a pattern in speech that will be easier for him to adopt successfully. Most of all we need to accept the fact that such speech is a sign that pressures and demands made on this child must be reduced if his speech patterns are to change.

Infantile mispronunciations are common and reflect patterns of feeling as well as of speech. They may indicate that the child is clinging to babyhood. The independence offered by going to a school will itself be of help to the child. We need to read and talk a great deal to the child whose speech has misarticulated sounds in it, enunciating clearly as we speak.

It is of interest that types of speech defects vary in different cultures. Among certain Eskimo and Indian tribes, for example, no case of disfluency has ever been recorded. In our culture, disfluency is much more common among boys than girls, while there are cultures where the reverse is true. Speech seems to be a sensitive index or response to the pressures that an individual feels. We need to try to understand more than just the words that are spoken.

There Are Cues to the Child's Feelings in His Behavior

Children who feel insecure are likely to face a new situation or a difficult problem by defending themselves. They may retreat, avoid the activity, resist, or attack. Their defensiveness may make it difficult for them in the situation. Children who feel secure, on the other hand, do not feel the need to defend themselves. They are free to look for ways of coping with the situation. They often seek out new experiences.

Bill (4.4), whom we mentioned on page 126, was able to cope with Kim's (4.1) interference at the blackboard in a variety of ways. A less secure child might have defended himself by crying or attacking. Ralph (3.1) bursts into tears when someone knocks against the tower he is building, and then he hits out frantically at the offender. He has little confidence in his ability to cope with interference. It is worth noting that Ralph feels sufficiently secure with a few children in the group to be able to accept interference when he is with these friends, without being overwhelmed by feelings of helplessness.

When people lack confidence in themselves, they usually act defensively in many situations. Jane (5.4), who is new in day care, begins to cry when the teacher asks her to be quiet at rest time. She is too insecure yet to accept any indication that she is behaving unacceptably. The teacher's suggestion that it was time to settle down and rest would have helped a child who felt at home in the school. The comfortable child can cope with demands. The insecure child tries to defend himself against them.

Sometimes we meet a child who is unable to accept comforting even from a familiar teacher. This child may not welcome a friendly pat, or may avoid an expression of closeness such as an arm around him. He usually is an insecure child who has found close relationships unreliable and unsatisfying. Only slowly does he come to trust adults. Occasionally we find a child striving for autonomy who resents comforting. He has developed patterns for finding his own way and sees the adult's approach as encroaching on his independence. Only careful observation can give us a cue as to each child's needs.

The secure child finds it easy to be friendly. He can share with others because he does not fear loss. He does not need to defend his rights. The insecure child cannot afford to share. His problem is not one of selfishness or unfriendliness, but one of degree of security. We need to handle the real problem, not the symptom, in such cases.

SOMETIMES THE CUES ARE INDIRECT ONES

Peter (3.11) had a hard time separating from his mother when she started to leave the school. He cried and protested. His mother was distressed and felt she could not leave him. One day he had this conversation with his teacher as she was helping him get ready to go home:

> Peter (half teasingly): Miss Williams, will my locker be here when I come back?
> Miss W.: Yes, Peter, it will be right here waiting for you.
> Peter: If my locker starts to run away, will you hold It?
> Miss W.: Yes, I'll hold it tight and tell it to stay right here because Peter is coming tomorrow.
> Peter: You just hold it. I want it right here.

As the teacher thought about the conversation, she felt that in an indirect way Peter was telling her that although he wanted to run away home, he wanted more to stay at school. He needed more help from her in resolving the conflict he felt in separating from his mother. He wanted his teacher to "hold" him, like the locker.

She telephoned his mother and suggested that the mother try leaving, even though Peter protested, for Peter really was enjoying school and might be ready to stay by himself. The mother left him the next day, a bit reluctantly, for he was crying and struggling. Almost immediately he relaxed and was ready for play under the watchful eye of his teacher. She had given him the help he wanted.

John (4.0) shows us what a name tag can symbolize to a child. He was proud of the name tag he wore to help the assistant teachers identify him. He reminded the teacher to put it on each morning. During the morning, one of the teachers reproved him for something he did. John said nothing, but a few minutes later this teacher observed that he had taken off the name tag. She felt that it was as though he did not want his name to be associated with misbehavior. He could remove his guilty self by removing the name tag.

THUMBSUCKING MAY BE A SYMPTOM OF INSECURITY

In school, one may see a child sucking his thumb at rest time or when the group is listening to a story or even during a play period. Like all behavior, thumbsucking is a symptom and may indicate a need in the child for more reassurance and greater security than he has found in his experience. It may be a difficult world for him because he is expected to be more grown-up than he is ready to be. He may be expected to be quiet, to inhibit his impulses for touching things, to take over adult ways of behaving at the table or in social situations, to comprehend and maintain the rules for property rights, and so forth. The strain of living up to all these demands or of failing to live up to them may be so great that the child seeks an infantile source of comfort. He turns to this thumb as a refuge.

The child is telling us something through his thumbsucking, and we need to understand. Adults should not increase his strain by taking away the avenue of comfort that he has found, but should try to make his life simpler and more comfortable. They should try to reduce the tensions he is under and offer him a greater opportunity for feeling secure and adequate, so that he may seek other kinds of satisfactions.

Mary Lou Took Her Own Thumb Out of Her Mouth

Mary Lou (3.6) was a round little girl who sucked her thumb most of the time at school. She was timid and often held onto the teacher's skirt with her free hand. She didn't venture into activity with other children or even play alone actively.

Mary Lou was the oldest of three children and had always been a "good" girl according to her mother. She had been easy to care for and could even be depended on to watch out for her little sister while her mother was busy with the baby. She seemed content with little to do and never disturbed the babies. It was not hard to imagine that Mary Lou had had very little chance to have the satisfactions that usually come with being a baby. She had had to grow up very quickly and had had to seek approval by behaving in unchildlike ways.

She remained dependent on the teacher at school for many weeks, but her interest in the children was plain as she watched a group having fun together. Sitting close to the teacher, she sometimes became part of a group at the piano or at the clay table. She had a real capacity for enjoying what she was doing and a sense of humor which became evident as she felt freer to act. She thoroughly enjoyed the clay, the sandbox, and the mud hole in the schoolyard. She often played alone in the homemaking area after she felt more comfortable at school.

Later she ventured into more active play. She still stood watching activities with her thumb in her mouth part of the time, but she was busy in the sandbox or riding the tricycles more of the time. The most marked change came in her behavior after she gained enough courage to use the slide. Sliding was a popular activity, and Mary Lou would often stand watching, but resisted any suggestion that she join the group at the slide. At last on a day when no one else was at the slide, she tried it, with her favorite teacher near to hold her hand. It was an effort, but she succeeded and went down again and again. She waved gaily to her mother when she came that day and showed off her newly acquired skill. From then on she participated more freely in every group. Mastering the slide seemed to give her a great deal of confidence. She even did a little pushing to hold her place in line at the slide and began to stand up for herself in other ways. She was active and happy. She hardly ever had time for her thumb. By the end of a year some of the adults had even forgotten that she used to suck her thumb. The fact that she no longer needed her thumb told a great deal about the change in Mary Lou, and what school had meant to her.

ALL NERVOUS HABITS ARE SYMPTOMS

Some children may express the tensions they are feeling by biting their nails, twisting on their clothing, or sucking other objects. Masturbation is another means of finding satisfaction and a defense against strain. We may do a great deal of harm by attacking the symptom directly and denying the child an avenue of expression while he is still feeling tension and seeking relief and satisfaction. We need to look on all of these so-called nervous habits as symptoms whose cause must be sought and treated before the symptom itself can be expected to disappear. Treating only the symptom will tend to make some other form of expression necessary for the child and increase the strain he feels. The thumbsucking child may become a nailbiting child or a masturbating child, for example, if the symptom and not the cause is attacked. We must keep in mind the fact that all kinds of behavior have meanings which we cannot afford to ignore.

ACCEPTING THE CHILD'S FEELINGS

In all these ways, a child shows us how he feels. After we have learned to recognize the child's feelings, we must find ways of adding to his feelings of security and confidence and reducing his feelings of insecurity.

What are some of the ways in which we can do this in the school?

We Must Face and Accept Feelings If We Are To Help

The most important step is to make sure that we really accept the child's feelings and that we do not condemn or blame him for them. Perhaps he feels afraid or angry or unfriendly. These may be feelings of which we do not approve, but approval and acceptance are different things. Acceptance means recognizing without blaming. It does not mean permitting the child to act out his feelings as he may wish, but it does mean acknowledging that he has the right to feel as he does without being ashamed of it. We may not approve, but we must accept the feelings that the child has if we are going to help him with them. Our very acceptance often reduces the feeling and makes the child less defensive about his insecurity, fear, or anger. Instead of hiding his feelings, he can bring them out where he, and we, can do more about them.

Accepting Our Own Feelings May Be Difficult

We usually find it difficult to be accepting of feelings that we have had to deny in ourselves. When we were children, we often felt jealous, resentful, or hostile, but we may not have been permitted any expression of these feelings. We had to act as though we loved a little sister, for example, and were willing to share our dolls with her, or we had to let the neighbor boy ride in our wagon because the adults insisted that children must be generous. Now, as adults, we find it hard to be accepting of the child who refuses to share her doll or who pushes another out of the wagon. We feel like punishing this child. This helps us to deny that we were ever like this little girl. If we handle our feelings by denying them, we cannot offer help to children who face problems with their feelings.

The story of what goes on unconsciously is oversimplified by the description we have given, of course, but we can be sure that whenever we strongly reject a bit of behavior, there are deep emotional reasons from our past experience for such a rejection. For some of us there will be more of these emotionally toned areas than for others, and our feelings will be stronger. Few of us will have escaped without some areas of behavior which we find it hard to accept.

If, on the other hand, we were helped to accept our real feelings when we were children, we will now find it easier to be accepting of children as they show their feelings. If the adults with us when we were children said, "It's easy to get angry at someone who takes your things, I know," instead of saying, "She's your sister, and you must love her and share with her," then we would have felt understood and could have faced our feelings with this kind of support. It would have seemed easier to feel and act more generously. This is the kind of help that we want to offer the children we are caring for today.

It is important if we are to help children in this way that we free ourselves of our old defenses. As adults we can now take the step of accepting the reality of any feelings that exist. We know that we all find sharing and loving difficult at times. Some jealousy is almost inevitable as children adjust to changing patterns in the family or at school. It is not necessary to deny the existence of feelings. Hostile, aggressive feelings exist in all of us.

Acceptance Helps the Child

The child who refuses to share a toy is not helped by disapproval and shaming. Neither is the child who is afraid. All these children need to be accepted as they are if they are to feel secure. There is always a reason for their behavior. As we work with the little girl who refuses to share her doll or who pushes her companion out of the wagon, we will accept her feelings and use her behavior as a cue to understanding. We will ask ourselves some questions. What kind of little girl is it who is trying to keep the doll? Is she craving affection and substituting the doll for the love she seeks? Does she depend on possessing things to give herself a feeling of security? How can we help her?

We Can Voice Our Acceptance of Feelings

We can express our acceptance in words: "I know how you feel. It makes you cross because it's Timmy's turn on the swing and you want it to be yours," or, "It makes you feel cross to have your blocks tumble over, I know," or, "You're pretty angry with me right now because I can't let you play outdoors." Words like these help if they express a real acceptance of the feelings that exist. They are different from words like, "You didn't mean to hit Bobby, did you?" that are untrue, as the child's reply, "I did, too" tells us. We must be honest and state what is true.

CONFIDENCE THROUGH EXPRESSION

Next comes the question of what can be done about a feeling after it has been accepted. The answer is that feelings must be expressed in some way if we are to be secure and confident. If feelings are not expressed, they remain with us to be carried around until they come out unexpectedly in ways that may make us unhappy and less sure of ourselves.

Feelings must be expressed, and they are best expressed at the time they occur. The child who says, "I'm afraid," is already less troubled by the feeling of fear. The child who says, "I don't like you," to someone who frightens him may be managing his feeling better than the child who says nothing, but then bursts into tears when the person tries to make his acquaintance. The child who is angry needs to do something about the way he feels at the time, rather than keep his anger hidden where it may come out in more damaging ways later; by that time, his anger may have grown and spread.

When we can do something about the way we feel, we are more confident. Psychiatrists tell us that the child who has been aggressive in his early years and whose behavior has been met with understanding has a better chance to

Children who are friends can discuss plans freely together.

make a good adjustment in adolescence than the submissive child. The aggressive child has done something about his feelings and has had an opportunity to identify them and to learn how to manage them.

It Is Essential To Express Feelings in Words

There are many ways in which feelings can be expressed. Most importantly, it is essential to learn to put negative feelings into words if we are to manage them constructively. When children can use language to drain off negative feeling, they have taken a step toward being able to control feelings. Their later responses will be more reasonable.

As adults, we often put our feelings into words to ourselves, silently, and then we know how we feel. We may feel even better if we have an opportunity to talk to a friend about our feelings. Putting a feeling into words makes it clear to us, and thus it seems more manageable. It helps drain it off. Knowing how one feels is tremendously important. It is a dangerous thing to try to fool ourselves about our feelings. We must understand and face our feelings if we are to be secure, comfortable people.

The child needs help in understanding what he feels, and he also needs help in putting his feelings into words. We should welcome his verbal expressions of feeling, for this way of expressing feelings means a step in his growth toward maturity and control of feelings. Children usually find it easy to talk things out directly, on the spot. They call people names or shout insults to one another. They may be using the best means of handling feelings that they have at their disposal, for they are not grown-up people yet. They are controlling the impulse to hit or attack, and they are expressing, not hiding, their feelings.

Jill (4.10) gives us *an example of what putting feelings into words can do for a child.* Jill had been in school about six months and had been developing very well. She was a friendly, active child who enjoyed play with other children, and she was eager and curious.

During one holiday period Jill had an experience in the doctor's office that had left her very frightened and upset. Her parents had comforted her as well as they could and tried to interest her in other things. Since they were very disturbed themselves about the affair, they preferred not to talk about it. They did not mention it to the teacher when Jill returned to school after the holiday. The teacher noticed a change in Jill's behavior. She was quiet and passive. She clung to the teacher and cried easily. Her teacher felt sure that something was wrong and asked the parents for a conference. They were glad to come and talk with her, and they told her about the incident. They, too, had felt that Jill was acting differently, and they were eager to help her. The teacher pointed out that it was important for Jill to feel able to talk to someone about her fears. Jill's mother seemed understanding, although she felt it might be hard for her to talk with Jill about the matter. The teacher suggested that the next time Jill got upset and cried, her mother might tell her that she, too, had been upset in the doctor's office, that she understood how Jill had felt, and that it was good to talk about the matter.

A few days later the mother telephoned to report that she had had a talk with Jill the night before. The parents were preparing to go to bed and had found Jill still awake. She seemed unhappy. The mother had gone into the room and, sitting on Jill's bed, she had begun to talk with her about the frightening experience. She said that at first Jill did not seem able to put anything into words, but as they continued talking, she became freer and finally went over all the details. Her mother told Jill that whenever she felt unhappy and afraid, she could come and talk with her, that she would understand, for she felt the same way sometimes.

At rest time that day in school, Jill said to the teacher, "You know what happened? Last night I was unhappy, and I told Mummy." The teacher asked, "And Mummy understood?" "Yes," said Jill, "she asked me why I was unhappy, and I couldn't say, but she knew it was about the doctor." The teacher answered, "Mummies do understand and know, and you can tell Mummy when you feel that way again." Jill went on, "And she said that at night when I am unhappy to come and tell Mummy and Daddy, but I wasn't unhappy anymore. I was just a little unhappy, and now I'm happy." The teacher repeated, "Mummies and daddies do understand, don't they! You can always tell them."

That evening the teacher telephoned Jill's mother to tell her about the conversation. Jill's mother could hardly believe that Jill had repeated this conversation, even using the same words that the mother had used to her. She realized that it had made a deep impression on the child. She felt that she herself could talk to the child more easily now. In school and at home Jill's behavior began to change rapidly. She had played and laughed that day at school, jumping in and out of a box with two other children. She began to assert herself more and to take her place in the activities of the school. She became more like her old self. It seemed wonderful to the teachers, too, that a conversation with a mother who understood could do so much to relieve a child. Putting her fears into words with the help of someone she trusted had drained off much of the disturbing feeling and had left the little girl free to grow as before. Her mother had learned from the experience. It gave her confidence. She knew better how to help her child.

THERE ARE OTHER WAYS TO EXPRESS FEELINGS

Crying is another good way to express feelings, yet many times we hear people say to a crying child, "That didn't hurt. You're too big to cry." The crying may come because there have been too many failures or too much deprivation or frustration. Whatever the reason, the feeling of wanting to cry is there and needs to be accepted, not denied. No one can handle with wisdom feelings he isn't supposed to have. Words like "I know how you feel," when they are said by a person who really accepts the feeling help a good deal more than words like "You're too big to cry."

Motor forms of expression of feelings are common forms for expression. A young child may kick, hit, or throw. Our job is to help him use motor outlets in a way that will not be damaging to others. He may even need to be put by himself so that he can act in these ways without hurting anyone. If he is older, he may be able to take a suggestion about using a punching bag to advantage. Vigorous physical activity, such as pounding or throwing a ball hard against something, will serve as an outlet for feelings.

If there is a warm, understanding relationship between child and adult, the child can accept many types of suggestion for draining off negative feelings. The teacher may be successful when she says, "You feel just like hitting someone, I know, but you must not do it. Try hitting the target over there with these beanbags. See how many times you can hit it. I'll count the hits." The child may be able to handle his feelings with the help of an understanding, accepting teacher. Our job is to see that he does not use destructive outlets. It is also our job to direct him to outlets that are possible and acceptable.

Creative expression can be used to drain off feelings and make them more manageable. Finger painting, painting at the easel, working with clay, playing in water, even the sandbox or a good old mud hole, will help a child to relax as he expresses feelings through these media. Music offers still another possibility and is often used this way by children.

Creative materials should be freely available to children because of the value they have as avenues for the expression of feelings. Adults use these same outlets. The child who has found he can turn his feelings into such creative channels has discovered an outlet which will serve him all his life. A child is more secure if he has many avenues of expression open to him. He grows when he can express himself and his feelings through art media. When he is denied self-expression in art media because models are set for him, he loses a valuable avenue for the relief of feelings which might help to safeguard him all his life.

THE TIMID CHILD CAN LEARN HOW TO EXPRESS HIS FEELINGS

We will often see a timid, inhibited child swing over into unduly aggressive behavior as he begins to gain confidence in himself. This may be the first step in gaining confidence. He must first express his feelings and find acceptance for them. Then he can proceed to modify them. The child who has been inhibited may express his feelings in clumsy and inappropriate ways in the beginning. His first expression of feeling may seem exaggerated. This expression may belong at a much younger level than his present chronological age. If his timidity developed in an earlier period when he was afraid of his feelings and the way people would react to them, and was thus unable to express feelings, he will need to go back and act as he wanted to act earlier. With understanding guidance he will come through this stage quickly, but he must "live out," for however brief a time, a period of expression at the less mature level. He must try out being "bad" and discover that he is accepted and that his "badness" does not frighten the adult. It can be managed.

"Transitional Objects" Give Security

Children sometimes use "transitional objects" to help themselves *feel more secure* and better able to cope with new or difficult situations. For some children it may be a blanket they have had from babyhood. For others it may be a cuddly toy. Carrying it or knowing that it is easily available may help the child weather the strains he feels. The object is a device for coping with a difficult world. It has symbolic value for the child.

Transitional objects help in the "weaning" process that is part of growing. They are useful in periods of change when the child must let go or leave behind his old sources of security. They signal to us the child's need for support, as well as indicate the effort he is making to deal with change. One two-year-old in a group could not part with his sweater for several weeks after he entered the group. It may have represented his mother or his home. He wore the sweater or carried it, and became very anxious if it was out of his sight. The way a child uses a transitional object gives us cues about his feelings.

A Child Feels More Secure When He Is Having Satisfying Experiences

Having his needs met applies to the child's experience in school as well as to his experience at home. If the school is providing satisfying, stimulating opportunities, it makes it easier for the child to be happy and secure. The whole program of the school, as well as the equipment provided, will contribute to the child's growth in feeling more secure and more adequate. Learning opportunities adapted to the child's level of development, equipment that fits him and makes it easy for him to solve problems, support from adults who understand what his needs are, all make it easier for a child to gain the feeling of security and adequacy that he needs.

Most important of all, in the school the child is with others who are on about the same level of development. He can have fun doing things with other children. Among this group of equals he does not need to feel inadequate, for he *can* keep up with them. He can do things as well as many of the others. He gains strength from the feeling that he is like others, from being able to identify himself with people who are at his stage of growth. Belonging to a group of equals constitutes one of the best forms of insurance against feeling little and helpless.

Conversation between friends at snack time in a comfortable atmosphere.

The child needs to find teachers in the school who will accept his positive feelings, too. As teachers, we must be ready to return his smile, to take his hand when he slips it into ours, to take him into our arms, or to talk with him when he seems to feel the need of such closeness. We must respond to his warm, friendly feelings. If it is his need and not ours that we are meeting in responding, we can be sure that he is helped to be more independent by what we do. He will gain confidence as he feels sure of having a warm response from us when he wants it.

GOOD TEACHING CONTRIBUTES TO DEVELOPMENT OF CONFIDENCE

By the techniques we use as teachers we will also help the child grow more secure and confident. Let us take the situation of a child climbing on the jungle gym as one example, and see what it may mean.

Joan (2.8), is just learning to climb; she cautiously and awkwardly manages to get halfway up in the jungle gym and then calls for help, "Help me! I want down!" An adult comes to her rescue and answers the cry by lifting her down. Joan is on the ground, safe, but with all feeling of achievement lost! On another occasion a different adult comes to the rescue. She stands beside the child and says reassuringly, "I'll help you, Joan. Hang on to this bar and put your foot here," thus guiding Joan's climbing back to the ground. Safe on the ground, Joan is elated. She starts right up again and this time is successful in reaching the top. When her mother comes, she can scarcely wait to show her this new achievement.

If, when Joan starts to climb the jungle gym, her mother says in a disgusted voice, "Come on, Joan, you've had all morning to play. I'm in a hurry. You can show me tomorrow," Joan may again lose the feeling that she is a person who can achieve. If her mother is eager to share the experience and watches her, exclaiming, "That's fine, Joan, you've learned to climb way up high," Joan takes another step in growing confident.

Let us summarize briefly some of the things that we can do in the school to increase a child's feelings of security and confidence.

1. *Accept him* as he is, his feelings and his behavior, knowing that there are reasons for the way he feels and acts. Recognize that hitting and other forms of motor expression of feelings are normal for the young child. Stop his unacceptable actions without blaming him or shaming him. We can expect him to change his behavior, but he has a right to his feelings. We want him to respect himself and have confidence in himself. We want him to feel that we have confidence in him.

2. Help him find *acceptable outlets for his feelings.* Help him put his feelings into words, not only as a way of identifying what he feels but also as a step toward control. Help him use many avenues for the expression of feelings, especially the creative avenues, but be sure that feelings are expressed. The really destructive feelings are those that have no recognized outlets.

3. Try to *meet the child's needs* as he indicates what his needs are and leave him free to develop in accordance with his own growth patterns at his own rate. Thus, we will give him confidence and the feeling that he is an adequate person. Refrain from "nudging" him. Instead, try to understand him.

4. *Acquire skills in handling him* that will increase his confidence, making suggestions to him in a positive way, reducing the difficulties of the situations he faces, adjusting demands to fit his capacities, and forestalling trouble when possible.

SITUATION FOR DISCUSSION

*Gilbert: Feelings Are Strong**

9:35 Ginger, a student, had brought her riding equipment into the playroom. The saddle, the bridle, her riding boots, and a brightly colored horse blanket were on a low table. The children crowded around the table, pointing and talking about the articles there.

As Ginger showed the children the blanket, Gilbert (3.6) reached out and patted the blanket, saying, "Pretty, pretty." He pushed another child aside so that he could touch the saddle also. He ran his hand along the leather side of the saddle caressingly. "Mine, mine," he shouted at Nels (3.3) when Nels tried to climb on the saddle. Glaring at Nels, Gilbert pushed him away and climbed up on the saddle himself, hanging on as tight as he could. "Mine, mine," he repeated. Without a word Nels walked away. Pam (4.0) and Ann (4.3) tried to get him to give them a turn in sitting on the saddle. The answer each time was an emphatic "No" from Gilbert.

9:48 The teacher entered the situation. "Gilbert, let's put the saddle across this plank (a board with ends resting on two chairs). Then when you sit on the saddle your feet will fit in the stirrups," she said. Very reluctantly Gilbert climbed off the saddle and turned his attention to the blanket and the rest of the equipment on the table. Many of the children tried "riding the horse," climbing on and off the saddle. Gilbert stayed by the blanket, rubbing it with both hands.

10:00 Ginger's mother came into the playroom to help Ginger take the equipment to the car. She picked up the blanket along with the boots and walked into the hall. Gilbert rushed after her, grabbing the blanket and shouting, "Mine, mine." Softly Ginger said, "Gilbert, we must take the blanket home to the horse." Gilbert screamed, "No, no," as he tugged at the

---

* Recorded by Jane Martin

blanket and began to cry, to the surprise of Ginger's mother. Connie, another student, picked Gilbert up and said, "Come, Gilbert. I'll read you a story." He kicked at her, screaming, "Mine, mine." Connie had no success in trying to quiet him. He sobbed for about 10 minutes after Ginger had left. At juice time Gilbert joined the other children.

Comment

How might this situation have been managed to make it a more constructive one?

We find a child who evidently is attracted to the color and texture of the blanket and saddle. "Pretty, pretty." He feels the leather saddle caressingly and rubs his hands on the blanket.

What he enjoys, he also seems to want to possess. "Mine, mine," he shouts. His feelings are strong as he reveals by the long period of sobbing. He shows little confidence in his ability to possess what he wants, so he must act aggressively, pushing other children and shouting.

Our goal in this situation will be to preserve the sense of pleasure Gilbert feels and at the same time help him gain confidence that there is enough for him and for the others to enjoy, in other words, to help him feel better able to share experiences with others while still enjoying them himself.

The first opportunity to help came when Gilbert pushed Nels away and climbed into the saddle himself. At this point Ginger might have stepped in, saying, "Nels is taking his turn on the saddle. It will be your turn next." To help Gilbert accept waiting for a turn, she might have put her arm around him and told him how she used the blanket and the saddle when she rode her horse, describing the hard, smooth leather so different from the soft blanket. She could have carried on a conversation with him, enriching the experience by her comments. Then she would make sure that Gilbert *did* have the next turn and that he did not have too long to wait. He might feel more confident if Ginger or another adult had maintained his right to sit there when the others wanted to use the saddle, "It's Gilbert's turn now." He might then have been better able to give it up when the end of his turn came.

It is not clear from the record whether Gilbert did have a turn after the teacher asked him to get off so that the saddle could be placed on the board. If not, this experience would have contributed to his despair at losing the blanket in the end. Gilbert had turned to the blanket after having to leave the saddle and seemed to be using the blanket as a comfort or security object, rubbing it with his hand. It became one more loss for him. We notice that, according to the record, there was no help given to prepare him for its loss and no explanation until *after* it had gone.

When he began to cry, Ginger told him that the blanket belonged to the horse, a fact, but not one that helped him with his own feelings. She might have said, "I wish I could leave the blanket here for you, but the horse needs it. It is his blanket." She might have given him a hug as she said, "Feel it once again before I have to take it.'' By a hug and such words she might have shown him that she understood his feelings, that she wished she could give him what he wanted so much to have.

When Connie picked Gilbert up and offered to read a story to him, she was really denying his feelings and avoiding facing them. It was as though she did not understand what he was feeling. A child can face and manage feelings with help. It would have been more helpful to Gilbert if Connie had knelt down, and put her arms around him rather than pick him up (which may have made him feel more helpless). She might have said, ''I'm so sorry that they have to take away the saddle and blanket. You liked them, didn't you! It is hard to see them leave. Maybe Ginger can bring them again someday.'' If his sobbing lessened, she might continue, ''What did you like best, the saddle or the blanket?'' as she tried to get him thinking in different ways about the experience, recreating it and capturing the enjoyment in recall, recovering and dealing with the loss.

It is evident that Gilbert could make use of a greater variety of materials with texture and color. The equipment in the play group might include a box with a variety of fabrics: a piece of velvet, silk, fine cotton, textured material; squares of brightly colored gauze; scraps of colored pieces; and scraps of leather. Some blankets for the cradle, in colors, could be added in the homemaking area. Plenty of opportunity to work with collage materials and to use paints should be satisfying to Gilbert. An excursion to the barn to visit Ginger's horse would be a valuable trip for all the children, including Gilbert, with some preparation beforehand about what to expect and about what the children would be allowed to do there.

PROJECTS

1. Observe and record three situations in which the guidance given by the adult was directed toward helping the child to feel more secure and confident. Estimate how successful it was in its effect on the child.

2. Listen to the quality and pitch of the children's voices. List the names of children whose voices are high pitched or strained, soft and indistinct, loud and somewhat harsh, and easy and pleasant. How would you relate what the child's voice seems to reveal with what you know of the child's adjustment and his feelings about himself? Do the same with motor forms of behavior such as posture, hand movement, or body tension.

3. Make a list of emotionally loaded words sometimes used in describing behavior of a child, such as spoiled, stubborn, selfish. Indicate briefly how the use of such words may influence objective observation of behavior. Give an example of some descriptive terms which might be used to describe the same behavior in the case of some of the words listed above.

SUPPLEMENTARY READING

Arnstein, H., and others. *What To Tell Your Child about Birth, Death, Illness, Divorce and Other Family Crises.* Indianapolis: Bobbs-Merrill, 1962.

Bowlby, J. Security and anxiety. In D. Edge, ed., *The Formative Years.* New York: Schocken Books, 1970.

Butler, A. Today's child—tomorrow's world. *Young Children,* 1976, *32* (1):4–11.

Gonzalez-Meno, J. What is a good beginning? *Young Children,* 1979, *34* (3):47–53.

Murphy, L. *The Widening World of Childhood.* New York: Basic Books, 1962. Parts 3 and 4.

Yamamoto, K., ed. *The Child and His Image: Self-concept in the Early Years.* Boston: Houghton Mifflin, 1972.

13

Scribbles
(girl, 2.0)
Mother said child was
angry over arrival of baby.

Feelings of Hostility and Aggression

The problem of what to do about feelings of hostility and aggression is a difficult one for individuals and for groups. It is not likely to be solved by avoidance or by denying the existence of these feelings. As we have pointed out, the existence of a feeling must be accepted before there is much chance that it can be handled constructively. Only when we have accepted our hostile, aggressive feelings can we discover: (1) the best ways to handle them and (2) the best ways to prevent them from multiplying.

We can use the school as a laboratory to study the problems of hostile and aggressive feelings and to try to understand them. Resentment and hostility expressed aggressively are evident in the behavior of children whenever the situation is one which is not rigidly controlled by adults, whenever children are free to show us how they feel. A child who is angry may address the teacher as "You dummy," and this teacher will be the one in whom he has some confidence. He is likely to be more polite to the teacher with whom he does not feel as safe. "We don't like you," sing out two children to a third. Occasionally, a chorus of "name calling" greets the visitor to the school. Some children do not reveal hostile feelings by such direct expressions, but they may have these same feelings anyway. We can learn to recognize their less direct expressions, too, and how to prevent more hostility and aggressiveness from developing.

HOSTILITY AND AGGRESSION ARE TIED UP WITH GROWTH

A certain amount of hostile feeling in all of us results from the growing-up process. As infants we were helpless and often our needs were not met. We felt threatened by the greater strength of the people around us. There were many frustrations and interferences for us all. Frustrations breed resentment when the frustrated person is little and helpless.

Some aggressiveness is necessary, for growth itself is a going-forward process which demands it. Dr. Kubie states, "The acquisition of positive, self-assertive, commanding and demanding attitudes in the first two years of human life is an essential step in the development of every child" (1948, p. 67). But we now realize that much unnecessary aggressiveness, as well as hostility, is aroused by some of the traditional methods of handling children at home and at school. Healthy aggression becomes unhealthy. Resentment develops which interferes with healthy growth. As we apply better methods of guiding children in the growing-up processes, we should be able to reduce the amount of hostility and unproductive aggression in the world with increasing effectiveness, as our knowledge and understanding grow.

RESENTMENT IS INCREASED BY INCONSISTENT EXPECTATIONS

The amount of resentment and aggression, as well as the amount of confusion and guilt over these feelings, is perhaps greater in our society than in some others because a child will be in a variety of social situations, each with its own behavioral expectations. In one situation, as with parents at home, the child is supposed to be obedient. In another situation, as on the playground, he is expected to "stand up for himself" and come out ahead in highly competitive types of situations. The same bit of behavior is wrong in one place and right in another. These inconsistencies make learning difficult for the child and may increase the number of his mistakes and the resultant guilt that he may feel.

Children in our culture also carry a handicapping load of resentment when parental management is harsh and when standards are rigidly or inconsistently enforced. Such methods may arouse a great deal of hostile aggressiveness in individuals. We have usually refused to acknowledge the extent of these feelings and have gone on multiplying them—in children and in ourselves. The result is that they are spilling over constantly in all kinds of unsuspected ways in our personal lives as well as in our group life. Few problems are more important than the problem of facing and reducing the hostility we feel.

PATTERNS OF VIOLENCE IN A SOCIETY MAKE CONTROL OF AGGRESSION DIFFICULT

Managing feelings of hostility and aggression in constructive ways is made more difficult for the child who is exposed to patterns of violence in behavior in the society. Many children today watch programs on television that are full of brutal attacks on people, cruelty, and disrespect for the dignity of human beings. The example set by these patterns of behavior in television programs, or on the street, makes it only too easy for children to follow these patterns themselves when their own controls break down.

There are uncontrolled, violent ways of expressing the negative feelings within us, and there are more ''civilized'' ways that require understanding and control. Feelings must be expressed, but this can be done in words or art forms or actions that do no harm to others. With the help of adults, this energy can be channeled into constructive achievements.

CHILDREN NEED TO EXPRESS HOSTILE FEELINGS

It is safe to say that *all* children at times feel aggressive and hostile, but that not all children act out these feelings. In the past we have tended to give approval to the children who did not act out their negative feelings. From what we now know about mental health, we realize that it is essential that feelings be expressed if a person is to remain mentally healthy. The problem is to discover avenues of expression that are not destructive to the child or others, rather than to deny expression to these feelings. It is unlikely that we can have a peaceful world for long, while the individuals in it are carrying around a load of hostility with the added guilt that having such feelings and denying them is sure to create. We must help children to face and to express their hostile feelings.

It is worth quoting part of the aforementioned discussion by Dr. Kubie (1948) as follows:

> Repeatedly in the early years of life anger must be liquidated at its birth or it will plague us to the grave. . . . If we are even to lessen the neurotic distortions of human aggression, then it seems clear that the anger must be allowed and encouraged to express itself in early childhood, not in blindly destructive acts but in words, so as to keep it on the fullest possible level of conscious awareness. Furthermore such conscious ventilation of feelings must be encouraged in the very situations in which they have arisen, and toward those adults and children who have been either the active or the innocent sources of the feelings. Only in this way can we lessen the burden of unconscious aggression which every human being carries from infancy to the grave. (pp. 70; 89)

ADULTS MUST ACCEPT HOSTILE FEELINGS IN THEMSELVES

The important job of parent and teacher, then, becomes one of encouraging expression of feeling in nondamaging ways and of diminishing the number of situations in which negative feelings are developed. Our ability to do this will depend in part on our ability to accept our own feelings or we will find ourselves meeting aggression by aggression and hostility by hostility. When a child calls us ''You dummy,'' we must be able to accept the fact of the child's feeling of anger without getting it tangled up with our own angry feelings. This will be easier as we realize that his words offer no real threat to us as such words might have in the past or under other circumstances. We happen to be the recipient of his anger and hostility at the moment, but they have been generated by many factors in his past experiences just as our own have been.

To the extent that we were punished or shamed for the expression of our own hostile feelings, we may find it hard to accept the fact that the child needs to express such feelings. If our own defenses against such feelings are strong, if we have permitted ourselves little expression, it may be difficult for us to permit expression for others. It remains important for us to achieve this acceptance if we are to be of help to the child.

MARVIN COULD COPE WITH STRONG FEELINGS BECAUSE HE COULD EXPRESS THEM

Let us look at an example of the steps one child took to master his anxiety and resentment as he prepared himself to cope with a situation. The year before, Marvin (4.6) had attended a child-care center for five days. He had objected to going and had cried each day. His parents had not stayed with him, but the director had reported he was "a nice quiet little boy." However, the parents learned that on the fifth day he had climbed into a chair and stayed in it all day, clutching his teddy bear. He had not eaten lunch or taken a nap. As he was a lively, active three-year-old at home, the youngest of three children, they realized that he had really been unhappy and arranged for his care with a baby sitter in the neighborhood while they were at work.

They talked over plans the next year and decided to try the center again. Marvin was now four, and there was to be another teacher, whom they knew, in charge. Here is the father's report of what happened when he broached the subject to Marvin.

> Marvin was eating his breakfast. He was in his usual exuberant mood while eating his cereal. He was dive-bombing his spoon into the bowl with appropriate sound effects.
> "Marvin," I said, "one of Daddy's friends is going to be working in the school you went to with Tommy. Would you like to visit her with me sometime?"
> Marvin stopped eating, his spoon poised in midair. His eyes grew wide with alarm. His body tensed and he almost visibly drew into himself. He continued to stare at me and his lower lip began to tremble.
> "If you take me to that school again I'll throw a bomb at it and break it all up!" he blurted.
> "We could go just for a visit," I said somewhat uneasily, not at all prepared for the impact the idea school still held for him.
> "They're bad there! Those children don't like me! That lady doesn't like me!"
> "You liked Tommy. Didn't Tommy play with you?"
> Marvin was breathing heavily. After a pause he said, "Tommy could come to my house and play with me. I won't go to that school again!"
> "You didn't like that school?"

"No! I will take my axe and chop it all up!"

"You don't want to go there again?"

He was a bit more relaxed. "No." A pause. "No. They don't have good toys. Or good boys and girls. Or good people."

"You didn't have fun there?"

"No." He became quite agitated again. Then, in a quiet voice, he said, "I'm tired of eating." He put down his spoon, climbed down from his chair and walked into our bedroom. He climbed into our bed and covered himself up.

I sat down on the bed beside him. "Pat me," he said.

I patted him and told him we would not visit the school until he wanted to and that I would stay with him while he visited when we did go.

"But not today?" he asked.

"No, not today," I agreed.

"Not for this many days?" He carefully arranged his fingers so that he could hold up three.

"Not for many days," I agreed.

He lay still for a moment. "I better finish my cereal," he said, throwing back the blankets. He climbed out of bed and went back to the table. "Not for *many* days," he said to himself as he climbed into his chair.

We see that Marvin's first response is a rush of strong feeling. Then he mobilizes his forces and asserts himself. He attacks aggressively, "I'll throw a bomb at it and break it all up." He will solve the problem by destroying it. Wisely, his father does not resist but retreats a bit. Marvin then tries to think of reasons why this going to school must not happen. He does this effectively. Not only is the school "bad" and the lady there "doesn't like me," but his friend could come to his house to play. His father tries to put Marvin's feelings into words more directly, "You didn't like that school." Marvin's aggressiveness returns, "I will take my axe and chop it all up." His father then states the heart of the problem, "You don't want to go there again." Marvin seems a bit more relaxed as it is put into words by his father. He can count on his father's understanding. This time he is less negative. He says they don't have good people there rather than saying they are bad.

His acceptance begins but his appetite has gone. He leaves the table and goes to his parents' bed, climbs in, and covers himself up. He goes to the most comforting place available to him and hides himself. His father follows silently, taken aback by the intensity of the child's feeling, appreciative of the difficulty of the problem that the child must struggle with. "Pat me," says Marvin, needing and able to use the support he knows an understanding father can give. Now the father suggests a compromise. They will not visit until Marvin feels ready and he, the father, will stay with him. We see the "mutual regulation," the working out of a problem together which brings good solutions and good relations when there is understanding. Marvin tests it out, "But not today?" and his father agrees. Then Marvin asserts himself again, but this time it is in having a share in the decision. "Not for this many days," holding up three fingers. When his father says, "Not for many days," Marvin's response is, "I better finish my cereal." He climbs out of bed and returns to the table, saying, "Not for *many* days," as he climbs into his chair. He has coped with the situation actively and constructively. His self-respect and confidence remain. His father has stood by him in the steps he took to master his anxieties. One suspects there has been a mutual growth in understanding and both will be able to meet the situation when the "many days" are over and it becomes a reality. They are better prepared.

SOURCES OF HOSTILE FEELINGS

Let us discuss some of the common situations in which resentment is felt by children, how feelings develop in these situations, and how they may be liquidated.

A NEW BABY AT HOME CAN CREATE FEELINGS OF HOSTILITY

A common occasion outside the school in which the child will feel hostility is when a new baby arrives in his home. Parents are often afraid that the older child will be jealous and may reassure themselves that he "doesn't seem the

A baby is interesting to children.

least bit jealous.'' Yet it is inevitable that an older child will resent in some respects the coming of a new baby however much he may also enjoy other aspects of the changed situation. Julia (3.5), a well-adjusted child, was not eager to receive a baby sister into her home. She was at school when her grandmother came with the news of the arrival of the long-awaited baby. After hearing about her and asking some questions, Julia reassured herself, ''She won't come home today, will she?'' and when her grandmother affirmed this, she added, ''I don't want her to,'' and returned to her play. Julia could express her feelings.

If parents are afraid of a child's jealousy, he may have to conceal it from them. It can only come out indirectly, in his too rough hugging of the baby, in ''accidentally'' hurting it, and in an increased cruelty in his play with other children. These indirect ways are not as healthy as a direct expression, for they are less understandable and less likely to drain off feelings of jealousy and may even add to feelings of guilt. There is less need to be afraid of hostile feelings themselves than of what they do to us when we try to hide them and thus lose control over them.

LIQUIDATING HOSTILE FEELINGS IN SCHOOL

When there is a new baby at home, the child's feelings often spill out in his behavior at school. He will act them out in the doll corner, perhaps, spanking the dolls frequently, smothering them with blankets, or throwing one on the floor and stamping on it. In this way he relieves himself by draining off some of the hostility he may be feeling, making it easier to face the real situation. A school should have some dolls that can stand this kind of treatment. A direct ''draining off'' of feelings in this way may be about the only means some children have of expressing the conflict they feel. Many parents do not, as Julia's parents could, understand and accept expressions of feeling at home.

If our interest is in sound personality development, it is not hard to see how little real value there would be in emphasizing the proper care of dolls at this point. If one did insist that dolls were not to be treated in this way, one would block for the child this avenue of expression, leaving him in an emotionally dangerous situation. There might be a good deal of trouble ahead for him in his relationship with the real baby. It is worth noting that anthropologists report that certain very gentle Indian tribes permit young children to show great cruelty to animals, which, they suggest, may serve the purpose of draining off some of the hostility which children feel, and account in part for the Indians' friendly behavior with each other.

Rubber dolls and other rubber toys serve as a good medium for the release of hostile aggressive feelings. They can be pinched and bitten with a good deal of satisfaction. Jeremy (3.6), whose relationships at home had been tense and strained, had felt his position in the family threatened by the return of a father who was almost a stranger to him, and then even more threatened by the arrival of a new baby. His insecurity and hostility came out in the readiness with which he attacked and bit other children in the school. The teacher had to watch him constantly to prevent his attacking others. She found that she could substitute a rubber doll and that he seemed to find relief in biting it. Biting is usually done by a child who feels helpless. He can see no other way to meet his problems. She carried the doll in her pocket for a time so that it would be instantly available, and she gave it to him when she saw his tension mounting, saying, "I know! You feel just like biting someone. Here's the doll. It's all right to bite the doll." The least interference or the smallest suggestion of a rejection filled his already full cup of negative feelings to overflowing. He had to do something, and biting on the doll served to reduce the feeling to more manageable proportions. The teacher's acceptance and her understanding of the way he felt gave him confidence. The day came when he ran to her himself because he knew that he needed to bite the doll. He could recognize his feelings and handle them in a way that was not damaging to the other children. He began to have more success and find more satisfaction in his play. Steadily he had less hostile feelings to handle.

During this time, Jeremy had also been engaging in a great deal of verbal aggression against the adults in the school. When he was faced with the necessity of limiting his activity during the rest period, for example, he would lie on his bed and attack the teacher verbally, "cut her up, her legs, her head, her arms," and would sometimes, "put her in the garbage can," or sometimes, "put her in the toilet." His words revealed the extent to which he himself had been hurt and the anger and fear he had felt. Very slowly, with many avenues of expression open to him, he drained off some of his resentful feelings, and the acceptance and success he had in the school helped him to build other kinds of feelings. He discovered other kinds of relationships, and the warm, supporting relationship he had with his teacher left him free to find friends among the children.

ANOTHER SOURCE OF RESENTMENT IS THE NECESSITY FOR KEEPING CLEAN

Another source of resentment in children, in addition to changing positions in the family, lies in the demands made on them to "keep clean" and the fear and guilt they often feel when they yield to the impulse to play in dirt.

Ruth (3.6) was a child whose mother had emphasized cleanliness and proper behavior, including a strict toilet-training regimen. Ruth showed as much hostility and resentment toward adults as did any child in the group at first. She refused requests or suggestions which came from an adult, even though they might be ones she really wanted to carry out. Her mother characterized her behavior as "just plain stubbornness." Their life together had been a succession of issues over one habit or the other. The following incident occurred after she had been in school a year and had begun to participate in activities with confidence; at this point she was even affectionate with the teachers she knew, saying, "I like you," with real feeling. Even then she still grew disturbed and anxious when faced with a little dirt.

A child who need not stay clean can explore materials thoroughly.

Ruth happened to be on the playground with a student teacher. She was swinging. It was muddy and as Ruth's boots swept through the puddle under the swing, they splashed mud on her and on the teacher. Ruth looked disturbed. "What will your Dad say?" she asked the student teacher anxiously. The teacher assured her that he wouldn't say anything and that it was just an accident and couldn't be helped. But Ruth answered darkly, "Oh yes, he'll say something."

She again tried swinging but once more they both got splashed. Ruth said warmly, "I'm sorry," and she repeated, "What will your Dad say?"

This time the teacher replied by asking Ruth what she thought he would say. Ruth answered, "He'll say you're all dirty and will have to clean up and take a bath," and then she added, "I'm going inside and stay in, if you don't mind." She went in and did not come outside again during the morning.

Even though she expected no punishment for splashing the mud in this situation, it was a "bad" thing to her. It meant disapproval from the adults on whom this insecure little girl had to depend. Standards for behavior were high and punishment severe. Her anxiety was apparent in her words and her behavior. It was not hard to see why she had shown hostility and unfriendliness.

In this situation, a more experienced teacher not only would have recognized the extent of the anxiety the child was showing by her questions, but would have tried to help her put it into words so that it might have become more understandable and manageable—she would not have needed to run away from it. She might have verbalized in some such way as this, "Does your Dad get mad when you're dirty? Mothers and Dads often do, don't they, when children get dirty?" This might have given Ruth the help she did not find in the student's denial that *her* Dad would be mad. Ruth knew better about hers! It would have made it a common experience, easier to face. The teacher might have continued, "Sometimes it is all right to get dirty because we can get cleaned up afterward just as we can now. Sometimes it's even fun to get dirty. I used to like to myself," and this might have relieved the child. She might have been able to stay outdoors and have fun. She might have been better able to trust herself.

THE CUE MAY BE A SMALL ONE

Sometimes it is harder to identify the feelings that lie behind words or acts. The child may be afraid to express his hostility or his aggression openly. We have to find the meaning from a very small cue. Grace (4.2), for example, had always been very "good." This meant that she was not able to be very expressive or creative. In the school she gradually began to find it possible to act with greater freedom. It was clear to anyone watching her that she often wanted to act differently but did not dare.

One day the teacher observed Grace carefully laying several chairs on their sides on the floor. The teacher made no comment, not understanding the meaning of this behavior. The next day Grace's mother asked anxiously about how Grace was behaving in school. She was worried because Grace had told her that the day before she had "knocked over all the chairs at school." It was then clear to the teacher that this careful laying of a few chairs on their sides was in reality an aggressive act for Grace. It was as far as she dared to go in expressing her aggressive feelings, and she would have liked to have made it a much bigger act than it was.

Grace needed to be helped to see that she could express aggressive feelings, that she could really be accepted as a little girl who had "bad" feelings as well as "good" ones, that there were safe limits at school, too. Her parents needed to have more understanding of the importance of accepting all of Grace's feelings.

Henry (3.9), who was very timid, showed much the same kind of need when he declared, "I'm going to make a lot of noise," and then took one block and carefully threw it on the floor. His parents approved of quiet boys. He had few opportunities to be noisy, and he was trying to show that he really dared to be the kind of person he wanted to be.

In the cases of children like Grace and Henry it may be important to accept their "acting out" of feelings without doing anything about limiting or redirecting them at first, provided the behavior does not do them or others harm. When the child has an opportunity to convince himself that the "bad" part of him is accepted, then he is ready to take the more constructive step of putting the feelings into words, of talking about the feeling as Marvin did with his father. Then the child can begin to manage such feelings more acceptably.

Late four- and five-year-old children are usually ready for more immediate help in putting their feelings into words. They have a better mastery of language and can discuss feelings and impulses more directly with an accepting adult who is not condemning them. If we are able to listen to the child, we may be able to help him grow in understanding himself and in self-control.

FAILURE TO GET ATTENTION AND RESPONSE

Failure to get attention and response will arouse resentment and hostility in children, too, especially in insecure children who are seeking reassurance through getting attention. Their feelings are involved in a way that makes them sensitive to failure. Situations are constantly arising in which children want attention from the teacher or from other children, want to feel important and needed—and fail. They are resentful and hostile as a result.

Whenever the situation is a competitive one, there is more likelihood for failures. A child may want the attention of the teacher and, not getting it, may attack either the child, whom he feels is his rival, or the teacher, whom he feels is deserting him. A child like this needs to have his confidence built up so that he will see others as less of a threat to him. He needs help in accepting and finding better outlets for his feelings. When it is all right to admit the feeling of wanting the teacher all to yourself, it becomes easier to work out a better solution than attacking others.

As teachers, we should be aware of the strong need most children have to feel sure of their place and to receive a share of our attention. When we give attention to one child, we need to remember that other children may be feeling left out. We saw an example in Betsy (4.2), who untied her shoe so that the teacher could tie it for her just as the teacher had done for another child. Not many children can deal with their feelings as directly as Betsy. They may need some help from us. A teacher may say, "I think you'd like me to do something with you sometimes. I've been doing a lot with Helen lately because she is new and isn't sure about what we do. Of course I like helping you, too. Remember when you first came and I had to show you what to do? Now it's different, and you sometimes help the new children."

And she can add, "But you tell me when you really want me to do something for you and I'll do it if I can." This attention helps a child feel sure that there is a place for him and that he can have attention, too.

"NUDGING" AND HARSH METHODS OF CONTROL

Children who have been "nudged" from one stage of development to the next, who have had high standards set for their behavior, may feel a great deal of resentment which they often cannot express directly. One way that these children may try to handle the feeling is by reproving others. They identify with the teacher to escape from the feeling of being helpless. Joshua (4.8), for example, has received a great deal of punishment from parents who have never heard of any methods of discipline except the "good old-fashioned ones." Joshua was playing with Larry (5.0), and the two were building a block tower to dangerous heights. The teacher warned, "Not so high." Joshua immediately turned to Larry and said severely, "The teacher said no more blocks and when she says something you mind her." Thus he got rid of some of his resentment, but his "punishing" attitude makes it hard for any but the most comfortable children to play with him. Incidentally, in Joshua's behavior we get some insight into the quality of control which harshly disciplined people impose when they themselves are in power, and the need they often feel to identify with the controlling authority. Children who are harshly punished often identify with the aggressor and become punishing people themselves.

Sam Wanted Desperately To Feel Big

Sam (4.10) is an outstanding example of a child who had been pushed around in many ways without much loving and giving on the part of the adults in return for their heavy demands. He was expected to behave like a little gentleman on every occasion when there were visitors at home, and he usually came to school in his best clothing instead of dressing in play clothes like the other children. His speech was more like that of an adult—even his vocabulary of swear words. He was advanced in his development, but he was also burdened with a tremendous load of hostility. It came out in the frequency and the cruelty with which he attacked younger children and animals, and in his many verbal attacks against the adults when he discovered that these would not be punished. Instead of trying to identify with the teacher, he fought her on every occasion.

As the group was coming in from the playground one day, he savagely attacked a friendly little boy who got in his way. The teacher separated them quickly and firmly. Sam exclaimed, "That was fun." The teacher merely said, "It wasn't fun for Jim. It hurt him," and told Sam to wait outside. As soon as the others were taken care of, she returned and sat down beside him. They knew each other well, and she felt sure that he could accept her presence without feeling threatened by it.

"I wonder why it makes you feel good to hurt Jim and the other children," she speculated quietly, not knowing whether he could give her any cue. He immediately launched into a description of how his uncle had brought him a gun, and he and his "little friend" (an imaginary friend) could use it.

Again the teacher answered, "Sometimes it makes children feel big to have a gun and it makes them feel big to hurt someone. Do you ever feel that way?"

With apparent relief the child answered, "Yes." They discussed how people wanted to feel big and how sometimes it wasn't fun to be little. The teacher mentioned that being friendly sometimes made people feel big. Sam stuttered as he talked and was near tears, something that almost never happened with him. He seldom dared to relax his defenses enough to cry.

At last the teacher told Sam that it was about time for them to go inside. He said, almost crying, "I could stay out here until afternoon." "Yes," she said, "you could." She busied herself picking things up and then asked, "Well, now you can either come in with me or stay outside. I wonder which you are going to do?"

He got up and said rather sadly, "I don't know." At that the teacher knelt down and put her arms around this hurt, bewildered little boy and for the first time he could accept her loving and nestled close against her, no longer "tough." She said, "I know how it is," and then suggested, "You might paint a big picture inside." He nodded and took her hand, and they went inside. He went straight to the finger-painting table where there was an opportunity for him to express more of what he felt.

Sam gained in school and became better able to play with others. He was imaginative and resourceful and found a place for himself as his hostility decreased. When he left school, he was a less hostile child but still needed sensitive understanding. Although his mother had gained some insight into the child's problems, his father would accept none of this "sissy stuff" and continued to rely on repression and a generous use of the rod to bully his son into "good" behavior. It is interesting to note that when Sam was in high school some years later he excelled in athletics and became a person of importance there. He also received several awards for his artwork. He seemed to have found outlets for some of his earlier hostile aggressiveness.

To the Child, Even Friendly Adults May Seem To Be a Threat

All children, to some extent, are struggling with feelings of being little and helpless. Even friendly adults are so much stronger and more powerful than the child that they represent a potential threat. Children handle their feelings in different ways. When they are together in groups, they are quick to blame the adult for things that happen. We may overhear the following when Ricky (5.3) comes out on the playground and says to Nate (5.5), "Who covered up our holes?" "Oh, some teacher probably," replies Nate. Both these boys are friends with teachers, but they recognize in them the source of many interferences and frustrations as well as the source of needed support. They are glad to identify with each other against the teacher at times.

Craig (5.9) gives us another amusing example. He happened to throw some sand, which got into Celia's eye. Celia had to go inside and have the sand washed out of her eye. When she came back on the playground, Craig was very sympathetic and wanted to look into her eye. He said to her comfortingly, "I should have thrown it in the teacher's eye and then it wouldn't have hurt you, Celia."

Two children, Sandra (4.7) and Jennifer (4.5), are playing in the homemaking corner. Jennifer has set the table. Sandra sits down, saying, "I'm the father." They go through the motions of eating soup and as they pretend to eat, they turn to the mirror hanging on the wall by the table and talk to their reflections. Sandra says, "Shut up and eat your soup."

We see thus some of the sources of the child's hostility and resistances, some of the situations out of which these feelings arise. As adults we are concerned with helping children to express these feelings in ways that will not be damaging and yet will serve to reduce them or turn them into constructive channels. We need to understand the possible avenues of expression.

WHAT ARE POSSIBLE AVENUES FOR EXPRESSION OF FEELINGS?

Recognition of the feeling which needs to be changed is the first step the child must take if he is to "liquidate the feeling at its source," as Kubie (1948) suggests. The teacher who stops a child who is about to hit another child who has his favorite tricycle will say, "I know, Alan, you want the tricycle. It makes you cross at Will because he has it, but you must not hit. When you feel cross at someone because he has what you want, you can go over and take a good whack at our punching bag. That may help you." By words like these the teacher is helping the child identify his feelings. The child needs to know what feeling he is taking out on the punching bag. He needs to be *clear about the source of his feeling.*

Motor expressions, of course, offer the simplest, most direct means of draining off feeling for children. That is why hitting, pushing, and biting are common among young children. However, other more acceptable forms of expression along these lines can be utilized instead. Pounding at the workbench, hitting a soft material like clay, using a punching bag, biting on a rubber toy, throwing a ball against a backstop, or even running and digging can serve as an outlet for feelings in ways that do no damage to anyone. Some children give vent to their resentment at adult interferences by the hard pats they give each piece of paper they paste or by pounding clay.

The skillful teacher will accept the feeling and put it into words: "I know you feel like hitting him because he has the tricycle you want." She will channel the expression into acceptable behavior. "When you feel like that, you can hit our punching bag or pound the clay."

LANGUAGE IS ANOTHER AVENUE FOR EXPRESSION

Language is another type of outlet. The crying child relieves himself of a lot of feeling; so does the child who hurls angry words at an offender.

Young children may verbally destroy the teacher in all kinds of ways and tell her "to get dead." Such verbal expression relieves their feelings. They can see that it results in no harm to the teacher. She remains their friend. It is a satisfactory way at the child's level of "liquidating" feelings which might otherwise be a source of trouble. Later, as adults, these same children may use fantasy rather than verbal expression and be helped in relieving serious irritations, as Chisholm indicates in his *Prescription for Survival* (1957).

ART AND MUSIC ARE AVENUES, TOO

Art and music offer avenues for the expression of feeling. These avenues of expression are important because they may extend into the adult years and serve as a protection against the emotional load which adults must carry. If opportunities with art are to have value as a means of release for feeling, they must be experiences in which the child uses the medium in his own way. The child who paints the same motif or theme again and again is saying something about the way he feels through his pictures. He may do this through his work with clay or music, too. We need to conserve the values of art as an avenue of expression of feelings. These values are lost if art consists of copying patterns or models.

HOW THE TEACHER MEETS AGGRESSIVE BEHAVIOR

When feelings have many avenues of expression, they do not pile up and become so unmanageable. The teacher encourages expression even though she may face problems within the group situation. How can the teacher meet the needs of individuals and of groups?

THE TEACHER HELPS THE CHILDREN BY HER EXAMPLE

The teacher helps all children when she remains undisturbed herself in the face of aggressive behavior and does not meet anger with angry feelings in return. Because of her example, the children will find it less disturbing to meet the inevitable aggressions that occur in their world. The child who is most disturbed over being called a name is probably a child who has been severely reproved for name calling himself. Adults have attached importance to this kind of behavior. Children are likely to meet some rejection and some angry responses wherever they happen to be. If their own aggressive behavior has been met casually, they will find it easier to accept unruffled the attacks they receive. They are less afraid and better able to take the world as it is. In responding to aggressive behavior, the teacher can say, "We all feel this way sometimes." She is not upset by it because she does not accept it as a personal attack.

The Teacher Helps When She Accepts and Interprets Behavior

An important way to help is by interpreting to one child some reasons why another child is behaving as he is. She may reassure the first child by saying, "Never mind. He's calling you names because he's mad. It's your turn on the swing and he wants it to be his. It makes him feel better to call you 'dope.' You don't need to let it bother you."

She may help a child by showing him how to meet the rejection by explaining, "They want to play by themselves. It's all right. I'll help you find another place to play and you can look for someone who does want to play with you." She does not say, "But you must let him play," to the angry child who has shouted at another child, "You go away!" The newcomer will not be likely to have a successful experience with a person who feels unfriendly toward him.

There are solutions which protect the group while still respecting the needs of individuals. If the child who is excluding others is monopolizing the homemaking corner, the sandbox, or some other area, the teacher can say, "It's all right if you want to play by yourself, but all the children use the homemaking corner or the sandbox. You can make a house over in this corner and leave the rest for the children who do want to play together."

The Teacher May Need To Help Hostile and Insecure Children by Giving Them Techniques for Cooperating

Children need protection when they are unsure and suspicious of others, not denial of the way they feel. The demands of group life are complex. Children who are hostile and lacking in social skills may not be able to play with more than one child at a time. They may need to exclude others. The teacher helps when she accepts exclusion and makes it possible for them to be successful at their level.

Helping a child who is insecure and hostile to be successful may mean reducing the difficulties he faces. He may need to play with just one child at a time or with materials that can be shared easily or in situations that make few demands for adaptation. It may mean suggesting a desirable way to approach others before he fails in his approach. The teacher may say, "You might get a block and help John build the road," or, when another child approaches,

A child may cooperate by not interfering with his friend's work.

she may forestall failure by interpreting, "I think he would like to dig with you. I will help him find another shovel." Reducing the difficulty of a situation, forestalling and preventing failure are helpful techniques to use with children who find it difficult to accept others.

THE TEACHER HELPS BY PROVIDING A SUITABLE ENVIRONMENT

The teacher also helps the child handle the problem of his hostility and aggressiveness by a thoughtful planning of the environment and the program in the school. In a physical setup which is designed for him, the child will feel less hostility because he will meet fewer frustrations. He can get his own coat, find the play materials he wants within reach, solve his own problems in many ways, and submit to fewer limitations. The program, as well as the physical setup, can be designed to reduce, rather than increase, interferences and frustrations. If it is flexible and imposes only essential limitations, it meets individual needs in a way that minimizes hostility. Under this kind of program, teachers become people who help rather than people who interfere with the child.

THE TEACHER ACTS WITH FIRMNESS

The teacher helps the aggressive, resentful child when she is confident and firm in her management. The child needs firmness, not punishment. He may want to feel that someone else is to blame, but his teacher will accept only his need to wish that this were so; she does not accept this as fact. She is sympathetic but firm in dealing with his behavior and in facing the reality of the situation. She states it clearly for him. She has confidence that he will be able to face it, too. She tries to help him deal with his feelings directly, in a constructive way. Her firmness helps steady the angry child and reassure the insecure child.

Punishment does not help a hostile, resentful child. It only increases his burden of feeling. Firm action by the teacher may be essential for him so that he does not hurt others and thus add to his burden of guilt. For example, the teacher acted firmly, in the case of Sam, who used biting as a way of attacking. She knew she must prevent biting when she could, and yet she had to help him use acceptable means of relieving himself of the tremendous load of resentment and the feeling of helplessness he carried. If she had punished or rejected this child because of his behavior, she could have offered him no help. The already overburdened little boy would have had to find his way out alone, or fail.

We should act promptly to stop some kinds of behavior, but we need not do this in a punishing way. We can remove a disturbing child from the group or hold him firmly, but we do not have to blame him for his actions. We do not try to make him feel more ashamed or even to apologize. Making a child say he is sorry usually means making him say something false. Truth is important. Later he may say he is sorry when he really feels this way. Our responsibility is to help him find nondamaging channels for the expression of the resentment he is feeling. When he is relieved of this feeling, he is ready for other feelings and other expressions of feelings.

SOME CHILDREN NEED SPECIAL HELP

When a child is very seriously burdened with hostile feelings, he may need special help. He may be given this help within the group by assigning one teacher or an aide to be with him and to help him manage his feelings. With this kind of individual help, he may be successful. A teacher reported this observation of a child who attacked others on little or no apparent provocation. He had had a great deal of punishment and little real discipline. As he started to hit savagely another child who interfered with him, the teacher caught his arm and held it firmly, saying at the same time, "I think you must feel very angry." He looked at her in surprise, without resisting, and then nodded in agreement. Suddenly he turned and hugged her. The teacher knew how he felt and he was safe. She returned his hug and added, "Next time you feel angry, I will try to help you again."

The child who acts out his hostility may be serving a function for the whole group. He is acting it out for them, in a sense, and they learn what happens by watching him and the way his behavior is handled. If it is handled firmly, without anger, all children feel more comfortable. They have more confidence that their own angry feelings can be managed, if not by them at least by the teacher. We can observe this behavior when one child takes the place of another who misbehaves if the latter child is absent. There is always a "difficult" child. The children are learning how to manage their feelings by observing each other and by responding to others.

Every group will contain some children who are likely to express hostility in aggressive ways. Most of them can be helped within the framework of the group to handle their hostile feelings acceptably. An occasional child may need individual therapy outside the group in addition to help within the group.

PARTICIPATION IN A GROUP HAS SPECIAL VALUE FOR THE TIMID CHILD

The value that group participation possesses for many timid children is worth attention. Timid, inhibited children are greatly helped in expressing their feelings by the safety they find within the group. It provides them with an environment in which it is easier for them to accept their hostile feelings. These children will benefit greatly from the "freeing" of expression that comes in attending a good school. Children in groups may resort to verbal defiance of the teacher when there is some reason for resisting her. They feel strength in being together, and this feeling is one of the values that group experience holds for them. With people of their own age who are also feeling and expressing hostility, they are no longer so afraid of their feelings and behavior. Not as "good" in the conventional sense, they become healthier from the mental hygiene standpoint and capable of achieving a higher degree of emotional maturity.

Ben (3.3) is an example of a child who learned to express his real feelings. He was a quiet, timid child who remained dependent on the teacher for a long time after he entered the school. He usually found a place beside her when she sat down, and often held onto her skirt when she moved around the school. When he played, he would select the small toys and take them into a corner. He was not active and vigorous and was never aggressive toward others. Very slowly he began to join the other children in play and to identify himself with the group. He seemed pleased when they shouted names or chanted silly or "naughty" words. Finally he dared to express himself in this way, too. One day he was even a member of a group who defied the teacher from the safe height of the jungle gym.

It was at about this time that some movies taken at the school happened to be shown one morning. A picture of Ben's teacher appeared on the screen. Laughing, Ben went up to the screen and slapped her image. It was probably no accident that he chose the teacher's image. That act may have symbolized the strength and the freedom to be aggressive which he was feeling. With that slap he proved that he had left his dependence behind. His relationship with the teacher was a friendly one, but he was no longer tied to her skirt as he had been in the beginning. Ben had known plenty of love at home but not much chance to express the resentments that he inevitably felt. As soon as he dared to be aggressive, to express what he felt, he became more active and social. He had no great amount of hostility to release. Soon he was able to maintain and accept the limits which the teachers set for the group. He developed rapidly.

We may summarize what we have been saying about hostility and aggression by pointing out that we must: (1) accept the existence of these feelings; (2) see that they are expressed in some acceptable way, but as directly as possible, so that the individual will be freed from the emotional load that he will otherwise carry; and (3) learn how to handle children without creating in them unnecessary feelings of hostility and resentment which make good social adjustment difficult.

Reducing the amount of frustration a young child has to meet, building up his feelings of security and confidence, accepting him as he is rather than "nudging" him into being something different will all help in the solution of the problems which these feelings present to any individual or any form of group life.

PROJECTS

1. Observe and record two situations in which a child faced frustration (was unable to carry out a purpose). How did he try to cope with the situation? What feelings did he express at the time? Later?

2. Report an observation of a child using an appropriate defense; an inappropriate defense. Give reasons for your evaluation in each case. Describe the different kinds of defenses which you have observed children using. Why were they used?

3. Observe and record a situation in which a teacher helped an angry child put his feelings into words.

SUPPLEMENTARY READING

Child Study Association of America. *Behavior: The Unspoken Language of Children.* New York: CSAA, 1967.

Escalona, S. *Understanding Hostility in Children.* Chicago: Science Research, 1954.

Issacs, S. *Childhood and After.* New York: International Universities Press, 1949, Chapter 3.

Redl, F. *When We Deal with Children.* New York: Free Press, 1966.

Sears, R., E. Macoby, and H. Levin. *Patterns of Child Rearing.* Evanston, Ill.: Row Peterson, 1957, Chapter 7.

14

Cinderalla
(girl, 4.2)

Dramatic Play—
Avenue for Insight

Susan (2.11) was in the kitchen with her mother who was preparing for a tea party. "You may put the cup cakes on this big plate," said her mother in answer to Susan's wish to "help." Pleased at the task, Susan carefully placed the cakes one by one on the plate until it was covered. Then she faced a dilemma. There were several cup cakes left, but there was no more space to fit them on the plate. She stood looking, uncertain and thoughtful, and then she began placing each remaining cup cake exactly on top of one of those already on the plate. They fit, and Susan exclaimed with delight, "Look, caps!"

This incident illustrates how a young child treats a simple task in a playful way, solving a problem with imagination and enjoying achievement. Healthy children spend much of their waking time in play. Play lies at the heart of a school program for young children. It becomes important for the teacher of young children to observe and try to understand what play reveals.

In this chapter we will look at children's dramatic play and the contribution it makes to healthy personality development, as well as the insight it gives us into what the child is thinking and feeling. In a later section on Curriculum we will be considering play as a mode of learning.

Dramatic play consists of activities that are imitative or representational, in which the child assumes the roles of people whom he knows as he under-

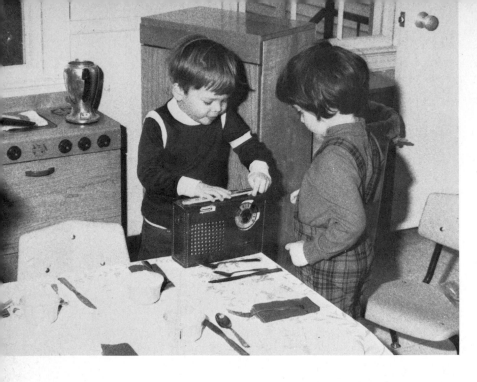

Children enact roles as they understand them.

stands their roles. It may also involve activities in which the child tries to communicate thoughts and feelings symbolically through the use of objects or actions. Dramatic play may be carried on by a child aione or by several children together, in which case it becomes sociodramatic play.

CHILDREN PLAY FOR MANY REASONS

There are many reasons why children play. They play because it gives them *pleasure,* as was the case with the child who was delighted with her creation of "caps." They play because they have an *urge to explore and discover.* The infant discovers his fingers at one stage and spends time moving them and gazing at them intently. The preschool child is absorbed as he pours water into the sand, watching how it runs down the channels he has dug. Children also play because of an urge to *master a skill* or *solve a problem.* A toddler will return again and again to a stairway, climbing up and coming down until he does it easily. Another child will persist in riding a tricycle until he rides with skill. Children play *to make friends* for it is one important way that young children form relationships with one another. Play also serves as a means of *mastering the emotional problems* that inevitably come with growth. It is essentially *creative,* involving all the child's capacities. Play leads to the integration of personality.

Dramatic play may occur as part of any activity. It is most likely to occur when children are playing together, trying to understand and make sense out of what they see and hear, and mastering feelings of fear, anxiety, or anger.

Children Use Dramatic Play as a Way To Master Feelings

As we have pointed out in previous chapters, every child has feelings which he needs to drain off. Children have many fears—the fear of being left or deserted, the fear of being little and helpless, or of being hurt, and sometimes the fear of their own violent impulses. As we watch children at play, we observe how often they take the role of the one who goes away and leaves or the one who punishes or controls. By reversing roles in play the child restores his own confidence.

Here is an example of a child's play that shows us his efforts to master conflict by reversing roles. David (3.3) is playing by himself with some small doll figures and furniture, while the teacher sits nearby. He talks to himself as he plays. A comfortable, happy child, his words nevertheless reveal something of the conflict all children feel during the process of socialization. He puts the smallest doll in a bed, saying, "She has to stay right in her bed. If she makes a noise, I'm going to spank her little bottom—spank her little bottom—spank her little bottom." He turns to the teacher. "She's a nasty little girl because she got up and made a noise, didn't she? She's a nasty little girl. She has to go sound to sleep." He turns back to the doll and continues as if two people were talking together. "Quit doing that. I'm just going to stay downstairs all day. Shut up. It's not daytime. It's still nighttime. I want to stay up all day. Do you want to peepee or not? You're not going to peepee. Stay right in your bed." In this play David is handling some of his feelings about toilet training and going to bed. He is probably reassured by the teacher's presence, although she makes no comments. He feels her acceptance. She is there to steady him if the play should become too disturbing.

In dramatic play children often act out aggressive, destructive feelings. It is important to accept them in play, being sure only that the children are safe and that the impulses are under control and kept on the pretend level. An adult may need to remain near to "steady" a group that is acting out negative feeling, as in a war game or a fire play. It is important to the children to know that they can stop or that they will be stopped before they do real harm. Without this help the play may not serve the purpose of draining off hostility and keeping it within manageable proportion. It may only increase the anxiety of some children about their ability to handle their impulses. As adults we should have no hesitation about making a suggestion, redirecting or limiting play which we can see is going "out of bounds."

In redirecting play, we do not want to deny expression to negative feeling. We must avoid an adult tendency to want only "good" behavior. Here is an example. Ruth, Marilyn, and Gordon are pretending they are lions. Marilyn, who is an inhibited child, says, "I'm a good lion." Gordon says, "Don't eat me up." Lions seem to fascinate him because of their dangerous possibilities. Marilyn changes her role. It's safer. "Don't eat me up," she says.

Ruth boldly says, "I'm a mean lion," and chases Gordon. Then she stops and asks him, "Are you a mean lion?" When he answers "Yes," Marilyn feels braver and says, "I am too." "Pretend you can't get us," says Ruth. Gordon answers with, "I'm going to eat you up." Unfortunately, at this point a teacher steps in and tells them to be "good lions," and they drop the lion play. It no longer serves a purpose for them. Marilyn, who has conformed to high standards of good behavior and has paid a price in loss of creativity, had just reached the point of joining Ruth and Gordon in daring to be a "mean" lion. The teacher's words close this avenue of escape from adult demands for Marilyn. It is interesting to get further insight into what Marilyn is seeking by watching her subsequent play. A few minutes later she climbed up high in the jungle gym and says, "This is dangerous."

Being little and often helpless, and being unable to comprehend fully what is taking place inevitably creates some degree of anxiety and resentment in every child. Life becomes more manageable for the child because he can escape at times into play. Winnicott (1957) tells us that, "In the preschool years play is the child's principal means of solving the emotional problems that belong to development" (p. 22).

Play which is repeated by individuals and by groups is almost sure to have meaning for them. We need to try to understand what its meaning is if we are to offer sound help. It is probably neither accident nor perversity that makes a child knock over things or throw them down. We must remember that he himself has tumbled many times. He has been startled, and perhaps hurt, by falling in the course of learning to walk. He may recover some assurance by making other things fall and thus reduce the threat which falls have offered to him. We know that children are frightened by sudden, loud noises and yet as soon as they are able, they pound and bang, making all the noise they can. In this way they may be better able to handle the fear they have felt. Because they can make noises themselves, they are less disturbed by noise. The child who lives with adults who disapprove of noisemaking on his part, or who consider knocking over block towers as destructive and useless play, may carry a burden of unresolved fear and anxiety.

Guns are one of the props in play which children use in coping with the feelings which go with being little or helpless. The smallest boy may be the one who uses the biggest gun or perhaps two guns. Guns are a part of the world we live in, and we can hardly deny them to children as they try to recreate this world. They serve a role in helping a child to overcome the feeling of being little and help in the efforts he makes to find his place in the adult world. We can, however, verbalize to him our own feelings about guns and our hope that some day they will not have such a place in the world. We can disapprove of guns just as we show our disapproval of expressions of violence. We can also set limits on where guns may be used, limits such as use outdoors only or not to frighten other children, in order to reduce the stimulation which guns often produce and which sometimes becomes more than a hostile child can manage.

Many Kinds of Feelings Are Revealed in Play

Unable to bring out feelings directly, children sometimes hide them under what they feel is the safer guise of pretending to make a joke, just as adults often do, or they may pretend that they are acting a part. A three-year-old, who had been hurt and frightened repeatedly by what had happened in his world until he could not bear to face reality, used to deny that he was "Bill" and insisted that he was an "elephant." As an elephant he felt free to trample over the other children's materials, to resist the adults, and to escape from being the poor, frightened little boy that he really was. In time he grew to feel more secure with one of the teachers and sure of her support. This relationship gave him confidence. He began to drop the role of an elephant and dared to be Bill, taking some responsibility for his own behavior.

It is always interesting to note what children consider funny. Understanding humor is one cue in understanding the kind of adjustment a person is making. Children's dramatic play often has a humorous quality, but underneath the humor may lie disguised meanings. We must be aware that feelings of many kinds are likely to be expressed under the acceptable guise of a joke.

One child tickles another with a leaf that he is carrying. They both laugh, for his gesture expressed friendliness. Another child tickles a companion with a leaf and the child objects. He senses the attacking quality which exists under the apparent playfulness of the gesture and resents it.

Simon (4.6), who is struggling hard to establish a sense of a masculine role in the world, is making a mask at Halloween. He says, "I want a *man* witch. I don't like girls." His father is a withdrawn person, defensive and aloof. His mother clings to Simon, is overdirective, and possessive. But Simon is valiantly making the effort to identify himself with male things, even male witches. At times he dresses up in skirts and then tries to defend himself by rejecting all girls. His conflicts are revealed in his play.

It has been clearly established that dramatic play has therapeutic value for children. We need to recognize and accept this fact. Such acceptance does not imply that teachers are in a position to undertake play therapy in the more technical sense of the term. But in school, however, children need to have plenty of opportunity to play out feelings, try out roles, clarify concepts through their own spontaneous dramatizations, and thus benefit from the therapeutic values of dramatic play.

Through his dramatic play the child may also be communicating feelings and ideas. With only limited ability to express himself in language or words, he uses actions to represent in symbolic ways what he is feeling and thinking. The child's struggle with jealous feelings after the arrival of a new baby, for example, may be expressed in his destructive behavior with some object which he uses as an outlet. His apparent fascination with covering up objects may be a communication about his concern over the disappearance of people important to him or with finding an answer to something hidden from him. We should look carefully at play behavior which occurs repeatedly and try to understand what the child may be trying to tell us.

CHILDREN WHO ARE UNABLE TO PLAY

Sometimes we find a child who seems to be unable to enter into play, whether on his own or with others. He is likely to be a child who lacks a basic sense of trust in some respect. He may be overwhelmed by the anxieties or the anger he feels. One child whose parent sometimes acted with violence, shouting or throwing objects, was unable to engage in much play at home or at school. In the nursery school his play was limited to riding a tricycle around in circles or just watching other children. He seldom explored materials, and he had not developed much speech. He seemed to feel the world was a dangerous place. He trusted no one, including himself. His teacher's first task was to establish herself as a completely reliable person who accepted him in every way, whatever he did. After many weeks he began, hesitantly, to play near other children when his teacher was with him. Then he began to use materials more aggressively and to act out some of his fears. Before many months, he was playing almost joyfully with other children although he needed "his" teacher with him at first. He had learned to trust in this situation and had begun to reach out to play with others. He also began to communicate with speech.

Murphy (1956, 1962) provides us with vivid descriptions of normal children of this age coping with stress. Her case studies of children with her interpretations of their behavior help us understand better how children can use play to help them cope with crises such as the arrival of a new baby in the home, entering a new school, going to a birthday party, or having a seriously ill parent.

There are times in the lives of all children when they are not free to play because they are overwhelmed by the new, the strange, or the feared. A child may become overwhelmed at times of illness, accidents, death, or family problems. Demands to perform beyond his ability or teasing can overwhelm him. Economically disadvantaged families are more likely to have chronic stress, but some chronic stress can be found across all economic groups. Situational stress will affect all children from time to time. It is critical that all children who cannot play or whose play is disorganized and aggressive find a trustworthy, reliable adult in their school or day-care center. They need a teacher who will not push them to be busy, but rather one who will take time to build a trusting relationship and will help them find ways to cope with their particular stresses.

FANTASY AND IMAGINATION IN DRAMATIC PLAY

Fantasy and reality are often confused in young children's thinking. What they think seems true to them whether or not it is true in reality. Children need help and time to make the distinction between reality and fantasy without having to reject their fantasies. They have a right to imagine and to create fantasies as well as a need to learn to identify reality.

Francis (3.3) is at the table playing with the playdough. He rolls it with a rolling pin and pats it. He talks softly to himself. "Is that a birthday cake? Where are some candles?" He reaches and gets some cut straws and places them on the playdough. He then turns to a teacher sitting near and says, "I don't want to sing." The teacher assures him that it is all right to have a birthday cake and not sing. He blows two very hard puffs and says, "I blew it out," adding, "Where is the knife?" The teacher hands the knife to him. He says, "A *really* birthday because I'm cutting the cake. It must be real because I'm cutting it. I blew out the candles and I'm cutting it."
Teacher: "You pretended to blow out the candles, didn't you?"
Francis: "Yes, but I'm really cutting it." He hands the teacher a piece, and he keeps a piece.
Teacher: "You really cut it, but we'll have to pretend to eat it."
Francis: "Ya." A slight frown comes across his face. He then runs across the room to Jamie, who is building with blocks. "Superman, I cut the cake for you. I pretended it was my birthday."
Jamie smiles but makes no comment. Francis runs back to the table, picks up the clock, and runs to Jamie with it. "See what I got for my birthday?"
Jamie: "Why?"
Francis: "Because it's my birthday, and it's brand new."
Jamie: "Not your birthday."
Francis: "I pretended. I made a cake."

Francis, as are most three- and four-year-old children, is coping with the problem of the real and the pretend, and is well on his way to finding pleasure in both. He makes the distinction in "I cut the cake. I pretended it was my birthday."

At five years of age, Valerie finds it easier to differentiate fantasy and reality.

Valerie (5.3), who is very fond of a teacher in a younger group, visits the group often. Today she enters with a tool box in her hand and smiles at Mrs. M who is very involved with a group of toddlers, but says hello to Valerie. Valerie says to Mrs. M in a businesslike way, "What's to fix?" Mrs. M responds, "The door knob; it's very loose." Valerie spends a few minutes pretending to fix the door knob, and then asks, "What else?" "My car; it has a new squeak," replies the teacher and gestures toward the driving bench. Valerie walks about halfway across the room, stops, and says to the teacher, "Are you pretending the radiator is your car?" "No," answers the teacher, "the driving bench." Valerie continues across the room to the driving bench.

Valerie's thinking is flexible enough that she can step out of her role in the play, ask a reality question, and then return to her role again. She can step in and out of pretend when she is the initiator of the change—that is, when she controls the flow of the play. In situations where she does not have such control, she may not differentiate reality and fantasy so easily. For example, she knows that the superheroes are pretend characters, but she can still be frightened by their awesome power.

It is sometimes a struggle for children to get the real world and the world of magic into their proper places. A child is fortunate when he has help from a parent or a teacher in this learning. His imaginative tales can be valued for what they are, delightful figments of the imagination, a method of escape which we can all profit from at times. It is fun to make up stories, but one should be clear about the differences between the "pretend" and the factual. A few children will "turn their backs" on reality and use fantasy to escape from painful experience. Such fantasy isolates the child from his peers, his teacher, and the learning situation. A lonely, isolated child who consistently escapes into fantasy requires professional assessment.

The teacher does not discourage the use of imagination by children; rather, she encourages it. Imagination is valuable. We know that "hunches" and "brain storming" often produce worthwhile ideas with adults. Children are naturally good at using their imaginations. As they become clearer about reality and fantasy, they have fun making up fanciful stories as well as describing real experiences. They enjoy games of pretending such as, "Wouldn't it be funny if. . . ." or, "This looks like a. . . ."

SOCIODRAMATIC PLAY

Four- and five-year-old children spend more time in sociodramatic play than do three-year-olds. They are capable of more sustained relationships with their peers. They find friends in play and accommodate their desires. They have a better command of language, which enables them to share ideas. In playing they recreate homemaking scenes, scenes from television, or scenes from stories, and often mix them in rapid shifts. They plan and make decisions,

Properties may help four- and five-year-old children sustain relationships in play.

that quickly change as the drama unfolds. They are resourceful and imaginative in using props and actions. In playing with others, a child begins to understand that others may be sad, happy, frustrated, afraid, or that others may want to possess or be first. He learns, too, that he can stand up for himself and find ways to influence others. Children often develop remarkable social skills as they play together. Play with others seems to be essential for healthy personality development.

Smilansky (1971:42–43), after a study of children's self-initiated socio-dramatic play, concluded that, "Socio-dramatic play behavior develops three main areas in a child, all of which are essential parts, not only of play, but also of the school game and the game of life."

According to Smilansky, "The first main aspect is *creativity,* based on utilization of past experience and controlled by the demands of the framework." The imaginative "Let's pretend," which is based on understanding and modified by the necessity of adjusting to the ideas of others, is an important part of living itself. This imaginative element in spontaneous play is part of the creative approach to experience so valuable in the scientist and artist.

"The second aspect is *intellectual growth,* which includes the power of abstraction, widening of concept and acquisition of new knowledge." In

The group is re-creating a social gathering with the usual telephone conversation.

playing together children share their ideas and concepts about the world around them. Language is important here, and children use language more freely in sociodramatic play than at most other times.

"The third aspect is *social skills,* which includes positive give and take, tolerance and consideration." These social skills develop in carrying on episodes of family or community life when children must use techniques for getting along with others for achieving purposes or constructing settings.

As teachers we enrich the play by supplying needed accessories and by suggesting techniques that seem to be lacking in getting along with others. Thoughtful observation before stepping in to make suggestions or offer materials is as important as in material in any other area. Later, children will go on to playing group games with rules, a very different kind of play and one which emphasizes only a few skills at a time.

Here is an example of the play of two four-year-old boys which seems influenced by television in the beginning, but turns into a familiar picnic situation in the end.

Kevin and Michael were playing together in the housekeeping corner. After rearranging the furniture, they picked up the suitcases. Michael opened his. It was full of clothes and other articles. Kevin opened his and seemed disappointed because it was empty. Michael poured some of the contents of his suitcase into Kevin's. He then proceeded to put on some dark glasses and picked up the suitcase and left. Kevin called good-bye to him.

Michael came back into the housekeeping corner, saying to Kevin, who was playing with a string of beads, "We're robbers. Come on, robber."

"They'll be here in seven minutes. Call the police," Kevin answered him.

Michael picked up the phone and pretended he was calling the police.

"They're coming right away," said Michael.

"Call the cowboys," said Kevin. "Come on, let's hurry; go on outside and I'll be there in a minute before the cowboys come. Go on outside, don't walk on the lawn. I'll be with you in a moment." Michael went outside the housekeeping corner.

"Come on back in; we'll eat a light supper first," Kevin said. "Hurry up, now, hurry up. If you don't want to set the table, I will," he added. (All this time Kevin was separating the plastic beads as he talked.)

Kevin told Michael to get some more silverware and put it in the suitcase.

Michael made a sound like a siren.

Kevin said, "Put more silverware in the suitcase."

"Let's take the plates, too," Michael replied. He got the cups, more plates, and silverware. They worked together to shut the suitcase.

"Now let's go," said Kevin, and they ran out of the housekeeping corner into the adjoining room and unpacked the suitcase.

"We're having a picnic," said Kevin. Kevin filled the sugar and creamer with water. They set out the dishes. Michael had previously put a phone in the suitcase, so he took it out. They pretended to eat. Michael picked up the phone and made a call. "Let's drink some more tea," said Kevin, and they did.

"Would you help me snap these beads together, Michael?" asked Kevin. "You'd better."

So Michael started putting the beads together. "You make you a string, and I'll add onto mine," Kevin said.

Michael replied, "Leave a lot for me. Here, I'll put some more in a cup for you and some for me." They put the beads together, working very hard.

Kim came in and Michael popped up and said, "We're playing house, and you can't come in."

Kevin repeated this.

Kim stood on one side watching. Kevin and Michael then packed everything in the suitcase and returned to the other room.

Kevin and Michael are friends. Each makes suggestions that the other accepts. They improvise as they play. Themes and roles change. Robbers, cowboys, police, and family roles mix. Michael refers to Kevin who seems to be the leader, but who does not dominate the play. Michael makes his own suggestions, too. They start by playing together in the housekeeping area and sharing materials there. Then Michael leaves, putting on dark glasses and carrying a suitcase, perhaps taking the role of a father leaving for work, but he soon returns with the suggestion, "We're robbers." The play becomes more animated. They hurry. They call the police, then the cowboys, while Kevin warns, "Don't walk on the lawn," a prohibition which may have puzzled him at some time. They both seem to feel that in being robbers they are playing a dangerous role, and calling the police helps them. After each move made as robbers, they seem to find reassurance in deciding to pretend to eat, a familiar homemaking activity. Having called the police, they decide to "have a light supper first." After having taken the silverware and dishes, they decide to have a picnic and they pretend to eat and later begin playing with beads in a very ordinary play situation.

They have played out a series of situations which have an element of fear and anxiety and which they do not understand. They have found some resolution. They are ready for less exciting play. One feels they are reassured and ready to end the episodes. They have made a point of sharing with each other, but they exclude Kim when she tries to join them. They show us how much confusion exists for them in regard to roles different people play. Their play illustrates the creativity, the sharing of ideas, the use of language, and the social relationships which take place during dramatic play among children who are friends.

TELEVISION IS LIKELY TO IMPOVERISH AND DISTORT PLAY

Television is having an effect on the dramatic play of young children. Patterns appear in the child's play that are a reflection of what he has seen on the screen. In some of the portrayals of aggressive behavior on television programs, children seem to find patterns for playing out their own aggressive feelings. While we are not sure what the effect of television may be on young children, we can be certain that it is desirable for the child to reenact what he sees on television programs. In this way he is doing something about what he sees, trying to understand it better and make it less frightening. At the same time it is important to remember that if these roles are too frightening, disorganizing, or cause a child to lose control, playing them out will not enable him to cope. Rather, it will do the very opposite. Teachers must redirect, limit, or stop this play, as well as accept the child's feelings and let him know she is protecting him. The evidence from studies so far suggests that parents are wise to protect young children from the terrifying, incomprehensible material which too often makes up television viewing for them.

Most children today do a lot of television viewing. The viewing limits a child's time for play, which is his natural avenue for learning. Play is an active process in which the child is doing and imagining, while television viewing is a passive process.

Television is a mass media. It cannot be adapted to the individual needs of children and their individual readiness to cope or to learn. The personal element so necessary for the young child is lacking. Misconceptions may not be discovered and cleared up. Amassing facts, partially understood, does not promote sound learning. For older children television can and does offer material that broadens their horizons, just as reading does, with television adding the vividness of pictures and movement. For young children, however, the excitement, speed, noise, and constantly changing stimuli are probably bewildering and overwhelming. Children lack the background for interpreting the rapidly changing sequence of events. Children need actual, concrete experiences that they can control in some way, and television does not offer such experiences. Young children believe what they see on television. They are still trying to sort out what is actual from what is fantasy or fiction, and television does not make this process easier for them.

Violence is often what children see as they watch television. Young children are still in an "acting out" stage, and have not developed much "inner control" as yet. Their impulses are strong. They tend to hit, bite, or kick. They are not sure of the difference between acceptable and unacceptable behavior. With few exceptions, television makes little distinction between acceptable and unacceptable behavior. Conflicts are resolved by violence. One must conclude that television viewing does not belong in a good school program for young children.

THE TEACHER'S ROLE IN DRAMATIC PLAY

The teacher who values the spontaneous play of young children provides plenty of uninterrupted time in the schedule for such play. She may find that there will be more of this kind of play after the children become acquainted with each other and thus better able to sustain constructive, creative relationships with small groups of friends. Some children need a more structured situation than others. They may not trust themselves enough at first to play freely in an unstructured situation. Children differ in their play needs as they do in other ways. In providing for play, the teacher makes it possible for children to satisfy different styles of playing behavior.

Besides allowing time for play the teacher provides the properties needed to encourage dramatic play as she observes the themes or roles in which the children seem interested. Homemaking play is a universal theme and should be well provided for from the beginning. The properties should include dolls and doll clothes, dishes, a table, chairs, stove, sink, two telephones, and so on. The doll family should be large with more than one "baby." In one group the favorite doll was a baby doll with eyes painted shut as though she were sleeping. There should be black and brown dolls. A full length mirror with a box of "dress up" clothes, including masculine items like ties, belts, caps as well as feminine items like scarves and shawls, all add to the play possibilities. Most four- and five-year-old children improvise in their play. Items which suggest themes such as a fireman's hat or a painter's cap and some large paint brushes can enhance their imaginations.

Dramatic play will be enriched by trips in the community to observe what goes on there. Trips to a fire station, to a building under construction, to a farm or dairy, and to a store broaden the children's horizons and add to the roles they may rehearse in play. The teacher helps make more explicit what they may have experienced by recalling with them afterward what they saw or did on the trip.

Play supervision that is thoughtful and unobtrusive is important. Children may need and welcome a suggestion, but they may not need or want direction. They may want to feel sure there is a teacher available and interested. The teacher may participate in a role in dramatic play, in which case she guides rather than directs. Turning this kind of play into a teaching situation may distort the value of the play for the children involved. Children enjoy learning, and they enjoy playing.

Teachers and also parents learn from spending as much time as possible observing unobtrusively and making notes on the play behavior of children. Reading over a series of notes about the play of an individual or of a group may give the teacher insight into the children's concerns and interests and indicate where help may be needed. Staff members can discuss the notes, and they may find they understand better a child's behavior or learning difficulties. Dramatic play offers an avenue for insight for the attentive teacher. She will be rewarded by this glimpse into the spontaneous play world of childhood.

PROJECTS

During an observation period in nursery school, day-care center, or kindergarten, observe and record a dramatic play situation which occurs. What roles do the children take? Is there a leader? What seems to hold the group together? What ideas or feeling do they seem to be expressing? What kinds of satisfactions does the play seem to be giving them?

SUPPLEMENTARY READING

Axline, V. *Play Therapy*. New York: Ballantine, 1969.

Cuffaro, H. K. Re-evaluating basic premises: Curricula free of sexism. *Young Children*, 1975, *30* (6):469–477.

Curry, N. E. *Current issues in play: Theoretical and practical considerations for its use as a curricular tool in the pre-school*. Pittsburgh: Arsenal Family and Children's Center, 1972.

Hartley, R., L. Frank, and R. Goldenson. *Understanding Children's Play*. New York: Columbia Univ. Press, 1957, Chapter 5.

Peller, L. E. Models of children's play. In R. E. Herron and B. Sutton-Smith, eds., *Child's Play*. New York: Wiley, 1971.

Winn, M. *The Plug-in Drug: Television, Childhood and the Family*. New York: Viking, 1977.

Part Four

CURRICULUM

15

*Self Portrait
(girl, 5.0)*

The Process of Learning
in Early Childhood

The organization of the physical environment, ways of teaching and guidance procedures are all geared to a common aim: to support the young child's learning. It is now time to look more closely at the learning process itself and how children are helped to develop strategies for thinking and reasoning, to cope with feelings, and to learn adaptive ways of behaving.

DEFINITION OF LEARNING

Learning is a change in behavior that occurs as a result of experience. To be useful to teachers two words from this definition need further explanation: *change* and *behavior*.

In learning we are concerned about change with regard to its direction and its description. The change should be in the direction of competence, coping, and adaptation. To describe change we must be able to describe what the child can do at one point in time and then describe what he can do at a later time. That is, knowing that a child can make a loose knot when tying his shoes tells his teacher just where he is in the process of learning to tie his shoes. When with time and practice he can tie a firm knot consistently, we can say his skills have changed or that he has learned to tie his shoe.

247

Learning and behavior are not the same. A child's behavior may change as a result of fatigue, hunger, illness, medication, level of motivation, or affective state. For example, the child who can usually tie his shoe may not be able to perform at his usual level of competence for any one of the above reasons. Learning cannot be observed; what can be observed is the behavior or performance of the child. We make inferences about learning on the basis of what the child does or does not do, says or does not say.

INDIVIDUAL DIFFERENCES IN PACE AND RATE OF LEARNING

At any age there are large individual differences in the pace, rate, and efficiency of learning. As a child matures, his learning proceeds with increased efficiency. Each child has his own pace, and this pace may be constant for similar tasks, although different in varied tasks. For example, Evie (5.10) was already learning to read. Her motivation was great, her pace was fast, and she mastered to a high degree each new learning related to reading. Her mastery of gross motor learning was slow. She had learned to walk late, and each subsequent motor skill was slowly acquired and then utilized at a methodical pace. Her quick-moving teacher was challenged to supply meaningful materials and activities to support Evie's interest and rapid rate in learning to read. At the same time, her teacher also had to help Evie to learn that she moved more slowly than her teacher and most of her peers. Evie was helped to learn to plan, anticipate, and begin action ahead of others in situations that mattered to her. The teacher took into account the child's feelings, and this support later enabled the child to take into account others' feelings. It is difficult for a child to speed up or slow down his pace. Being constantly reminded to hurry up or to slow down is damaging to one's self-esteem and takes the pleasure out of doing. Gradually, over time, children can learn to anticipate, plan ahead, maintain their own speed, and take others into account.

CONDITIONS THAT FACILITATE LEARNING

Learning is best carried on under relatively conflict-free conditions. For the best use of the child's capacities, there should be an element of surprise or uncertainty or some disequilibrium in the learning situation, such as an unanswered question or an unresolved ambiguity. Conditions that favor intellectual growth are those in which the child feels secure and relatively free from conflicts and has confidence in himself and in his ability to cope with the problems presented. He does not learn readily when he is discouraged and sees little hope of success, or when he feels alienated from others.

In order to learn, the child must want to learn. A motivated child who is actively involved with people, objects, and events is the most efficient learner. His activity must include both motor and mental involvement with his environment. Young children enjoy all kinds of movement, both fine and gross motor activities, indoors and outdoors. They learn by being active, exploring what they can do with their own bodies, and discovering what they can do with materials and equipment.

Children also learn by attending to selected aspects of their environment; attention implies active selection on the part of the child. Active minds and bodies construct and reconstruct relationships among people, objects, and events.

In order to be on the side of the child who wishes to learn, we must remember that the child has learned a great deal before he enters school. He has had many experiences, and he understands his world on the basis of these experiences. He already "knows" a great deal, and our teaching must be based on a knowledge of and a feeling for his understandings. It is important for him not to skip any stages, psychosocial or intellectual, in his development.

These ideas about learning apply to all children, but with special force to those children whom we have labeled "deprived" or "underprivileged." They are children who, at earlier stages, have missed opportunities for experiences that are important to their functioning well in school. They need to go back and experience what was lacking rather than attempt learning at a higher level. Some of these children need opportunities to learn to trust adults and themselves before they are ready to make choices and become responsible for their own learning. Learning depends on a measure of autonomy built on trust. Children need firsthand opportunities on which to build the concepts required for understanding number, for reading, or for any other traditional concepts and skills that the culture requires.

Our task, then, is to understand where the child is with regard to his feelings, his competencies, and his understandings. We need to observe children, consult with parents who have guided their children's earlier learning, and build a teacher-child relationship that is beneficial for each child. On this basis, we are ready to guide the child's learning in a group.

PERCEIVING: FOUNDATIONS FOR LEARNING

The child learns about the world around him through his perceptions—looking, listening, feeling, tasting, smelling, and moving. His interactions with people, his actions on objects and events, and his observation of his impact on his world, help him to construct and reconstruct his reality over time.

A child with a perceptual defect, such as a partially sighted child or a hearing-impaired child, is handicapped because he assimilates incomplete or inaccurate information. Some children, because of their experience, do not trust their perceptions. The handicapped child must be supported to use the perceptions available to him to his best advantage. The child who lacks trust needs to be supported in trusting all of his abilities to perceive. All children need to be encouraged to use the perceptual information available to them when acting on objects, interacting with people, and taking part in or observing events in order to "know" their world.

Looking, listening, feeling, tasting, smelling, and moving are not totally separate in the real world. By the time a child comes to school he is well on his way toward organizing his physical and social environments. It may be useful at this point, however, to separate and discuss briefly each perceptual system available to the child to organize and build concepts about his world.

LOOKING

Looking, watching, and observing are the most constant and readily available sources of learning for most children. An infant responds in an excited way to the sight of the breast or bottle being brought near him. He has learned a sequence of sights and sounds, that allows him to anticipate and predict this event. A well-nurtured toddler given a toy will look at and explore the toy from all angles until he has assimilated or understands it to the extent that he is able. Nursery and kindergarten children continue to utilize looking, watching, and observing as primary ways of finding out or understanding the potential of their worlds. Teachers of young children come to respect the adaptive, reflective behavior of the child who observes a bit before he uses a material or joins a group.

Seeing is important in organizing perceptions. Teachers who are accurate observers of children's behavior will be alert to any signs that may indicate the child does not see well; for example, a child who consistently pours milk to the right or left of his glass, a child who often squints in situations where others do not. Any one or a combination of symptoms can alert a thoughtful teacher. This information should be shared with parents and the child should be referred for vision screening.

In favorable conditions children have many opportunities to look at and to know the formal, functional, and physical properties of objects and materials at their own pace. The result is that they are able to organize and move about in their environment with considerable precision, security, and confidence. In unfavorable environments children may have fewer of these opportunities. The effect may be to discourage their curiosity and urge to explore.

In a program for children who were failing in their early school experiences, teachers at Bank Street College of Education, in New York City, found that some of these children were helped when they were given cameras and taken in small groups on trips to photograph their own neighborhoods. These children then became interested again in looking. Encouraged to look, discover, and find meaning in experiences, they began to respond to opportunities that were offered to them in school and to learn from them.

Watching to see where
the water goes.

Beauty in line, form, texture, color, and arrangement are important for children to see in order to develop an aesthetic sense. They are helped to become aware of beauty by having lovely things to look at in their school—a bowl of flowers or autumn leaves, a beautiful picture in the entrance hall, a lovely print hanging on the wall, some of their own paintings attractively mounted and changed frequently, pleasing lines in furniture design, materials and toys organized in interesting ways, pleasing colors, and orderly surroundings.

Shapes and forms interest children. Big and small, long and short, wide and narrow, curved and straight, corners and edges are terms to learn in relation to objects to be seen and felt. Differences in textures should also be looked at as well as felt, such as the bark on trees, the tracks in sand or mud, or ripples in water. By experimenting with shadows, children can change shapes and sizes.

Discovering shadows.

Young children watch and imitate adults with whom they have a warm, supportive relationship. Nursery and kindergarten children are not skilled at selecting the relevant aspects of another's behavior to imitate. For example, when singing with a group of children and combining movement with the music, many a teacher has rubbed an itching nose or brushed her hair back and had at least half the group of children reproduce these irrelevant movements! Because many young children pay close attention to what their valued and predictable teachers say and do, the teacher must be very thoughtful about what she models.

LISTENING

Sounds are important to children. Interest in sounds and the capacity to listen and to discriminate sounds contribute to the development of language. Pleasure in sound is the basis for the enjoyment of music.

Children discover many sounds on their own as they explore materials. The teacher can support and extend these opportunities by her questions and comments: "You made a different sound when you hit the spoon against the cask," or "What does it sound like to you?" or "Is the sound high or low this time?"

Children make the sounds of a truck or siren to accompany their play or make the sounds of animals as they look through a picture book. Teachers who enjoy onomatopoeia (words that imitate natural sounds) can help children to listen and produce these sounds with pleasure. Playing with words and making up nonsense rhymes are other ways children represent their world. Reading poems and stories in which the words are pleasing to the ear further encourages children to experiment with the sounds and meanings of words. A keen ear can be a source of pleasure and an aid in learning the sounds of woodwinds, strings, and brasses and later in distinguishing the differences among such instruments as the violin, cello, and viola.

The teacher provides many opportunities for listening and encourages sound making. She helps children discriminate differences in sound and pitch. She helps children attend to sounds—bird songs; the sounds of an airplane, an eggbeater, a clock, a whisper, a rumble of a truck, the swish of feet in leaves; the silence of the falling snow; and the rain as it courses through the drain. She helps them make a variety of sounds—hitting two things together, ringing a bell, and making musical sounds with a variety of instruments. She helps children notate sounds by placing pictures of musical instruments such as a triangle, a bell, tambourines, and maracas in a series so that their original patterns of sound can be reproduced.

The teacher is in a position to detect hearing impairments early. A child may seem inattentive and sometimes defiant because he does not hear. The teacher can make a simple test such as speaking to him in a normal tone when his back is turned, or move a ticking clock toward him and noting when he pays attention. If she suspects a hearing loss, she can consult with his parents. He may need hearing tests by a professional. If he has a hearing loss, his teacher will need to take this handicap into account and help him learn some ways to compensate for the loss.

FEELING AND TOUCHING

Children are very responsive to the feel of objects. This mode of perception is a valuable one for organizing the world about them. They need help in naming the feel of things that they have identified by touch, for language can help facilitate and direct their thinking. A teacher can exercise ingenuity in providing children with opportunities to touch and feel and encouraging their personal descriptions of the feel of things.

Objects feel hard, soft, rough, smooth, firm, spongy, warm, and cold. A "feel box" with different objects hidden in it gives a child an opportunity to try to identify objects by their feel and to use descriptive words relating to texture, size, and shape. Sorting games based on shape, size, or on the feel of materials with different textures are interesting and instructive to children as they group objects on the basis of commonalities and differences. Children like to collect different objects which have special "feels" such as stones, shells, and glass made smooth by sand and water, beechnuts or horse-chestnuts, and other objects that are both smooth and hard. They enjoy the sensory delights of feeling things.

The same object feels different at different temperatures, as the handlebars of a tricycle in the sun or shade. Water feels different when it has turned to ice. The feel of a leaf when it is green and when it is dry is different, as is the feel of bark on different trees or the feel of different animals—a worm, a baby chick, a turtle, a kitten. Food can be identified by its texture as well as by its taste. Some foods are soft, and some are crunchy. The feel of clay when it is dry is different from its feel when it is "gooshy."

The teacher can provide a variety of materials of different textures in the homemaking area, such as squares of filmy gauze or chiffon, velvet, silk, soft and scratchy wools or cottons along with synthetic fabrics. In each case the teacher uses the correct word as she and the child talk about the feel of the different materials. These same textured materials and others can be used for collage and construction in art activities.

The teacher can encourage the child to experience the feel of things. She supports and extends his experience by her descriptive comments. She may also feel things herself, describing her experience without asking for any response from the child. The teacher models a way of learning. Children organize their world and learn by touching and feeling.

TASTING

Children often comment on taste saying, "It tastes bad," or "good." There are more accurate terms, however, to describe the discrimination of tastes, and the teacher can introduce children to the terms "sweet," "sour," "bitter," and "salty" with samples. Things that look the same do not always taste the same, such as pineapple and grapefruit juice, or a pinch of sugar and a pinch of salt. The most likely place for children to be interested in taste discrimination is at the table when they are eating. Still, most of us know the taste of paste, playdough, and a wide variety of other things we use in the school setting. Many young children also will bring objects and materials to their mouths to explore their taste and feel. All materials used in a school should be safe for mouthing. Being discriminating about what is for eating and what is not is learned by a well-nurtured child long before he comes to school. Indiscriminate eating is a symptom of deprivation and requires some special attention.

Experiencing and describing tastes not only increase the child's awareness, but also challenge his ability to express his perceptions. Enjoying tastes and flavors increases enjoyment in eating.

SMELLING

There are many kinds of smells—the smell of food or flowers, the smell of clay, paint, or soap, the smell of freshly washed towels, the smell of wool when it is wet, and the smell of new shoes. Some smells are pleasant; some are not. The smell of food is good when one is hungry. The odor of a skunk is offensive. Some flowers have a strong, pungent fragrance; some have a delicate fragrance. Almost everything has an odor which helps us to identify places, things, people, and animals.

Describing smells challenges children's ability to express their perceptions in precise ways. The teacher will support the child's discrimination and organization of odors by asking questions, such as: "Do you notice that odor?" "Do you smell something?" "What does the juice smell like?" "What does that odor come from, I wonder?" "Can you find where the odor comes from?"

MOVING

A child's kinesthetic perception is a result of using his body, for example, knowing what it feels like to lift a weight, to race down a slope, to swing on a swing, or to throw a ball. Running, jumping, climbing, bending, stretching, twisting, turning, spinning, balancing, and a host of other movements allow the child to learn the kinesthetic discriminations necessary to organize and control his own body in and through space.

ORGANIZING AND INTEGRATING PERCEPTIONS: FORMING CONCEPTS

As a child moves about his social and physical world, he is using his perceptions and forming concepts. He is learning to recognize objects, people, places, events, and feelings. He is building a repertoire of behaviors that can help him deal effectively with his environment. These behaviors, which include perceiving, thinking, feeling, and doing, are integrated and synthesized to comprise personal and impersonal experiences as well as objective and subjective reality. For example, in pursuing a task or playing, a child may have strong feelings, strivings, or he may encounter problems. As he feels and acts, he may also talk. These behaviors usually occur altogether. At any point in time one may be dominant. As teachers, we separate behaviors into well-defined, discrete categories in our own thinking—not because they are separate entities—but in order to try to understand and describe a complex interactive system of behaviors.

Organizing and integrating perceptions over time and through experience result in the formation of concepts. The child gradually learns that *people, objects, places, and events have an independent existence from him.* He comes to understand that *people, objects, places, and events differ from one another and that they have labels or names.* His dog is just the right size to sit on his lap and is called Brandy. His neighbor's dog is big, jumps on him, and is called Mac. Mac both frightens and fascinates him. In the course of learning he discovers that *people, objects, places, and events have multiple functions, attributes, or characteristics.* He learns that his dog is a pet, and the dog next door is a watchdog; his dog is small and black, and his neighbor's dog is big and thin with brown and white spots; his dog wags his tail and licks his hands to greet him, yet growls when squeezed. He plays with his dog, but he wants to hold his daddy's hand when the dog next door jumps on the garden fence. Out of experience with a wide variety of *people, objects, places, and events, the child learns to perceive common elements.* Many objects that bark and have a body, a head, four legs, a tail, and fur are called dogs. The child who is usually accurate in identifying a wide variety of dogs as "dogs" has a concept of dog. He is perceiving commonality from diverse stimuli and *grouping them into a class*—dogs.

Concepts are not limited to those ideas relating to people, objects, places, and events. Perceptions of feelings are also formed into concepts. Concepts about feelings, too, are expanded and integrated through experience. The toddler who crawls up a long stairway and looks back over his shoulder to smile at his teacher who in turn responds with a smile and says, "You're pretty pleased with yourself, aren't you?" may well be learning one meaning of the idea *pleased*. The idea or concept of "pleased" becomes, over time, more differentiated, consistent, and finally, articulated as a result of many experiences such as, "You look pleased when you see Jon" by an adult who recognizes and acknowledges the child's pleasure; or a teacher who says, "Look at Jon's face, Mary. I think it pleased him for you to give him a shovel" or "When you ask me so kindly I'm pleased to snap your apron."

As children organize their perceptions they need the tool of language to support their thinking. Roger Brown (1958) in an essay on "How Shall a Thing Be Called?" says: "It seems likely that things are first named so as to categorize them in a maximally useful way. . . . The categorization that is most useful for young children (money) may change as they grow older (dime and nickel)" (p. 20). Thoughtful teachers who are helping children learn the names of objects, events, and feelings in their daily lives at school will select the most meaningful and useful words for each child's thinking and communication. For example, the cello, violin, and trumpet are better examples of the class musical instruments than a piano, because a piano is a piece of furniture as well as a musical instrument. The best opportunity to learn what a feeling is called may occur when the child has just experienced a particular feeling strongly or has watched another child experiencing the feeling acutely. Comments similar to: "I thought you were feeling very sad," or "Look at Betsy; I think she is feeling very sad," can be helpful to the child in discriminating feelings in himself and in others.

Language provides a way for the child to identify people, objects, places, and events as well as their function and attributes. For example, a child may learn the distinctive features of a cello and be able to distinguish cellos from violins. He may be able to call both the cello and the violin by their appropriate names. Sometimes he may call them "musical instruments." Yet one cannot safely assume that the child understands musical instruments as a class concept. He may have a good memory and be reporting what he has heard, or he may be using the term "musical instruments" in a limited way. Teachers concerned with the development of thought and language make an effort to distinguish between the child's use of words and his grasp of a concept. Teachers will provide opportunities over time that enlarge the child's perception of feelings, people, places, objects, and events and that support the integration of his perceptions.

Shared meanings of spoken words allow the child to communicate his ideas, feelings, needs, and wants and to understand communication from others. Lars (3.2), on his first visit to school, asked to play with bricks. His teacher was puzzled, but asked, "Do you see what you want to play with?" Lars immediately went to the blocks. "There, the bricks," he said. His teacher commented, "I learned something new, Lars, I call these blocks. You call them bricks." Lars chuckled, he seemed surprised and pleased. "Bricks and blocks," he said. They had both learned from each other. It was important for Lars' teacher to give him the word that other children used, while at the same time it was important for her to respect the word that he had learned previously.

As children learn and grow, perceptions, concepts, language, and feelings are joined together. Feelings and thoughts about oneself are integrated with feelings and thoughts about others. At the same time concepts are enlarged and integrated with other concepts.

HOW CHILDREN ARE MOTIVATED TO LEARN

As we observe children, we see that they are most absorbed when they are most interested; they can concentrate and persist just as we ourselves do. If we are to teach effectively, we need to understand the interests children are likely to have and the particular interests of the individual child. Only when we make available materials and opportunities in which the child is truly interested can we facilitate his learning.

A child's interests are dependent on the experiences he has had and on the pleasantness of those experiences. Children who have had pleasant experiences with a variety of objects and people are very likely to have a variety of interests. Sometimes teachers say, "He is not interested," but it is helpful for us to know that interest results from experience, that familiarity causes liking, and that new interests are often linked to old ones. A teacher's responsibility includes knowing each child's present interest and helping each child to develop new interests.

The child must want to learn in order to learn. Perhaps the most lasting contributions a teacher can make to a child are to support his wish to learn, to help him develop interests, and to learn how to learn. In infancy, a child learns in order to please his mother and father. The teacher will support the child in wanting to learn because learning can be pleasurable. In this sense,

A magnet fascinates
this boy.

the child learns to please himself. A child also learns for a variety of other reasons—to increase his own feelings of competency, to pursue an interest because of previous success, to imitate or be liked by someone important to him, to win praise, or to avoid displeasure. No one of the above reasons is good or bad in itself. Any one may be useful to a particular child at a particular time. It is important for a teacher to try to understand a child's motivations. If his motivation is weak, he is not likely to persist in a task. If the tension from his desire to learn is too great, his learning can be disrupted. Sometimes children release tension as aggression directed toward objects or people. Children vary widely in their motivations, and teachers need to be alert to individual behavior relating to motivation.

The desire for love and appreciation is a strong motivating force in young children. It is a need that can easily be exploited unless we keep clearly in mind the child's purposes and his level of development. Too often we may be more concerned with our own purposes than with his. If we give the child approval only for being "good" by our standards or for doing what we think is best, we may be limiting his development as an individual in his own right. We need to make sure that we acknowledge with approval—for example, the effort a child put into dictating a story that satisfied him, or the control he exercised in not acting on the impulse to hit an offending companion, or the spontaneous sharing done among friends, or the imaginative observation—rather than giving approval only for achievements that satisfy us.

A well-informed teacher is generous in the attention or approval she gives for effort as well as success. Too often attention is reserved for success, and the child's efforts are not rewarded if they do not achieve the expected results. Giving attention for efforts as well as for success are desirable teacher behaviors.

Praise and success both facilitate learning. Such rewards are more effective when related to a specific effort or act. A teacher might say, "You asked me so kindly. The 'please' and your kind tone of voice make me want to read you this story." When the rewards are given in the context of a life situation, the transfer of that learning to other life situations will be more likely. The child speaks clearly so that he can be understood. He asks kindly because people are responsive to kindness. He attends to stories because they tell him something he is interested in hearing. He reads a sentence because he wants to find out what it says.

The teacher will always try to help children succeed in what they undertake. A child, or any of us, needs a large measure of success if he is to bear inevitable failures. Occasionally, we see people who are so afraid of making mistakes that they have stopped attempting anything difficult. These people have had too few successes, or their failures have seemed too significant to them. The teacher of young children will make sure that a child's mistakes are not too serious, and she will encourage his efforts that will lead to success.

When the teacher approves with a smile or a nod, she will want the child to be clear about what he has done that results in her approval. The more specific and immediate she makes the evaluation, the more relevant it is to the child's motives, and the more supportive it is of his learning.

For every task to be mastered by the child there is the possibility of a supportive response on the part of the teacher. Warm, honest, specific support is an effective means of making sure that behavior is repeated. The support may be an approving nod or verbal encouragement. The teacher may say to a fearful child who is making an effort to climb up high, "You've come up seven steps, another step and you will be at the top!" The teacher, on the other hand, who says, "Don't be afraid, you are almost to the top," is calling attention to the child's fear. What he may learn is that climbing makes him feel afraid. To focus on what he has accomplished and the next goal can help him learn that he can climb; this mastery brings him feelings of competence. Such competence serves the child for this specific task now and may transfer to other learning in the future.

Already, by three years of age, children vary in their estimate of what they can and should be able to do. Already, there may be unrealistic expectations in what the child hopes for and expects. The same activity and performance may bring one child a feeling of failure and another a feeling of success.

Unrealistic expectations can be detrimental to the child's self-esteem. They can be disturbing to perception, memory, and learning. Failure to meet his own expectations can depress the child's potential for being actively involved in his own learning. The introduction of opportunities for repeated successes can restore a child's self-esteem, self-direction, and adaptive behavior. The teacher will encourage children and, in addition, she will provide well-organized, intact materials matched to the child's ability and interest. She will plan opportunities that allow success for individuals and small groups of children.

When the child has enough self-esteem and views the teacher as a supporter of his learning, she can help him face failure in a positive and productive way. She can then venture to say, for example, to the child who is having some difficulty in woodworking: "Next time hold the hammer here, close to the head. I believe you will have better control, and the nail may go in straight. Try it, and see if that helps." In making these comments the teacher helps the child look for causes, consider what has happened, and improve his performance. His errors become a means of learning. He gains new perspective and can use his experiences more positively.

A problem-solving attitude is necessary to much of learning. Children need to learn to take a less subjective view of matters and become emotionally and intellectually involved in problem solving. For example, when a sign that has been made for a block building keeps falling over because it is too heavy for the support, a child's first response may be to blame "someone." If the teacher asks, "I wonder why that happened?" she may help the child take a problem-solving attitude to consider alternative reasons for the sign falling. When the child can figure out why it falls, he may gain new confidence in his own capacities.

Some of the strongest motivations are the urge toward mastery of a problem and the satisfaction which comes from performing with skill. We see these motivations in a young child, for example, as he persists in working on a fastening until he succeeds in opening it and then turns to fresh fields of endeavor.

This urge toward competency, as R. W. White (1960) has called it, is a strong motivating force as long as we feel that there is a hope of success. The strength of the urge diminishes if our efforts are continually blocked. The child who has lost hope of any success is not motivated to try. He has lost this powerful urge. When a child has lived in an environment that is largely unfavorable for successful learning, the teacher must work to reawaken his curiosity and zest for exploring and discovering. Above all, she must help him rediscover his faith in his own competence. He must believe that he can succeed if he tries. He must see himself as someone who is able to achieve by his own effort. He must realize that that effort is under his control. If the teacher is to help him, she must believe herself that this child can learn.

Under favorable conditions the child's natural curiosity and his urge toward competency motivate him. He wants to learn and to gain skills. The teacher does not need to depend on extrinsic forms of motivation for the child wants to grow to be like the important adults around him. When these adults present themselves as "models," who work and achieve and who take pleasure in the process, they give direction to the child's efforts. He can work and become competent.

Bruner (1966) comments: "The will to learn is an intrinsic motive, one that finds its source and its reward in its own exercise" (p. 127). He points out that the most lasting satisfactions lie in learning itself. Extrinsic rewards do not give reliable nourishment "over the long course of learning." The urge toward competence is strong in a healthy child. He needs little else except encouragement to sustain his learning.

The teacher has a responsibility to guard this precious "will to learn" that motivates the child, or to reawaken it in children who may have lost this desire. She needs to help these children find "the confidence to try and to make mistakes, and the confidence to know that it is worth doing for its own sake" (Carroll, 1969).

Some people feel it is necessary to introduce children to competition early. If we think about the stages in development, we see the fallacy in this kind of thinking. The child advances stage by stage. Because our culture is competitive, it is all the more important to protect children from having to face competitive situations until they have progressed through the stages of developing a sense of trust, of acquiring some degree of independence, and of finding the rewards of individual initiative. It is more useful to the child to begin by learning to cooperate and help others than to compete with them.

The teacher who understands young children's emotional development will not use competitive methods for motivation. She will know that nursery and kindergarten children have not yet developed enough confidence in themselves to gain anything constructive in competing with each other. They are not yet ready to make use of failure as a spur to further efforts. They only see themselves as nonwinners and often cease to try. Cooperation is more important to children and brings more rewards.

Rather than trying to motivate children by using competition with others in which case someone must fail, teachers will put a great deal of effort into helping children succeed. The pleasant feelings that accompany success will enable children to repeat and expand experiences that are pleasurable to them. It is in this way that teachers can best help children develop interest and abilities. Success leads to realistic goals and increases the probability for more success.

SUPPLEMENTARY READING

Blank M. *Teaching Learning in the Preschool: A Dialogue Approach.* Columbus, Ohio: Merill, 1970.

Brearley, M. *The Teaching of Young Children: Some Applications of Piaget's Learning Theory.* New York: Schocken Books, 1970.

Cohen, D. H. *The Learning Child.* New York: Vintage, 1973, pp. 1–118.

Dinkmeyer, D., and R. Dreikurs. *Encouraging Children To Learn: The Encouragement Process.* Englewood Cliffs, N.J.: Prentice-Hall, 1963.

Seagoe, M. V. *A Teacher's Guide to the Learning Process,* 2d ed. Dubuque, Iowa: William C. Brown Company, 1961.

Sigel, I. E. The attainment of concepts. In M. L. Hoffman, and L. W. Hoffman, eds., *Review of Child Development Research,* vol. 1. New York: Russell Sage, 1964.

16

Car with Mouse on Top
(girl, 2.5)

Play as a Mode of Learning

The whole panorama of life is lived over again in the play of children. If there is any way of gaining knowledge particularly suitable to this stage of development, it is in the play which they spontaneously devise but which needs nevertheless an attentive teacher for its support and nourishment. (BIBER, 1967:6)

There have been many explanations of play during the past 140 years since Froebel began his kindergarten. Play continues to be a familiar but little understood activity of children. It is well known to all of us, but it is difficult to find a definition that proves satisfactory. Therefore, it seems reasonable to avoid the strict definitional question and ask: How do we recognize play when we see it?

HOW TEACHERS CAN RECOGNIZE PLAY

Neumann (cited by Spodek, 1974:13–14) after analyzing the literature on play, outlined a set of three criteria for determining whether or not a child's activity is play. Her criteria are as follows: (1) *control*—to the extent that the activity is determined by the player rather than being determined by someone else, it is play; (2) *reality*—to the extent that the activity has an "as if" or pretense quality rather than being real, it is play; (3) *motivation*—to the extent that the motivation is within the player rather than originating from outside forces, it is play. Neumann views each of these points as a continuum rather than as all or nothing. That is, any activity may be judged as having more or less control by the player, more or less pretense, and more or less internal motivation.

An Application of the Criteria of Play

As a further explanation of the above criteria, we will apply them to the child's activity described below. Again, the question being asked is, "Is this activity play?" To answer that question we will use Neumann's criteria.

> Jeanette (4.0) is in the homemaking corner rocking and feeding the baby doll using a shampoo bottle as a feeding bottle. She rocks and feeds the baby for five minutes. From time to time she speaks softly to the baby and adjusts the baby's blanket. Then she gets up and carefully tucks the baby into bed. She is very gentle as if not to wake the baby. From a nearby clothes rack she takes a pink, lacey party dress and puts it over her head skillfully. Reaching her hand to the back of her neck, she tries to find the zipper. She cannot reach it. "Could you help me?" she asks as she backs up toward the teacher so she can reach the zipper. The teacher zips the dress, and Jeanette goes back to the baby's bed, puts her hand on the baby's back, and gently pats her. "Go to sleep, sweetheart," she says softly. She turns from the bed, furrows her brow, and looks thoughtful. She picks up a pocketbook and says to the teacher, "I'm going to my wedding." The teacher asks, "You're going to meet the bridegroom?" "What?" says Jeanette, looking rather puzzled. "You're going to meet the man you're going to marry, the bridegroom?" At this question Jeanette smiles a truly coy smile, but remains silent. She turns slowly away from the teacher, who says, "I'll baby-sit for you so don't worry about your baby." Jeanette turns, smiles, and nods (and goes to the wedding?).

Is this activity play? To what extent is Jeanette playing in the situation described above? We need to ask and answer three questions about her activity.

First, was the activity *self-motivated?* Yes, Jeanette chose it freely; no one suggested the play. At least it seems from the information given that she decided for herself what she was going to do. Without more information, however, we do not know for certain who if anyone might have influenced her selection.

Secondly, was the activity under the child's *control?* Yes, Jeanette was alone, and no one intruded until the teacher asked her a question, used a word she did not know (i.e., bridegroom), and perhaps did not respond to Jeanette's intent.

Thirdly, was the activity *pretend?* Yes, Jeanette is not an adult, but she acted "as if" she were an adult lady. She dressed in a party dress, took a pocketbook, and announced that she was going to her wedding. She used the shampoo bottle "as if" it were a baby bottle, fed the baby, put the baby to bed, covered the baby tenderly, and returned to be sure the baby was all right. In reality, Jeanette knew the bottle was a shampoo bottle and the baby was a doll. She was pretending.

On the basis of the criteria, then, it would seem that Jeanette's activity was play.

PLAY IS PLEASURABLE

Pleasure or the appearance of pleasure often accompanies play, but pleasure is an internal feeling that takes many forms and may or may not be observable. As one observes a child playing, the child is usually quite serious. "Play is pleasurable, enjoyable. Even when it is not accompanied by signs of mirth, it is still positively valued by the players" (Garvey, 1977:4). We infer that play is valued by the child because it is self-motivated, under his own control, and continues over time.

TYPES OF PLAY

One way to understand play is to classify it on the basis of what the child may be learning from being involved in play. That is, to view play as a mode of learning and to classify it in terms of what the child is doing and what he may be learning. Any system of classification is arbitrary, because it is imposed on the child's play and does not necessarily reflect the child's intent. A young child's play is not easily placed into one of a number of

Learning to swing can be challenging.

mutually exclusive categories. Nevertheless, accepting the following categories of play may help teachers understand children as they play.

Exploratory play is play in which children explore the properties of their world. They discover the relationships among people, places, and things outside of themselves. They use objects in novel and unique ways, for example, wearing a plastic bucket for a hard hat or using a piece of rope for a gas hose. They play with language to make the sounds of animals and vehicles, to rhyme, and to make jokes. They discover that blocks can fall, that glass can break, that clay is malleable, and that a sow bug contracts into a small ball when touched.

Skill mastery play is play in which children become proficient at physical skills, such as scampering up an agility net, riding a tricycle, or climbing in, under, and through objects. In such play children also become skilled with a variety of materials as they practice drawing, cutting, writing, or building. The examples in the second chapter, of Clark riding a tricycle, painting, and digging involve skill mastery play, as does the example of Louise reading the recipe.

Construction play is play in which children represent their ideas about the world by putting objects and materials together in their own way. They organize and reorganize their concepts of the world as they construct and reconstruct with a variety of materials, such as blocks, sand, building game sets, and art materials. Examples of this type of play are, again, found in Chapter 2 as Louise makes the "book" and as the kindergarten children make the "school."

Imitative, symbolic, dramatic play is play in which children take roles from the adult, roles of important and powerful people. In dramatic play children can be the actors and the observers at the same time. They define the roles,

Learning to write can be challenging and lead to mastery.

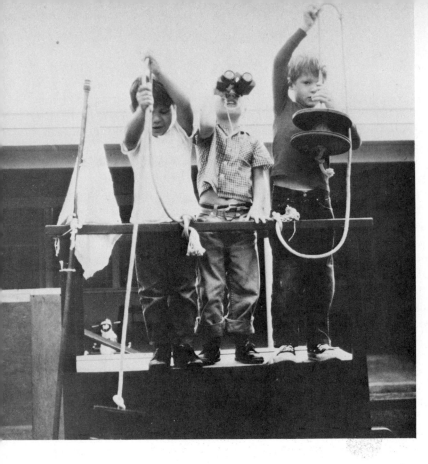

These children are using their imaginations and interacting with each other in dramatic play.

use real properties, use their imaginations, and often interact with others in the play as they use language for communication. The example of Jeanette's play, earlier in this chapter, is dramatic play.

Using this classification system will help the teacher understand that children may gain abilities, skills, and understanding through play. Many people have and are studying children's play in an effort to understand its function in children's learning. The central role of play in children's learning makes it a critical area that demands constant study by the teacher.

THEORIES OF PLAY

Piaget's theory and the psychoanalytic theory of play may contribute additional insights into the teacher's understanding of play as a mode of learning. Selected aspects of Piaget's theory of intellectual development and Freud's view of personality development are presented in Chapter 3. The discussions of Piagetian and psychoanalytic views of play, given below, are only small aspects of the two theories.

PIAGET'S THEORY OF PLAY

Piaget (1962) defines three stages in the development of play, each of which parallels a stage in intellectual development. The first stage, *sensorimotor*, begins when the parent imitates the child, and the child repeats the parent's actions. For example, the child smacks his lips and the parent smacks her lips in imitation of the child; then, the child repeats the parent's action. The parent imitates what the child can already do in a playful way. Both child and parent smile or laugh as they mutually enjoy the play. Over time many such sequences of play are established. These sequences seem to contribute to new sequences as the child begins to invent patterns himself.

Symbolic play, the second stage, begins as the child imitates the important and powerful people in his life. Without a model for the play being present, he pretends to drink from a cup, for example, or to "turn on" a toy stove. At the beginning of this stage much of the child's play is in imitation of what people important to him have done with him, such as, feeding, bathing, dressing, playing, and offering affection. As the child imitates, he differentiates, integrates, and expands his understanding. He pretends, makes believe, imagines, and invents in his play. Most well-developing, well-nurtured nursery and kindergarten age children are in this second stage.

The last stage is *games with rules.* Late nursery school and kindergarten age children enjoy an occasional game with rules, but it is the six-, seven-, and eight-year-olds who are truly involved in being inventive with rules and games.

Play becomes an intellectual activity as the child is able to represent his world in play; to manipulate his ideas about objects, events, people, and places and to fit these representations into his organized schema. Piaget views *representation* of objects, events, people, and places as an important function of play, which in turn is an important aspect in the intellectual life of the young child.

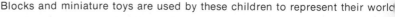

Blocks and miniature toys are used by these children to represent their world

Psychoanalytic View of Play

Psychoanalytic theory (Erikson, 1950, 1972; Lidz, 1968) views play as a mode for healthful release of feelings and ideas through "acting out" unconscious feelings and ideas accompanied by appropriate emotional release. Opportunities to "play out" confusing, distressing, or shocking feelings may enable a child to gain insight and assimilate painful, distressing, or traumatic experiences.

Erikson (1972) says of themes in play:

> we recognize . . . "working through" of a *traumatic* experience: but they (themes) also express a playful *renewal*. If they seem to be governed by some need to *communicate,* or even *confess,* they also seem to serve the joy of *self-expression*. If they seem dedicated to the *exercise* of growing faculties they also seem to serve the *mastery* of a complex life situation." (p. 131)

Erikson does not settle for one of these functions, but sees all as important. Central to this point of view is the idea that through fantasy play, children can play out the roles of powerful and important people and feel a sense of *mastery,* which makes it possible to cope with the reality.

Both the Piagetian and psychoanalytic perspectives respect the integrity of the child and his play. Piaget offers a structure to help us understand how the child uses play to gain knowledge about his world. The psychoanalytic view offers us a way to help children cope with stress and to gain mastery. It also helps us to appreciate children's needs to communicate feelings. Chapters 9, 12, and 13 contain many examples of children's play and ways adults can be helpful to them in draining off feelings through play. Examples of how play can be extended on behalf of the children's intellectual development are provided in chapters 17, 18, and 19. Again, we have classified children's learning into two categories: affect or feelings, and intelligence or cognition. In the real world, children learn and develop as total persons. Thoughtful attention to each aspect of development—affective, cognitive, social, and physical—as well as attention to the interrelationship among the aspects, is essential if the teacher is to plan for total development.

OBSERVING PLAY BEHAVIOR

Perhaps in no other area will a teacher or parent find more cues to help her understand the individual child's skills, abilities, understandings, and feelings than in his play. By careful observation, she can begin to evaluate the progress a child is making in reaching his potential. Observing a child's play will help define a child's strengths, vulnerabilities, and interests. The teacher can become more aware of what materials or opportunities she may provide that will match his interests and needs. Observing and recording the child's play behavior increases the adult's insight into the child. Teaching cannot proceed in a purposeful way without such observation.

Assessing Children's Play

Teachers observe children's play to learn where children are with regard to their learning at a particular point in time. Knowing where a child is in his learning is essential in matching learning opportunities to a particular child's skills, abilities, and understanding. Sara Smilansky (1968:9) has defined six elements of play. These elements are as follows: (1) imitative role play; (2) make believe with regard to objects; (3) make believe with regard to action; (4) persistence; (5) interaction; and (6) verbal communication. Each of these elements can be described more specifically by stating the place *from* where the child may begin *to* where the child may progress (the long-term goals for children's play).

1. imitation—*from* imitation of discrete actions of important adults *to* playing complex roles and playing a wide variety of roles elaborated by language
2. make believe with regard to objects—*from* using actual objects much as adults do *to* using objects to represent real and imagined objects and using language and gesture to elaborate ideas
3. make believe with regard to actions and situations—*from* imitating others' actions and situations *to* playing out a wide variety of real and imaginary actions and situations, and using language to communicate imagination to others
4. persistence—*from* playing for a few moments *to* playing over an extended time within a day or over several days
5. interaction—*from* playing alongside another child *to* playing out a complex play episode with several children and using many verbal interactions
6. verbal communication—*from* not speaking to another person *to* using verbal interaction to communicate a wide variety of ideas in play

An Example: Assessing Kim's Play

As a further explanation of how these elements can be useful in assessing where a child is along a continuum *from* one level of complexity *to* another, we will apply them to Kim in the play episode that follows.

2:30   Kim (4.6), Nancy (5.1), and Barbara (5.3) are outside playing house under a tent made of two little screens covered with a blanket.
   Kim: "There is a lion outside the house. We are frightened so we stay in."
   Barbara: "Yes, and we have to take care of baby sister, too, or else the bad lion will get her."
   Kim comes out of the house. She finds another child, Bonnie (5.4), standing near the tent. Kim goes up to her, takes her hand, and says, "You are a bad lion. You frighten people, so they lock you up in a cage. Now you go to your cage"—Pauses, leads Bonnie to the other room, saying, "Come, I will make you a cage." She puts four long blocks together and tells Bonnie, "Now you get in there. That's your cage." Bonnie stands in the enclosure, and Kim goes back to the house. Kim says, "The lion is locked in the cage, so we are safe."
   In the meantime, Barbara, still in the house, says to Nancy, "Now you better listen to your big sister like a good girl, or else the lion will catch you. Mommy will be back home soon." Kim, returning home, calls out to Bonnie from inside the tent. "You have escaped from the cage. You have unlocked the cage, and you have escaped."

As Bonnie walks toward the tent, Kim shouts to the others, "The lion has escaped, the lion has escaped." They all three scream and shout.

Kim: "I must call the zoo and tell the manager." She picks up the telephone and calls. "There is a big lion escaped from the zoo, and he is frightening us. Please get him, will you?" She puts down the receiver.

Barbara: "Now they will come and get him and put him back in the cage. Ha! Ha!"

Everything quiets down, and the play shifts.

Nancy: "I am the mother."

Kim (pointing): "No. You (Barbara) are the big sister, and you (Nancy) are the little sister. You are eight, and she is five. You better mind her while I go out." She goes out for a few seconds and comes back.

Kim to Barbara: "Did she (Nancy) mind?"

Barbara: "No, she was a very bad girl."

Kim to Nancy: "Mommy is not mad at you, but next time you must mind." 2:35   Nancy: "I will."

Kim goes out for a few seconds and returns. Kim to Nancy: "Did you do what mother said?"

Nancy: "Yes."

Barbara says, "I know. When you go somewhere like downtown, we could play ring around roses."

Kim answers, "But be careful, big sister, because she is only three, and she might fall down and get hurt."

Kim to Nancy: "You didn't behave, and we spanked you—not real hard—I'll show you how. It doesn't hurt, does it?"

Nancy: "No—But don't spank too hard, OK?"

Kim: "And then you played with the telephone."

Barbara to Nancy: "You better not. You are too little to play with the telephone."

Kim to Nancy: "You were playing in the street, and we caught you."

Nancy: "I have to go out to pick berries."

Kim: "No, because you fooled us (pauses) Why do you have to pick berries?"

Barbara: "I want to call Grandma." Picking up the telephone receiver, dials 1, 2, 5, 8. Puts down the receiver. "I called, but the line is busy."

Barbara: "I am going to pick berries."

Kim to Nancy: "You also go to pick berries. When we are not looking."

Kim: "We must sleep now. Curl up, honey."

Nancy walks out on tiptoe. Suddenly Kim and Barbara rush out shouting, "Where is she? Where is she?" Both of them run out looking for Nancy. Barbara finds Nancy behind the door and shouts excitedly, "Here she is, Mom—Hurry, Mommy." Barbara and Kim hold Nancy's hands on either side and drag her into the house. Kim pretends to lock the door of the house and tells Nancy, "You have been a bad girl. Now you have to stay in all day." 2:40

Now, we can assess Kim's play using each continuum previously described.

1. Imitation: *Her portrayal of the mother role is beyond imitation, and it is elaborated by her language.* Kim first plays the role of a protector who cages the lion and calls the zookeeper when it escapes. She then defines roles for all and takes on the role of a protective mother, who assigns responsibility to the older child, goes out, and returns to check up on her children. In this role

she is permissive and suspicious; she is firm and spanks. As a mother, she puts her child to bed and brings her home when she runs away.

2. Make believe with regard to objects: *She uses real objects to represent other objects and imagined objects. She elaborates her imagined use of objects with language.* One real object, the telephone, is used. Kim uses an imaginary house made of two screens and a blanket. She pretends there is a lion's cage, and she pretends to lock a door, which does not exist.

3. Make believe with regard to actions and situations: *Kim plays out a wide variety of actions and uses language to communicate her pretense as the play develops.* She pretends that a child is a lion, that the four blocks are a cage, and that the lion escapes. She pretends to call the zookeeper. She pretends to be a mother who assigns pretend ages and roles to the children. She pretends that one of the children misbehaves, that she reprimands her, and that she spanks the child. She pretends a child runs away and that she looks for her.

4. Persistence: *Kim persisted in this play for 10 minutes.* She persisted in another sense, too. When Nancy seems to want to change the play with, "I have to go out to pick berries," there is a pause and some action by Barbara, but Kim returns the other children back to the theme of the play.

5. Interaction and 6. Verbal communication: *She plays out a complex episode with three other children. She communicates verbally to others sixteen times during this episode.* Kim interacts with three children and an imaginary zookeeper.

It is interesting to note the children's concern about misbehavior—playing with the telephone, playing in the street, and running away. They cope with the problem of being little and the temptations they often face by creating a "bad lion," and by dealing with him, and by being the punishing parent. They recreate their world; only this time they are in control. Sociodramatic play serves to build confidence in them as they deal with and master the situations they reenact.

CHILDREN WHO CANNOT PLAY

All children do not play. Some children seem unable to enter into play whether on their own or with others. Mattick (1965) and Pavenstedt (1965), working with economically disadvantaged families who were under great stress, observed that the children from these families did not play well. Smilansky (1968), studying both advantaged and disadvantaged children in Israel, found that advantaged children spent 78 percent of the time in sociodramatic play while disadvantaged children used only 10 percent of the time in that manner.

During many years of observing and teaching children across all socioeconomic groups, we have found children in *all* groups who do not play well or do not play spontaneously. Some children are not free to play because of short-term stress, such as illness or fatigue; other children are not free to play

Playing the doctor's role is common in young children's play.

because of continuous, long-term stress. In both cases, the inability to play is a serious handicap to communicating with other children, to the imaginative use and exploration of materials, and to developing problem-solving strategies. Being unable to play establishes patterns of behavior that continue as learning problems into the elementary school years.

A primary goal for the child who is unable to play is to *learn to play*. The learning opportunities planned for him can be based on the teacher's determination of the types of play the child can engage in, and her assessment of the elements in his play (see pp. 270–272). The teacher's general role in facilitating play is outlined below. The specific learning opportunities and the emphasis in the teacher's role will depend on the particular child.

Some children do not respond to stressful situations by being unable to play but, rather, their play is often disorganized and aggressive. Chapters 13 and 14 will be helpful to teachers working with such frightened children.

THE TEACHER'S ROLE IN FACILITATING PLAY

Throughout this book many references are made to what teachers can do to facilitate children's learning. It seems important, however, to make explicit some ways teachers can be particularly helpful to children in developing rich, well-elaborated play. Our suggestions for the teacher are as follows.

1. She will develop with each child a relationship that allows him to play freely.
2. She will observe each child's play to determine his interests and abilities.
3. She will arrange attractive, well-organized, inviting play spaces based on children's interests and make educated judgments about how to extend these interests.
4. She will provide realistic materials for the youngest children or for children who are learning to play.
5. As children are able to use realistic materials in imaginative and flexible ways, she will provide props that enable them to keep track of other children's roles in interactive play. For example, clothing or tools may help children keep in mind the roles being played.
6. She will encourage flexible thinking and the use of imagination by supplying raw materials that can be used in a variety of ways.
7. She will model language that facilitates children's interactions with each other in play.
8. She will join in pretend play, but she will not regress to childish behavior.
9. She will plan large blocks of time for play to develop.

SUPPLEMENTARY READING

Biber, B. *Play as a Growth Process*. New York: Bank Street College of Education, 1959.

Hartley, R., L. Frank, and R. Goldenson. *Understanding Children's Play*. New York: Columbia University Press, 1952.

Murphy, L. B. Infant's Play and Cognitive Development. In M. W. Piers, ed., *Play and development*. New York: Norton, 1972.

Omwake, E. B. The Child's Estate. In A. J. Solnit, and S. A. Provence, eds., *Modern Perspectives in Child Development*. New York: International Universities Press, 1963.

Sponseller, D., Ed. *Play as a Learning Medium*. Washington, D.C.: National Association for the Education of Young Children, 1974.

Space Man
(boy, 3.3)

Curriculum Areas:
Mathematics and Science

MATHEMATICS

As young children play they handle objects and become aware of quantity. While building with blocks they find out about enclosed spaces and estimate lengths. They learn that some objects are large, some are small, and some are middle sized. All of these understandings are basic to the child's comprehension of mathematical ideas.

The concepts from mathematics that can serve as organizing ideas for a school program for young children are: classification, seriation, number, time, space, and measurement. These ideas are not only basic to mathematics, but they build on the understandings that the child already has when he enters school at age three.

CLASSIFICATION

Ordering objects, people, events, and ideas pervades the daily life of adults. We group objects or ideas together that share a common property or characteristic. In general, groupings or classifications are made on the basis of *functional* characteristics or on the basis of *formal* properties. For example, if we put all of the paint brushes on the same shelf and further group them so that the easel brushes are in one box and the watercolor brushes are in another box, we have grouped the objects on the basis of a functional characteristic. Objects classified on the basis of formal properties may be grouped according to size, color, shape, or weight. For example, we may group the paint jars by the color of paint, putting all the reds together, all the blues together, etc.

As logical thinkers, adults can think of many ways to group the same collection of objects, events, people, and ideas. Most adults need not literally move the objects together; they have the mobility of thought that allows them to mentally group and regroup. A teacher may use such flexibility as she mentally groups and regroups her class many times a day. She thinks, "there are 14 children in my group, seven boys and seven girls. Four children are just turning three years old; six are between three and three-and-a-half years old; four are between three-and-a-half years and four years old. Six need a great deal of help with the order of dressing; five need help with boots, zippers, and buttons; three are independent in dressing except when they are tired or under stress."

Knowing objects well is a necessary prerequisite to comparing objects, making relationships among objects, and grouping objects according to common properties or characteristics. The objects and materials in the room and playground can become well known to the children. These objects have characteristics which can be seen, felt, heard, tasted, or smelled; they have color, shape, size, texture, actions, and reactions. Out of these readily perceivable characteristics children discover commonalities and differences.

A two-, three-, or four-year-old child is still learning who he belongs to and who belongs to him; what objects are his and what objects belong to others; where a whole variety of objects belong, and how these objects are used. Belonging is a relationship that can define a group or a set. For example, "This is my new coat; it belongs in my locker." "This is John's car; it belongs to him." "This is a tricycle; it belongs outside." As a child knows he has a "place" and things have a "place," his ideas of belonging can become a useful way to organize objects and understand their relationships. He can describe or characterize objects as belonging to someone (possession) or belonging somewhere (location); he can group objects together that share a common belongingness.

Other concepts a child learns related to classification are that of "likeness" and "difference," or the ability to match or find an object that is like another and the ability to exclude the different object. For example, finding a hat that is like the one a friend is wearing; being able to sort out a truck from a group of cars as the one that does not belong in the basket. From these beginnings the child develops the related concepts: "like," "almost the same," "just alike," "exactly alike," "things that go together," "not alike," "not the same," "unlike," and "different from." At the same time a child is learning the above relationships he is learning the relationship between the concepts "same" and "different."

The development of the concepts "same" and "different" and the development of the ideas related to them are dependent on the child having opportunities to work with a variety of materials and people, in a variety of contexts, over a long period of time. This time span generally includes the nursery and kindergarten years. To facilitate the development of these concepts the teacher plans an environment where there are many opportunities in the normal course of the day for children to sort and match objects. The room, yard, and storage closets are organized into functional units where objects related to a specific function are kept. For example, toys that are used with blocks are in baskets or on shelves in the block corner; blocks are stored by size and shape; dishes are sorted into cups, saucers, and plates; hats are placed together separate from shoes and purses. In a room so organized, sorting and matching may take place many times a day as a child replaces materials after use and at general clean-up times.

To advance beyond sorting or grouping objects on the basis of one common characteristic a child needs many opportunities to learn fine discriminations among objects and to express precisely what he perceives. For this purpose, it is particularly helpful for a teacher of three- and four-year-old children to model thinking and language. For example, while looking at a collection of buttons, the teacher says, "I wonder if there are any white buttons? Here's one! Here's another; this one is smaller than the first one I found." Honest questions and real comparisons model behavior and convey to the child a teacher's interest in learning.

For a four- or five-year-old it is important for a teacher to ask the *child* questions so that *he* makes statements about *his* observations. For example, after a child has sorted buttons putting all the green together and all the gold together, the teacher might ask, "Are all the green buttons alike? Are they just the same?" or "Are any of the green and gold buttons alike in some way?" The purpose of the teacher's question is not only to give the child an opportunity to be explicit about his observations but also to provide the teacher with information about the child's thinking process. "Open ended" questions are more likely to serve this purpose than are questions that require a relatively simple "Yes" or "No."

A five-and-a-half-year-old who can respond to the questions, "Are all the green buttons alike? Are they just the same?" with, "No, this one has two holes." and then, after he inspects other buttons, comments, "These don't have any holes!" is ready for the teacher to ask, "Can you think of another way to sort all the green buttons?" At this point he will probably respond, "No." Although he identifies another difference, he is not able yet to abandon the criterion of color and sort them into another set.

Another child, who is six-and-a-half years old, and who is also sorting buttons by color, might look at his two piles of buttons and resort them on the basis of those with two holes and those with shanks. He then notices that some buttons are large and some are small, and he resorts them on the basis of size. When asked, "Could you tell me why all these go together?" He responds, "Well, these are big and these are little." He has been able to change criteria and regroup the buttons three times. In addition, he has been able to explain the basis for his grouping. He has done this sorting while using familiar materials. Before a teacher could be sure that this child had the mobility of thought to sort on the basis of three properties, the child would have to be able to repeat this behavior with a variety of materials.

The next step in classification is being able to make two sets from a collection of objects and compare "all" and "some." Using the buttons as an example, a child can say, "All of the buttons are plastic and some are green." When asked if there are more plastic buttons or more green buttons, he can answer, "More plastic buttons." In addition, he can tell you he knows, "Because *all* of the buttons are plastic and only *some* are green." This step is rarely demonstrated with a wide variety of materials before nine years of age.

SERIATION

Seriation is comparing objects along a particular dimension and ordering them according to their relative difference. Examples of common dimensions adults use for seriation are: size (length, height, width), weight, shades of color, texture, sound, hardness, and temperature. A teacher uses the concept of *ordering* objects and ideas in many ways each day. When she decides how to order in the storage closet she may place the large, heavy packages of paper on the bottom shelf, the somewhat smaller, lighter packages on the shelf above it, and on the next shelf the smallest, lightest paper. When ordering the paper this way she coordinates the relative differences to determine the appropriate shelf placement.

Concepts related to seriation assist the child in understanding and *ordering* his world. For example, he is learning the concepts of: "big-little," "big-bigger-biggest," "long-short," "long-longer-longest," "short-shorter-shortest," "wide-narrow," "wide-wider-widest," "loud-soft," "loud-louder-loudest," "soft-softer-softest." Interactions with many objects differing along a variety of dimensions and interactions with others in a social setting are paramount to the child's learning and understanding these relationships. For notions of *ordering* to be useful to the child, he must have continuous opportunities to arrange what he sees along appropriate dimensions, such as size or shades of color, to order what he hears in terms of pitch or intensity, and to order textures, smells, and tastes. All of these opportunities would contribute to the child's understanding of seriation; however, size is a dimension that is particularly related to mathematics and, therefore, it will be the focus of the following discussion.

A three-year-old child uses the idea of "big" and "little" in relation to himself and personal things. He recognizes big and little objects and can recall that he is larger than his baby brother at home. He can arrange a group of three objects in the order of size; for example, a baby, a mother, and a father. He can say that his mother is bigger than he is and that his father is even bigger. He may know in this instance that his mother is middle sized, but will probably not be able to use the word middle appropriately in another context. If he is given a larger group to order on the basis of size, the child does not order the objects logically and he may make a task of his own playing with the objects.

With many opportunities to make objects smaller and larger than another and to order objects by size, the child of about four-and-a-half years can arrange a group of six or eight graduated bowls or toy people into a series by trial and error: He tries one, and if it is not the next tallest in the series he proceeds to try another.

By the time the child is about seven years old he can arrange six or eight objects in ascending or descending order without resorting to trial and error. The child is now in the stage of *concrete operations*. He has a concept that he can use with facility with real objects. That is, when arranging a group of toy people he understands and uses the idea that the second person is taller than the first person, that the third person is taller than the second person as well as taller than the first person.

NUMBER

The concept of number is built by bringing together the ideas of classification and seriation. In other words the understanding of the number four depends on mentally *grouping* four objects to form a class and the *relationships* between four, three, and five. When we speak of number we usually mean how many objects or people in a group. *Cardinal number* has its roots in classification: We put objects or people into groups or classes and answer the question: "how many?" *Ordinal number* ideas are built by putting objects in a series and determining the order of each object. First, second, third, and so on tells us where an object is in a series of objects and its relationship to the other objects. A child's own action on materials builds the mental organization that allows him to understand number. There are no shortcuts to this mental process. A child is supported in matching, sorting, grouping, and ordering objects when he has ample opportunities to use materials that are interesting to him. Telling him the "right way to do it" or the "right answer" will only lessen his confidence in his ability to learn.

A two-year-old child can hold up two fingers and say, "Two"; he can point to his nose and say, "One" or to his eyes and say, "Two." At three he can say, "one-two-three-four-five-six-seven-eight-nine." The numerals can be memorized without understanding that the numeral which represents the set is two, and that two is independent of the set it represents. Many three-year-olds "count" to ten or more by rote, but this does not mean that they understand the numbers taken out of the context of the memorized chain. When asked how many blocks he has, the three-year-old is likely to give a number name, but not the actual number of blocks he has. A young child needs many opportunities to associate the name of the number with the objects it represents, and later, the name of the number with the numeral.

The three- to four-and-a-half-year-old child needs many opportunities to make gross comparisons of the quantity of two sets. All of us make gross comparisons in the process of learning precise comparisons. The first such comparisons children hear and begin to learn are: "enough," "not enough," "too much," "a little," "a lot," "a little more," "large," "small," "more," "fewer," "greater than," "less than," "the same as," and "equal." There are many quantitative relations to learn and these are best learned in life situations with objects that matter to the child and with people who are meaningful to him. The social setting of a school should offer rich opportunities for a child to make comparisons within the context of the reality of other people.

One-to-one correspondence or matching objects is a useful way to introduce exact comparisons. Natural relationships like a napkin and a cup at snack, or cups and saucers in the homemaking area allow for matching objects from one set to objects of another set. A teacher who understands that matching object to object is important to a child's learning to make exact comparisons will select materials for each area in the classroom that have many such relationships. As a child understands exact comparisons by

Reflection is required to determine the equivalence of sets.

matching objects, he may use this idea to settle disputes over who has the most by matching.

A late five-year-old child who has had many opportunities to make gross comparisons and then exact comparisons will be ready to use opportunities planned especially for matching sets. Miniature objects that relate to a child's interest can be used such as: a set of adult animals and a set of baby animals; a set of boats and a set of sails; a set of umbrellas and a set of children; a set of workers and a set of caps. The child is shown the sets and asked to compare the sets. For example, he is asked, "Are there just enough mothers for all the babies?" This child will probably be able to determine the equivalence or lack of equivalence of sets that contain four or five objects. He may say, "There are four mothers and five babies; we need another mother for them to be the same." With sets of six or eight this same child will use matching to determine equivalence and say, "There are enough mothers for babies." If the teacher moves all the mothers together and asks, "Are there still just enough mothers for all the babies?" or "Are they still the same?" the physical arrangement of the objects may be so salient as to influence the child's response. The mothers spread out seem to be more to him or the babies bunched close together seem less. If this is so, he will respond, "No, there are not enough babies." He will need to restore the original physical correspondence by matching each mother to each baby. With maturity and experience he will not need to literally match objects. He will know that the number of objects stays the same no matter what their arrangement. He will be able to say, "You just moved the babies," or "You didn't put out another mother so they are just the same."

It is important for teachers to accept the responses a child gives to her questions. To tell the child he is wrong by facial expression or words makes him doubt himself and his thinking. We must remember a child thinks differently from adults. We can show our interest in him by raising a question such as: "I wonder what you were thinking" or "Tell me what you were thinking." For many children under six thinking about their thinking is a task beyond them. It will be helpful to these children to have whatever they say accepted however poorly they express their ideas. Acceptance of what the child says with positive feelings toward him can be a support to his intellectual and emotional development.

After matching many objects a kindergarten child can learn to match the numerals to objects. Even children who are rational counters will need to learn to match numerals to objects. For example, children can use small mailboxes with the numerals 1–10 written on them and ample letters to fill each mailbox with the appropriate number. Some children can write their own numerals, and some children can write the numeral names on the mailboxes for themselves and others. Children who do this task well can help others who are learning. Whether or not a child can read or write the number names should not exclude him from such tasks. A variety of such materials can be made with the ability and interests of particular children in mind.

After matching numerals to objects with ease and accuracy, a child finds it interesting to match numerals to pictures of sets of objects. Numerals may be written on small cards that can be placed on the pictures. Some children can write the numeral and/or the number name themselves. However, not being able to write or not being a skilled writer does not interfere or exclude a child from this opportunity. Teachers often use work sheets consisting of interesting groups of objects with numerals and number names written along the side or across the top of the page. Children who cannot write for themselves can draw a line to connect the appropriate numeral with the appropriate group of objects.

Children who can count rationally are ready to manipulate objects such as an abacus for simple addition and subtraction. Many children discover addition and subtraction as they count up and down. Most children who do not grasp the idea of putting a set together and taking a set apart will discover it as they work with more sets. With a spirit of cooperation in a common learning opportunity, children learn from each other.

After this understanding of addition and subtraction has developed, the child is ready to practice computational skills. Some children will be able to make their own cards with two numbers each that total from zero to ten. These cards can be used as an aid in memorizing these combinations. The process of making the cards can be a cooperative venture between two children or a teacher and a child. Although this task is time consuming, the thinking for a child that goes into it is well worth the time spent completing it.

Teachers must remember that mathematical knowledge is based on understanding seriation, classification, and number. No step in the process of learning can be hurried. Telling a child will not replace his own discovery nor

Pegs and fingers can be helpful in simple addition and subtraction.

will it add to his understanding. Each step in the process must have meaning to a child. He must have time to practice using these ideas in a variety of settings with a variety of materials.

TIME

Time has several meanings: (1) a period or instance in time; (2) a point in duration, occasion, moment, or instant; (3) continuance. Adults in everday life speak of setting a time, an opportune time, calculating time, in no time, time payments, the time of our life, and the time that hung heavy.

For nursery, kindergarten, first-, and second-grade children, time is a difficult concept to grasp. It takes approximately until about the age of 10 or 11 years to coordinate the concepts related to time. However, there are important opportunities appropriate throughout infancy and early childhood that enable children to gain in understandings that will contribute to their fully developed concept of time.

As a child is bathed, dressed, played with, fed, and put to bed at somewhat regular times from birth, he is having opportunities for experiences that begin to form the basis for time perception. A child builds the idea of order and duration through hearing sounds of varying lengths, seeing the actions of people and toys start and stop, being in control of starting and stopping his own action and the action of objects, and participating in activities that begin, continue, and stop.

By the time a child is two he has learned to anticipate an immediate event, and he refers to time in the present—"now." By the time he is three he has learned to place events in the past, present, and future correctly. He lacks precision about these ideas and "a long time ago" may mean yesterday or last week and "soon" may mean in the immediate future or in the next week.

A three-year-old child understands time in terms of events that relate to him—"time to get dressed," "time to play," "time for breakfast," etc. The three-year-old speaks of "a day," "all week," "all time," "long time," but he does not understand these words as adults do. He asks, "What time is it?" but he does not mean is it 10 or 10:30 o'clock. He may be asking, "When is my mommie coming?" or "Is it time to go outside?" A teacher who responds with a simple sequence of events is most helpful in teaching the child about time, because her answers are understood by the child. When a child says, "Help me, teacher!" it is helpful to the child's learning about time to be precise and say, "I'm helping John; I'll help you next," rather than saying, "In a minute" or "Soon, Betsy." Sometimes our "moments" get long and our "soon" becomes later. It is helpful to a child learning about time, learning to wait, and learning the language of time for a teacher to be precise in her responses.

As a three-year-old enters school there are many "times" for him to learn as he encounters a whole new series of events. The gradual introduction to school described in Chapter 9 is designed, in part, to help a child gradually learn about the time at school and its relationship to time at home. A child, like adults, experiences time that is stressful as too long and time that is pleasant as too short. Unlike an adult who has had a great deal of experience with duration and understands it, a young child becomes overwhelmed by stress that seems too long. The discussion in Chapter 9 is important to consider for a child's adaptation to school as it relates to his understanding of time.

For a child to have the time and opportunity to learn the sequence of the day should be a consideration in each subsequent group he enters. Such opportunities provide positive experience for the cognitive and affective aspects of learning about time.

While helping him in routine situations such as dressing, eating, and toileting, there are many opportunities for teachers to help a child learn sequences within events. For example, when dressing, a child can learn that underpants go on first and pants second; first snowpants, followed by boots, jacket, cap, and finally mittens. Children need to find out for themselves that these sequences are useful. A child needs to make reasonable to himself what adults have learned long ago. The learning is the child's and with understanding on the part of his teacher a child very gradually learns the logical orders for routines and becomes *autonomous* from adults. Such learning is well worth a teacher's planning time for leisurely dressing, eating, and toileting.

As a child has opportunities to associate the name of the day of the week with particular events, he learns the names of the days. "Monday my daddy comes for me!" "Thursday Steve makes music with us." Yesterday, today, and tomorrow become more precise ideas as they are associated with many events important to the child. A child often makes interesting errors at three and four; for example, John (3.9) said, "Lasterday I visited my friend." A thoughtful teacher recognizes such errors as reasonable for a child learning the complexities of the language. She does not focus on the error but, rather, accepts the child's intent.

By four a child is learning about and uses the words: weeks, month, and year. He seems to know the relationship of these intervals and usually uses them correctly, if not precisely. Conversations and stories that include next month, next summer, last winter, and birthday months can help to add meaning and precision to these ideas. A practiced three- and four-year-old emerges as a five-year-old child who understands and is able to verbalize and spontaneously refer to the sequence of his daily schedule. He usually states it in terms of large blocks of time and still in terms of the activities that take place. A major change in schedule, such as being outside the first of the day when the sequence of events has usually been to be inside first, confuses the child. He does not fully understand that the order of things in time can be reversed and the interval of being at school remains the same. A teacher repeating the different sequence and how it is different from other days helps him to accept a "backward" day and he gradually learns to understand the reversal of activities in time.

A late five-year-old child may seem to understand months, years, and seasons. These ideas are only understood in relation to him and what he has experienced. He does not have a long enough personal history to bring full meaning to them. He can represent a sequence of events with which he is very familar. Pictographs are helpful learning opportunities for him now. For example, four pictures, each one portraying a step in the process of building a block structure, or four pictures representing getting dressed, may be used. Pictographs need to be selected with a child's experience in mind. Calendars can be used to keep account of special events, but they have limited meaning for even a near six-year-old. The symbol and systems for calendars and clocks need to be thoroughly understood and not memorized.

SPACE

Space is generally thought of as distance between or within things, as area or room for some purpose. Adults use the term space in various ways, such as "parking space," "booked space," and "outer space."

Concepts related to space are another way we order the world around us. Some of the concepts a child is learning are "in–out," "in back of," "in front of," "up-down," "around," "through," "in-between," "on top," "on the bottom," "by the side of," "inside–outside," "parts," and "wholes."

Just as with time, infants and young children gain an understanding of space through their own movements and actions. Looking, touching, mouthing, hearing, moving through space, and acting in space enable a child to build up ideas about distance and the spaces within and between objects.

As a three-year-old enters school, he needs time to learn the location and purpose of many spaces: the location of the toilet, of the playroom, of the yard, of objects important to him in the room, and of the place to put his own belongings. As discussed in Chapter 9, a visit to school when no other children are present and the child's gradual introduction to school provide opportunities for him to gain a sense of "knowing" the place. A part of knowing the place is knowing the space. Space needs to be arranged in such a way that it is easily knowable to the child. The child's introduction to school time and space are second only in importance to his introduction to the people who will be with him in school.

Thoughtful teachers will help children new to school, whatever age, learn the names of the areas in the room and in the playground. In a school some of the areas will be the locker area, the homemaking area, the block area, the climbing area, and the sandbox. Learning the areas' names can help focus the child's attention on space and enables him to understand where people, objects, and choices for the day are located.

Opportunities for children to learn about location in space are natural in the social setting of a school. As children work with other children and have needs for particular materials, they turn to the teacher. To support the child's developing concept of space, the teacher responds to the child's inquiries with precise statements like, "Yes, they are in the block area, on the bottom shelf in the small basket." The teacher's gestures, indicating location, are needed cues for the young child. As children learn the *ideas* of bottom, top, side, etc., they can respond to the verbal directions without the support of gestures. Precise directions, as given above, enable children to grasp the ideas of location and to learn the words that represent the ideas.

A late three- or four-year-old can show others where materials and places are located. but it takes a long time for him to be able to put them into words. A five-year-old can begin to use the language related to location and positions in space to help others, just as his teacher has helped him.

Three-, four-, and five-year-old children can learn about *parts* and *wholes* in a variety of practical ways as they use floor blocks, parquetry blocks, and building game sets. The three-year-old fits blocks together to make new shapes, a whole made from parts. However, it should not be assumed that he has planned to use the parts to make the wholes; rather, he is building with blocks in ways that please him. As he constructs his own building, he makes new shapes and forms. From this activity he begins to understand the relationship between these particular blocks (i.e., parts) and this particular building (i.e., whole). The generalization of the relationship between parts and wholes will be at least three years away.

By five, a child may be challenged to replicate printed designs. Parquetry blocks and colored one-inch cubes are examples of materials that can be used for this purpose. At the same time, children of this age continue to be interested in making their own designs and thus should not be limited to copying.

Using parquetry blocks is one way to learn about parts and wholes.

MEASUREMENT

Measurement is a system for determining the extent, the quantity, or the size of something. There are standard instruments and units for linear, volume, weight, and square measurements, as well as for dry and liquid measures. Although one's occupation may determine one's knowledge of the tools and units used for some measuring, all of us measure and estimate measurements in our daily lives (e.g., buying groceries, buying clothing, and placing the dinner leftovers in a bowl to be put in the refrigerator).

The concepts of "alike–different," "larger–smaller," "more-less," and all the related concepts discussed with regard to classification, seriation, and number are fundamental to measurement. As adults we have been well schooled in the exactness of measurement, and thus we are likely to overlook estimates and comparisons as related to the topic of measurement. Also, for most adults measurement seems very concrete, as indeed it is for any given instance of measuring something. However, as we work with children, it is important to remember that measurement units, even though universally agreed upon, are arbitrary and abstract.

Linear Measurement

Three-, four-, and five-year-old children are very accurate in judging that one object is larger, smaller, or the same size as another if the objects are side by side and oriented in the same direction. However, if one of the two objects is on its side or if one is placed at a different level, the children are unable to accurately compare the objects because they are unable to mentally coordinate two dimensions, namely, height and width. For most children the ability to coordinate two dimensions does not develop until well into the elementary school years.

What young children can learn is that the size, height or width, of objects can be compared by placing the objects side by side. Learning to use this method of comparison requires many opportunities for children to use comparison with a great variety of objects and materials in a large number of meaningful, real, problem-solving situations. For example, on a rainy day Abbie (3.2), was making an "umbrella" from tinker toys. She picked up a dowel and fit it into a sprocket, then she took another dowel that was longer than the first and put it into the sprocket. Her brow wrinkled and she pulled out the second rib and reached for another. She repeated her effort several times. Each time the second dowel was longer than the first. Abbie had not compared the lengths of the dowels. Yet, when she saw them in place, close together, she could recognize that the second one was too long. Her teacher asked, "Do you want all the ribs of your umbrella to be just the same length?" Abbie replied, "Yes!" Her teacher demonstrated to Abbie how she could place a dowel next to the first one and judge whether it was too long, too short, or the same length. In this instance Abbie could use that method of comparison to complete the umbrella she was making. It takes solving many

How long is the space?

such problems over several years before a child can spontaneously use this method for comparing lengths, as well as for comparing other dimensions of size.

Five-year-olds often begin to use their own bodies as units for measurement in situations meaningful to them. Michael (5.2), exclaimed about an airplane he had just constructed, "It's big! It's four hands long!" Such interest in "exact" measurement may be fleeting or related only to specific situations or tasks, but a thoughtful teacher will watch, listen, and expand the child's interest in it. At the same time, she will not push the idea because she knows five-year-olds are still *initiators* of many ideas that they are not intellectually or emotionally able to pursue. Well into the kindergarten year, after a child spontaneously has used hands and feet to measure a large number of objects, a teacher might introduce the idea of measuring objects by a standard, objective unit. A good introduction to such measuring units is a stick which the child can mark and use to measure and compare many objects in the classroom.

Learning measurement is progressing from the direct comparison of objects laid side by side to comparing the recorded standard unit measurements of two or more objects. Exact measurement involves understanding rational counting and being able to use it as an operational technique.

Weight

Very young children, as well as adults, can accurately judge the weight of most objects they lift. That is, they apply an appropriate amount of muscular force to lift objects.

Weight and size tend to be related so that, in general, large objects are judged to be heavier than small objects. However, as adults, we know that there are many exceptions. We know that weight depends not so much on size as on density and on the material out of which the object is made. Young children, three- and four-year-olds, are just beginning to understand the exceptions and often find it interesting and challenging to discover which objects are heavier and which lighter as they compare objects of various sizes and materials—styrofoam, wood, and plastic, for example. Rocks of different density as they exist in the natural environment make interesting objects to compare.

When children are about five-and-a-half, balance scales can be useful instruments for making exact comparisons. For example, using a balance scale, a child can discover how many little pebbles it takes to balance a large stone. The concepts of "lighter than," "heavier than," and "the same weight as" can have fuller meaning as children use balance scales.

The child plays with balance scales, trying them out.

Volume

Volume is the amount of space occupied in three dimensions. It involves both the amount of space enclosed within the boundaries of an object or container and the amount of space displaced by the object. To understand the measurement of volume, it is necessary to be able to coordinate three dimensions (e.g., height, length, and width). For most children such abilities do not develop until the end of elementary school.

Three-, four-, and five-year-old children can gain an understanding of how much can be held within an enclosed space by working with containers of various sizes and building block structures. Water-play or play with corn meal or rice offers children opportunities to fill and empty jars, cups, bottles—containers of various sizes. A block building may be a garage filled with cars, or a furnished house, or a farmyard filled with animals. Children late in the kindergarten year may be interested in making more exact comparisons of volumes by using standard measuring containers. A few kindergarten children may discover that the shape of the container does not determine the volume. All such activities may add to the child's concept of occupied space, which will later contribute to the development of the concept of volume and its measurement.

SCIENCE

Discovery is fundamental to science. Regardless of the specialization, a scientist's sense of wonder and curiosity motivates her to describe her observations, to explain relationships, and to postulate cause and effects. The young child's natural curiosity motivates him in the same way the adult scientist's curiosity motivates her; that is, the young child, too, finds pleasure in describing and explaining his observations.

The young infant observes nonliving and living things; he is both a physical scientist and a life scientist. The infant investigates the physical properties of nonliving things: solid objects, such as rattles, mobiles, and balls; liquids, such as milk, syrup, and his bath water; and gas, such as odors and air. He investigates the world of living things: animals, such as, dogs, birds, and his parent's face; and plants, such as grass, leaves, and flowers.

An older infant or toddler extends his observations of his world and begins to understand some relationships and systems, such as a light and switch; a clapper and bell; and his coat and going outside. What the child learns from his interactions with objects, people, and events depends, in part, on how he relates what he currently sees, hears, touches, tastes, and smells to what he has previously experienced. For example, a child who sees a lamb for the first time and calls it a dog has classified this new animal by relating it to what he already terms "dog." An adult who enjoys the excitement of discovery will find the child's relationship an interesting one and may say, "Yes, it does look like a dog; it has four legs and a tail, but it's called a lamb." She will

Children observe eggs and tadpoles and use sequence cards to learn about the life cycle of a frog.

enjoy the child's thinking and, although she may smile, she will not laugh at him. She will recognize his serious and thoughtful attempt to make sense of his observation.

The infant or toddler who has found his observations of the world about him interesting and rewarding will be a nursery school and kindergarten child interested in observing and interacting with more complex systems, such as ropes, pulleys, inclined planes, or the life cycle of a frog from egg to tadpole to frog. He will be interested in life and death; he will be interested in the difference between alive things and dead things and in the difference between things once alive and things that never were alive. He will wonder, be curious, and ask questions, the answers to some of which he should be encouraged to discover from his own observations and actions.

CLASSIFICATION AND PHYSICAL PROPERTIES

In the previous section, mathematics, we discussed the development of the concepts of classification, seriation, number, measurement, and time. These concepts are relevant to science because they are ways to organize observations and knowledge. For the young child, one of the most useful of these concepts is classification, the grouping of objects on the basis of shared functional or formal properties. In science, functional properties become known to the child as he *uses* objects, or as he *acts with* objects; whereas formal properties become known to him as he *perceives objects,* as he looks at, listens to, tastes, or feels objects.

In addition to functional and formal properties, objects may be classified on the basis of *physical properties,* a fundamental scheme in science. Physical properties become known to the child as he observes his actions on objects and the reactions of the objects. For example, if a rubber ball is dropped, it bounces; if a glass is dropped, it breaks. The ball is resilient, a physical property not shared by glass.

Classification is the core of the young child's learning in science. He uses it to order his observations. It involves both the content of science and a method of scientific inquiry. Through the process of classification the child learns the characteristics of a wide variety of objects. He is learning that objects may share a common formal property, but not necessarily a common physical property; for example, all red objects do not bounce. He is learning to describe not only objects, but also events, the sequence of actions and reactions. He is learning to compare events, and he is learning to predict outcomes.

CAUSATION

In addition to classification, a central concept in science is *causation.* Causation involves phenomena that take place in space through time. The child builds a concept of spatial-temporal relationships as he has opportunities to observe change in objects over time, as well as in and through space. He needs opportunities to ask questions and to plan ways of answering them. The young child must be an active participant in the question and answer process.

As a beginning nursery school child confronts natural events each day, he is unaware of all that is relevant to a particular happening. Nevertheless, he is ready to begin the long process of learning to test his predictions. He confronts cause and effect as *he personally* is the cause. Out of a large number of opportunities to observe the effect *he* causes and to observe objects change, he will emerge as a six- or seven-year-old child who is able to take a more objective view of cause and effect. The child three through five years of age builds his *own knowledge* from his *own* experience. He learns through his own direct involvement with the objects and through changes in the objects that are meaningful to him. Telling him answers that we have discovered ourselves will not help him in this process. The child has to structure his knowledge for himself. A teacher can be helpful in providing the opportunities for a child to learn ways of thinking, to learn ways to ask and answer questions, but she cannot shortcut the process for him.

During his third and fourth year the child can learn to extend his powers of

A garden is a natural opportunity for observing change over time.

observation and begin to order the evidence from his perceptions. He can pose a question and learn to consider ways to find an answer. For example, what does a rabbit eat? Various foods can be placed in the rabbit cage, where the rabbit can be watched to see what he chooses to eat. The teacher can help the child to develop a "wait and see" attitude rather than jumping to conclusions. The child can observe what the rabbit eats over a period of a few days. Children who share an interest in this project may, with the teacher's help, make pictorial representations as a record of their observations. They are gathering evidence and then drawing conclusions. Success in discovering what the rabbit likes to eat may bring pleasure and interest in future inquiries.

A four- or five-year-old child who has learned to be an accurate observer may use observations to reason about a single cause. That is, he can reason about a single cause that results in a predictable effect. For the purpose of aiding this beginning learning of objective cause and effect, opportunities should be planned that make a single cause clearly discernible to the child. The event can be clearly discovered by the child if the opportunity is stripped of any phenomena that is extraneous to the particular cause and effect being studied. For example, when planning an opportunity for children to observe floating and sinking objects, the selection of the objects is critical. The teacher wants the child to *discover a cause* of sinking or floating through his own observations of the action of the objects. The sinking objects must have a common characteristic that is reasonably related to sinking. It should be the only characteristic common to the sinking objects. The same should hold for the floating objects. In this plan the child will not inadvertently "discover" that color is what makes objects sink or float.

THE SCHOOL ENVIRONMENT IS AN INTERESTING RESOURCE FOR SCIENCE

The environment of the school provides a number of natural phenomena that attract the interests of young children. There are living things, such as earthworms, ants, flowering weeds, caterpillars, leaves, sowbugs, birds, and spiders. There are nonliving things, such as sand, gravel, rock, concrete, and ice. All of these things, living and nonliving, may be found in the playground and can be observed and talked about as they exist in their natural conditions.

Sand is an example of a substance commonly found in playgrounds that can offer many learning opportunities as it is naturally used by children in their play. As a child plays with water and sand, he may notice that a large amount of water can be added to a pail full of sand. How much water? One bucket full? One-half a pitcher? He can find out by doing it, by adding water until it flows over the top of the pail. A child may notice that dirt will wash out of sand. What happens when he stirs a magnet through the sand? How does sand compare to dirt? As the child explores sand, more questions and possibilities may occur to him.

The school environment is, indeed, a natural science laboratory for young children. The alert teacher is aware of each child's curiosity and interests. She helps the child expand in his initial explorations while at the same time allowing him to control the extent and direction of the activity.

SOME SCIENCE INTERESTS IN COMMON TO YOUNG CHILDREN

The three-, four-, or five-year-old child finds himself a particularly interesting subject to study. His own body is a serious subject for serious observation and description—saliva, blood, urine, feces, genitals, bone, hair, skin, and fingernails. Sometimes a child is frightened when he gets a scratch and bleeds. It is important for him to learn how to take care of cuts and bumps. For example, most young children can wash the cut, apply antiseptic, and place a bandage on the cut. Allowing the child to do as much self-help as is possible will allow him to learn about himself and to reassure him. Being hurt is a threat to a child's autonomy; helping himself whenever possible can help restore confidence in his ability to act on his own behalf. The child can learn about swelling, bleeding, and healing in a simple straightforward way. A good teacher will help a child to observe, to appreciate, and to understand his own body, inside and outside. In addition, he will have the opportunity to observe, to appreciate, and to understand others.

Nursery school and kindergarten age children are interested in the subject of where babies come from and how they grow. Specifically, a child is interested in how *he* was born. Simple, factual information such as, "You started growing inside your mother's uterus. Your daddy started the egg growing," is a good beginning in relating such knowledge. A next step might be, "You grew from an egg fertilized (or started growing) by your daddy and were protected in a special place in your mother called the uterus until you were big enough to be born. Then you were born, fed, and taken care of by your parents."

Young children are interested in knowing the ways babies are fed. Watching a mother nursing is a fascinating experience for a group of children as one can see on page 296. These children are absorbed by what they see. The child in the first picture has never seen an infant nursing before. His response seems to be one of great interest. The mother explains, and the children listen as they watch the infant. They are observing the way this baby is fed. Are there other ways to feed infants? Are baby animals fed this way? What other animals are fed this way? How can he find out?

Watching animals and caring for them can provide a wealth of learning opportunities for a child to learn about living things, such as their natural habitats; what they eat; how they eat; how, when, and for how long they sleep; how they move; what kind of tracks they make; how they eliminate; how much they grow; and how they reproduce. A child can observe, make charts, predict, and discuss his observations and predictions about a pet. Over time he will organize a great deal of knowledge if he has the opportunities to observe and to interact with animals. Kindergarten children can begin to make comparisons of the animals with which they are familiar. Some animals that are appropriate to have at school are rabbits, guinea pigs, lambs, pigs, turtles, lizzards, or snakes.

When an animal is brought to school, it is important to make adequate provisions for caring for it, such as a proper shelter, as natural as possible, that can be cleaned easily and thoroughly. Helping to take care of an animal makes it possible for children to learn about the needs and habits of particular animals.

Animals that cannot be housed at school for a long time can be brought for a visit. Some science centers loan animals such as turtles, lambs, guinea pigs, mice, and snakes. In one school it was possible to have a goat visit for a few weeks. The children learned that the goat drank milk from a bottle each morning. He played with the children and often managed to slip in an unguarded door and make straight for the kitchen, the place his bottle came from each morning! This young kid proved as adept as the children in walk-

These children learn about one way a baby is fed.

These children are learning to handle and care for baby chicks.

ing on boards and jumping over objects. The children learned about the kid's ability to find his food and to handle his body. They found him to be a fine companion.

If there is a farm nearby the children can visit on a regular basis in order to become familiar with the smells, sights, and sounds of the animals, as well as with the needs and habits of farm animals.

As children have opportunities to observe and take care of animals, they are sure to come into contact with death. Baby mice will sometimes die; or a dog may get into the pen and kill the chicken. The children may find a dead bird in the playground or a dead fish in the aquarium. A child's response to death will reflect the attitude of the adults around him. There is no need to hide the fact of death from a child or try to escape from facing it. A child will usually want to understand why the animal died. He may be helped in his acceptance of the reality by feeling how the dead animal differs from a live one he has known. The child will not be greatly disturbed if the adult does not need to dramatize, distort, or escape from the fact of death herself. If a child can have a sound, reassuring experience with death, he will be able to face life, as well as death, with less fear.

The teacher who poses problems and takes advantage of spontaneous problems helps a child discover relationships out of his own experience. Ways of discovering are supported and answers are left open so the child does not necessarily settle for the first answer. The child can determine for himself what is interesting to him. The teacher may state her interests in an honest way; she may point out the interests of others. In this way, the child

Finding out what's in the shell
is interesting to both the
teacher and the child.

can learn that there are other interests while at the same time he knows he may pursue his own. Teachers provide a model for ways and means of stating questions and pursuing discovery. A teacher who injects a substantial element of honest doubt, "I do not know. Let's see if we can discover . . . ," helps the child learn the value of inquiry and the joy of discovery.

Making new connections depends on knowing enough about something in the first place to be able to think of other things to do, of other questions to ask, which demand the more complex connections in order to make sense of it all. The more ideas a person has at his disposal, the more new ideas occur, and the more he can coordinate to build up still more complicated schemes. (Duckworth, 1972:231)

SUPPLEMENTARY READING

MATHEMATICS

Copeland, R. W. *How Children Learn Mathematics,* 2nd ed. New York: Macmillan, 1974.

Education Development Center. *Teacher's Guide for Geo Blocks.* New York: McGraw-Hill, 1967.

Education Development Center. *Teacher's Guide for Pattern Blocks.* New York: McGraw-Hill, 1968.

Ginsburg, H., *Children's Arithmetic.* New York: Van Nostrand, 1977.

Kamii, C., and R. DeVries. *Piaget, Children, and Number.* Washington, D.C.: National Association for the Education of Young Children, 1976.

SCIENCE

Althouse, R., and C. Main. *Science Experiences for Young Children.* New York: Teachers College Press, 1975.

Holt, B. G. *Science with Young Children.* Washington, D.C.: National Association for the Education of Young Children, 1977.

Kamii, C., and R. DeVries. *Physical Knowledge in Preschool Education: Implications of Piaget's Theory.* Englewood Cliffs, N.J.: Prentice-Hall, 1978.

Pratt-Butler, G. K. *How To Care for Living Things in the Classroom,* rev. ed. Washington, D.C.: National Science Teachers Association, 1978.

Waters, B. S. *Science Can Be Elementary: Discovery-Action Programs for K-3.* New York: Citation Press, 1973.

House, Sun, and Sky
(girl, 3.9)

Curriculum Areas:
Language Arts
and Social Studies

LANGUAGE ARTS

Language arts is a broad term which includes four general areas: speaking, listening–attending, writing, and reading. All of these areas are a part of the process of thinking and communication, and each area is interrelated with the other. In nursery school and kindergarten these areas merge, as language arts is learned in the context of ongoing, everyday activities. Language arts pervade the total curriculum. Like other modes of art, language arts involve self-expression and the mastery of techniques to produce artistic forms.

SPEAKING

A healthy, well-developed infant can see, hear, and vocalize. He differentiates various visual patterns, attends to the face of his caretaker, responds to the affect expressed by her face, and attends to and visually follows moving objects. He responds to different sounds by being soothed, alerted, or distressed and by turning his head or looking in the direction of a sound. Although he may look at the face of an unfamiliar person, he smiles at the face of his caretaker. He vocalizes by crying, babbling, and cooing in a differential manner (Appleton, Clifton, Greenberg, 1975).

At about one year of age, as the result of verbal interactions with his caregiver, the infant says single words. During his second year of life, the child learns many words which he uses to make requests to call attention to an object, a person, or an event, and to express feelings. He begins to put words together to ask questions and to make statements: "Where daddy?" "Read book!" "Daddy's hat?" and "Nice kitty." During the last quarter of his first year and during his second year, the child can understand and respond to a wide variety of simple instructions, discussions, reproofs, and warnings, such as: "Bring Daddy the ball." "Please, drink your milk." "Sit in your chair! You're making mommie angry." and "Careful, the stove is hot!" He uses intonation, gesture, and language to communicate; for example, depending on his intonation, gesture, and the context of the situation, "Daddy's hat" may mean "This is daddy's hat," "Is this daddy's hat?" "Where is daddy's hat?" "Give me daddy's hat!" or "Get your hat daddy, and let's go!"

All of this language learning takes place by hearing language in the social and concrete context of people, actions, objects, gestures, and feelings. The child is not limited by imitation of language he has heard, but rather he combines words to construct his own original statements and questions. During the later half of the second year, language becomes a powerful tool for the child, as well as a pleasure. He plays with sounds; he understands the difference between real words and his own delightful inventions, and is amused by them.

When children come to school at about three years of age, we observe great individual differences in their competence with language and their verbal "styles." Some children are always talking or singing to themselves as they play. When they are with other children, they talk to them, describing what they are doing, giving directions, agreeing, and disagreeing. Other children use very few words in the same situation, and go quietly about the business of play. Nevertheless, their facial response or actions indicate they are listening and understand.

Children all go through stages in learning language that are strikingly similar from child to child. Each child actively discovers the structure of the language he hears and tries to make sense out of it. In this effort, he applies his own rules to the language he speaks. At some point, he might say "foots" or "mouses." These are not words he is likely to have heard, but his use of them shows that he has observed that an "s" sound is used to mean more than one object. He applies this rule, an intelligent action, only later to discover that there are exceptions. The same thing happens when he concludes that "-ed" refers to something in the past. He overgeneralizes a rule and says, for example, "comed," "goed," and "teached." This attempt to construct a logical grammar is evidence of an advance in thinking, although to adults unfamiliar with language development, these errors seem like a regression. Overgeneralizations of rules drop out as the child's language matures. This language learning goes on, not in a conscious way, but as a formulation out of tacit knowledge gleaned from listening and speaking.

During the nursery school years, children are likely to misplace or omit sounds in syllables in words as in "hangerburger" and "saghetti." It is difficult for children to learn pronouns because of their relational use. Young children do not fully understand time, space, and number concepts; they may express their understanding of these concepts by invented words, such as "lasterday." They often define words in terms of function, such as "a broom is for sweeping." They may use analogies from their personal experience. One day, for example, a child who sat on his foot so long that the circulation was impaired for a time said, "I have bees in my shoes!" Children repeat words as they hear them, for example, "the starched spangled banner."

The Teacher's Role as a Speaking and Listening Partner with Children

The teacher who enjoys children's picturesque, inventive, and often poetic speech is an ideal language partner for the child. She takes pleasure in the child's developing abilities and understands that language learning is a life-long process. She provides a good model and is a consistent source of corrective feedback for attending and speaking. The eight points discussed below are offered as guides for the teacher as she enacts the role of a speaking and listening partner with children (Provence, Naylor, and Patterson, 1977:174–176).

1. *Attend to and respond to the intent of each child's nonverbal and verbal communication.* Teachers of three-year-old children have to become skillful at understanding the child's nonverbal communications, as well as the words they say. They must look beyond the words and endeavor to discover the child's meaning. For example, the child who asks, "Will the swing break?" may really be asking "Will you keep me safe?" In this way the teacher can extend the child's use of relevant language. She can encourage children's language by paying close attention to both nonverbal and verbal behavior and by responding appropriately, the communication is rewarding for them both.

A teacher who respects the child and wishes to be a model the child can imitate will not directly correct a child's grammar or speech pattern. She will use acceptable forms and supply correct names. She will respond to his intent. For example, Bill (5.6) said to his teacher, "It don't work," when telling her the pencil sharpener was broken. The teacher's response was, "The pencil sharpener doesn't work. Open it and see if you can find out what is wrong." Bill communicated his idea to his teacher, and she responded to his intent.

Children appear to imitate some people and not others, depending on affectional ties. A child selects his own speech models, and the teacher who respects the child's intent is in a better position to be imitated.

2. *Teach language casually and spontaneously in a setting mutually pleasurable to both the child and adult.* One-to-one conversation with an adult on a subject of real interest to the child can provide language practice that over time can lead to increasing mastery for the child. A teacher will find *time* and *opportunities* for conversation with each child in mutually pleasurable situations: as they wash paint brushes together; as they plan a surprise for someone; as they plan a project together; or as they prepare a snack.

A child learns the words he puts to use; therefore, a teacher will provide opportunities for the child to speak and encourage his use of language. For example, at lunch a teacher will encourage children to recall their experiences saying, "Do you remember when. . . ." or "Tell us about the. . . ." and encourage each child to respond. The teacher's statements or questions should reflect honest interest rather than empty exercises in teaching language.

3. *Express appropriate effect for the verbal and nonverbal messages received from the child or given to the child.* As a teacher converses with a child she should not be a bland person; rather, she should express a wide range of effect appropriate to the communication. For example, Stacey (4.5), who needed to be a very "good" girl, was angry with her teacher and gave her a hard hug. Her teacher responded, "That was a very hard hug, and it hurt me. I wonder if you aren't angry with me because you wanted to help set up the snack?" The teacher's tone of voice, facial expression, and body movement showed that the hug hurt and her honest wonder about the cause of the anger. She did not confuse the child by accepting the hug as affection, but conveyed to the child in a kind, honest manner that hurt and anger are appropriate feelings and can be expressed in a straightforward way.

Feelings as well as thoughts can be expressed in words. The child takes an important step in recognizing and controlling his feelings when he can put them into words rather than expressing them through action. He can ask for what he wants rather than grab. He can express sorrow and pleasure. An appropriate affective response from the teacher helps the child to understand and accept his feelings, particularly for children whose language skills are not developed, although appropriate responses are important to all children.

4. *Speak with clear articulation whatever the dialect or regional accent.* "The language variety one learns simply reflects where and with whom one lives, not the intelligence with which one is endowed" (Cazden, 1972:23). Teachers may have dialects and are certain to have some regional accent. Because ours is a highly mobile society, teachers' speech often contains traces of many accents.

When a teacher speaks a dialect, she may have syntactical differences from standard English. Teachers will need to be aware that the structure of their statements and questions may be confusing to the child. It is the teacher's responsibility to communicate her intent clearly and in ways children can understand.

If a teacher comes from another region, she may pronounce words differently or have different names for familiar objects. When teaching children language, it is important to articulate words clearly so that children hear the words being said. If a teacher has a different name for familiar objects, children can learn that an object is called by several names. In this way a child's language may be extended and enriched.

5. *Match words, phrases, and sentences closely to those of the child and then expand these with functional words while maintaining the order of the child's speech.* When the child's language is nonspecific, the teacher can use precise language to teach the child new words and meanings. For example, if a child says, "I put it over there, Miss C.," the teacher can respond by using specific referrents: "Thank you, Jim, for putting the pitcher on the tray." The teacher uses *complete sentences* with *precise* words when talking to children, as "Please, bring me the red truck on the top shelf," rather than "Please, bring me that truck over there." In the first example, the child has a pattern of exact speech to learn from.

6. *Elaborate the child's speech and ideas in conversation.* For example, if a child questions, "What's that?" The teacher can say: "This is a saw. Would you like to cut a piece of wood with it? See how it cuts when you move it back and forth." In this way the child will learn new words in the context of action and experiences meaningful to him.

7. *Teach differentiation of similar objects and ideas.* In the example above a child might be reminded of other tools he has used for cutting. "Can you think of anything else used for cutting?" The child might recall the knife used to cut carrots and the potato peelers. The teacher might add: "You know lots of tools for cutting." The conversation could move on to how the objects are alike in function, but how they look very different. Some child will surely have the idea that knives are not safe. Such an *idea* can be discussed in terms of when and where knives can be safely used.

8. *Ask questions to stimulate children's thinking.* Open-ended questions, such as, "What do you notice about the rabbit, John?" require the child to observe and think. There are many things to observe about a rabbit: He has fur; he wiggles his nose; he eats lettuce, but not hamburger; he has strong back legs; and he jumps. When a teacher wants a child to learn to think and put his thoughts into words, she asks a question to stimulate his thinking. The child's response may tell the teacher something about the child's thinking, too. Noting children's responses to such questions over time provides a great deal of information about how well a child is able to verbalize his observations. If the question, "Tell me all you see when you look at the rabbit," appears to overwhelm the child, the teacher may revise her question to, "What sounds do you hear? Feel him, what can you find out about by feeling the rabbit?" Questions like, "What do you think will happen now?" can cause a child to wonder, whereas questions such as, "Do you think the rabbit likes lettuce?" call for "yes" or "no" answers and give the teacher few cues to the child's thinking.

Taken together the eight guides above are intended to reflect our belief that a fundamental purpose of language is communication, communication between people who both speak and listen. Listening in the communication process means attending to what the other person says and, at the same time, attending to the nonverbal signs in order to respond to intent, as well as to words. Therefore, in addition to speech skills, the teacher models the skill of listening. She understands that it is important for the child to practice listening to be reflective, and she will use spontaneous situations and plan opportunities for that purpose.

LITERATURE

Opportunities to look at books and to hear stories and poems are a part of the daily program in a school that values language development and the language arts.

SELECTING BOOKS

In selecting books the teacher will find the *Horn Book* magazine, resource books, such as those by Arbuthnot (1971, 1976), Anderson and Groff (1972), and MacCann and Richards (1973), and the local library sources for help in becoming acquainted with new books being published for children and with children's literature in general. A useful criteria for selecting children's books can be found in *The Child's First Books* (McCann & Richards, 1973). The book, *Helping Children Cope* (Fassler, 1978), in which children's books are organized according to topic, will be particularly useful to teachers who are helping children cope with problems and conflicts. Many schools depend on the local library for most of their books. These books can be selected with the interests of individual children in mind. We recommend that all schools purchase a few story, poetry, and informational or resource books each year. It is very helpful to a child's learning if a teacher can locate and use an informational or resource book with him when his interest in a particular subject is at a peak.

Characteristics of three-, four-, and five-year-old children can be used as a basis for the selections of books to be read to them. *Children these ages are rapidly acquiring language:* Books with language slightly more complex than the child uses with some new words, repetition, and rhyming can add to his pleasure in learning language. *The attention span of preschool children is relatively short:* Matching the length of the book to their ability to attend will allow them to find pleasure in stories. *They are curious about their world:* Books about people with experiences similar to their own and books that reflect the daily lives of children and parents are often good choices. *They are imaginative:* Stories that personify animals or inanimate objects peak their interest. *They are learning to distinguish reality from fantasy:* Stories that are make-believe, that portray danger, death, strife, generosity, and kindness, but end with a sensible resolution help children to separate reality from fantasy. *They seek warmth, affection, and secure relationships:* Stories that have happy or just endings, or that portray mastery or heroic action appeal to children. *They are developing autonomy:* Stories that portray other children, animals, or people who are coping with the stresses of growing up lessen their feelings of being dependent. Choosing books for a particular child or a group of children requires a thorough knowledge of the children's interests, abilities, and understandings.

Books should be changed weekly in order to extend children's interest. Some picture and story books become such favorites that they should be left in the classroom until they no longer attract children's attention. Books, like old friends, are a pleasure to see and hear over and over again. Most children enjoy a whole series of books written by a favorite author or illustrator. Children who have learned to enjoy books can participate in the selection of those to be included in the weekly supply and those to be purchased.

A Place for Books and Browsing

Bookshelves or a rack for books with plenty of adjacent table space and chairs make it possible for a child to look at books comfortably. Some children prefer a cozy spot with a deep pile rug and pillows to lie on while

A place to browse supports this child's interest in books.

they browse. Children cannot be expected to handle books carefully if the space is crowded, or where books are heaped on a shelf; nor can they be expected to be interested in books for long if they are not comfortable. Books, attractively displayed, and a comfortable spot to browse promote children's interest in books.

STORY GROUPS

Story groups should be small for three-year-old children. Knowing how long the children can attend and matching the story to their interests are important factors in planning a group story. Comfortably seated, a whole group of four- and five-year-olds usually can attend to a well-selected, well-read story. Spontaneous comments by the children at any age will be accepted by the teacher. Three-, four-, and five-year-old children are egocentric and identify with the characters and situations in literature. Spontaneous comments result from this identification. Teachers will try to preserve the continuity for the whole group, but not at the expense of the individual child's spontaneity. Reading stories need not be confined to one story time. Some children will want many opportunities to look at books and listen to a favorite one. Small, informal groups that are formed when there is an interest meet this need.

LISTENING CENTERS

Four- and five-year-old children often enjoy listening centers. Some tape recordings can be made of the teacher reading. Many excellent recordings of children's stories are available, too. In classrooms where there is a minimum of adult help, listening centers enable children to hear stories and poetry when they are interested in doing so. Children can look at the book and follow the story as it is being read. Children can easily learn how to use record players, tape recorders, and earphones.

FILM STRIPS AND MOVIES

Many local libraries loan short film strips and movies of books. Late four- and five-year-old children find film strips and movies particularly interesting. Some children who enter school and are not interested in books can be helped to enjoy stories first in the animated form and then in book form. Recordings and films should be a supplement to, rather than the primary source of, stories.

CHILDREN WHO FIND IT DIFFICULT TO LISTEN

Some children may find listening to a story even on a one-to-one basis difficult. It is important to understand why a child is unable to attend to stories or has little interest in books. Perhaps the books are beyond his develop-

A story for an individual child often attracts another.

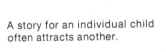

mental level. Does he hear well? Has he had little experience being read to or seeing books? Are there no books available that match his interests? Has a book or a story been frightening to him? These are some of the questions a teacher can ask herself or parents in order to find ways to help a child enjoy, even love books. A child who does not enjoy books misses opportunities to enrich his life each day and will be handicapped throughout school. A teacher should try to find ways to invest books with value for each child in her group.

POETRY

Children appreciate poetry that contains imagery within the range of their imaginations, that expresses their own feelings and fantasies, that has humor they can understand, and that contains rhythm in repetition. Poetry can be introduced early, long before children enter school. The alliteration and repetition of poetry begin with Mother Goose rhymes and go on to the delightful verse of Kenneth Grahame, A. A. Milne, John Ciardi, or Robert Frost. Poetry is a marvelous way to learn language because poetry depends on words with precise meanings. Children who are familiar with and enjoy poetry will often go on to create beauty with words themselves. In the process they enhance their language skills and find a lifelong source of aesthetic enjoyment.

DRAMATIC PLAY

In Chapter 16 dramatic play has been discussed as a mode of learning. It is important to make explicit that in dramatic play language is learned as children interact in spontaneous ways and communicate their ideas to others. Usually, in order to continue the play, children must communicate with each other. With four- and five-year-old children language is often used to substitute for actions and to define the setting. For example, a child might say, "Now, this will be grandmother's house. I'm the big sister, and you are the little sister. I'm making supper. You pretend you get hurt and cry, and I take care of you." With the stage set, the play continues. During 10 or 15 minutes of play this kind of resetting the stage may take place several times.

Because language is often used freely in dramatic play, play provides an opportunity for a teacher to listen and write down what a child is saying. An accurate record of the child's *exact words* is very helpful in making an assessment of the articulation, structure, and use of his language. In some settings students or parents can make these records for the teacher.

DRAMATIZING A STORY OR EVENT

Most children enjoy dramatizing favorite stories and familiar events. Dramatizing a story is another way of knowing literature and language. Dramatizing an event clarifies the child's thinking about what happened and what was or could be said. It is a way for him to become active in telling a story.

The first step in dramatizing a story can be for the children to join the teacher in repeating a recurring story line. One group of children we knew enjoyed being the chorus, as the teacher read *Millions of Cats* (Gag, 1928). After hearing *Mr. Gumpy's Outing* (Burmingham, 1971) a few times these children were able to assume roles and use simple properties to dramatize this story. Dramatizing stories became an activity they thoroughly enjoyed. During their second year at school, as four-year-olds, most of these children took delight in gathering props and acting out more complex stories and events. When they knew a story well, the children would discuss the characters; for example, the troll and the billy goats in *The Three Billy Goats Gruff* (Brown, 1957). Then they dramatized the story often adding to the story line. As kindergarteners their pleasure increased in creating drama as they acted out events such as family picnics or an angry encounter with a friend. Sometimes they were the actors, and sometimes the audience. Their teacher found two books particularly helpful to her in supporting these children's interests, *Using Literature with Young Children* (Jacobs, 1965) and *Creative Dramatics for Children* (Durland, 1952).

Through hearing stories individually, in small groups, and large groups, as well as through discussion of stories, participation in experiences described in literature, and dramatization of stories and events, many of these children were able to express the main ideas of a story in their own words. They could request books by a particular author or illustrator, describe the characters in a story read to them, state which elements in a story were real and which ones were make-believe, and tell which character they liked best and why. Many enjoyed predicting the outcome of a story or suggesting other possible endings.

LISTENING-ATTENDING

Attending is implicitly central to all areas of learning in the school program. What differs among the areas is the predominant perceptual system the child uses to attend. For example, in science the child acts on objects and attends to the results primarily by looking. In language the child attends by listening to the sound of another's speech and looking for nonverbal cues. It is also important to realize that the child learns to monitor his own speech by listening.

FOLLOWING AND GIVING ORAL DIRECTIONS

Following directions becomes a part of a child's life before he understands words; he responds to intonation and gesture. Care-givers talk with a child as if he understands, and this can be an important part of his learning about making requests of and receiving requests from others. The toddler's behavior is characterized by ambivalence—the wish to please and the wish to be autonomous. Inevitable conflicts arise when adult directions have to be given. How well these conflicts are resolved will affect the child's willingness and ability to tolerate, accept, or hear directions.

The well-developing three-year-old can respond to a single direction, for example, "Get your sweater, and you will be ready to go outside," or "Put your juice cup in the wastebasket." It is helpful to a young child in new settings to accompany the words with gestures. As soon as he is familiar with the place and teacher, the words alone will usually suffice. As his ability to attend, his memory, and his language develop, he can act on and be given two-part directions, such as "Put your apron in the basket, and then choose a book to read." If following the first part of a direction takes more than a few seconds, the second part may be forgotten; for instance, "Wash your hands, and then choose a book to read." Handwashing may take several minutes and the second statement may thus be forgotten.

As a child is able to follow one- or two-part directions, he can learn to relay a short message to another person, such as "Please, tell Mark it is his turn on the swing," or "When you finish with the tricycle, tell Mark it is his turn." Children need practice giving and following directions. The social setting of the school provides many opportunities to give and to accept directions from both children and adults. Increasing the complexity of directions as the child is able to follow them is important to his learning. With such practice and self-confidence, a child can relay important messages to his classmates and to children and adults in other classrooms. He can use giving and following directions as a social skill in play and in simple games, such as lotto. With continued practice and learning he will eventually be able to use directions to play dominoes, candyland, and other simple games. Some children will be able to teach other children how to play a game or how to use a piece of equipment.

ALLITERATION AND RHYMING

Poetry and stories for children are filled with opportunities for teachers to direct children's attention to sounds; for example, "A lovely, light, luscious, delectable cake" (Kahl, 1955), or "What's all the clatter? asked the platter" (Cameron, 1961). Many children attend to and take pleasure in the repetition of the beginning consonant sound and the repetition of the sound in the last syllable. Sometimes teachers need to overemphasize these sounds slightly when reading to help children focus on and enjoy the sounds of the language. Even the youngest children in school can attend to and enjoy the sound of alliteration and rhyming. With age and experience, attention to longer, more complex story lines and poems, and to the placement of the repetition (the beginning sound, the ending sound, or the specific sound repeated) will increase.

MAKING AND IDENTIFYING COMMON SOUNDS

Toddlers enjoy reproducing the sounds of animals and the sounds of cars and trucks. Three-year-old children in dramatic play often make the sounds of common objects, such as eggbeaters, sirens, horns, and airplanes. It is important to support children in these vocal activities, for they enrich their play and help to focus their attention on the natural sounds associated with objects and actions, or onomatopoeia. Four- and five-year-old children accustomed to playing with sound use it in increasingly complex ways in play: to make a door bell or phone ring, to make the sound of a dentist's drill, or to make the sound of a space ship taking off. Making a game of identifying a child's voice or identifying common sounds played back on a tape recorder tests a child's increasing ability to discriminate common sounds in his environment.

MAKING AND REPEATING SOUND PATTERNS

Music presents many opportunities for children to reproduce pitch, and to repeat and create melodies and patterns of sound. Identifying rhythm and musical instruments by their sound can start with bells, tambourines, and other common rhythm instruments. Introducing, one at a time, instruments of the orchestra that are distinctive in sound, such as a clarinet and a violin, and repeating their performance over time might be a next step. Through the nursery and kindergarten years children can learn to discriminate the sounds of some woodwinds, brasses, and strings by hearing real instruments and then listening to recorded music.

WRITING

By one year of age a well-developing infant has a well-defined pincer grasp; by 18 months he scribbles spontaneously and can imitate a decisive vertical stroke; by 24 months he can imitate circular strokes; and by three years he can copy a circle and imitate a + (Gesell and Amatruda, 1941).

The three-year-old child enters school with well-developed eye-hand coordination and is able to scribble and draw. If he has looked at books and been read to, he knows something about the written word. He often pretends to write in dramatic play or "writes" his name on a picture he makes; that is, he makes some marks on his paper and refers to them as his name.

Long before a child learns to write, he can learn some of the many uses of writing. He can learn that its central purpose is to communicate ideas to others. There are many opportunities for teachers to help children learn that writing is for communication. If a child wants a turn at the swing, the teacher might say, "I'll write your name on this card, and that way I can remember that you want a turn," and she writes as the child watches. Then she uses this list to help her recall whose turn is next. Or, perhaps there are lots of paintings and the teacher says, "I'll write your name on the back of the paper, so I'll know this is your painting."

Block buildings can be identified by a card with a child's name written on it and attached to the building. Children can take a walk, and when they return, the teacher can write all the things they recall on the chalkboard. She reads the list back to them and comments that the list is long and that writing things down helps everyone remember. She suggests that the children's parents might be interested in seeing the list so they will know what the class saw on the trip. The list could be dittoed and sent home with a note from the teacher.

If a visitor has (a musician, fireman, etc.) come to school, whom the children have enjoyed having, the teacher can tell the children that a kind, friendly way to thank the visitor is by writing him a letter. The children who wish to say thank you in this way can tell her what they would like to say, as she writes down each child's words. They then mail the letter to him.

A three- or four-year-old child can learn that his name is written on a card identifying his locker. We recommend that each child's locker have a card with his name written both in all capital letters and in manuscript, as well as some other means of identification, such as his photograph. Some three- and four-year-old children recognize their names in capital letters, but not in manuscript. To write each child's name both ways provides an opportunity for him to learn that there are different ways to write. One does not expect a three- or four-year-old to recognize his name, but he can and will learn that writing can communicate the idea—my locker. Sometime during the year a child may begin to write the first letter of his name. It is helpful to provide him with a model of his first name or of the letter he is learning to make. One child may work for a few minutes one day and then abandon the task. Another child may work a little each day until he makes a clear letter or his whole name. There is no hurry, and a wise teacher helps just as much as is needed and *no more*.

Eventually by or during the kindergarten year almost all children will learn to write their names. Many children will learn to write the names of the people in their family and the names of friends. Learning to write takes a great deal of fine muscle control as well as eye-hand coordination. It requires the wish to learn to write and the persistence to practice. When learning to write, children make errors in spatial judgment. Errors occur, too, because children forget just how a letter or word looks. Models of the child's name are useful to the child in learning because they help to keep him from practicing errors. Each time an error is made a child is more likely to repeat it, for he is practicing errors. A basket of name models kept near the paper and writing or drawing tools will be handy for the child to use. Some children will be helped in learning to write by tracing letters and words with a china marking pencil over a model placed under a mylar sheet. In this way children can be immediately successful in writing.

It seems wise for children to learn to write both capital and manuscript letters because they will be using both as they continue to write. Some children can write manuscript first. Others can write capitals with greater ease. To be successful is important for the child's persistence in learning to write, and so he writes the way he can write best. We know children will eventually learn both ways of writing. Models of both manuscript and capital letters can be sent home with children. Few children limit their practice to school, and it is helpful to the child's learning if parents understand that both manuscript and capital letters will need to be learned. By writing their names, the names of their family members, and the names of their friends, children can perfect their writing skills and can learn names using many letters of the alphabet.

COMPOSITION

As children learn that writing communicates ideas, they will become interested in using it for that purpose. A child might say, "Teacher write, John Edwards Building Keep Off," or "Miss B., write Colored Bubbles on my picture." In dramatic play a child may request a sign: "Picnic Place," "Res-

Using a typewriter can be absorbing and challenging for a kindergarten child.

taurant,'' or ''C-3PO.'' As signs are written and read, children can learn letters and words.

Children enjoy making their own books. These can be made by stapling paper together. Children accustomed to adults writing often like to dictate stories to their teachers. Teachers may type them or write them quickly in manuscript. At first the dictation might be a caption for a picture or a simple statement, such as ''This boy is asleep.''

Many kindergarten children want to compose stories. Their writing skills are usually labored, and the words they use are beyond their ability to write on their own. Dictation to a teacher, who writes the story in manuscript, can take the place of the child writing at this particular time. Also, in only a few days a child can learn to use a primary typewriter to make his own copy of the story. By using a typewriter, a child can learn that each word is separate from the others with a space between, and that writing proceeds from left to right—one can only write from left to right on a typewriter. It is delightful to read children's dictated or typed stories back to them. They enjoy reading them with the teacher and to others, and they usually want to take them home for parents to read. Some teachers like to keep copies of children's stories. Carbons can be made as the teacher writes and can be placed in the child's folder. Often children illustrate their stories and sometimes they are willing to place their book in the bookshelf for others to look at as they browse.

PUNCTUATION AND CAPITAL LETTERS

As a teacher writes or types a child's dictation, she starts the statements or questions with a capital letter and capitalizes the proper names. She inserts commas between words in a series and puts the proper punctuation mark (period, exclamation point, or question mark) at the end of a statement or question, or she may put quotation marks around a caption. Children discover punctuation marks and are curious about what these marks mean. The teacher explains their use, and can show them how punctuation is used by opening almost any book. Most children will not pursue the use of punctuation marks further at this time.

READING

Reading is an active decision-making process in which the reader must differentiate, categorize, and integrate information in order to identify a letter, a word, or a meaning (Smith, 1971). Before learning to read a child needs a wide variety of first-hand experience. During his nursery and kindergarten years, he will have many opportunities to put his thoughts and feelings into words, to build concepts, and to solve problems. He will have many opportunities to use and enjoy books, to dictate signs, captions, and stories, to make his own books with his thoughts and words written down, and to listen when his and others' stories are read. He will have many opportunities for visual and auditory discrimination and eye-hand coordination. In addition to these opportunities, the child needs teachers whom he can trust; teachers with realistic expectations for him.

Following Top-to-Bottom, Left-to-Right Sequence

As children begin to look at books with adults, the adult starts at the front of a book and looks from left to right. Some children enter nursery school knowing where the story starts, but many do not. It is helpful to children's later learning and need not interfere with their present pleasure in books for the *adult* to start at the front of a book. The child can start wherever he chooses just as adults often do with magazines. An important beginning is for adults to enjoy books with children because it is through a pleasant, affectional relation that children identify with and imitate the adult actions. As books with story lines are read to and looked at with children individually and in small groups, the teacher can place her finger on the left side of the page and move it across to the right to indicate the direction of reading. She can also put what she is doing into words, "The writing begins here," or "I start reading here; this is where the story begins." This action does not need to be done every time, for it can begin to interfere with the child's pleasure, but often enough for the teacher to be sure that the idea is conveyed to each child.

As children begin to look at pictures and tell themselves the stories that have been read to them, they are likely to imitate the teacher by starting at the front of the book and looking at the words as if they are reading. Observing the direction of the child's head, eyes, and hand or finger movements provides useful cues about the child's understanding of following left-to-right and top-to-bottom sequence.

Richard Scarry's books are excellent for helping a child learn to scan a page from left to right and top to bottom. *Cars, Trucks, and Things That Go* (Scarry, 1974) has a tiny bug that can be found in a different place on each page. Looking at this book with a child, a teacher can move her finger across the page at about one inch intervals searching for the bug. Such an orderly search is rewarded quickly when the bug is found. This book is an interesting one, and its many details appeal to a child. Finding the bug is delightful. Most children will imitate the teacher's orderly searching because they want to find the bug. As teachers look at many books with children and make opportunities to point out the process of following left-to-right, and top-to-bottom sequence in ways that enhance their interest and pleasure in books, children will learn to do the same. A three-year-old child can learn to scan a page.

Arranging pictographs or sequence cards in order from left to right is an activity four- and five-year-old children enjoy. Such cards provide an opportunity for children to think through the order of the sequence left to right, first to last, and attend to fine detail. The teacher can begin with a series of three cards expressing an idea familiar to the child, such as putting a sock and shoe on a foot. As children learn to arrange these cards and tell their reasons for their left-to-right arrangement attending to fine details, the complexity of the task can be increased gradually to four then six cards with each successive set containing more detail. Some late fives like to make their own series of pictures, such as comic strips or moving pictures.

Associating the Written Word with the Spoken Word

As soon as a child understands that written words can express ideas the way the spoken word does, he is beginning to understand reading. Most children have been read to a long time before they realize that the written words correspond to what the reader is saying. Most parents and teachers of two- and three-year-old children have had the experience of a child turning a page before they have finished reading the text on that page. Sometimes the child turns the page because the text is too long, and he is ready to move on to look at the next pictures. Sometimes he turns the page because he is reading the pictures himself. There is a time when a parent or teacher says, "Wait, I have to look at the words that tell us about this picture," and the child looks very thoughtful. He may look intently at the printing as if to understand her statement. This is an opportune time to say, "All these words are a part of the story. They tell what is happening in this picture."

As a child begins to learn to write letters, he may combine them at random and ask "What does this say?"—AME. This action provides an opportunity to respond that he has written three letters, but they do not spell any word. One can cover the A and say that these two letters make a word: ME. Many children will experiment with combining letters in this way as a way of trying to understand the written word. It does not mean they are ready to learn to spell.

The child who recognizes his name in his locker, who refers to a list to find out when his turn will be, who writes a sign for a building or a caption for a story, who reads a recipe with words and pictures, who makes his choices for the day from a chart with pictures and words, who dictates a story to a teacher and reads it back with her, and who asks a teacher to read the directions for a game is well on his way to associating the written with the spoken word.

In this section on Language Arts our emphasis has been on providing children with many opportunities to use and explore language. Many kindergarten children may wish to read. Some pursue a variety of prereading tasks for several weeks and then move on to other interests. These children find out for themselves that they are not ready to pursue reading. A *very few* children learn to read before they enter first grade. A teacher may find a child in her classroom who is ready for reading instruction. Such a child can

Reading together can be fun!

probably listen, follow directions, attend to detail, and can work in a group of three or four children at several tasks. He will have the courage to make errors and to fail publicly. He will have had many opportunities to make visual and auditory discriminations, as well as being competent in eye-hand coordination. Reading instruction for such young children should be individualized. In planning an individualized program, a teacher will find it helpful to seek the guidance of a reading specialist.

SOCIAL STUDIES

The subject matter of social studies is drawn from the various social sciences: anthropology, economics, geography, history, philosophy, political science, social psychology, and sociology. It is the facts and understandings furnished by each of these sciences, as well as the interrelationship among them, that adults use to resolve problems facing a society and the individuals in that society.

Social studies are a way for a child to learn about himself, his relationships to other children and adults, and his relationship to objects, events, and places in his world. Through interacting in the world, children are in constant contact with the content and substance of social studies. As we have said before, the child learns best from the people he trusts and cares about, who spend a lot of time with him. The people he finds trustworthy are people who are responsive to his needs, reasonably consistent, and predictable. He cares about whether or not he pleases them, what they say and do with him, and if they are present or not. These people are his primary resource for learning about his worth and competence.

CONCEPTS ARE USED TO ORDER KNOWLEDGE IN THE SOCIAL STUDIES

Adults organize their ideas about social studies through the use of the concepts of classification, seriation, number, time, space, measurement, and causation. Man has invented objects, materials, and places to help him adapt to the particular environment in which he lives, to lighten the burden of his work, and to enhance his play. A child begins to learn about his social world concretely by *using* and *acting with* particular objects and materials in particular places and in specific situations. For example, he learns the function of a chair by having many opportunities to sit in different chairs. Whatever his life space has been before he comes to school, each three-year-old will have had interactions with many of these inventions, such as clothing, tools, housing, paper, paint, appliances, furniture, transportation, roads, sidewalks, signs, farms, factories, airports, marinas, schools, post offices, supermarkets, gas stations, hospitals, jails, offices, malls, libraries, museums, or zoos. The child's interest in and knowledge about his social

The child learns from experiences with everyday objects.

world will be determined by where he lives and the opportunities he has had to use these social inventions.

As a child interacts with people who are important to him, he learns about *social roles,* about what people do in the world, and about the customs, rituals, and values associated with what they do. He learns, first, what the people in his family do. For example, he may learn that mommie cooks the dinner, and daddy washes the dishes. The young child will assume that the behavior of other mothers and fathers is like the behavior of his. As the child has opportunities to move and visit outside his home, he learns that there are people other than his parents who "work"; he learns something about where they work and what they do. The beginnings of his knowledge and understandings will be a result of what his parents say and do. Later, as he has more contact with people and places outside his parents and home, his ideas and beliefs will be a result of *his* interaction, of where *he* goes, and of what happens to *him.* A child may learn, for example, that the doctor works at a special place called "the clinic" and that people who work there take care of people who are sick or hurt. After his visit to the clinic he will have an expectation of what happens there. He will come to know it as a pleasant or a scary place; he will know the people there as kind and helpful, or unpredictable and frightening. He may look forward to another visit or be apprehensive about returning. In general, the child is learning what people do and where they work. He is learning what work means to *him;* that is, what happens to him, how he is supposed to act, and whether it is good or bad, pleasant or unpleasant, fun or tiresome to *him.*

Although a young child has the rudiments of the concept of social roles, he does not comprehend readily that a person may have more than one role. At first, he will understand this concept as it applies to the important people in his life, the people with whom he identifies, the people who are responsible for him over a long time.

Kathleen (5.4) told her teacher, "You know, my mommie is a mommie and a doctor!" Kathleen knows her mother can be both things and still be the same person. She is beginning to understand that people may have more than one role. She understands this idea for the people who are important to her and whom she has known for a long time. When, during the first week of school, her father tells her that her teacher is one of his students, she says in disbelief, "How can that happen? She is my teacher!" It will probably be two or three years before Kathleen is able to conceptualize that *all* people have multiple roles.

REPRESENTATION AS AN EFFECTIVE SUPPORT FOR LEARNING IN SOCIAL STUDIES

Representing or presenting anew the mental images and sounds of his social world is an important mode for a child's learning. In Chapter 16 we spoke of play as a mode of learning and described four types of play: exploratory play; skill mastery play; construction play; and imitative, symbolic, and

These children are using miniature toys and blocks to represent their neighborhood.

dramatic play. Each type of play offers a child opportunities to represent his social world. As he represents his world in play his images become clearer, take on more detail, and become an effective support to his language and thought. In exploratory play children can use language to make sounds, such as the sounds of telephones, fire engines, and jack hammers to represent objects. In mastery play children can use drawing, painting, and writing to represent people, objects, places, and events. In construction play children use building sets, blocks, woodworking, art materials, and sand to represent objects, people, and places. In imitative, symbolic, and dramatic play the child uses himself to represent other people's roles, values, customs, taboos, and language.

Play provides an opportunity for the symbolic representation of all the child has experienced. It can provide an opportunity for him to put his experiences into words and actions. He may enact the roles of family members as they interact with each other in everyday situations or in special events, such as picnics, camping, or birthdays. His play may revolve around his experience of taking a trip by train, subway, or boat. Children often recreate community resources and services they know, such as grocery store, post office, or hospital. Dramatic play offers a truly unique mode for the child's learning as he integrates and synthesizes his understandings, perceptions, feelings, and fantasies of the world. Play allows the child to explore alternative solutions and behavior to social as well as to personal problems and conflicts, without having to deal with the reality of an unsuccessful solution.

SOCIAL LEARNING: I. CHILDREN'S RELATIONSHIPS WITH TEACHERS

The child entering school is dependent on finding trustworthy teachers; teachers who are responsive to his needs, who are reasonably consistent in their expectations of him, and who are predictable in their responses to him. If he has had many experiences at home that have supported his self-esteem and the development of realistic competencies, he comes to school anticipating play with others. He expects the school to be a safe place. He will probably relate to his teacher in very much the same way as he does to his primary care-giver at home.

The primary responsibility for building a child-teacher relationship rests on the teacher. There is a wide range of individual difference in the way children relate to adults. The child's relationships with parents and other people who have shared large portions of his life influence his expectations of a teacher and his ways of relating to her. One child may require a great deal of thought and effort from the teacher for her to build a relationship with him. Another child may find the transition from home to school and from parent to teacher an easy, natural one. Most children's ways of relating to new adults lie in between these two extremes. Each child deserves our thoughtful attention and support in building a positive relationship with him. In Chapter 9 there are many examples of individual children's responses to new situations and some ways for a teacher to help a child as he joins others in the social setting of the school. Each child has his own particular way of relating to adults; teachers will find ways of relating to each child that suit his particular needs.

The teacher helps the child to feel secure and confident and to build social skills. The teacher's first task is to help the child feel good about himself. Children who are secure, confident, and like themselves find it easier to like other people. They will be free to use their energy to learn social skills, and will be more skillful in social situations.

The "forms" of getting along with others are of little use when they are imposed on a background of insecurity and distrust of others. A common mistake of adults, teachers, and parents is to directly attack the lack of skill, the inability to take turns, or the tendency to exclude others, and to try to change these shortcomings. We must stop and think about the feelings that have brought about such behavior. We must first help the child to feel sufficiently secure, adequate, and free of hostility so that he can like others and not have to act defensively. Then he will be ready to learn social skills. With a relationship based upon trust and confidence between himself and his teacher, the child can utilize the teacher as a model for learning social skills. Many suggestions for ways teachers can build feelings of security and confidence in children are presented in Chapter 12.

The teacher is helpful to the child in learning to share attention and like others. A child in a group has the opportunity to face and manage the feelings he may have about wanting a large share of the adult's attention. Sharing the teacher's attention is less difficult than sharing the attention of one's parent. If the teacher gives her attention generously when a child asks for it, she helps him feel that there is enough attention for all. He is less likely to feel deprived at the times when he cannot have her full attention.

A child may also take a step in learning that it is possible to like many people—adults as well as children. As a child's relationship with the teacher develops, he finds he can like and depend on different people. He usually finds a teacher on whom he depends, and may want this teacher and no other to help him. He may seek her out when he comes to school. As he grows more sure of himself, he has less need to depend on her, and he begins to reach out to others. It is important for him to feel that this is the step to take.

The teacher helps by accepting the child's right to be resistant. For many adults the phase in a child's development when he "talks back" and is resistant or defiant is a distressing one. It takes experience with the preschool-age child, as well as confidence in ourselves, to value behavior that is usually considered unacceptable. When a quiet child who has usually complied with adult requests begins to "talk back" and resist, some adults meet the child's resistance with anger and aggression. Such behavior will probably only increase the child's resistance. It takes knowledge about the age group and insight into that child's behavior to understand that his resistant behavior may mean growth for him as a self-controlled person. It takes insight into both the child's feelings and our own feelings in order to meet resistance without resistance or anger. It may take a teacher time to guide a child through periods of such resistance in a manner that safeguards his self-respect and allows him to become self-controlled. At the same time, it is important that she sets safe and realistic limits. Guidance that meets the child's needs will support the child-teacher relationship. Chapter 13 has suggestions for a teacher as she thinks about and interacts with a child who is resistant.

Sometimes children gain strength from others and resist as a group. A child often feels less helpless in a group of other children. Compared to adults the child is helpless. In a group of children he compares more favorably with them. He may feel able to act in ways that he would not dare on his own. A child gains courage from realizing that he is liked and can like other children.

These feelings are evident in the following incident. Six children had gathered at a table and were working puzzles, talking, and helping each other. The teacher sat nearby. Suddenly, Nancy remarked, "I like you, Andy," and Andy replied, "I like you." Nancy went on, "And I like Jane and Larry and Linda and Debby." The others began naming each other as people they liked. Then Nancy began again, "But we don't like her, do we?" pointing to the teacher. "We only like children." Everyone laughed and seemed very pleased.

It is difficult for a teacher to accept group defiance unless she appreciates what it may mean to the child. A small group of four-year-olds, for example, may climb to the top of the jungle gym when they are told it is time to come inside. They are playing a new role, doing the thing they may have wanted to do many times in the past. They are no longer helpless children. They are powerful people, high above the adult, asserting themselves.

The teacher in such a situation does not need to feel threatened in her authority, although it is easy to have this feeling. She can allow them their moment of power. Inside themselves, they know they are children, and she knows that she is an adult, responsible for bringing them inside. She may perhaps manage the matter in a playful way, pretending they are paramedics waiting for an emergency, or she may say, "I'm ready to pull you home in the wagon," or she may seriously discuss with them, "I wonder why it is that you don't want to come in now." To this question she may get some replies that help her to understand just how they feel in face of an adult who seems so powerful, but does not use her power against children.

Through the preschool years, as the child becomes increasingly self-reliant, the teacher-child relationship will change. The teacher will become less of a substitute for parents. Her role will become one of a resource person to the child. That is, the child will ask her for assistance, evaluation, or information. He will offer her assistance or information. He will find her a help in solving problems, and he will help her to solve problems. He will listen to her and state his own point of view. He will raise questions with the teacher about reasons for school policy, procedure, limits, and rules. Because he has increased understanding, self-control, skills, and abilities, some limits and rules will be revised as a result of his questions. At times when his self-confidence is shaken, when he is fatigued, ill, or physically hurt, he may regress and need the emotional support that was characteristic of his earlier relationships with teachers.

The following are some teacher behaviors that may support the child's self-reliance and understanding of the teacher's role:

1. The teacher demonstrates by her actions her concern for the care, safety, and welfare of each child in the class.
2. The teacher observes and identifies the child's strengths; she is on the side of his strengths, helping him to build on them.
3. The teacher observes and becomes aware of the child's vulnerabilities and limitations; she gives him support in learning to cope with his vulnerabilities rather than deny them or blame him.
4. The teacher encourages the child's self-reliant and independent action and thought. At the same time, she accepts his regression under stress.
5. The teacher is realistic, clear, and flexible about expectations in terms of the child's needs at any point in time, as well as responding to his increased understanding, abilities, and skills over time.
6. The teacher is imaginative about finding ways to help each child build skills and be realistic about expectations for himself.
7. The teacher includes children in adult conversation and activity.
8. The teacher brings humor and imagination into her relationships with children.
9. The teacher demonstrates to children specific skills and approaches or ways of relating to other people.

Throughout the preschool years the child is learning about his role as a learner in school, and he is learning about the teacher's role. He is, also, learning about the changing relationships of these roles. Roles and their relationships are central to the social studies.

SOCIAL LEARNING: II. CHILDREN'S RELATIONSHIP TO OTHER CHILDREN

Within a group there will be a wide range of difference in children's skills and abilities to relate to others. Each child will have learned some ways of relating to other children before he comes to school. To be helpful to a particular child in building social skills, a teacher will need to observe him. Her observations may be gathered by looking at the child's interactions across many situations. She can make observations in terms of the *amount* and *quality* of his interaction with others. She may also note the child's actions in situations where *conflict* arises and that call for *sharing* and *taking turns*. Using these elements of interaction the teacher can determine where a child is in his learning to relate to others and make decisions about how she will act and how the environment can be organized to help him to learn ways of relating to others.

A more realistic self-concept may evolve as a child has an experience in a group. In a group of contemporaries the place each one of us holds depends

Family play: a boy and a girl cook together.

on our skills and what we have to offer the group. We must demonstrate our worth. We must measure ourselves against others who are like us, finding our strengths and facing our weaknesses, winning some acceptance and meeting some rejection. When we experience success, it is based to a great extent on achievement. The limitations we face are likely to be real rather than arbitrarily imposed. A favorable family situation helps us to feel secure, but experiences with our own age group help to develop an awareness of ourselves and of social reality that family experience alone cannot give. One of the most significant values for the child in being a member of a group of equals lies in the fact that he has an opportunity to build a more realistic concept of himself as a person apart from his membership in a family. Both family and outside group experience are necessary for complete social development.

Teachers can support friendships among children even though most young children's relationships with other children in school are temporary or shifting. Two children, drawn by a mutual interest, may play together for a morning or for a few days. Then each may have an equally close but short-lasting friendship with someone else. Yet even in these shifting relationships, there are likely to be certain children who are consistently attracted to or antagonistic toward each other for reasons we may not fully understand. We can help children better if we are aware of their feelings of liking and disliking, so that we can be careful to use the one wisely and not to contribute to the other.

There is nothing much better at any age level than having a friend. The confidence and assurance that come from feeling that one is liked, sought after, and depended on by an equal make possible a great deal of development. Such friendships are worth encouraging, even though at one stage they may mean that the two exclude others. The friendship is likely to lead later on to a growth in friendliness.

Close friends often have conflicts with one another, especially if they are beginning to play more with other children. They may quarrel frequently and call each other all the current names, such as "dummy," "mashed potato head," and separate with: "I won't play with you any more." They are still best friends, however, quick to defend each other against outsiders.

While close friendships offer real support to children, the teacher needs to be alert to offer help at the point at which one of the pair may be ready for new contacts. Janice (4.6) and Jerry (4.5) had both developed confidence after they began playing together. It was several weeks before Jerry began to assert himself. One morning he announced, "I'm going out." Janice had previously decided she didn't want to go out. Janice complained, "Jerry shouldn't go out when I don't go out." The teacher pointed out to her, "But you could go out." Jerry persisted, "But I want to go out. I'm going out with Timmy." Janice protested again, and Jerry finally went out. Neither child was very happy. A wiser teacher might have recognized the real problem, which the situation presented for the two children. Instead of pointing out to

Janice that she too could go out, she might have said, "You like to have Jerry with you, don't you? He's going out now, but he'll be back. You and he will play together again." She would then have tried to help Janice have fun away from Jerry, so that the two children might find satisfaction in greater independence while still remaining friends.

Teachers can help children develop skills, abilities, and interests that enable them to be interesting to others. Children are often attracted to the child who can contribute a good idea to an ongoing activity or who can be instrumental in providing the impetus for involvement in an interesting task.

As less sought after children's ideas are used, these children become important people to others. For example, Benjamin (5.3) was quite an isolated fellow. His teacher found it difficult to find an important role for him. Talking with his mother, his teacher found out that Benjamin and his father went lobstering, which was something they both enjoyed very much. His mother said she would ask Benjamin if he would like to bring a lobster trap to school. Benjamin was pleased to bring his trap to school. The children were fascinated with what Benjamin had to show them. They played "lobstering"; they made bait bags; they looked at books about lobsters; they made lobster traps with building sets; they drew pictures of traps and lobsters. Benjamin's contribution was a major one, and it was the focus of a week's activity in the classroom.

Benjamin found this role rewarding. He was more willing to participate with others who had ideas because he had learned that he had ideas to offer also. For the same reason, other children were pleased to have him participate in activities they suggested.

When children are *successful,* they build confidence, which enables them to be less self-conscious about themselves and free to relate to others. The aggressive child, on the other hand, is likely to be rejected. In Chapter 13 we discussed how to help the child handle feelings of hostility and aggressiveness, but one idea with regard to such a child seems especially useful here. As children change, it is very important for teachers to help other children take into account that that child is less often or is no longer afraid and aggressive. It is very easy for a child to be cast into a role by his own behavior and then have to live up to that role. Teachers can honestly point out to children, "Yes, Lucy used to hit a lot, but now she only talks loudly when she is angry. All of us are learning. I learned how to help Lucy; and I learned how to help you not to be afraid of climbing. Remember? We've all learned and changed."

The kind of *activities* or options a teacher plans for a day or through a week can influence the social interaction of children. In Chapter 5, when discussing the building, time, space, and materials, we described an environment planned for social interaction, as well as provision for time and places to be alone. Some activities, such as dramatic play in the homemaking corner and block building seem to promote more interactions than other activities, such as painting, assembling puzzles, and listening to stories. Thoughtful and careful attention to what activities seem to facilitate children relating to each other in positive ways within a particular group is worth the teacher's effort.

The child's progress in group relationships will be facilitated by our suggestions of ways to approach and interact with other children. When a child is successful in approaching other children, he will tend to use the approaches that have been successful. A child learns social skills from experiences that are within his ability to comprehend.

What are some of the social skills that we can suggest to a child who is ready for our help? We can suggest positive ways of approaching others or help them to understand the feelings that lie behind the approaches of other children.

An approach is usually more successful if the child can make some contribution to the play in progress. A straight request "May I play with you?" is often doomed to fail even if it is accompanied by the adult word "please." The adult offers more help to the child if she can suggest something specific to him that he might be or do. Another advantage in this approach is that if one is rejected in one role, one can always find another role or a different activity to suggest.

Sometimes the teacher may need to enter the play, taking a role herself and withdrawing when she is no longer needed to help the less skillful child. She may demonstrate a skill by modeling words for the child, for example, saying, "Doctor, I think my baby needs a shot," to help carry on "doctor" play. She may forestall difficulty by suggesting, "There will be more room for the building on this side of the rug," when two builders are encroaching on the territory of others.

Children are often realistic and successful. Terry calls to Tommy, "Say, Tommy, you'd better let Doug play with us because he won't let me have the rope unless he plays, and I want it."

Possessing something desired by others is as much a social advantage at age three as at age thirty-three. A wise teacher may utilize this fact in helping the shy child. Allowing the child to introduce a new piece of equipment or to bring something from home for the group to use may help him feel more accepted and give him more confidence. Obviously, such a crutch should not be depended on too heavily, but it can sometimes be the basis for a social start.

Offering something in return for something else is often successful. Some children have amazing skill in making a second object appear desirable when they want the first. Even secondary roles can be made attractive by an imaginative child. For example, Regan (5.1) wanted to join the group playing "police officer," mounted on tricycles, but there were no other tricycles. Terry encouraged her to join anyway, saying, "You can be a walking policeman, Regan. They have walking policemen. You can play if you are a walking policeman," and he made it sound worthwhile, for Regan became a "walking policeman."

Some children are too compliant. They may need the teacher's help in asserting themselves. Matt (3.8) seemed to find it hard to express his own desires. One day he and Mary were painting at the easels, side by side. Matt was very absorbed in his picture. Suddenly Mary (3.8) reached over and painted a green spot on his paper. The teacher, observing this, asked him if he wanted Mary to do this. Matt only looked at it and said, "That's a funny spot." The teacher replied, "Yes, it is a funny spot, but do you want Mary to paint on your picture?" Matt hesitated a minute and then said, "No." "Then you can tell Mary you want to paint this picture by yourself," the teacher said. Mary was listening intently to the conversation. She began to paint again on her own side. The two children went on to paint more pictures side by side, each more aware of the other.

Whenever possible the teacher leaves the children free to work out their own solutions. She does not interfere unless her help is needed. For example, Cindy (4.2) and Larry (4.7) are riding tricycles. Debby (4.4) wants to ride with them, but there is only a small tricycle left that she doesn't want to use. She is unhappy and tries to take the tricycle from Larry. Cindy settles the matter by saying, "If there's not any big ones, then you can't ride one now. But if you will wait, then Larry will get tired, and then you can ride with me." Debby appears convinced and lets go of Larry's tricycle.

Adjustments like these are likely to be reached only when the children involved *like* each other. When they have had pleasant experiences together in the past, they can make compromises more easily.

Terry (5.0) is already a past master at working out compromises. On another occasion he was busily building with blocks when Regan wanted him to play house with her again. He satisfied her by saying, "I'll live over there with you, but I'll work here, and I'm working now," and he went on with his building. Terry has had many successful experiences of getting along with others. He has confidence, and his confidence shows in the way he solves his problems.

As we listen to children in their play, we find that they approach others in friendly ways far more frequently than we may have been aware. We may not have noticed their considerations for each other because our attention is more likely to be directed to the times when they hit or grab. We will also find that there is more friendly behavior in a group where the children are treated with courtesy and consideration by the adults. Children adopt the patterns of behavior of the important people around them.

Children need help from the adults in learning about property rights, taking turns, and sharing. Living in a group of equals provides many opportunities for learning these social behaviors.

Since property rights are considered important in our society, the child must begin early to learn about possession. In his home he discovers that some things are not his to touch. The wise parent helps him accept this fact by giving him something that is his when she takes away something that he cannot have, and she does not insist that he share the things that are his until he is willing and ready to share. Pushing him into sharing before he is ready will only confuse him and may prevent sound learning. She will find that he can share first with people he knows, trusts, and likes, and then he can slowly broaden his ability to share in other situations.

The school provides an excellent place for the child to continue his learning about sharing, taking turns, and possessions. Equipment at the school does not belong to individuals, but to the group as a whole. Two simple principles can be established to cover most situations. First, when a child is through using a piece of equipment, such as a tricycle or swing, it "belongs" to the next person who may wish to use it. No child has the right to claim something he is no longer using. Second, after the child has used a piece of equipment for a time, he may have to let someone else use it even though he is not through, and he can expect to get it back again.

If these principles can be translated into very specific terms, they will be easier for the child to understand; for example, "After he rides around the circle once, you may have a turn. You can ride around the circle once and then give it to him." Words like these are easier for the child to understand than, "You must take turns with him." A group at the slide will be helped more when the teacher says, "First you go down and then Jim and then Lucy." They will not understand when she says, "You must all take turns at the slide."

The teacher often needs to interpret situations to less skillful children to prevent misunderstanding. Bill (4.4) was pulling a wagon when he observed Rickey on the tricycle he had been riding earlier. Rickey (3.9) was new in the group and uncertain. Bill approached him aggressively; "I was riding that," he said. Rickey just smiled, and the teacher replied, "You are pulling the wagon now, Bill." "Yes, I am," said Bill, half surprised, but satisfied. In a few minutes both boys were playing together on the jungle gym.

When we try to teach children about "turns," we must be sure to follow through. If a child gives up a swing so that another child may have a turn, we must see that the first child gets it back afterward if he still wants it. Even if he isn't standing there waiting, it may be wise to say, "Johnny, Jane has had her turn now, and you can have the swing back again if you wish." This verbalization clarifies the concept and prevents the child from feeling that taking turns means losing something.

A group of four-year-olds were playing with boats in a large pan of water where there were also two turtles. Michelle had a boat, but wanted a turtle. She picked up the turtle that Davy was playing with. "Hey, that's mine," said Davy, and he quickly grabbed it back.

The teacher accepted his assertion of his right to the turtle, but she commented to Michelle, "It's hard to want a turtle and find that someone else is playing with it."

Davy then turned to Michelle, "Here, this one will be for both of us. I'll give you a turn with it," and he shoved it across to her. It often happens that the child who can assert himself freely can also take turns easily.

An interesting situation is sometimes created by the children themselves.

An aggressive child may prefer a certain piece of equipment. Almost before the teacher is fully aware of what is happening, he may establish that it is "his," and the other children, fearing his attack, may prefer to leave it for him and give up their turn with this piece of equipment. The teacher must be alert to such situations and protect the other children in their right to use all equipment equally. She must see that they suffer no retaliation later. Charles (4.2), whose aggressiveness was making him unpopular, preferred a red tricycle. With his usual lack of awareness of the needs and feelings of others, he proceeded to take it when he could. It became important for the teacher to accept responsibility for maintaining the right of others to use the coveted red tricycle. It was important because Charles needed to have other children feel friendly toward him. No one in the group was more eager to be liked. The fact that there were occasions when he possessed the red tricycle legitimately made it easier for him to bear the limitation of not having it every time. It was also important for the teacher to watch this situation because the other children needed to be successful in standing up for themselves in the face of the threat Charles posed to them.

A slightly different situation exists when a timid child may depend on a particular piece of equipment for a feeling of security. He may cling to a tricycle or a doll because he feels safer with it. It may happen to be the first thing he played with or the toy with which he had his most satisfying experience. It is important for him to have the teacher protect him in his possession of this piece of equipment until he has found other areas of security. The teacher must suspend the rules in his case, interpreting to the other children: "We will let him keep the doll because he's new in our school and still feels strange. Remember when you were new? When he knows that we're friends, he can take turns with you." In responding to and verbalizing individual needs, the teacher helps other children to understand and accept differences too.

Bill, for example, was a quiet, thin child who stayed aloof from the children and teachers. One day he discovered the large red wagon. It may have been like one he had at home. Whatever the reason, he began to play with it almost exclusively and could not bear to give it up to another child. The teacher felt that it was important to protect Bill in his use of the wagon for a time. She helped the more secure children find a substitute whenever possible and allowed Bill time to grow more sure of himself at school before she expected him to take turns with the wagon.

The time comes, of course, when a child like this should be ready to accept the standards of the group. The teacher must watch for this readiness and, for the sake of his relationships with others, not prolong the child's dependence on one piece of equipment.

Usually a child gains more from being helped in a situation than from being taken out of it, because most of the child's learning about how to live in a social group comes from the responses of other children to him. As he faces the consequences of what he does by the reactions of others, he learns what is acceptable and what is not. We may need to temper these consequences for him, but for the most part we can leave the child free to find his own way if the group is one of equals. We help him most when we help him discover that being with other people is fun. Then he will want to modify his behavior to fit the pattern of the group in order to belong.

When the situation is too difficult for the child, he will show us by his behavior that he needs help. Aggressive, attacking behavior is often a sign that the child feels helpless and is seeking a way out of the situation. The teacher needs to step in with the words such as, "I'll help you." A child will stop hitting if he sees some hope of getting help. He can wait while the adult helps him work out a solution. He cannot be expected to trust the adult, however, if she blames him for the difficulty. He must have confidence in her acceptance of him and her willingness to help. Confidence is based on past experience, and we must remember that the present experience will itself become a past experience, which will either help or hinder the child the next time. To condemn a child, to blame him for his social inadequacies, will only lessen his chances of success and our chances of offering help that he can accept.

Following the example of some adults, children may be overly concerned with "bad" behavior. Giving undue attention to a child's undesirable behavior may make it difficult for that child to find his place again in the group. We sometimes see a parent or teacher isolating a child as punishment for not getting along with others. Punishment may be undesirable because of the load of resentment and hostility that may accompany it. While the child may not repeat a particular act after being punished, he is not likely to feel more friendly toward others or to get along better with them because of it. Isolation or being made to sit on a chair deprives him of the chance to have other, and perhaps better, experiences. It also labels him as "bad" in the eyes of the group and thus adds to his difficulties in getting along with others.

Isolation may be desirable when it is used with a child whose difficulties are the result of overstimulation and fatigue. In this case, the teacher may accept the child's need for a simpler environment. She will try to achieve it without giving him a feeling that isolation is a form of punishment. She may explain to him that he will get along better with others after a time of relief from the pressures of the group. She may give him a choice between a story or a walk with an adult, or she may suggest a time apart from the group with a quiet activity of his choice. Thus, she may remove a child who is disturbing other children, but she will not do so as punishment for his failure.

Judy (4.10) is a tense child, very jealous of her twin brother whom she feels her parents prefer. She has trouble getting along with other children because she seems to see them as rivals. One day she put it this way to the teacher.

> Judy: "I want to be a wicked witch."
> Teacher: "I wonder why you want to be a wicked witch?"
> Judy: "Because they cause spells on people."

Teacher: "You mean there are really too many people around, and you would like to get rid of them?"

Judy: "Yes, there are too many, and I'm going to be a witch and get rid of them."

Teacher: "Sometimes it is hard to have so many people around. When you feel like that, we could go off by ourselves where it is quiet until you feel better."

They went to the clay table where Judy worked with clay. By the time she had finished, she was quite relaxed. Her voice was pitched lower, and she said she wanted to go back with the others.

The teacher must be aware that young children, in part because of their dependency, will be competing for her attention. Comparisons increase the rivalry they feel. She should be very careful to do nothing to increase jealous feelings. These feelings can cause unhappiness. Often a child will misbehave at rest or at the table because he wants the attention that the teacher is giving another child. His teacher must be ready to reassure him by a word or a smile that she cares about him too.

One of the least helpful things that the teacher can do is to encourage direct competition among children. Competitive situations breed ill will. Comparing children by holding one up as an example to others is unfair to all because of the hostility it arouses. The following comments are likely to make children like each other less rather than more: "See who will finish first," or "See how much faster Jane is dressing," or "See how quiet John is." They make others appear to be rivals or competitors rather than friends.

Conflicts will keep arising when children are in groups because it is difficult to solve all the problems that exist when people actively play and work together. Because children are in the process of learning, they meet many situations that are beyond their skills to handle constructively. It is the teacher's responsibility to help the children understand themselves and others better, so that they can solve their own problems.

As we observe children in school, we are aware that the satisfaction they find in all activity is enhanced by the fact that other children are sharing it, just as we ourselves enjoy experiences that we can share with others. Whether children play cooperatively or merely side by side, they show us that each experience has more meaning for them when it occurs in a group. Children belong together.

Kay expressed in her own way what should be our goal in group relationships. She and another child were on a walk with their teacher when they met a stranger who stopped to inquire whether the girls were sisters. "No," replied the teacher, "just friends." Kay smiled at him and said, "We make friends out of people at school."

In sum, our goal for children in groups is that children should get to like each other more. We might use this question as a yardstick for our teaching: Will the children like each other better if we do this? If children are friends, they will find it easier to get along together. If the approaches they use are constructive ones, they will find it easier to live with others.

SOCIAL LEARNING: III. BASIC PRIVILEGES AND RESPONSIBILITIES AS A GROUP MEMBER AND AS A PARTICIPANT IN GROUP ACTIVITY

As a child enters a school group, he has some ideas about the privileges and responsibilities that are a part of group membership. He has been a member of a family where some things belong to him and some things belong to others. He will have been a participant in family activities, such as meals or a trip to grandmother's house. As a participant in a family, he constructs his ideas of how to be a participant in group activity and about the value, importance, use, and care of objects and materials. The social setting of the school offers many opportunities for the child to extend his ideas of privileges and responsibilities as he participates with a group of peers.

The classroom and the playground are provided for children and teachers to use. The school is, in a sense, on loan to both children and teachers. The privilege of using it implies a responsibility for preserving and caring for the playground and classroom. In some settings the teacher takes all the responsibility for the care of materials and equipment. In so doing, we believe that the teacher denies the children the opportunity to learn the socially valued behavior of becoming responsible people. We believe that the teacher has the responsibility of helping children to learn to use equipment and materials in socially acceptable ways, that is, to preserve and care for them.

How can a child learn to become a socially responsible person? The first step in such learning is for the teacher to establish a climate of mutual trust and responsibility. She will be kind to all children and thank them for their kindnesses to her. She will work alongside them and demonstrate ways to take care of materials and equipment. Direct teaching or *telling* children how to be group members, without demonstrating this quality, will have a limited effect on their behavior, thinking, and learning. Given a trusted teacher, who models the behavior she wishes the children to learn, most children will imitate her behavior patterns rather rapidly.

In Chapter 5 we spoke of the playrooms and playgrounds as centers for the child's daily life in school. We emphasized the importance of the selection and arrangement of materials and equipment as well as the use of space and time so as to facilitate the child's growing ability to be self-directed. We view the school as a place where a child can practice social behaviors that are relevant to him in the school as well as in other social settings. What are these social behaviors that relate to privileges and responsibilities in a group? For the sake of discussion, privileges and responsibilities will be grouped in the following manner: (1) using materials and equipment on an individual basis; (2) using materials and equipment with several others; (3) recurring activities for the group that involve the participation of several members on a voluntary or rotating basis; and (4) group activities that require interdependent action by all.

Using Materials and Equipment on an Individual Basis

There are many materials used by a child that will later be used by another, for example, a paint apron, a puzzle, or a lump of clay. Teachers can help children learn to leave these materials ready for the next child. In the case of the paint aprons, having a basket near where the aprons are to be used is helpful. The child can get an apron from the basket himself. As a three-year-old child or a new child in any preschool group, he may need help learning to put on a particular kind of apron. This help can be given by a teacher or child. When the child is finished, a teacher might say, "Please put the apron back in the basket, John. Then it will be there for you the next time you want to use it."

With each material used the teacher plans a place where the material is easily replaced. She needs to plan time to demonstrate and help children learn how to be socially responsible members of the group. With the same material and with each new material this process will have to be carefully repeated. The child will come to understand the reasons for replacing material. There will be times when he will not want to take the time to ride a tricycle back to the shed or return a book to a shelf, and the teacher will say, "I'll do it for you this time; you do lots of kind things for me." She makes this statement because it is true.

Using Materials and Equipment with Several Others

When several children are using materials, it is difficult for a child to know just which ones he actually was using. For example, a child may build a block building and then move on to the homemaking area. The goal is to keep each area organized enough so that the space looks attractive and invites use. During the block building a teacher might ask, "Kathleen, are you using these blocks?" If Kathleen's response is, "No," the teacher might say, "These blocks are not being used, Mark. Please help me put them back on the shelf." As they work together, she might say, "Thank you for helping me, Mark. With so many blocks on the floor there is not much space to build." As they finish she can say, "Well, that was a lot of work we did! Now they are ready to be used again." It does not matter that Mark did not get the blocks out. Perhaps he had been using material in the sandbox or homemaking corner. It is not important to put away just what one uses; the spirit of cooperation in keeping the room or yard usable for all is the goal.

Recurring Activities for the Group That Involve the Participation of Several Members on a Voluntary or Rotating Basis

In every school there will be some tasks that need to be done on a regular basis, such as watering plants, feeding animals, preparing snack or lunch tables, or putting out cots for rest. These tasks can be shared by the children and adults who make up the group. Usually a teacher enlists the help of a child or two, and the task is accomplished with all working together. Some

The teacher models ways of working together.

children will enjoy a particular task and look forward to helping with it each time it needs to be done. Sometimes a task such as putting out the cots or setting a table becomes valued and can be done on a rotating basis. The goal is not to pressure a child, but to help him learn to participate with pride and pleasure in the acceptance of what will be during the preschool years a limited responsibility. It is not helpful to the child's assumption of responsibility with pride and pleasure if the tasks become mandatory.

Group Activities That Require Interdependent Action by All

Examples of such activities are story, music and movement groups, and trips. In order to make it possible for children to learn to take part in group activity, teachers must arrange the environment, model behavior, and plan opportunities that are within each child's ability. Groups must be small enough for every child to be personally and directly involved in the activity for which the group is designed. Such groups enable the child to learn socially acceptable group behavior, such as the following: (1) to take turns for making comments or asking questions, yet being spontaneous and flexible; (2) to leave and join a group in such a manner that the group is not disturbed; (3) to stay with a group and to observe the safety rules on a trip.

Children who are not familiar with group activity will need to begin in small groups perhaps as small as two or three children. As children gain competence in small groups in a variety of situations, the groups can gradually be enlarged.

As teachers we are concerned that the self-control required for being in a group comes from the child's ability to regulate his own behavior. The responsibility for self-regulation and for holding himself to certain standards develops very gradually in the child. His emotional and cognitive development enable him to become a more self-disciplined person, particularly in areas requiring delay in fulfilling immediate needs and pleasures. For this reason, the teacher plans for slow, steady progress, trying not to impose the control by virtue of her role as the authority.

The Home, the School, and the Community as Organizing Ideas for Social Studies

A general principle of learning that we have stated before is that learning builds on what is known and familiar. For social studies this principle implies that the young child entering school is ready to expand his understandings from his family, home, and community to the environment and people of the classroom and the school. He learns that there are adults in school who do a variety of jobs, that is, have a variety of roles: secretary, principal, custodian, teachers. He learns that the space and materials of the classroom are organized. He learns that he has a role as a learner, a participant in the classroom, and how this role interrelates with other roles. In other words, he learns the social structure and the social dynamics of the school. It is important for teachers to introduce the people and their roles as a way to facilitate each child's learning about the roles they play.

Some schools are fortunate in having children of different origins within the groups. Most children know that all people do not have the same color skin or hair, that people do not all dress alike, or eat the same foods, or even respond in the same way. They also know that with all these differences the children come to the same school and make friends there. If every child feels that his differences are valued and accepted, he can readily accept differences in others. All can enjoy what these differences may offer. Children may enjoy eating different ethnic foods and become aware of eating patterns among people. Another culture may be more fully appreciated as the children have the opportunity to see and hear that culture's art and music. The group may have a piñata party with the help of the children and parents of Mexican heritage or a luau if there is a family from Hawaii. It is important to provide the opportunities for children to know from their own involvement that people are different, as well as similar, to one another.

The school environment offers innumerable naturally occurring learning opportunities related to social studies. Children can participate in the selection and ordering or purchasing of food for snack, lunch, or a particular cooking activity. They can receive and store food purchased for the school. They can assist in the selection, ordering, receiving, and storing of some of the materials and equipment needed for their classroom and playground.

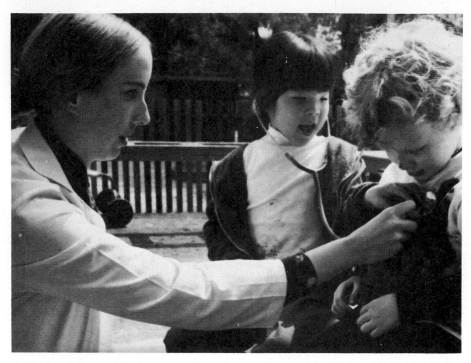

A new experience: listening to a heart beating. A mother who is a physician brings her stethoscope to school.

They can be active in the ongoing tasks that allow them to meet and learn about the work roles of people and businesses that serve their classroom and school.

Children live in a community, and they wish to understand it. Teachers can see through observing spontaneous play how children work on trying to understand the roles of different people. In dramatic play children include not only family roles, but also the roles of firefighters, bus drivers, doctors, service station attendants, astronauts, and repair persons.

As children learn social roles, they also learn about the places where people work, the physical structures, and the surrounding environment. Building with unit blocks and other construction toys can be used to represent or to recreate the physical structures associated with social roles.

The child beginning to use blocks builds towers and rows and, as in art, his intentions may not be represented by what he builds. He may call a row of blocks a gas station or a farm, and so it is! A well-stocked shelf with transportation toys, farm animals, people, gas pumps, and the like offers the child properties to remind him of his experience and enhance his play. As a child comes to enjoy blocks as a mode of representation, as he has experience in and around buildings and is able to recall more detail, his buildings come closer to his intent. Often several children cooperate to build a structure

Trips around the block provide valuable information for social studies.

together. The building may represent their collective ideas about a particular place. For example, several children may build a farm, a house, or their classroom. These constructions may be elaborated with signs, interior furnishings and, perhaps, roads or playground equipment. Such constructions, together with the related dramatic play, offer unique opportunities for children to integrate their learning from social studies, art, mathematics, language arts, and the sciences. In turn, the teacher gains insights into each child's understandings and misunderstandings as she observes the process, as well as the product, of the child's activity.

Children's learning may be enriched by having visitors come to school. The person who delivers the milk may be willing to stop and show the children his truck and tell them about what he does each day. The mailcarrier, the service station attendant, the librarian, and the checker in the grocery store are all people that adults may take for granted, but their roles are fresh and interesting to children. Meeting them, talking with them, and watching them carry out their work will make community services better understood by children. Such contacts will provide content for dramatic play. Some of these contacts with people who work may come from the child's day-to-day activity. Some may be provided by trips for small groups of children or the whole class depending on the needs of a particular group.

The teacher can plan opportunities for children to play these roles. She can observe their play to determine where they lack understanding of the roles. She can help them understand social roles and their interrelatedness by taking and repeating trips and by reading stories. She can discuss with children the details of how the work is done, where it takes place, and how it fits into a larger sequence of work. Sometimes a teacher will take a role in play. In so doing, she may play a role faithfully and help to clarify the children's concepts of the roles that they are enacting. At such times, the teacher's part in the play should supplement and enhance the children's play and involvement, rather than be dominant. Through dramatic play children represent their ideas of the social world in which they live; it is an ideal mode for social learning.

SUPPLEMENTARY READING

Language Arts

Cawley, M. Connecting words with real ideas. *Young Children,* 1978, *33* (2):20–25.

Davis, F. R. Writing development in some British infant schools. *Young Children,* 1977, *32* (3):55–61.

Mattick, I. The teacher's role in helping young children develop language competence. In C. B. Cazden, ed., *Language in Early Childhood Education.* Washington, D.C.: National Association for the Education of Young Children, 1972.

Smith, F. *Understanding Reading.* New York: Holt, Rinehart and Winston, 1971.

Wyatt, G. L. *Language Learning and Communication Disorders in Children.* New York: Free Press, 1969, Chapter 1.

Social Studies

Asher, S. R., S. L. Oden, and J. M. Gottman. Children's friendships in school settings. In L. G. Katz, ed., *Current Topics in Early Childhood Education,* Vol. 1. Norwood, N.J.: Ablex, 1977.

Hirsch, E. S., ed. *The Block Book.* Washington, D.C.: National Association for the Education of Young Children, 1974.

Richards, B. Mapping: An introduction to symbols. *Young Children,* 1976, *31* (2):145–156.

Seefeldt, C. *Social Studies for the Preschool-Primary Child.* Columbus, Ohio: Merrill, 1977.

19

Santa Claus
(girl, 4.4)

Curriculum Areas:
Art, Music, and Movement

ART

Art to the young child is more than making objects or painting pictures. Through art a child can *express* his thoughts, feelings, individuality, and *represent* his world. Art is an avenue that the child can use to *communicate* his ideas about himself and his world. Encouraging him to work in *his own* way will enable him to become self-sustaining in his art work. With such experience he will begin to work easily and focus on what he is doing. As he gains confidence and skills, he will be able to work with sureness and absorption. His ideas will begin to flow freely, and he will be more concerned with his own standards than with the standards of others (Bland, 1957).

WHAT TO EXPECT OF CHILDREN AS THEY DEVELOP

There are wide individual differences in children's experience, perceptions, and maturity in the use of art materials. A knowledge of some of the characteristics of three-, four-, and five-year-old children can be helpful to teachers as they plan an art program. Teachers use their knowledge of these characteristics as a way of understanding where a child is in his development of representation and to plan opportunities. Learning opportunities in art

341

should build the child's confidence in his subjective experience and allow him to express feelings and ideas through gradual mastery of materials. *"The mastery of the medium is only a result of the need of expression"* (Lowenfeld, 1952:58). The teacher is most helpful to the child in art as she enables him to discover and invent lines, colors, textures, and forms; to put them together in ways that satisfy him; and to develop his sensitivity to the quality of the materials.

Lowenfeld (1952) described the developmental stages in artistic representation as follows:

1. *Scribbling stage:* The young child practices scribbling and discovers the connection between his marks on the paper and the motion he makes. He gains control and confidence in his mastery of the material and enjoys the kinesthetic sensation of scribbling and its mastery. Pleasure in discovering contributes to the child's making new motions, usually using his whole arm. Based on his experience, the child begins to name his scribblings, and now imagination and representation enter his scribbling activity.
2. *Pre-schematic stage:* Over time the child discovers the *relationship* between drawing, thinking, and reality. At the beginning of this stage, he may intend for the symbols he makes to represent something, but his representations usually do

A child expresses his thoughts and feelings in painting.

not reveal his intentions. Gradually, as he searches for symbols to represent his feelings and ideas, he develops representational forms and concepts of form.

3. *Schematic stage:* As the child moves into this stage, he begins to discover and create definite ideas of man and his environment. He uses line, color, and space to help him depict his ideas of objects and people; he establishes a baseline and indicates movement in his representations.

Lark-Horovitz (1973) studied individual development in art from toddlerhood to adolescence. She collected spontaneous drawings and paintings that children had done in their own homes. She found individual differences in the age and peak of productivity and creativity. This same study gives some evidence of a relationship between expression in art and language. That is, all the children whose home art was creative and abundant were later rated by their schools as superior in language and vocabulary. It was as if the children's spontaneous expression in creating pictures had contributed to later expression in language.

INDIVIDUAL DIFFERENCES IN PACE AND RATE OF LEARNING IN ART

In art as in other areas of learning there are wide individual differences in *pace* and *rate* of learning. One child may paint a single picture carefully and slowly. One picture is enough for him. His pace is slow and methodical. Another child may paint a series of pictures, in rapid succession. Some children move through the stages to representation rapidly. Other children scribble for a long time seeming to enjoy changing the paper. Still other children become absorbed in using color or texture and may explore these variables for several years. No one way is necessarily best; each child has his own pace of working and his own rate of development.

Children Have Preferences for Art Medium and for Tools

No one art activity is equally satisfying to all children. One child may prefer to use a pencil to draw intricate lines, seeming to plan each stroke. He may prefer a small piece of paper. Another child may prefer paint and a wide brush. He may use a large piece of paper, cover it quickly, and allow his colors to drip. Another child may find that clay allows him to express his ideas and feelings best. He may enjoy the feel of clay or its potential for three-dimensional representation. Clay may be most useful to him as a means of expression.

Young children need drawing tools which allow an easy grip for spontaneous drawing. Crayons are a resistant medium in that they require tight, cramped movements in order to draw. In addition, crayons do not make satisfactory line drawings and the colors do not blend. Avoid crayons for young children! Flopens, soft lead pencils, pastel pencils, colored ink pens, and pastels move easily across the paper. Pens or pencils are usually selected by children who are interested in line. Often their products are remarkably detailed and complex. Given choices of drawing tools, each child may select the particular ones which meet his need for self-expression.

Children May Enjoy Painting on a Flat Surface or at an Easel

Painting on a flat surface, such as the floor or a table and painting at an easel are very different experiences. Children should have opportunities to try painting in both positions and then be able to choose which one serves their purpose best. One child enjoyed painting and found he could control the drips better on a flat surface, and he therefore preferred that position for a time.

Two-Dimensional Representation in Art

Scribbling is a very important activity for the young child. It is not "just scribbling." By making scribbles, the child realizes that through his own power *he can change* a blank piece of paper. The child at this stage needs a large piece of paper, at least $12'' \times 18''$, and one oil pastel or flo-pen. The pastel or flo-pen should be nontoxic, for the young child is likely to put it in his mouth. The large piece of paper allows him to use the full sweep of his arm without being distracted from his task by going off the paper. A single color does not divert his attention to the same extent that having several colors to use will. The pastel or flo-pen moves across the paper easily without resistance and allows free, easy movements. An accomplished scribbler, one who has gained control to the extent that he can place lines where he wishes them to be, is ready for several colors. Teachers can be most helpful by providing materials for *drawing* in a place where children are not distracted or disrupted in their task. It may be helpful to an inhibited or disorganized child for a teacher to use materials alongside him. She can make free, easy movements and lines no more complex than the child can do. At the same time, she looks at what she is doing and models attention to the task.

As the child brings imagination to his drawings and begins to intend for his symbols to represent something, he is ready to learn about the quality of the materials. Gradually the teacher can vary the shape, size, color, and texture of the paper and also provide colored chalk, colored oil, and water soluble pencils for his use. Wet and dry paper can also be made available to him. It is helpful to the child's learning for the teacher to vary one material at a time until the child becomes thoroughly familiar with the quality and the effect of each one. A child enjoys using the same material over and over again, perhaps because the repeated use allows him to master the material or because he likes to repeat a pleasurable experience. Teachers can plan learning opportunities in art that continue over two or three days to allow time for mastery and repeated pleasure. Teachers can demonstrate simple techniques such as blending pastels; however, the child should be encouraged to explore and experiment with the materials in order to find out the characteristics of the materials for himself. As a child comes to know the characteristics of the individual materials, he can combine them as he wishes, in ways that satisfy him. The materials can help serve *his purpose* to express and represent *his feelings* and ideas.

Painting with tempera on a flat surface or at an easel can be introduced to children when they become accomplished scribblers. Large sheets of newsprint (18″ × 24″), a brush (with handle cut to 10″), and one clear color mixed to the consistency of heavy cream provide a good beginning step. With a location relatively free from distraction, newspaper on the floor to catch drips, and an apron to protect his clothing, the stage is set for the child to begin painting. The teacher can show her interest and appreciation as the child learns to use brush and paint; she refrains from asking questions about *what* he is painting. Beginning painters usually do not intend to paint anything; they are learning to use paint.

Sometimes a child does not want to wear an apron. He may think that the apron is a bib and cannot tolerate wearing one, for it seems like a regression to him. Painting is more important than wearing an apron. We suggest putting a tablespoon of soap, adding hot water to melt the soap, and then adding tempera when mixing the paint. The soap facilitates washing paint from clothing. Eventually the child will come to accept putting on an apron to protect his clothing as a part of the preparation for painting.

As the child becomes skilled with the paint and brush, he will take pleasure in using color and line. We suggest providing two primary colors that will combine to make a third color. Presenting paint in this way allows the child to *discover* the properties of colors. Mixing colors can become a real adventure as the child becomes aware that he has made the new colors all by himself. Providing three primary colors is a next step in introducing the child to painting. These three colors enable the child to mix a wider variety of colors. As he mixes colors and experiments with line, he may overlay a painting, which we think is lovely, with paint. This process is very important for the child, and we must remember that the painting belongs to the child. Although the painting may be less attractive to us when overlayed, the process is valuable to the child's learning to make and to change colors. Some children discover texture in this process of overlaying paint and experiment with it. One child who had made a well-defined car covered it over with a thick layer of dark blue paint which he had carefully mixed. At the end of the day he showed the painting to his mother and said, ''Uncle Ned's car is under this blanket.'' He had covered the car for a purpose, and he knew the car was still there.

Gradually the colors, the consistency of the paint, the texture of the paper, and the size of the brushes can be varied. As with drawing, one variable at a time can be introduced until the child is thoroughly familiar with the quality of the materials. The materials can come to serve *his purposes,* to express and represent *his feelings* and *ideas.*

Each child applies paint in his own way. One child may use daubs of paint;

one may use wide, bold strokes; one may place one color beside another color; one may overlap color; one may repeat patterns in a way that is characteristic to him; or one may paint in different ways at different times. It is important to the child that his teacher allow him to work through each stage in his own way and at his own pace.

A teacher can be helpful at each stage in the child's development by standing back, looking at the painting from a distance, and discussing with the child what he has done. For example, she might say to him, "You made pink and orange and put them side by side," or "You filled all the space by placing one color beside another," or "You used two broad strokes of black and some dots of red and yellow." It can also be helpful to a child's learning to be explicit about the process of looking at a painting. For example, a teacher might say to a child, "Let's look at your painting, I'm going to look at it very carefully. Is there anything that you'd like to add? Is it all finished?" The child will be able to decide. Sometimes he will say it is all done or add a finishing touch. It is important that these questions are honest requests for information from the child or asked as a way to help him think about his painting rather than a way to impose adult standards on his work.

The experienced painter at five years of age will probably do some pre-planning or work with a plan that he changes as he proceeds. He is likely to work from fifteen minutes to half an hour, and he continues to profit from his own exploring and working in his own way. *Watercolors* may be added as a new form to an old medium at this time.

Fingerpainting is another form of painting that allows valuable, spontaneous expression. Some children find it difficult to put their hands into what

Finger painting is a satisfying activity.

seems to them to be messy substance. We have used shaving cream or soap flakes and food coloring in hot water and whipped it to a whipped cream consistency to help a reluctant child to feel comfortable with fingerpaint. This painting can be done directly on a table top with children standing to allow for freedom of movement. A teacher can work alongside children using the palms of both her hands and fingers to demonstrate how hands can be used to paint. Her use of the paint also reflects the fact that such painting is an appropriate activity for both children and adults. Children and adults both wear aprons at this activity. Setting up fingerpainting with a bucket of water or a sink nearby is helpful, for some children will need to stop and wash their hands, perhaps, to assure themselves that this form of painting is all right. Such fingerpainting can be repeated over time, and children learn how to manage aprons, handwashing, and cleanup through this simple process.

The next step could be to use fingerpaint that can be made or purchased. Children can again use paint directly on the table. The paint can be set out in a squeeze bottle so that the child can help himself. Colors can be introduced one at a time; later two primary colors which will combine to make a third color can be introduced. Children will be involved in the process rather than the product; however, there will come a time when they will wish to save their painting. Monoprints can be made from their table paintings by placing a sheet of paper on the child's painting, smoothing it out to make the print, and removing it with a quick upward motion.

Fingerpainting directly on fingerpaint paper or butcher paper with the wax side up can be a next step. This process is similar to painting directly on a table, except that the table is wet with a sponge to keep the paper from slipping and the paper is wet to keep the paint pliable.

Five-year-old children who are experienced painters may enjoy using their finger paintings another day as a background for a collage. There are several illustrators of children's books who use painting in this way. If the child is familiar with a particular book a teacher can point out how the illustrator achieved the special effects in the illustrations. The child and teacher can plan an opportunity for the child to try this means of expression himself.

In general, there are two ways to *hold a brush:* one is a power grip, with the fingers wrapped around the handle with thumb and fingers in opposition; and the other is a precision grip, with the brush held with the fingertips like holding a pencil. Young children usually use the power grip. This grip allows control of the brush for bold strokes with use of the whole arm. The precision grip allows fine and accurate control of the end of the brush with use of the fingers and wrist. Children discover precision grips as they draw and write. They can use these grips in painting as they need to use bits of color or line with a particular kind of paper and brushes for expression. No one way of holding the brush is the "right" way. A grip is good only in the sense that it helps the child to accomplish the task he wishes to accomplish. If late four- and five-year-old children have not discovered these grips on their own, it may be helpful for the teacher to demonstrate the grip that will help them to accomplish what *they* wish to accomplish right at the time they need it. It is the child's choice to use the technique or not.

Cutting is a skill that is often used as children engage in art activities. Before children can use scissors as a tool, they can tear paper for their use. As children are learning to cut, this activity is important in and of itself and need not serve any other purpose. The child makes snips to change the appearance of the paper. Changing the paper into small or large pieces *is* the activity. Most children will learn to cut if the teacher sits with them and snips paper herself at *their* level of cutting. Over time, as children become skilled in using scissors, they can use them as a tool to make shapes for collage, assemblage, or other activities.

Well-constructed blunt scissors with sharp blades should be provided for preschool children. Scissors should cut paper easily, but they must also be safe for children to use. Some excellent plastic scissors that cut only paper are now available.

Some children will need help to learn to use their thumb and middle finger in opposition and to hold the scissors loosely for cutting. A few children will have great difficulty learning to cut. For them, there are dual scissors made

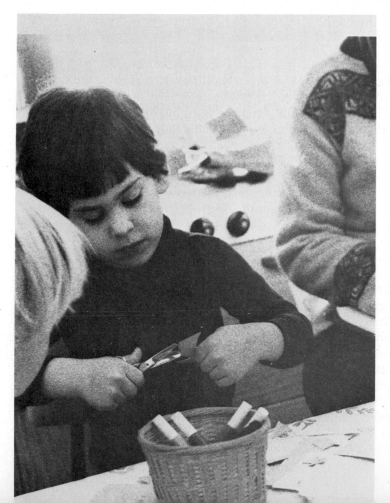

Skillful use of scissors requires practice.

Mastery of a skill: cutting takes concentration.

with places for both a child's and teacher's fingers. By using dual scissors children get the kinesthetic feeling of the finger movements, and they can then use regular scissors. Left-hand scissors are important to have on hand, too. It is nearly impossible for a left-handed child to cut with scissors designed for right-handed people. Generally, it is difficult for preschool children to cut fabric with children's scissors. Having some excellent, six-inch adult scissors available for special tasks is important.

Pasting, like cutting, starts out as an activity that young children enjoy for its own sake. Children often place one piece of material over another with paste sandwiched in between; in this way they learn about the quality of paste. By using paste over time to attach paper and fabric to a variety of background surfaces, children learn how to accomplish their particular purpose. They make two-dimensional compositions called *collages.* Children can start pasting with paper or cardboard as a background surface and attach materials of various colors, textures, and shapes prepared by the teacher. Mucilage or library paste is easy to handle and provides a beginning step in this learning process. As other materials and adhesives are used children can become more selective in choosing materials and adhesives. They learn to place the materials with greater thought and deliberation. Teachers can be helpful in this process by accepting and respecting what the *child* creates. Our goal is for the child to feel free and confident in his own expressions through collage. When he pleases himself, he pleases us, too.

There are many kinds of adhesives, such as library paste, mucilage, liquid starch, vinyl plastic, and rubber cement. Each has its own unique qualities and each is designed to accomplish a particular purpose. For example, a tissue paper collage can be made with liquid starch or library paste. Liquid starch will dry transparent and give a stained glass window effect to the tissue paper. As children use adhesives with various materials they can learn which ones produce the effect they desire.

Many kinds of materials can be used for collage, such as candy wrappers, wire screen, cotton balls, confetti, and velvet. Teachers will search for all sorts of interesting materials with a wide variety of textures, shapes, and colors for children to use and become sensitive to the quality of the materials.

In one school teachers use clear plastic shoe boxes to store collage material; parents, teachers, and children all gather materials to be used for this purpose. If a clock, radio, or other simple machine breaks, someone dismantles and collects all the usable parts for collage supplies.

Three-Dimensional Representation in Art

Clay is another medium that can be introduced to young children as they begin to use art as a mode of expression and representation of their world. In the stage comparable to scribbling, the child breaks clay apart, pounds, beats, and rolls it into balls or coils. The idea that one can squeeze, break, roll, pat, pound, or feel the clay without making anything may seem difficult for a well-intentioned adult to understand. There seems to be no art medium that is more likely to tempt an inexperienced teacher into model making. The teacher can be most helpful if she handles the clay in the same way the child does by exploring the properties of the material herself.

As a child begins to bring his imagination to clay, he may arrange small pieces and call them his family or build vertically and call it a building. He then usually pulls the clay apart and makes something else. It is helpful to the child's learning how to use clay for self-expression if the teacher follows his lead and takes pleasure along with him in his creations. After having time to use and explore clay by itself the child will enjoy using acorns, beads, pipe cleaners, plastic straws, and the like along with clay. Such materials are useful in encouraging the child to use his imagination.

With experience in using clay, the child will begin to use this medium to make objects modeled from his world. He will begin to add to rather than to take the clay apart. The objects that he makes begin to represent his intentions and come out of his experience with people, animals, objects, places, or events. The products may seem unfinished by adult standards, but he has enjoyed the process and his increasing powers to express ideas with the material. Gradually, more detail is added, and the objects made by the child become sturdy in construction. The straws or pipe cleaners become an integral part of the total representation. One child made a turtle, pulling out the legs and head and rolling a tiny tail. He had handled the school turtle many times and knew its shape both visually and kinesthetically. He used some simple tools for working with clay to make lines on his turtle. Another child made a bunny; he wanted the surface to be "furry" like the one he had observed and handled many times at school. His teacher supplied some steel wool and demonstrated how it could be used to roughen the surface. The effect he produced was just what he wanted. Both of these children were almost six years old. They had used clay for three years, and it was becoming a mode of representation for them.

With three-dimensional representation it is important for children to look at their work from all directions. Teachers can place a child's creations in a position so they both can walk around it and look at it from all perspectives. Children using clay boards can learn to rotate the board to look at their work themselves and build in corrections as they wish.

When children are at this stage in working with clay, it may be possible to fire the product. Many children we know have been very pleased to have their creations fired. There are several kinds of commercial clay that harden by drying and do not need to be fired, and which can be painted with tempera if children wish to add color to their work.

Assemblage, or a whole that results from parts fitted together, is another mode that can be used by children. The skills they have learned in working

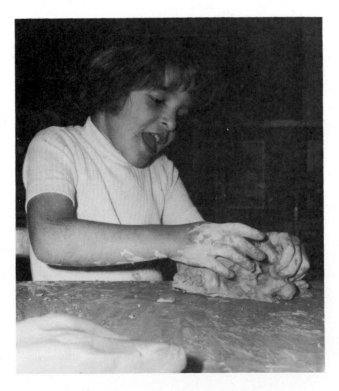

One can easily see how this child feels.

with paste and glue can be used to make three-dimensional creations. For example, a collage made on a piece of white drawing paper, with layers added by using liquid starch and torn tissue paper, can become an assemblage when the paper is twisted and projects upward from the flat surface. Children are often delighted with their discovery of such depth. With paper, clay, cardboard, wood, tiles, or shallow boxtops as a base an assemblage can be made of sand, sea shells, spools, pieces of wood, yarn, clock works, string, wire, buttons, driftwood, and a variety of other "found things." The assemblage does not necessarily require a base, and children can join objects together with glue, pliable wire, or staples to make creations of their choice.

It is important that teachers are thoughtful about the skills needed in using a particular material or tool for art. If a child needs to put two materials together that can be joined best by the use of a stapler, this need may be the motivation for him to learn to use the tool. The wish to connect two objects together may serve as the best motivation to learn to twist pliable wire. The introduction of one skill at a time, so that the skill can be mastered, is important for the child's learning. It is also important for his self-expression and representation. If he cannot get the help he needs to complete his idea, the child may think his ideas are not worthwhile. One can learn, for example,

Through exploration these children learn what they can do with clay.

to use a stapler in another situation and bring that skill to art. Teachers need to be certain that the child can learn rather quickly the skills needed for using any material. Also, there must be available enough help in learning new skills, as well as materials that are simple enough so as not to interfere with the child's being able to use his ideas to create.

Mobiles are another three-dimensional art form that can be made by children. The same materials for collage and assemblage can be used for mobiles. Starting with simple materials, such as string, paper, and pipe cleaners, facilitates children's understanding that mobiles can be made and hung. Late five-year-olds, who have acquired the skills of cutting, pasting, and joining and who understand the qualities of many materials, can use their skills and knowledge to create assemblages and mobiles in combination to represent their feelings and ideas.

Woodworking is an activity that the beginning nursery school child will enjoy. He can learn to use a hammer with soft wood and nails with large heads. Equipment needed for woodworking is as follows: a good quality lightweight hammer, a short cross-cut saw that is sharp, sandpaper, wood files, rasp, brace and drill bits, "C" clamps, woodworking bench with a vise, and saw horses. A place to store this equipment adjacent to where it will be used is helpful in assuring its safe use. A place where the noise of hammer and saw will not overstimulate others is important to plan too. A good supply of soft wood, such as pine, facilitates the child's learning to use tools. Hardwoods and plywood are difficult for even skilled carpenters to use with hand tools.

The youngest children or those unfamiliar with woodworking tools usually begin by learning to put a nail into wood. We have found that a cross-cut section of a tree can be used for years and is an excellent place to learn to drive nails. The process of nailing is exciting to beginners. The next step can be nailing pieces of wood already cut together to make simple constructions. Bottle caps, spools, pieces of cloth, and other "found materials" can be nailed on to create interesting effects. Many nails can be put into wood and string or yarn can be wound around them to make interesting patterns and shapes.

Sawing will be an activity in its own right over a long time as children increase their skill and power to cut the wood. Children can nail their cut pieces of wood together or they can save the cut pieces of wood to make assemblages with glue.

A child may name his representations made with wood, but as in drawing and painting, his intent may not be reflected in his product. The product, too, may seem unfinished from an adult point of view. Again, what is important to the child is the process and the fact that he has created. He has had a "wonderful idea!"

Over time, with use, the child can become skillful with hammer, nail, and saw. He may find that the saw cuts are rough and will learn to use sandpaper to smooth the rough places. As the need for a particular tool arises, a teacher can demonstrate its use, and the child can learn to use all of the above-mentioned tools. The teacher demonstrates the tools, but she does not define what the child is to make or if he is to make anything. Ideas come from the child, and the teacher helps him learn to use the tools he needs. A late five-year-old child, who is skillful with woodworking tools, may intend and succeed in making representative creations.

EXPRESSION IN ART SHOULD BE SPONTANEOUS

Art has value for the young child only when it is his own spontaneous expression and when it is his own exploration and discovery. We accept that what the young child produces is seldom art in the sense that it has lasting value on its own. Art is valuable to the young child and his development when it expresses his personal perceptions. We block or distort and diminish its value if we set patterns or models or give directions, such as, "This is the way to do it." Anxious attention on the product rather than the process, concern with skill or technique, the use of coloring books, or copying a model all hamper the child's spontaneous expression. When we hamper his spontaneous expression, we show we do not value what the child himself can conceive and produce.

ADULTS CAN HELP

The child needs uninterrupted *time,* a comfortable *place,* and *materials* to carry out his art work. The adult can provide such opportunities for a child to draw or paint and leave the child free to work in his own way. An adult

Children at the workbench with a teacher ready to help.

will show interest and encouragement, but she will not interfere with a child's work to teach him skills. She may ask questions to stimulate his thinking or to draw attention to the detail of his work. She may suggest observation of what he has done or exploration of the possibilities of the medium.

Sometimes adults try to supply the child with too many choices and too much variety. It is through using the same materials with slight variations over time that a child learns how to use art materials and what he can do with them. Too many materials and too much variety tend to confuse and distract the child from his purpose. It is a wise adult who observes to discover which materials seem best suited to what the child is trying to express and learn. She will provide choices which suit the child's stage of development both intellectually and physically. She will not impose choices based on her need for variety rather than the child's need for integration.

Art Materials Are "Messy"

Most art materials have the potential for being messy. As teachers we must look at our attitudes about messy materials. We may have had a high premium placed on keeping clean in our own childhood. It may be hard for us to see children delighting in using sticky clay, smearing finger paint, or using thick, creamy paint. Unless we accept our feelings, we may find ourselves avoiding the use of paint, finger paint, and clay, preferring play dough or flo-pens. We may find ourselves depriving the child of many opportunities for self-expression or, on the other hand, being unable to set limits when limitation is necessary. We need to cope with our own feelings apart from working with children if we are to offer a rich variety of opportunities to children for self-expression.

Some Children Enjoy Displaying Their Art Work

Children often want to take their art work home. They should be able to make this choice without feeling guilty. At other times they enjoy displaying their work at school.

Bulletin board space at the child's eye level is useful for displaying paintings, drawings, and collages. Frames or colored backing can enhance the child's work. Three-dimensional art work can be displayed on a low table or shelf where it can be viewed from all directions. Brightly colored pieces of wood or paper can serve as a base for clay or other three-dimensional art. Such displays can be valuable learning opportunities for all children as they look at, enjoy, and discuss the detail of a child's work. Teachers will need to be sure that all children who wish to display their work have an equal opportunity to do so.

MUSIC

Exposure to musical sounds often begins early in a child's life. There is a developmental significance to a mother's rocking and singing to her infant. The sound of the mother's voice, the feeling tone expressed in it, and the rhythm of the melody and rocking become important to the child early in his life. They may establish a base for aesthetic understanding. Using hearing and kinesthesis as primary modes of perception, music becomes a means of self-expression. Music is more than making sounds and melodies.

The Tone of the Human Voice Carries Meaning

All of us infer meaning from the tone of voice people use. Without language to rely on for communication, the young child learns to rely on intonation and tone of voice for meaning, and to respond to them before he learns to speak. The child in school will respond to the tone and intonation of the teacher's voice as much as to the words she is using. He can be reassured if her tone is confident and friendly, without regard to what she says. The "music" of the voice is an important mode for communicating feeling. As teachers, we need to be aware of the effect that the tone of our voice may have on children. There are cultural differences in what is considered a pleasant tone of voice, as well as differences in intonation and its meaning. Teachers must be sensitive to the cultural differences represented in the group she teaches. As we work with children and become sensitive to their perceptions of tone and intonation, we can learn to use the tool of voice quality to communicate with children. We can learn to communicate with them with respect for their feelings and in ways they understand.

Just as the child takes meaning from the intonation and tone quality of adult voices, so can we be alert to what the child is communicating through the use of his voice. The high-pitched, rapid speech of one child, the low, only half-articulated speech of another, and the strong full tones of another tell us something about each of these children and how they are feeling. The statement with the intonation of a question or the question with the intonation of a statement may need to be thought about in context in order to understand what the child is communicating to us. Through careful listening, we can learn to identify more and more accurately what the voices of children reveal.

The Child Is a Natural Maker of Sounds

Judy (18 mo.) sat on the floor striking a pan with a wooden spoon. She struck the pan at random and vocalized at the same time. Her attitude was one of intense concentration. As she struck the pan, she made two high-pitched sounds and then two low-pitched sounds. She then vocalized in the same pattern and repeated the pattern with spoon and pan; she repeated the pattern with spoon and pan and the voice pattern several times with intense concentration. She looked up at her mother and laughed with delight. "Pretty music," her mother said, "You made pretty music, Judy." Judy's mother enjoys experimentation and sound, and she is a good listener. Judy, like other children, is a natural maker of sound. Sometimes her sounds are pleasant to the adult ear, and sometimes they are not. Already at this early stage in her child's life, Judy's mother, taking the cue from her child's laughter, is appreciating her child's idea of pleasant sounds.

As teachers of preschool children, we can provide many opportunities for sound and music making and for listening to the sounds and music children make. We can offer opportunities for children to determine for themselves which sounds are pleasant or unpleasant to them. We can find ways to alert children to the similarities and differences in sound.

THE ABILITY TO KEEP TIME IMPROVES WITH MATURITY

There is evidence that the ability to keep time is not improved by practice, but that it depends on maturity and innate ability. At four, a child is more accurate in keeping time than he was at three, whether or not he has had training. One five-year-old will keep time better than another, regardless of practice, because of innate differences in ability. If a child is subjected to pressure to keep time to the music, he will probably find less enjoyment and feel less adequate in music. Even though there are individual differences in the rate at which a child develops a sense of time, all children can enjoy music and moving to music.

THE ABILITY TO MATCH TONES IMPROVES WITH PRACTICE

The ability to "carry a tune" does improve with practice. Singing along with a teacher who sings will give a child practice. If a teacher likes music and enjoys singing, she can help a child to use singing as self-expression. Children's voices are not usually high pitched, but some very young children have a surprisingly wide range of tones. Most three- and four-year-old children's voices range from middle C to C or D in the octave above. Songs that range within three to five tones are more easily learned by these young children. As children sing, the range of their voices gradually increases. Many children sing their own songs in a minor key, a contrast from the songs that they are often taught (Sheehy, 1968:60).

SONGS CHILDREN ENJOY

Singing simple songs related to young three-year-old children's activity or play adds enjoyment to the activity and builds their skills in singing. For example, the song, "Horsie, horsie, don't you stop! Let your feet go clippity clop," can add pleasure to a walk when children's shoes are making a clopping sound. "Warm kitty, soft kitty, little ball of fur, sleepy kitty, happy kitty, Purr . . ! Purr . . ! Purr . . !" is a song that can be sung when a snug little group gets drowsy at story time. Any melody that the words suggest to an individual teacher is fine for these simple songs. Songs about activities, such as dressing, undressing, jumping, running, or hopping, or songs about roles such as firefighters, farmers, or astronauts, and songs about vehicles, such as cars, boats, and airplanes are all interesting to three-year-old children and can be sung to and with them as they work and play. Young children enjoy songs that include their names: *Mary Wore A Red Dress;* ones with a visual aspect: *There Was a Little Turtle;* and ones that they can make up verses to: *The Wheels on the Bus Go Round and Round.*

As children begin to enjoy and gain skill in singing, they will be ready to learn a wide variety of songs. They enjoy lullabies, ethnic songs, folk songs, jazz songs, rock songs, patriotic songs, community songs, seasonal songs, holiday songs, action songs, contemporary songs, humorous songs, and songs in other languages. We believe it is important for late three-, four-, and five-year-old children to learn to sing songs that will be accepted and appreciated by older siblings and parents. An enthusiastic singer can lose his interest quickly when told by an older sibling, "That's a baby song." In the bibliography at the end of this book there are references for books with many songs people like to sing. Many adults are surprised at the number of songs they know when they skim through a song book. Often when looking at a song book, one recalls both the words and melodies to songs that they learned long ago. Browsing through song books can often enable a teacher to approach singing with fresh ideas about how to encourage children to sing.

TEACHING CHILDREN SONGS

When teaching children a song, a teacher should sing it clearly all the way through. In this way children can get the feeling for the sound and the movement. Often children join in before the teacher has finished singing. It is difficult to wait to sing a good song. The teacher can then sing it again and ask the children to sing it along with her, repeating it several times. On another day, the song can be sung again, and if there are parts that the children do not know, these can be worked on for a few seconds. Preschool children enjoy *repetition,* and one or two new songs each week are enough for them to learn and learn well. Children enjoy singing the old familiar songs, too. Songs like books become old friends, and children can easily learn songs that contain repeated word phrases and melodies, and music within their voice range. Teachers may use instruments to accompany singing, such as a piano, autoharp, guitar, or recorder. All of these instruments add interest and pleasure to singing. On the other hand, simply singing together without accompaniment is a delightful activity. Children need both kinds of opportunities.

MAKING MUSIC WITH OTHERS

Children enjoy group sings, too. Such opportunities can enhance children's interest and pleasure in music. One group can join another, singing together and singing for each other. Later, several groups can have sings together. One school we know began to have group sings, which lasted for ten to fifteen minutes, on Friday mornings. All children did not have to participate, but most children were delighted to visit other classrooms. Children learned songs, such as *Row, Row, Row Your Boat* and *White Coral Bells* in their own groups and then sang them together as rounds. They were delighted with their harmonious singing. Occasionally, a small group of adults who regularly sang together visited these Friday morning sings. They sang songs they liked to sing and often some of the children's songs. The children were delighted to have these adults make music with them in their school.

CHILDREN ENJOY USING INSTRUMENTS

Children enjoy instruments and need many opportunities to experiment and listen to the sounds they produce. A good supply of rhythm instruments with uninterrupted time and a place to use them freely allows such experimentation. Because instruments sound different in the open air, we suggest that

Children enjoy a variety of instruments as they move to music.

children use them both indoors and outdoors. Instruments that vary in tone quality and timbre are important to have in a collection. Teachers can help children think about which sounds are pleasant or unpleasant, and these sounds will not be the same for everyone. Teachers can ask children questions to help them discover how to make the tones that they like best. For example, on one day, a teacher may put out several drums of different sizes and shapes, rhythm sticks, a timpani stick, and a stick with a hard rubber head. She can encourage the children to strike the drums in different places, such as on its sides, edges, and in the center. She can encourage the children to try different sticks. The children can decide which sounds *they* prefer. They can discover that drums sound different when struck in different places, that different sticks make different tones, that a hard strike produces a different tone than a light tap, and that their hand is a fine instrument for striking a drum. No one child will discover all possibilities at one time, but over time by experimenting and listening, each child can discover many possibilities for making music with drums. Every instrument offers possibilities for discovering ways to use it to make music. Teachers should avoid telling children how to hold an instrument, allowing each child to discover ways he can produce the tones he enjoys.

When children have thoroughly explored the rhythm instruments, they can use them to compose their own sound patterns. They may enjoy using them along with a record, such as Ella Jenkins' record, *Play Your Instrument and Make a Pretty Sound* (Folkways Records, FC 7665, 1968).

Exploring and listening to the sounds of a piano are interesting to most young children. Children can investigate how a piano works. They enjoy looking at the hammer and strings and finding out how the sounds are made. If there is access to a grand piano, it is delightful to sit beneath it while it is being played and then to move away from it and hear the difference in the sound. A piece of paper placed on the strings of a piano can allow children to see as well as hear the result of the strings' vibrations. By exploring a piano, children can discover that the pedals control the duration of the sound. They can discover that the black keys always sound lovely when played together, for they make no dissonant sounds. Telling children all these facts may make the adult "expert," but children learn best when they make discoveries themselves. A teacher is most helpful to a child's learning when she can help him to discover all these interesting things about a piano himself.

With very little supervision, a child can use and enjoy the piano by himself. Often a child makes music by exploring on his own. Such music can be recorded and played back to him.

Children also enjoy making their own instruments, such as shakers, sand blocks, and drums. One group of kindergarten children we know made a homemade orchestra from pots, pans, buckets, corrugated metal, and pan tops. They often spent the last 15 minutes of the day making music with all their "found instruments." These instruments were treated with as much care as the piano.

Teachers Can Record Children's Music

Teachers can find ways to record the child's own pattern of sounds, music, and songs. One teacher with no musical training, but with an excellent memory for words and music immediately sang back the words and melody that a child produced. They practiced together so both could recall the composition as follows:

> Shadow, shadow,
> In shallow water.
> Let's go fishing.
> Yes, sir!
> Yes, sir!
> Let's go fishing.
> Yes, sir!
> Yes, sir!
> La la la la,
> La la la,
> La la la la,
> La la la.   Conrad Hampton, age 4.2.

Playing the piano is interesting to most young children.

This child is directing others to play her composition from the cards.

This song became a favorite of that group of children. Other groups of children have enjoyed it, too. Another teacher recorded children's sound patterns, melodies, and words on a tape recorder. These were played back for the children to learn and to sing.

One teacher found that by drawing the outlines of simple rhythm instruments, four-year-old children could use these drawings to record the order of patterns of sounds they enjoyed. A place and time to experiment with the instruments had been the first step. As children became interested in the patterns of sounds they made, the cards with pictures were added. The teacher demonstrated how the cards could be used to help the children remember the patterns of sounds they had made. For example, three rings of the bells, two beats on the drum, and one ring of the bell comprised one composition. After working individually with instruments and cards, a small group of children practiced playing the compositions and then played their music for the rest of the group.

A teacher with musical training can encourage self-expression in singing by notating the melody and writing the words of the melodies children spontaneously sing. These songs can be played for and sung with the children later. Nevertheless, a teacher without musical training who enjoys children and music can be inventive about ways of recording children's music and encourage children to make their own patterns of sound or music and songs.

LISTENING TO MUSIC IS IMPORTANT

Another important musical opportunity that the school can offer is that of listening to music played by a musician. In the chapter on language arts, under the heading *Making and Repeating Sound Patterns,* we discussed introducing musical instruments to children and suggested a sequence for children's learning. In this section we will discuss some other aspects of listening to instrumental music.

A teacher can usually find someone who likes children and who will enjoy making music for them. Finding out that many people enjoy music and play instruments can increase children's interest in exploring music for themselves. Not all children may wish to listen each time such a musical opportunity is offered. There should be no pressure for all children to attend, for this insistence does not build positive attitudes toward music. The child who does not wish to listen can respect the needs of the listening group for quiet by choosing an activity apart from the group. Many times curiosity about a new instrument or the sound of music will bring a nonlistener to the group for a time.

Listening centers are very useful for children who wish to hear records. A teacher needs to be sure that the earphones are *not* adjustable for sound. The amplification of sound in adjustable earphones is beyond the safety level for children's ears and should only be used by adults who know how to use them. If the school does not have a listening center, the record player will need to be in a place where children can hear the music undisturbed by others. Some children will want to listen more than others, and they should be free to listen without interfering with other ongoing activities. With the appropriate physical setting, listening to music may form a large part of the curriculum for some children.

Sometimes we find a child who spends a large portion of his time at school listening to music. He may be using listening as an escape from facing difficult situations, such as making the adaptations required to play with other children. The teacher will need to recognize this behavior and encourage the child to extend his interest and skills. She will give him more support in learning to relate to other children. It is important that the total pattern of a child's behavior for a day and a week be taken into consideration. Music should not serve *only* as an escape.

Records selected for listening should be varied. Musicals, operas, symphonies, jazz, folk, and ethnic music, as well as records especially recorded for children are important for children to hear. Teachers should try to find excellent recordings of the music selected. We have found librarians, music teachers, parents, and record store personnel to be interested and important resources for assistance in selecting records for children's use.

MOVEMENT

Acquiring skill in using his whole body is important to the child. With the acquisition of mastery and control of his body, the child increases his *freedom* and autonomy and gains *competence* and *confidence*. The goal is for the child to discover the potential of his body as he moves in space, through time, and with differing degrees of force. Opportunities to move that are pleasurable to children, as well as challenging to their changing abilities, are an important part of what a nursery school, day-care, or kindergarten program can offer.

Vocabulary of Movement Is Learned in the Context of Activities

The child will need to have a beginning vocabulary of body parts in order to understand his teacher as she guides him in movement exploration. The first step for the child is to begin to learn the names of the parts of his body: head, neck, shoulders, arms, elbows, wrists, hands, fingers, chest, back, waist, hips, legs, knees, ankles, feet, and toes. Most children will come to school already knowing some of these names. Other names can be learned in the context of a variety of activities. For example, he may learn fingers, hands, and elbows as he uses finger paint, crosses a ladder bar, or sings a song.

In addition to the names of body parts, the child needs to learn the names of skills, such as running, hopping, bending, and shaking. He needs to know the qualities of movement, such as high, light, and fast. All of the terms related to movement and its qualities can be learned in a variety of activities and in the context of moving.

When the child starts planned movement exploration, his vocabulary of body parts, skills, and qualities of movement can be a small one. The exploration of movement itself will provide opportunities for him to learn many related words.

The chart on p. 365 outlines examples of basic body movements and the qualities of movements. This outline may be helpful for a beginning teacher as a guide to selecting movements and qualities as she plans learning opportunities for children.

The Development of Basic Locomotor Skills

Adults are familiar with the walk of a late two- or three-year-old child with his feet flat on the floor, using a wide base of support, and with little lift of his knees. His run may emphasize the lack of lift or bend in his knee joints. When walking or running, he may not be skillful in using his arms and legs in opposition for balance. With growth and many opportunities for walking and running on different bases of support, his skill increases, and his walk and run become well developed. Usually by the end of his third year, a child walks with a smooth, easy transition in a heel-toe progression and skillfully

BASIC BODY MOVEMENTS		QUALITIES OF MOVEMENT		
Locomotor	Nonlocomotor	Space	Force	Time
Walk	Swing	Shape	Free to	Tempo
Run	Stretch	(body design)	restrained	(slow to fast)
Leap	Bend	Level	Light	Duration
Hop	Twist	(high to low)	(delicate) to	(long to short)
Jump	Spin	Direction	heavy (firm)	Beat
Skip	Sway	(toward front,		(accented or not)
Gallop	Shake	back, or side)		
Slide		Size		
		(small to		
		large)		
		Place		
		(in or through		
		space)		
		Pathway		
		(curved to		
		straight)		

uses his arms and legs in opposition for balance. He is beginning to gain control in stopping, starting, and turning as he runs.

A late three- or four-year-old perfects his run and gains control in stopping, starting, and turning. He probably has jumped by stepping down from a step with a slight jump motion. During the late third and fourth years, he may learn to jump and roll forward to spread the impetus over his ankle, knee, and hip joint. He probably has stood on one foot maintaining momentary balance, and by the end of the fourth year, he can hop several times on one foot. He now can use a gallop rhythm while walking, running, or leaping. Usually, he practices all these skills to master them. He often gains great pleasure through repetition in practice and gradual mastery.

As a five-year-old uses his skill in walking, he finds challenging ways to walk, such as walking sideways and backward. He runs and tests his powers of control in variations of speed for stopping, starting, and turning. He combines running, leaping, jumping, hopping, climbing, and galloping as he moves from place to place. The gallop, with its same foot lead, is a challenge to him. He gallops with variations in level, direction, distance, force, and tempo. He jumps from the ground with force and control and now begins to use a jump spontaneously as he throws or catches a ball or in other play. He will have learned to balance well enough to walk on a narrow, two-inch base of support. He may be able to balance walking on a rope with a rope extended above him to hold onto. He discovers a skip and may then have difficulty with the gallop until the skip is perfected.

TEACHERS PROVIDE OPPORTUNITIES TO INCREASE SKILLS AND TO EXPLORE MOVEMENT

Motor skills develop through active, vigorous play. Children need many opportuntities to practice motor skills and to feel free and comfortable in many kinds of movement. They need opportunities to see the world from many different perspectives. Teachers can be helpful to children's learning by setting the stage for play, encouraging children to move and play, and using the names of actions and relational words in the context of activity.

Some activities in a well-planned playground that encourage movement and the development of motor skills are:

Lifting and piling large hollow blocks
Pulling a loaded wagon
Pushing another child in a wagon or wheel toy
Crawling through or over sewer pipe
Digging with a spade
Shoveling snow or sand
Raking grass, leaves, or sand
Climbing steps to a tree house
Climbing a jungle gym, commando net, or rope ladder
Climbing a large rope
Climbing up a hill
Climbing on boxes and boards
Sledding and carrying a sled up a hill
Sliding down a pole or slide
Pumping a swing
Swinging by one's arms or legs on a ladder bar
"Skinning the cat"
Riding a see-saw

A commando net for climbing.

Riding tricycles, wheel toys, or bicycle
Pounding nails, sawing, and using other carpentry tools
Rolling down an incline or hill
Pencil rolling on a mat
Turning somersaults
Balancing on a low wall or walking boards
Balancing on jumping, bouncing, and balance boards
Jumping and balancing on a large inner tube
Jumping rope
Running on sand or grass
Throwing balls through a basketball net
Throwing and catching balls ("Nerf" balls, indoors)
Throwing bean bags at a target
Playing hop scotch
Hitting a tether ball
Swinging on a set of rings

Many of these activities occur naturally in a well-planned, well-equipped playground. A few are seasonal. Some activities are appropriate only for older kindergarten children. For the most part, all these vigorous activities could be a challenge to three- through six-year-old children and engaged in at whatever level possible.

Equipment may be used in a variety of ways.

To help the child to explore the qualities of a movement, the teacher can begin by planning a learning opportunity in which only one quality of movement is varied with several well-established basic skills. For example, the quality of time may be explored by varying the speed of a run, a jump, or a walk. Each quality can be explored with this approach using the same or other well-established skills. As the child explores the qualities of time, space, and force, he is discovering the potential of his own body.

To be consistent in the approach to movement that we have been discussing, a teacher will use the vocabulary and characteristics of movement as she works with children. She will avoid analogies such as, run like an elephant or jump like popcorn. Given directions by analogy the child will move, but he will probably imitate and the movement will be based on pantomime rather than on the characteristics of movement. The use of imagery will limit the child's movement exploration unless the directions focus on the movement rather than on the image.

> The teacher who says, "Jump like popcorn," must also say, "Jump like a firecracker," or "Jump like a kangaroo," or "Jump like a slow motion film." It must be clear that the thing to be explored is jumping, with its various time, space, and force possibilities: jumping lightly, using small space: jump suddenly and sharply: jump slowly. . . . If the focus is placed on the image—popcorn—you'll find children pretending they are popcorn (Joyce, 1973:24–25).

Movement exploration can take place in a variety of settings indoors and outdoors, individually and in small groups. It can take place as the child uses equipment designed or arranged for that purpose. Equipment is not necessary for the child can explore moving simply as he moves through space. For many young children accompaniment enhances their exploration. Percussion instruments or handclapping can accent a child's own rhythm as he moves or can establish a rhythm to which the child can respond.

For young children a beginning movement group should not be larger than six or eight children. This size group allows the teacher to respond to individuals. Small groups may join together after children become able to respond to the language of movement and gain skill.

During the nursery school years the emphasis will be on acquiring basic skills and exploring the qualities of movement one at a time. Children who enter kindergarten having had two years of movement exploration may be ready to combine two movements with variations in time, space, and force. These children will probably be inventive in their ability to combine movements and qualities. These combinations may result in dancelike patterns which are based on the characteristics of movement. At this point, some children will be able to express their personal ideas and feelings through movement.

During the preschool years the child learns to push, pull, lift, carry, turn, slide, throw, swing, leap, spin, dodge, and fall. By the end of his fifth year he may be agile in the use of speed, force, and space. He may use his body fully and skillfully in a variety of different ways with different bases of support. He may have more than usual skill in a particular activity; for example, he may run forward or sideways to catch a ball. He will probably be able to use the teacher's verbal directions that are kinesthetic cues, such as "move lightly," as well as visual models to learn new movement patterns. He may feel free at many levels in space, be agile as he moves, and use the appropriate tension and relaxation for a variety of tasks. He probably will have a great amount of energy and endurance.

THROUGH MOVEMENT CHILDREN CAN LEARN SOME CONCEPTS OF SPACE

As the child moves in and through space, he has the opportunity to learn *relational concepts* which are abstract. As he moves he may learn concepts such as up, down, above, below, inside, outside, side, middle, between, through, away from, next to, top, bottom, far, near, fartherest, nearest, over, under, around, most, least, corner, center, row, high, low, behind, in front, beside, forward, backward, front, back, straight, curved, round, crooked, in order, disorder, right, and left. As he has the opportunity to move through space and to see the world from many perspectives, he can learn about *topological or map space* in a very concrete way.

SOME CHILDREN ARE OVERCAUTIOUS; A FEW DISPLAY UNUSUAL LACK OF CAUTION

Most children practice motor skills on their own and use every opportunity to gain mastery of their bodies, and most are reasonably cautious. All three-year-old children have to be watched closely and be protected by an adult

The arrangement of equipment can offer challenges for even the youngest child.

because they may not attend to what is not directly related to their purpose. It is difficult to inhibit a movement after it has been started. A child may become aware of the danger, but his awareness may occur too late to stop the movement. He may not have enough skill to make a quick recovery to prevent a fall or to sidestep to miss an oncoming object.

The overcautious child may need a great deal of help to gain confidence in himself. It is important not to force a child, for example, down a slide. He may go down the slide if he is forced but then he may be afraid of something else. It is important for him to cope with and conquer his fear at his own pace with warm support.

The child who throws himself from a moving swing, who tries to jump from high places, or who often hurts himself and does not cry needs a great deal of protection. It is helpful to let him know he will be protected. For example, the teacher can say to such a child, "I am going to hold your hand to keep you safe, Bill," or "I like you too much to let you get hurt, Mary." A child may test the teacher to find out if she can protect him. We will have to prove to this child that we care enough about him to keep him safe. He may need to be protected and to learn self-protection in the same way a toddler learns to protect himself. Of course, he is not a toddler, but he will have to learn self-protection through being cared for and being protected.

At some time a child will need to be encouraged to engage in activity and to use his motor skills. At other times he may need help to lessen the intensity of his activity and movements. A well-planned movement program will offer space arrangements and alternatives that invite and encourage participation, while at the same time channel the participation into productive activity. It is important to provide learning opportunities that allow each child to practice and master new skills, as well as to practice well-established competencies. The equipment can be arranged so that it will offer increments in skill level that challenge each child without undue stress. The teacher will need to be ready to give physical support, encouragement, and verbal or kinesthetic cues that are appropriate for each child. Teaching motor skills demands careful observation and planning.

A HEALTHY CHILD PRACTICES MOTOR SKILLS AND EXPLORES MOVEMENT

A healthy child enjoys practicing until he masters a skill. The toddler goes up and down stairs or climbs over objects until he can climb easily. The preschool age child will try many ways to ride a tricycle after he has learned to pedal and guide. He rides fast, cuts corners, rides close to objects, and stops quickly. Mastering a tricycle is important to him. A five-year-old child will work until he has blisters on his hands to learn to cross a ladder bar or to climb a rope. A healthy child is delighted with this competence. His competence gives him confidence!

SUPPLEMENTARY READING

ART

Bland, J. C. *Art of the Young Child: Three to Five Years*. New York: Museum of Modern Art, 1957.

Davies, R. *Let's Build*. New York: Van Nostrand, 1974.

Davies, R. *Let's Paint*. New York: Van Nostrand, 1971.

Lark-Horovitz, B. *The Art of the Very Young—An Indicator of Individuality*. Columbus, Ohio: Merrill, 1976.

Tingle, R. *Let's Print*. New York: Van Nostrand, 1971.

MUSIC

Cline, D. *Cornstalk Fiddle and Other Homemade Instruments*. New York: Oak Publications, 1976.

Miller, M., and P. Zajan. *Finger Play*. New York: Schirmer, undated.

Sheehy, E. D. *Children Discover Music and Dance*. New York: Teachers College, 1977.

MOVEMENT

Espenschade, A. S., and H. M. Eckert. *Motor Development*. Columbus, Ohio: Merrill, 1967, Chapters 6–7.

Joyce, M. *First Steps in Teaching Creative Dance*. Palo Alto, Calif.: National Press Books, 1973.

Part Five

HOME-SCHOOL-COMMUNITY RELATIONS

20

Elephant
(boy, 2.11)

Teachers and Parents Work Together

To bring up children in personal and tolerant ways, based on information and education rather than tradition, is a very new way; it exposes parents to many additional insecurities. . . . (ERIK ERIKSON, 1959:99)

The twentieth century has brought us so much that is new that we may find it difficult to appreciate how the role of a parent has changed. Parents, as well as teachers, face difficulties in trying to follow new ways or patterns of behaving.

Through the centuries there have been traditional ways of bringing up children in different parts of the world. Parents for the most part have followed these traditions. Only recently has a body of knowledge been developing that might be useful for parents in the way that knowledge is useful to an engineer or a doctor. Being a parent is different from being an engineer or a doctor. Being a parent is a deeply personal experience as well as one that calls for information. It demands "personal and tolerant ways" as well as "informed ways" of functioning. We are just beginning to give attention to the possible ways in which parents can be helped, not only to gain the "information and education" available at present, but also to use the knowledge in their individual ways, with respect for the individuality of their child.

Parents have a tremendous job to do and they do it remarkably well. Some of them face many obstacles because of health, housing conditions, the demands of their jobs, and many other factors. We are interested in the problems of parents. We are interested in how schools or day-care centers may help parents do their job.

When a child enters a school or center, he begins living in two environments, each requiring somewhat different adjustments. The child's parents will continue to carry the primary responsibility. They are the ones who know the child more intimately. The teacher brings her knowledge of child growth and development and her understanding of a number of children. Many teachers are themselves parents. Teachers gain in understanding the children in their group when parents share with the teacher their knowledge of their individual child. The insights of both parent and teacher may grow in the sharing. Such sharing will depend on communication and also on the basic respect parents and teachers have for one another. If there is a sense of mutual respect, both parents and teacher will be able to give optimum support to the child as he moves from home to school and back home.

PARENTS ARE IMPORTANT PEOPLE TO A CHILD

We know that parents and what they think, feel, and do are most important to the child. Ricky (4.9), for example, spent most of the morning in school making a table. After he had made it, he painted it, working intently with long strokes of the brush. He asked the teacher if it could be painted different colors. When she agreed that would be a good idea, he used blue, yellow, orange, and then he painted a part with one color over another to make another color. He announced that he had made the table for his daddy. He asked the teacher almost pleadingly, "Do you think my Daddy will love it?" "Yes, I think he will love it," she answered.

As he intently brushed the table with paint he said, "I am doing a good job. A painter should do a good job. I can paint better than other children." He seemed satisfied as he looked at the table, and he said hopefully, "We'll wrap it up with a string around so it won't come open. It is a surprise. Will he know what it is?"

The teacher answered, "If he doesn't, you can tell him." Ricky excitedly answered, "I *can* tell him it is a table for him." Here we see a child eager to please a parent, putting his best effort into a product, planning and anticipating, hoping it will be a good thing.

Parents differ in their responses to the school situation when their child enters school. The teacher finds each parent responding in his or her own individual way to the experience of having a child enter school. Here are two examples of parents with children, getting acquainted with the school.

JEAN AND HER MOTHER

On their first day in school Jean (4.1) and her mother are obviously enjoying themselves. Jean has discovered the easel and uses the paints freely and systematically, one color after another in solid masses. She shows delight in painting and calls her mother over to see. Her mother comes readily, interrupting her own exploration of the library corner where she has been looking over the books. She shows pleasure in Jean's painting, and they smile at each other. One gets the impression of two independent people respecting each other and confident of the bond of love between them.

Jean's mother watches the other children, appears interested in the activities that are going on, and comments or questions the teachers as thoughts occur to her. She is dressed comfortably in clothing that will not be hurt by fingers covered with paint or wet sand. She does not direct Jean's attention to objects or children. She does not attempt to tell her what to do. On one occasion when Jean is hit by another child, her mother appears to take it in a matter-of-fact way, neither approving nor disapproving of the behavior. Later, when Jean pushes a child down, her mother shows no special concern. She leaves matters up to the teacher. She is friendly and outgoing. In her handling of Jean's vigorous protest at leaving, she is casual, "It has been fun, hasn't it! Of course you don't want to leave, but we're going now, and we'll be coming back tomorrow." Jean relaxes and smiles at the teacher as they go out.

After a couple of days of visiting, she and the teachers agree that Jean is ready to stay without her. Before the end of the week, Jean has stayed through the whole morning and has had her lunch there. In the following weeks Jean's mother often stays for a few minutes to watch. She greets the staff and the other children warmly and often shares incidents from home with the teachers. For example, she reported with appreciation one morning that Jean had remarked, "Mother, you do have such nice kids." The mother then added, "You know, she's right!"

This mother has a good deal to manage in a home with four children, but one feels that she respects herself and doesn't expect the impossible of herself or others. She is free to greet the teacher, say good-bye to Jean, and leave promptly to attend to other committments.

TOMMY AND HIS MOTHER

Tommy (3.3), who has never attended school before, and his mother arrive on the first morning with anxiety showing plainly on their faces. They had met the teacher and visited the school the day before, but they still do not seem to feel at all sure of what school will be like. Tommy's mother sits down on the chair the teacher indicates is for her. When Tommy finally leaves her to explore some trucks and calls for help, she only goes to him after she asks the teacher, "Is it all right for me to help him?"

She watches him closely and only occasionally appears to notice what other children are doing. She quickly turns away when she observes a dispute. Once another child grabbed the small truck Tommy was using. He burst into tears and rushed to his mother who held him tightly and did not conceal her concern. One feels her uncertainty and disapproval of many situations that occur. She does not seem comfortable with the teachers and volunteers few comments. When she related an incident about Tommy to the teacher, she said, "I know what I did was wrong." She seems to pass judgment on herself and others and expects the same from them. Perhaps a school situation makes her feel this way because of her own childhood experiences of feeling failure and distance between teachers and herself.

For Tommy and his mother, the process of adjusting to nursery school is a slow, difficult one. It is a long time before Tommy feels sufficiently at home to stay alone comfortably. He continues to get upset when something unpleasant happens and to need his mother again. Tommy's mother shows anxiety over what is happening and continues to need the teacher's reassurance.

As we can see, the experience of having a child enter school means different things to each parent. The wise teacher needs to understand that parents may have mixed feelings about the school and of having their child enter school.

In bringing a child to school, a mother is taking a step that will mean important changes in her relationship to the child who has only recently been a baby, completely dependent on her. Now the child will quickly become more independent than he has been. He will have experiences in which the parent does not share. If the child is developing well, he will find satisfying relationships with other children and with his teachers. Parents may find it hard to share responsibility for the child with the teacher.

The parent who has enjoyed her child's babyhood may find it difficult to accept the child's liking school and his readiness to leave her. The parent who may have found the care of a young child unusually difficult may also be reluctant to let him go. Parents may be afraid of shirking their responsibility. They may find it hard to accept their realistic need to have some time free from the demands that every young child makes. Schools can help meet this need of parents as well as the needs of children.

The mother who is enrolling a child in school because she expects to be working outside the home will be influenced in her feelings about the school by the way she feels about her job. She may be looking forward to working and may be satisfied about arrangements at home. She is likely to be glad to have the child enter school even though she has some regrets about the necessary separation. If she wishes she did not have to work, she may find it very difficult to help the child enter into the group, and she may need reassurance from the staff of the school. Most parents are able to help the child with separation if they themselves feel confident in the school or day-care center.

Children who have had brothers or sisters in school previously usually adapt more easily than those who have not, less because they themselves are familiar with the school than because their parents feel at home there. If the parent has accepted school experience for the child, the child is likely to find it easy to do the same.

Most parents enjoy watching the spurt in growth which usually occurs in the child during the first few months of school. Changes appear in the child's language, his social skills, his ideas about himself, and what he can do. He is no longer a baby, and he now appears more sure of himself. As one mother remarked, she found herself enjoying her child much more after he started attending school. He seemed more like a person to her.

TEACHERS NEED TO BE AWARE OF THE FEELINGS OF PARENTS

Most parents feel strongly about matters pertaining to health. Frequently teachers are less alert than parents to adjusting a child's clothing to changes in temperature or activities, or to avoiding drafts. They may be less concerned about wet feet or wet sleeves. Teachers are not the ones who are up at night with the sick child, nor do they have the same heavy emotional investment in the child as the parent. Good parent-teacher relations are based on mutual understanding. The inexperienced teacher must train herself to be very careful in matters involving health. With experience, she will come to appreciate the parent's viewpoint. If she is careful, she relieves the parent of a source of anxiety and makes a better relationship possible.

Parents who are older than the average parent of a preschool child or parents who have a background of professional experience, especially those who have been teachers of older children, are likely to feel anxious about the behavior of their children. They may have had little in their background to help them understand and have confidence in the growth impulses of young children. They are likely to see failure for themselves in the childlike behavior of their offspring. They need reassurance from a teacher who accepts them and their children as they are.

Parents from minority groups may differ in their cultural traditions and their attitudes about the child's school. They may have difficulty in understanding what the school is attempting to do for their child. They themselves are likely to have met discrimination and may find it difficult to trust the teacher and the school. The teacher needs to give special consideration to the needs of these parents. She must try to learn all she can from them about their expectations and make any suitable adjustment in her program. She should inform herself about the cultural patterns the parents represent. She can strengthen her own program for the children if she incorporates elements from the different cultures with the help of the parents. All parents will have something to contribute. Doing so helps confirm for the children the validity of the mixed culture in which they live.

PARENTS MAY BE CRITICAL

Parents are interested in what happens to their child in his first school experience. As they come with their child, they watch the teachers and the other children and parents. They see rapid changes taking place in their child. They have many questions.

Not all the changes taking place will seem like desirable ones to parents. Growth seldom proceeds smoothly or in one direction. They may find a quiet, docile child becoming more aggressive and defiant after he has been in school for a while. He may not share his toys as willingly as he did earlier. His vocabulary may be increasing rapidly, but it may contain words that the parents find quite unacceptable.

Parents may be critical of aspects of the program. These criticisms should be considered carefully by the teacher to see whether situations should be handled differently as well as to identify and understand what may lie behind the criticism or complaint. It usually represents a step in growth when a criticism is expressed by the parent, accepted by the teacher, and a mutual understanding reached. Negative feelings will appear, but can be changed and cleared away by frank discussion so that they do not block the growth of more positive attitudes. Resistance is an important part of learning.

It helps if the teacher is aware of the part her own feelings play. She has her resistances to learning and changing. She may find herself acting defensively with parents, being most critical of them when she is most unsure of herself. Teachers need to feel comfortable about the things they are doing so that they do not act defensively. The teacher may need to say, "I have the impression that there are some things we do at school that bother you. Tell me what these are, please. We can talk about them." Teachers too can change. A competent teacher learns a great deal from parents. She is helped in her work with individual children as she comes to understand the child better through contacts with his parents. She may ask for a parent's help. Working together with parents can be satisfying and rewarding as we watch them learn and change, and as we find ourselves learning and changing.

GOALS IN WORKING WITH PARENTS

In working with parents there are two main goals. The first goal is to help parents gain confidence. The parent who feels confident in herself is better able to enjoy her child and better able to learn about the needs of children and to use this knowledge more effectively.

The second goal is that of helping parents gain the insights and the knowledge that may improve their contribution to a child's development. The teacher who helps parents feel more confident and who is skillful in providing sound information has achieved important goals in her work.

How Do We Help Parents Gain More Confidence in Themselves?

There are many small but significant ways in which the school and the teacher may help parents feel that they are important.

Does the school provide a comfortable place for a parent to sit when she is waiting, a bulletin board with attractive, interesting material on it, and some magazines and books for browsing or lending?

In her informal contacts with parents, does the teacher try to make them welcome at school? Does she take time to point out something of interest that is happening? Is she clear in the directions she gives about the arrangements for visiting, the acceptable times to bring and call for the child, or the decisions that are hers to make and those that the parent should make?

The parent will feel more confident if she understands just what is expected of her at school. She will gain confidence if the teacher takes the time to listen to what the parent wants to tell her. The teacher will try to "listen with the third ear" to understand the meaning that may lie behind the words. It is important for the parent to feel that she is being understood. In her relationship with the parent, the teacher will show interest, give encouragement, and avoid blame and criticism. She will make supportive comments on sound methods. She will accept all the feelings the parent may have.

At times parents may ignore or resist a request the school makes, for example, by continually ignoring the time for calling for the child. The teacher must be able to meet negative attitudes and negative types of behavior with understanding and firmness. She does not feel personally responsible, for she knows that negative feelings are often displaced. She faces the irritation she may feel and deals with it, so that she can be of help to the parent in working out a more constructive solution for both of them.

In all our relationships as teachers with parents we must respect the deep feelings involved in any parent–child relationship. We must remember that life with young children brings many frustrations and makes many demands, although it also brings much satisfaction and joy. We must respect parents if we are to help them feel confident. Good relationships are built on awareness and sympathy.

The Teacher Offers a Professional Relationship to Parents

The relationship between teacher and parent differs from the personal relationship between friends; it is a professional relationship. Just as a child learns the possibilities of a new relationship when he starts school and finds that the relationship with his teacher differs from that which he has with his mother, so the parent and teacher should form a relationship on a professional basis. Some teachers are unaware of these possibilities and seek only to make friends with the parents. In these cases, the teacher's own need for friendship and for closeness to people may stand in her way of developing a professional relationship.

The teacher who can offer a professional relationship to parents must have a real understanding of herself. She must be able to recognize her own needs and feelings and the part they play in her relationships with others. She must have ways to handle these needs and feelings, leaving her free to offer her interest and skill as a professionally trained person. She must be able to offer what she has in response to the parents' needs, not to satisfy her own personal needs. She accepts the parents, but she does not depend on feeling accepted by them.

The inexperienced teacher will need to guard against becoming involved in personal relationships with the parents of the children in her group. She will want to know them as people and be a person herself with them, but she will not seek to satisfy her own need for close, personal relationships through these contacts. She will be careful never to discuss the problems of parents with others outside the professional staff. She will try to understand and learn to use the professional relationship wisely.

What Knowledge Will Be Useful to Parents?

Our second goal in working with parents is to help them gain more understanding about children and their needs. Along with the intuitive understanding most parents have about their own child, they can benefit from more information or added knowledge. Much of what we have learned as teachers of young children will also be useful to parents. We have a responsibility for sharing our knowledge of child development with them and for doing this in a way that does not interfere with the parents' own unique knowledge of their child.

What knowledge may be especially useful to parents? What might be included in a parent education program? We will suggest here some information that might be included in a discussion program:

1. The values of play and of activity for the young child, with emphasis on letting the child touch things and explore as much as possible.
2. The kinds of play materials and play opportunities that are appropriate at different ages and stages, with emphasis on simple, "raw" materials, dramatic and creative materials, and homemade equipment.
3. Ways in which a child is helped to develop competence in speech, including the importance of talking with a child and listening to his speech, the importance of opportunities with books and stories, and the importance of expanding the child's own language.
4. Information about the way in which a child learns, and the value of answering a child's questions, of helping him ask questions, and of helping him to discover for himself.
5. Understanding about the kind of help that promotes development, such as giving directions or making suggestions in a positive rather than in a negative way; giving a child enough, but not too much or too confusing kinds of experience; letting him take his time; preparing the child for new or difficult situations; playing a supporting role rather than a critical one.
6. The value of helping a child learn to distinguish between fantasy and reality while still enjoying and using his imagination.

7. The importance of putting feelings into words as a way of understanding and controlling action, and how this verbalization may be done.
8. The value of play with other children and ways in which a child is helped in getting along with others.
9. Information about development and growth needs, especially about the extent of individual differences in children.
10. Understanding of the stages in cognitive growth, concept formation, the value of imagination in the thought process, and the contribution a rich variety of experiences make to intellectual growth.

With more knowledge, parents' expectations for the child become more reasonable. Parents can take more interest in the child's development, watching growth patterns unfold that are reassuringly similar to those of all children, yet unique in wonderful ways. They are better able to treasure the individuality of their child as a result of their increased understanding of growth.

How Do We Help Parents Learn?

Parents, or any of us, learn in a variety of ways. We learn by *observing* a skillful person as he performs a job. We learn by *discussion,* raising questions, and expressing feelings and attitudes. We learn by *doing,* putting into practice what we have seen and discussed. When observation, discussion, and active participation take place under favorable conditions, they result in sound learning. A good parent education program will include opportunities for all three kinds of activities.

Observation in school is an important opportunity for parents. At school they can see their child with other children and find that in some respects he is like others and in some respects he is a unique individual. Through observation parents may find ideas for play materials, activities, and ways of handling situations. Sometimes the child's behavior with other children and adults will need to be interpreted by the teacher. She can explain why a situation was handled in one way and not another or what she believes a bit of behavior may mean. Observations may make clear the significance and value of behavior that before may have been unnoticed by parents.

Parents should be encouraged to observe and have an opportunity to talk with the teacher about what they see. Such discussions can be arranged after school. If the school has adequate observation space, which may not be a part of the classroom, parents will find it easier to observe without distracting their child and other children.

The teacher may wish to observe a child at home in order to gain insight into his behavior at school or to help build a relationship with the child. She will arrange with the parent and child for a visit. The teacher can gain understanding about the child's interests, skills, abilities, and relationships with others from a home visit.

For a child, and for the parents too, the visit of the teacher may have a great deal of significance. The visit demonstrates to the child that he is an important person to her. And parents, even though they may feel somewhat anxious and strained, may still appreciate the visit. Parent-teacher relationships can be more comfortable as a result of this opportunity to visit outside the school. Afterward, it may be easier for a parent to ask questions important to her and for the teacher to understand what these questions mean.

Individual conferences represent one of the most valuable ways in which teachers and parents can share their observations of the child. The teacher and the parent may hold many informal conferences at arrival or dismissal times or by telephone. Planned conferences will be held at regular intervals when both parent and teacher can become more aware of how each may be of help to the other. As parents and teachers look at what is happening and pool their thinking about the child, they may see new significance in what he does and find new suggestions for helping him, as well as gain new appreciation for what he is like.

Often the first contact will be one made by telephone. Initial contacts are important even if they take place over a telephone. The parent always hangs up with some kind of feeling that will influence her attitude toward the school and will somehow be conveyed to the child.

The first planned conference (described in Chapter 9) will probably occur as the child enters school. At this time parents have the opportunity to raise questions about the school and are encouraged to talk about their child. The teacher listens and together they try to understand what the experience of entering school may mean to the child. They decide the roles each will play in helping the child to make the adjustment to school. There may be several short conferences for parents and teacher to share information about the adjustment process. The communication between parents and teacher around this common goal may establish the idea that conferences are matter-of-course events. Teachers accept the responsibility for creating an atmosphere in which communication is easy, honest, and direct.

At regular intervals during the year, perhaps near the midpoint and at the end of the year for most parents, reporting conferences can be held. At these times, the teacher's observation of the child's progress on a variety of dimensions can be reported: independence in taking care of his personal needs, his language, the choices he is able to make, his problem solving with materials and with children, his persistence in a task, his relationship with teachers and children, his particular friends, the content of his play, his interest and ability in group activities, the materials he uses, the fine and gross motor skills he has attained, as well as his concept development. The teacher's observations of the child at school can be compared with the parent's observations of the child at home. The teacher knows the child at school, and the parent knows the child at home. Conferences can be honest sharing of information on behalf of the child.

In the conferences the teacher has with parents, she helps them approach problems, not by giving an answer, but by pointing out possible causes of the problem and perhaps suggesting several possible solutions. The parent may select a solution from those suggested by the teacher, but it will work in the end only if she makes it her own. She knows the child, the situation, and what she herself can do.

The responsibility for solving a problem belongs to the parent, and the teacher should not attempt to take over this responsibility any more than she should solve a child's problem for him. She only tries to help the parent to solve a problem by listening to her, asking questions to clarify a point, or suggesting factors that may be related. She may point out the possible meaning of a course of action to a child and help parents think about a variety of alternative solutions. The experienced teacher does not offer advice or pass judgment. Her interest, sympathetic understanding, and information and knowledge of alternatives help the parent. The parent is also helped if the teacher is not anxious, but seems to feel certain that there is a solution even if it takes time to find one.

Every teacher needs some training in conference methods. She also needs the opportunity, especially as a beginning teacher, to plan and later discuss conferences she has with a professional person, such as a supervisor or a consultant. She learns from analyzing her actual experience and identifying the meanings in both her responses and those of the parents. In-service training is needed here. Only a beginning can be made in learning as a student.

Group discussions can make an important contribution to parents as such discussions provide them with the opportunity to have contacts with other parents. These contacts are not the same as those in the ordinary social event. Here, they meet as parents. They can share their concerns. It is often a relief for them to know that they are not alone in facing some problems. They may get help from each other in solving a specific problem. A mother with young children is likely to be rather isolated and lonely, without many contacts outside her home. She needs contact with adults who are also interested in children.

In the group meetings held at school, the parents get together to talk about common problems. As a group they all have children at the same stage of development. They are all concerned with early childhood education. Each has taken a step in the process of giving a child more independence. With the support of other parents, a parent may find it easier to let the child be free. Since many adults live far from their own families, they cannot turn to their parents and may be relatively alone in facing uncertainties which they hesitate to share with friends. They are in need of the "extended family experience" which the school may offer. It lightens some of the drudgery which is part of caring for children if experiences can be shared in conversations with people who have the same interests.

There are many kinds of group experiences. Some schools have general group meetings, held in the evening, for mothers and fathers. The more chance for parent participation, the more the individual parent will gain. Techniques can be used to bring about participation even when groups are large. The whole matter of planning a series of programs for the year should be done in such a way as to bring out the real interests of the group and to provide for participation. If the parents share responsibility with the staff for making plans, or take on the responsibility themselves, the experiences are likely to come closer to what parents really want and thus be more valuable to them.

Sometimes parents bring up particular situations for discussion. It is only natural that parents will wish to discuss the particular problem of their own child, but the discussion leader will need to keep relating the specific example to general principles or group interests. "Is this a problem which occurs frequently?" "Have some of you met this problem in other types of situations?" "Shall we look at reasons why this behavior appears in children just at this point in their growth?" Parents may be encouraged to bring in *typical* situations for discussion at a meeting.

It may be helpful to have some agreement before discussion starts on the length of time any one person should talk and what the group wishes to do about handling questions on personal problems. It is seldom wise to have a discussion of more than an hour and a half. Frequently small groups will stay to talk more informally about points which have been raised, and this is a valuable part of the experience for them.

Other types of meetings include discussion groups held when the children are in school. These may be informal "coffee hours," with a discussion led by someone on the staff when parents bring up questions, or they may be planned to cover some definite subject. There are also "work meetings" in which parents and teachers repair equipment and talk as they work.

A lending library with books and pamphlets is useful to parents, as is a bulletin board where teachers and parents can share things which have stimulated their thinking.

A parent makes cookies with a group in the center.

Parents can also learn from *participating* in the school. Most schools welcome parents who come in as volunteers, helping in the program, such as on an excursion or field trip, bringing in a musical instrument to play, providing objects of interest, helping with a cooking project, storytelling, or dancing. Discussion and evaluation by parents and staff afterward make parents' participation a valuable experience for all.

Schools such as some Head Start programs employ parents as assistant teachers. Parents have a great deal to contribute to the school. They need an adequate orientation in the procedures of the program for the particular school in which they will be sharing responsibilities with a trained teacher. They need to attend regular meetings in which there is discussion of current problems, review and planning of learning opportunities for the children, and an opportunity to raise questions, especially those about their own uncertainties or resistances. In other words, they need the same opportunities the professionally trained staff members need.

In addition to the problems faced by teachers routinely, parents who participate in a group with their own child face the added problem of filling two roles, that of teacher and that of parent. Playing these two roles may be a formidable task, and in many cases the parent faces this task without realizing what is involved. Since both the need to learn about children and provide them with sound group experience and the interest in learning on the part of parents are great, we may hope that better programs for parent participation will develop steadily.

THE SCHOOL AS A CENTER WORKING WITH PARENTS

The school has a responsibility for acting as a center for the education of parents. More is being done today, and much more needs to be done in the future, as we learn more about ways of helping parents. A good way to think about the matter is to ask ourselves, "What would we like to find in a center to help us with the task of being a parent?"

Many nursery schools, day-care centers, and private kindergartens have waiting lists with names of parents who hope to put their children in the school. These parents are interested, and the school can offer them opportunities for learning through discussion groups, through conferences and consultation services, and, in some cases, through home visits and home teaching. Classes for expectant parents have proved to be of value; their content can be extended. Most schools need to be doing much more to help both fathers and mothers find success and satisfaction in carrying on their roles in "informed" ways.

Parents who have lacked educational opportunities themselves can learn ways of supporting their children's learning. In some experimental and federally sponsored programs teachers are going into homes and helping mothers of infants and very young children find ways of enriching the experiences there. In other programs, teachers are going into homes to work with the child at home to augment what the school is doing and to demonstrate to the individual parent how she may help her child.

With more general awareness of the role of education, more parents are becoming aware of the role they themselves can play in the process of helping children learn. Children will benefit from this greater awareness by parents if *all* aspects of learning are emphasized. They will also benefit if parents do not work too hard at trying to be teachers.

The teacher remains in a key position to help parents. She can help the parent value what the child is and does. She can help the parent see a relationship between a single bit of behavior and the total growth pattern. In this way she may help the parent gain a perspective and yet keep a sense of closeness to the child. She will not stress techniques. Techniques are not enough, however good they may be. They may even interfere with spontaneous relationships. It is not so much what people do as how they feel about what they do that is important. "What parents need all along is enlightenment about underlying causes, not advice and not instruction as to procedure" (Winnicott, 1957:10).

As the teacher works with different parents, she will strive to understand the differences in their feelings. She will gain much in working with them that will help her in her own understanding of children. She, in turn, may help the parents in their understanding of children. Working together, teachers and parents will find the satisfactions that come with confidence, skill, and understanding.

PROJECTS

1. Observe a group of children at the end of the school day. Note what individual parents do and say as they call for their children.

2. A parent has many roles. What conflicts may arise in playing these roles?

SUPPLEMENTARY READING

Arnstein, H. *What To Tell Your Child: About Birth, Illness, Death, Divorce and Other Family Crisis.* New York: Condor, 1978.

Lawrence, G., and M. Hunter. *Parent-Teacher Conferencing.* El Segundo, Calif.: TIP Publications, 1978.

Le Shan, E. *Learning To Say Good-bye: When a Parent Dies.* New York: Macmillan, 1976.

Le Shan, E. *What's Going To Happen to Me? When Parents Separate or Divorce.* New York: Four Winds, 1978.

Simon, S. B., and S. W. Olds. *Helping Your Child Learn Right from Wrong.* New York: McGraw-Hill, 1976.

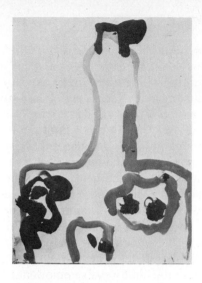

Church
(girl, 4.6)

21

Accepting Our Common Responsibilities

All through this book we have been looking for ways to increase our understanding of children and the ways in which they grow and learn. We have found that observing them will teach us a great deal about human behavior, and that if we are to handle children wisely, we must understand something about ourselves. The kind of people we are influences what we do for children.

The longer we study, the more we appreciate the complexities of human behavior, and the more we hesitate to propose ready-made formulas for solving problems or to set standards as to what a child ought or ought not do in a situation.

We have taken a big step forward when we have learned to *observe* children, to recognize the *uniqueness* of each individual, to search for the *meaning behind an act, to accept the child, and to have confidence in his potential for growth.* We have taken a big step when we have learned to make our contribution to the child through reducing the difficulty of the problems he must face, through enriching the experiences he has through providing him with optimum opportunities for learning, and through helping him to find avenues for creative satisfactions, rather than by depending on admonition and interference. We have also taken a big step when we can assume responsibility for

defining and maintaining limits for the child's behavior with confidence because we understand his developmental needs and his level of readiness.

Profound restructuring is occurring in many aspects of our living. New
possibilities are open in many fields. There is freedom from many old restrictions. Education plays an important role in helping to meet these changes.

Recent research findings call attention to the importance of infancy and
toddlerhood in giving direction to development, not only in physical growth,
but in intellectual and personality growth as well. Healthy parental bonds
established in this critical period influence all aspects of development.
Changes in hospital practices during childbirth are needed to avoid the long
hours of separation between mother and infant. Such practice may promote
satisfying relationships between parent and infant in the first months.

We also have evidence that opportunities to play with other children are
essential for sound personality development. Play alone, play with adults, as
well as with children, help the child resolve emotional problems arising out
of the developmental process itself. In the early years play is a most effective
mode of learning. Play, to be most useful to the child, needs the guidance of
an adult who is aware of its possibilities and a group small enough for the
adult to build a relationship of trust with each child. Evidence continues to
indicate that the early years are the important ones for learning and for
personality development.

Not all changes have brought improvements. The Secretary-General of the
United Nations has pointed out the tragic fact that more young children
lacked adequate nourishment during the last decade than during the previous
one. In spite of our advances, children today are in need of more help if they
are to develop in healthy ways. Parents have been concerned about their
children through the centuries, but today individual parents may be less
likely than formerly to be able to provide their children with a healthy environment. Families are in need of more support if they are to fulfill their
functions well.

Schools are an important part of a community. They reflect conditions
there. The community that does good planning in the direction of ensuring
adequate housing, adequate employment under conditions favorable for
everyone, and adequate community services and facilities usually values its
schools.

To the extent that a community fails to plan well, it handicaps the school in
carrying out its functions. The school suffers, too, as a result of divisions and
conflicts among the citizens, for the school does not exist as an agency apart
from the community. Schools are nurtured by their communities. They in
their turn should nurture community life.

The home and the school have a role to play in the improvement of the
community. They share responsibility for being aware of community needs
and for taking an active part in bringing about needed changes. The growing
interest in such matters as reducing air pollution and the shift toward more
community responsibility on the part of some business firms are examples of

such changes. The school as well as the home can support these efforts. Teachers and parents working together can support the positive advances that are occurring. They can also give leadership in identifying and working for other improvements in both local communities and the extended world community.

For more than 50 years teachers have been at work in the field of early childhood education. Books first published in 1930 have recently been reissued (Isaacs, 1966, 1968, 1972). The material is as sound today as when first published. *Parents and Children Go to School* (Baruch, 1939), indicates the early emphasis on working with parents. Today early childhood education has been "rediscovered," and the discovery has brought many newcomers into the field. There is need for a restatement of goals. We need to reaffirm our faith in the "whole child" and in the value of thinking of his physical, mental, and social well-being together as a whole. We need to act more effectively on the statement from the Universal Declaration of Human Rights, "Education shall be directed to the full development of the human personality and to the strengthening of respect for human rights and fundamental freedoms" (United Nations General Assembly Resolution, December 1948).

One of the strengths emerging from the flux of change is the fact that parents and teachers are finding it more possible to work together in planning a favorable environment for children. Together, parents and teachers may be better able to help children find the satisfaction and fulfillment that is possible in life. We live in one world, and our concern must include all children, all parents, and all teachers.

With many choices available, we must evaluate approaches critically if we are to meet our responsibility for bringing up children well. Only as we continue to study children and learn from them, only as we try to understand ourselves better, can we expect to judge wisely what will benefit each individual child. This is our responsibility today.

As students and teachers and parents we must accept the challenge put to us by Chisholm (1949), "Dare any of us say that he or she can do nothing about the desperate need of the world for better human relationships?" (p. 43).

SUPPLEMENTARY READING

Biber, B. *Challenges Ahead for Early Childhood Education.* Washington, D.C.: National Association for the Education of Young Children, 1969.

Education Commission of the States. *The Role of the Family in Child Development: Implications for State Policies and Programs.* Denver, Col.: Educational Commission of the States, 1975.

Erikson, E. *Insight and Responsibility.* New York: Norton, 1964.

References

Anderson, W., and P. Groff. *A New Look at Children's Literature.* Belmont, Calif.: Wadsworth, 1972.

Appleton, T., R. Clifton, and S. Goldberg. The development of behavioral competence in infancy. In F. D. Horonitz, ed., *Review of Child Development Research,* vol. 4. Chicago: University of Chicago, 1975.

Arbuthnot, M. H., comp. *The Arbuthnot Anthology of Children's Literature,* 4th ed. New York: Lothrop, 1976.

Arbuthnot, M. H., and others, eds. *Children's Books Too Good To Miss,* 6th ed. New York: University Book Press Service, 1971.

Baruch, D. *Parents and Children Go to School.* Glenview, Ill.: Scott, Foresman, 1939.

Biber, B. *Young Deprived Children and Their Educational Needs.* Washington, D.C.: Association for Childhood Education, 1967.

Bland, J. C. *Art of the Young Child: Three to Five Years.* New York: The Museum of Modern Art, 1957.

Bremner, R. H. ed. *Children and Youth in America: A Documentary History,* vol. 3. Cambridge, Mass.: Harvard University Press, 1974.

Brown, M. *The Three Billy-Goats Gruff.* New York: Harcourt, 1957.

Brown, R. How shall a thing be called? *Psychological Review,* 1958, *65*:14–21.

Bruner, J. S. *Toward a Theory of Instruction.* Cambridge, Mass.: Harvard University Press, 1966.

Burningham, J. *Mr. Gumpy's Outing.* New York: Holt, Rinehart and Winston, 1971.

Butts, R. F. *A Cultural History of the United States.* New York: McGraw-Hill, 1955.

Cameron, P. *I Can't, Said the Ant.* New York: Coward McCann, 1961.

Carroll, V. Quoted in *Christian Science Monitor,* November 29, 1969.

Cazden, C. B., ed. *Language in Early Childhood Education.* Washington, D.C.: National Association for Education of Young Child, 1972.

Chisholm, B. *Prescription for Survival.* New York: Columbia University Press, 1957.

Chisholm, G. B. Social responsibility. *Science,* 1949, *109*:27–30; 43.

Cohen, D. H., and V. Stern. *Observing and Recording the Behavior of Young Children,* 2d ed. New York: Teachers College, 1978.

Cuffaro, H. Dramatic play—the experience of block building. In E. Hirsch, ed., *The Block Book.* Washington, D.C.: National Association for the Education of Young Children, 1974.

Davis, M. D. *Nursery schools: Their Development and Current Practices in the United States.* United States Department of the Interior, Office of Education, Bulletin, No. 9, 1932.

Day, D., and R. Sheehan. Elements of a better preschool. *Young Children,* 1974, *30*:15–23.

Dewey, J., and E. Dewey. *Schools of Tomorrow.* New York: Dutton, 1919.

Duckworth, E. The having of wonderful ideas. *Harvard Educational Review,* 1972, *42*:217–231.

Durland, F. C. *Creative Dramatics for Children.* Kent, Ohio: The Kent State University Press, 1952.

Erikson, E. *Childhood and Society.* New York: Norton, 1950.

Erikson, E. *Identity and the Life Cycle.* New York: International Universities Press, 1959.

Erikson, E. Play and actuality. In M. Piers, ed., *Play and Development.* New York: Norton, 1972.

Fassler, J. *Helping Children Cope.* New York: Free Press, 1978.

Fein, G. G., and A. Clarke-Stewart. *Day Care in Context.* New York: Wiley, 1973.

Forest, I. *Preschool Education: A Historical and Critical Study.* New York: Macmillan, 1927.

Freud, S. *The Ego and the Id.* New York: Norton, 1960. (Originally published, 1923.)

Freud, S. *The Unconscious.* London: Hogarth, 1957. (Originally published, 1913.)

Gag, W. *Millions of Cats.* New York: Coward McCann, 1928.

Garvey, C. *Play*. Cambridge, Mass.: Harvard University Press, 1977.

Ginsberg, H., and S. Opper. *Piaget's Theory of Intellectual Development*. Englewood Cliffs, N.J.: Prentice-Hall, 1969.

Hill, P. S. Kindergarten. *American Educator's Encyclopedia*. Lake Bluff, Ill.: The United Educators, 1941.

Huck, C., and D. Young. *Children's Literature in the Elementary School*. New York: Holt, Rinehart and Winston, 1961.

Isaacs, S. *The Nursery Years*. New York: Schocken Books, 1968. (Originally published, 1929.)

Isaacs, S. *Intellectual Growth in Young Children*. New York: Schocken Books, 1966. (Originally published, 1930.)

Isaacs, S. *Social Development in Young Children*. New York: Schocken Books, 1972. (Originally published, 1933.)

Jacobs, L. B., ed. *Using Literature with Young Children*. New York: Teacher's College, 1965.

Joyce, M. *First Steps in Teaching Creative Dance*. Palo Alto, Calif.: National Press Books, 1973.

Kahl, V. *The Duchess Bakes a Cake*. New York: Scribner, 1955.

Keister, M. E. *The Good Life for Infants and Toddlers*. Washington, D.C.: National Association for the Education of Young Children, 1970.

Koch, H. L. The relation of certain formal attributes of siblings to attitudes held toward each other and toward their parents. *Monographs of the Society for Research in Child Development*, 1960, *25*, 4 (78).

Kritchevsky, S., E. Prescott, and L. S. Walling. *Planning Environments for Young Children: Physical Space*. Washington, D.C.: National Association for the Education of Young Children, 1969.

Kubie, L. S. The child's fifth freedom. *Child Study*, 1948, *25*:67–70; 88.

LaBarre, W. The age period of cultural fixation. *Mental Hygiene*, 1949, *33*:209–221.

Lark-Horovitz, B., and others. *Understanding Children's Art for Better Teaching*, 2d ed. Columbus, Ohio: Merrill, 1973.

Leighton, D., and C. Kluckhohn. *Children of the People: The Navaho Individual and His Development*. Cambridge, Mass.: Harvard University Press, 1947.

Lidz, T. *The Person*. New York: Basic Books, 1968.

Lowenfeld, V. *Creative and Mental Growth*, rev. ed. New York: Macmillan, 1952.

MacCann, D., and O. Richard. *The Child's First Books*. New York: H. W. Wilson, 1973.

Mattick, I. Adaptation of nursery school techniques to deprived children. *Journal of the American Academy of Child Psychiatry*, 1965, *4*:670–700.

Murphy, L. B. *Personality in Young Children: Colin—a Normal Child*, vol. 2. New York: Basic Books, 1956.

Murphy, L. B. *The Widening World of Childhood*. New York: Basic Books, 1962.

Patterson, J. M. Analyzing early childhood educational programs: Instructional procedures. *Educational Leadership*, 1971, *28*:802–805.

Pavenstedt, E. A comparison of the child-rearing environment of upper-lower and very low-lower class families. *American Journal of Orthopsychiatry*, 1965, *35*:89–98.

Pfluger, L. W., and J. M. Zola. A room planned by young children. *Young Children*, 1969, *24*:337–341.

Piaget, J. *Play, Dreams and Imitation in Childhood*. New York: Norton, 1962. (Originally published, 1945.)

Piaget, J. *The Language and Thought of the Child*. New York: Basic Books, 1954. (Originally published, 1924.)

Plant, J. *Personality and the Cultural Pattern*. New York: Commonwealth Fund, 1937.

Provence, S., A., Naylor, and J. Patterson. *The Challenge of Daycare*. New Haven, Conn.: Yale University Press, 1977.

Ross, E. D. *The Kindergarten Crusade: The Establishment of Preschool Education in the United States*. Athens: Ohio University Press, 1976.

Scarry, R. *Cars, Trucks, and Things That Go*. New York: Golden Press, 1974.

Senn, M. J. E. Insights on the child development movement in the United States. *Monographs of the Society for Research in Child Development*, 1975, *40* 3–4, (161).

Sheehy, E. D. *Children Discover Music and Dance*. New York: Teachers College, 1968.

Smilansky, S. *The Effect of Sociodramatic Play on Disadvantaged Preschool Children*. New York: Wiley, 1968.

Smilansky, S. Can adults facilitate play in children? Theoretical and practical considerations. In G. Engstrom, ed., *Play: The Child Strives toward Self-Realization*. Washington, D.C.: National Association for the Education of Young Children, 1971.

Smith, F. *Understanding Reading*. New York: Holt, Rinehart and Winston, 1972.

Spodek, B. The problem of play: Educational or recreational? In D. Sponseller, ed., *Play as a Learning Medium*. Washington, D.C.: National

Association for the Education of Young Children, 1974.

Steiner, G. Y. *The Children's Cause*. Washington, D.C.: Brookings Institute, 1976.

Stevens, J. H., and M. Mathews. *Mother/Child Father/Child Relationships*. Washington, D.C.: National Association for the Education of Young Children, 1978.

Sutherland, Z., and M. H. Arbuthnot. *Children and Books,* 5th ed. Glenview, Ill.: Scott, Foresman, 1977.

Weber, E. *The Kindergarten: Its Encounter with Educational Thought*. New York: Teachers College, 1969.

Whipple, G. M., ed. *The Twenty-Eighth Yearbook of the National Society for the Study of Education*. Bloomington, Ill.: Public School Publishing Company, 1929.

White, R. W. Competence and the psychosexual stages of development. In M. R. Jones, ed., *Nebraska Symposium on Motivation,* vol. 8. Lincoln: University of Nebraska Press, 1960.

Winnicott, D. W. *The Child and the Outside World*. New York: Basic Books, 1957.

Winnicott, D. W. *Playing and Reality*. New York: Basic Books, 1972.

Bibliography

Chapter 1 INTRODUCING THE PEOPLE IN THE SCHOOL OR DAY-CARE CENTER

Axline, V. *Dibs: In Search of Self.* Boston: Houghton Mifflin, 1964.

Biber, B. A view of preschool education. In B. D. Boegehold, H. F. Cuffaro, W. H. Hooks, and G. J. Klopf, eds., *Education before Five.* New York: Bank Street College of Education, 1977.

Coles, R. *Uprooted Children.* Pittsburgh: University of Pennsylvania Press, 1970.

Fleiss, B. A beginner's bibliography. *Young Children,* 1976, *31*:394–401.

Friedman, J., and A. L. Hauser. Developing a teacher resource center for preschool educators. *Young Children,* 1978, *34* (1):28–32.

Hymes, J. L. *Early Childhood Education: An Introduction to the Profession,* rev. ed. Washington, D.C.: National Association for the Education of Young Children, 1975.

Jones, E. Teacher education: Entertainment or interaction. *Young Children,* 1978, *33* (3):15–31.

Kenniston, K. Do Americans really like children? *Childhood Education,* 1975, *52*:4–13.

Ornstein, A. Who are the disadvantaged children? *Young Children,* 1971, *26*:264–272.

Scott, M., and S. Grimmett, eds. *Current Issues in Child Development.* Washington, D.C.: National Association for the Education of Young Children, 1977.

Senn, M. Early childhood education—for what goals? *Children,* 1969, *16*:8–13.

Smart, M. S., and R. C. Smart. *Children,* 3d ed. New York: Macmillan, 1977.

Todd, V. E., and H. Hefferman. *The Years before School: Guiding Preschool Children,* 2d ed. New York: Macmillan, 1970.

Zigler, E. Contemporary concerns in early childhood education. *Young Children,* 1971, *26*:141–156.

Chapter 2 PROGRAMS AND TYPES OF CENTERS

Association for Childhood Education, International. *A Lap To Sit on and Much More–Helps for Day Care Workers.* Washington, D.C.: author, 1971.

Association for Childhood Education, International. *Nursery school portfolio.* Washington, D.C.: Author, 1969.

Association for Childhood Education, International. *Toward better kindergartens.* Washington, D.C.: Author, 1966.

Austin, G. R. *Early Childhood Education: An International Perspective.* New York: Academic Press, 1976.

Boguslawski, D. *Guide for Establishing and Operating Day-Care Centers for Young Children.* New York: Child Welfare League of America, 1966.

Cohen, D. Continuity from prekindergarten to kindergarten. *Young Children,* 1971, *26*:282–286.

Committee on the Infant and Preschool Child, W. B. Forsythe, Chairman. *Standards for day care centers for infants and children under 3 years of age.* Evanston, Ill.: American Academy of Pediatrics, 1971.

Daily Program I, II, III. Washington, D.C.: H.E.W. Office of Child Development, Head Start Bureau, 1975.

Day Care for Your Children. Washington, D.C.: Department of Health, Education, and Welfare, Office of Child Development, Children's Bureau Pub. No. (OHD) 74–47, 1974.

Dittman, L. L. Migrant children in an early learning program. *Young Children,* 1976, *31*:218–228.

Dunlop, K. H. Mainstreaming: Valuing diversity. *Young Children,* 1977, *32*:26–31.

Durrett, M. E., and F. Pirofski. Effects of heterogeneous and homogeneous groupings on Mexican-American and Anglo children. *Young Children,* 1976, *31*:309–313.

Galinsky, E., and W. Hooks. *The New Extended Family–Day Care That Works.* Boston: Houghton Mifflin, 1977.

Huntington, D. S., S. Provence, and P. K. Parker. *Day Care, 2, Serving Infants.* Washington, D.C.: U.S. Government Printing Office, Department of Health, Education, and Welfare Publication No. (OCD) 73–14, 1971.

Keister, M. E. *"The Good Life" for Infants and Toddlers: Group Care of Infants.* Washington, D.C.: National Association for the Education of Young Children, 1970.

Kellog, E., and D. Hill. *Following through with Young Children.* Washington, D.C.: National Association for the Education of Young Children, 1969.

Keyserling, M. *Windows on Day Care.* New York: National Council of Jewish Women, 1972.

Klein, J. Mainstreaming the Preschooler. *Young Children,* 1975, *30*:317–326.

Leeper, S. H., and others. *Good Schools for Young Children,* 3d ed. New York: Macmillan, 1974.

Levine, J. A. *Day Care and the Public Schools.* Newton, Mass.: Educational Development Center, 1978.

McFadden, D., ed. *Early Childhood Development: Programs and Services: Planning for Action.* Washington, D.C.: National Association for the Education of Young Children, 1972.

Mindness, D., and M. Mindness. *Guide to an Effective Kindergarten Program.* West Nyack, N.Y.: Parker, 1972.

Moore, S. The effects of Head Start programs with different curricular and teaching strategies. *Young Children,* 1977, *32*:54–61.

Murphy, L. B. The stranglehold of norms on the individual child. *Childhood Education,* 1973, *49*:343–349.

Pizzo, P. D. *Operational Difficulties of Group Care.* Washington, D.C.: Day Care and Child Development Council of America, 1972.

Prescott, E. Approaches to quality in early childhood programs. *Childhood Education,* 1974, *50*:125–131.

Prescott, E., and E. Jones. *Day Care as a Child Rearing Environment,* vol. 1. Washington, D.C.: National Association for the Education of Young Children, 1972.

Prescott, E., and E. Jones. Day care for children—Assets and liabilities. *Children,* 1971, *18*:55–58.

Prosser, W., and F. Hoberkorn. The federal interaging day care requirements study, A dialogue with William Prosser. *Young Children,* 1976, *31*:385–392.

Provence, S. *Guide for the Care of Infants in Groups.* New York: Child Welfare League of America, 1967.

Sulby, A., and A. Diodati. Family day care: No longer day care's neglected child. *Young Children,* 1975, *30*:239–247.

Van Loon, E. *Perspectives on Child Care.* Washington, D.C.: National Association for the Education of Young Children, 1974.

Wakefield, A. P. Multiage grouping in day care. *Children Today,* 1979, *8*:26–28.

Ward, E. H., and CDA staff. The child development associate consortiums assessment system. *Young Children,* 1976, *31*:244–254.

Chapter 3 HISTORY AND THEORIES INFLUENCING CONTEMPORARY IDEAS IN EARLY EDUCATION

Almy, M. *The Work of the Early Childhood Educator.* New York: McGraw-Hill, 1975.

Baratz, S., and J. Baratz. Early childhood intervention: The social science base of institutional racism. *Harvard Educational Review,* 1970, *40*:29–50.

Bates, B. D. *Project Head Start 1969–70: A Descriptive Report of Programs and Participants.* Washington, D.C.: Office of Child Development, 1972.

Biber, B. Goals and methods in a preschool program for disadvantaged children. *Children,* 1970, *17*:15–20.

Biber, B. *Challenges Ahead for Early Childhood Education.* Washington, D.C.: National Association for the Education of Young Children, 1969.

Braun, S. J., and E. P. Edwards. *History and Theory of Early Childhood Education.* Worthington, Ohio: Charles A. Jones, 1972.

Cohen, D. J., and E. Zigler. Federal day care standards: Rationale and recommendations. *Young Children,* 1978, *33* (3):24–32.

Edwards, R. M. Role and class in early childhood education. *Young Children,* 1975, *30*:401–411.

Engstrom, G., ed. *Open education: The legacy of*

the progressive movement. Washington, D.C.: National Association for the Education of Young Children, 1970.

Erikson, E. Growth and crisis of the "healthy personality." In M. J. E. Senn, ed., *Symposium on the Healthy Personality*. New York: Macy, 1950.

Freud, A. *Normality and Pathology in Childhood*. London: Hogarth, 1965.

Freud, A. The ego and the mechanisms of defense. In O. Fenichel, and others, eds., *The Psychoanalytic Study of the Child*, vol. 1. New York: International Universities Press, 1945.

Greenleaf, B. K. *Children through the Ages: A History of Childhood*. New York: McGraw-Hill, 1978.

Hewes, D. W. Patty Smith Hill, pioneer for young children. *Young Children*, 1976, *31*:297–306.

Hodges, W. L., and R. Sheehan. Follow through as ten years of experimentation: What have we learned? *Young Children*, 1978, *34* (1):4–13.

Hymes, J. L. *Early Childhood Education: An Introduction to the Profession*, 2d ed. Washington, D.C.: National Association for the Education of Young Children, 1975.

Isaacs, N. *A Brief Introduction to Piaget*. New

York: Shocken Books, 1972. (Originally published, 1960.)

Johnson, H. *Children in the Nursery School*. New York: Agathon Press, 1972. (Originally published, 1928.)

Montessori in Perspective. Washington, D.C.: National Association for the Education of Young Children, 1966.

Piaget, J. *To Understand Is To Invent*. New York: Grossman, 1973.

Sears, R. R. Your ancients revisited: A history of child development. In E. M. Hetherington, ed., *Review of Child Development Research*, vol. 5. Chicago: University of Chicago Press, 1975.

Spodek, B. *Early Childhood Education*. Englewood Cliffs, N.J.: Prentice-Hall, 1973.

Spodek, B., and H. J. Walberg. *Early Childhood Education: Issues and Insights*. Berkeley, Calif.: McCutchan, 1977.

Weber, E. *Early Childhood Education: Perspectives on Change*. Worthington, Ohio: Charles A. Jones, 1970.

Zigler, E. America's Head Start program: An agenda for its second decade. *Young Children*, 1978, *33* (5):4–11.

Chapter 4   THE CHILDREN AND THE TEACHING STAFF

Baker, K. R., ed. *Ideas That Work with Young Children*. Washington, D.C.: National Association for the Education of Young Children, 1972.

Bently, R. J., E. Washington, and J. Young. Judging the educational progress of young children: Some cautions. *Young Children*, 1973, *29*:5–18.

Highberger, R., and C. Schramm. *Child Development for Day Care Workers*. Boston: Houghton Mifflin, 1976.

Johnson, H. *Children in the Nursery School*. New York: Agathon, 1972. (Originally published, 1928.)

Klein, J., and R. Weathersby. Child development

associates: New professionals, new training strategies. *Children Today*, 1973, *2* (5):2–6.

Landreth, C. *Preschool Learning and Teaching*. New York: Harper & Row, 1972.

Rudolph, M. *From Hand to Head: A Handbook for Teachers of Preschool Programs*. New York: McGraw-Hill, 1973.

Stinnet, T. M., and G. Pershing. *A Manual on Certification Requirements for School Personnel in the U.S.A.* Washington, D.C.: National Education Association, 1970.

Todd, V. E., and G. Hunter. *The Aide in Early Childhood Education*. New York: Macmillan, 1973.

Chapter 5   THE BUILDING; THE EQUIPMENT AND MATERIALS; THE USE OF SPACE AND TIME

Carmichael, V., and others. *Administration of Schools for Young Children*. Sierra Madre, Calif.: Southern California Association for the Education of Young Children, 1972.

Friedberg, M. P. *Handcrafted Playgrounds*. New York: Vintage Books, 1975.

Friedberg, M. P. *Playgrounds for City Children*.

Washington, D.C.: Association for Childhood Education International, 1969.

Frost, J. L., and B. L. Klein. *Children's Play and Playgrounds*. Boston: Allyn and Bacon, 1979.

Haase, R. W. *Designing the Child Development Center*. Washington, D. C.: Office of Economic Opportunity, 1968.

Helick, R. M. *Elements of Preschool Playards*. Swissvale, Pa.: Regent Graphic Services, 1973.

Hewes, D., and B. Hartman, *Early Childhood Education: A Workbook for Administrators*. San Francisco: R and E Associates, 1972.

Hewes, J. J. *Build Your Own Playground*. San Francisco: Houghton Mifflin, 1974.

Hill, D. M. *Mud, Sand and Water*. Washington, D.C.: National Association for the Education of Young Children, 1977.

Hirsch, E., ed. *The Block Book*. Washington, D.C.: National Association for the Education of Young Children, 1974.

McVickor, P., and others. *Imagination: Key to Human Potential*. Washington, D.C.: National Association for the Education of Young Children, 1972.

Osman, F. L. *Patterns for Designing Children's Centers*. New York: Educational Facilities Laboratories, 1971.

Rudolph, N. *Workyards–Playgrounds Planned for Adventure*. New York: Teachers College, 1974.

Stanton, J., and M. Rudolph. *Planning a Nursery School Building*. New York: Bank Street College of Education, 1962.

Stone, J. G., and N. Rudolph. *Play and Playgrounds*. Washington, D.C.: National Association for the Education of Young Children, 1970.

Whiren, A. Table toys: The underdeveloped resource. *Young Children*, 1975, *30*:413–419.

Chapter 6   INITIAL SUPPORT THROUGH GUIDES TO SPEECH AND ACTION

Beyer, E. *Teaching Young Children*. New York: Pegasus, 1968.

Beyers, P., and H. Beyers. Nonverbal communication and the education of children. In C. B. Cazden, V. P. John, and D. Hymes eds., *Functions of Language in the Classroom*. New York: Teachers College, 1972.

Bryan, J. H. Children's cooperation and helping behaviors. In E. M. Hetherington, ed., *Review of Child Development Research*, vol. 5. Chicago: University of Chicago Press, 1975.

Cohen, D. H. *The Learning Child: Guidelines for Parents and Teachers*. New York: Pantheon, 1972.

Freud, A. The emotional and social development of young children. In K. Read, ed., *Feeling and Learning*. Washington, D.C.: Association for Childhood International, 1965.

Ostler, R., and P. L. Kronz. More effective communication through understanding young children's nonverbal behavior. *Young Children*, 1976, *31*:113–120.

Samuels, S. C. *Enhancing Self-Concept in Early Childhood*. New York: Human Sciences Press, 1977.

Stein, M., E. Beyer, and P. Ronald. Beyond benevolence—The mental health role of the preschool teacher. *Young Children*, 1975, *30*:358–372.

Warren, R. *Caring, Supporting Children's Growth*. Washington, D.C.: National Association for the Education of Young Children, 1977.

Winnicott, D. W. *The Maturational Process and the Facilitating Environment*. New York: International Universities Press, 1974.

Chapter 7   DISCIPLINE, THE SETTING OF LIMITS, AND USING AUTHORITY

Becker, W. C. Consequences of different kinds of parental discipline. In M. Hoffman and L. M. Hoffman, eds., *Review of Child Development Research*, vol. 1. New York: Russell Sage, 1964.

Behavior: The Unspoken Language of Children. New York: Child Study Association of America, 1955.

Galambos, J. W. *A Guide to Discipline*. Washington, D.C.: National Association for the Education of Young Children, 1969.

Walker, H. M. *The Acting-Out Child: Coping with Classroom Disruption*. Boston: Allyn and Bacon, 1979.

Chapter 8   OBSERVING CHILDREN

Cohen, D. Learning to observe—Observing to learn. In G. Engstrom, ed., *The Significance of the Young Child's Motor Development*. Washing-

ton, D.C.: National Association for the Education of Young Children, 1971.

Read, Katherine. *A Guide for Recording in Day*

Care Agencies. New York: Child Welfare League of America, 1964.

Rowen, B. *The Children We See: An Observational Approach to Child Study.* New York: Holt, Rinehart and Winston, 1973.

Vasta, R. *Studying Children.* San Francisco: Freeman, 1979.

Wright, H. F. *Recording and Analyzing Child Behavior.* New York: Harper & Row, 1967.

Chapter 9 HELPING CHILDREN ADJUST TO NEW SITUATIONS

Anderson, J. W. Attachment behavior out-of-doors. In N. Blurton-Jones, ed., *Ethnological Studies of Child Behavior.* London: Cambridge University Press, 1972.

Baratz, S., and J. Baratz. Negro ghetto children and urban education: A cultural solution. *Social Education,* 1969, *33*:401–404.

Bowlby, J. *Attachment and Loss: Separation,* vol. 2. New York: Basic Books, 1973.

Bowlby, J. *Attachment and Loss: Attachment,* vol. 1. New York: Basic Books, 1969.

Curry, N. E., and E. M. Tittnich. *Ready or Not, Here We Come: The Dilemma of School Readiness,* rev. ed. Pittsburgh: Arsenal Family and Children's Center, University of Pittsburgh, 1975.

Heinicke, C., and I. J. Westheimer. *Brief Separations.* New York: International Universities Press, 1965.

Johnson, B. Before hospitalization: A preparation program for the child and his family. *Children Today,* 1974, *3*:18–21.

Jones, M. G. *A Two Year Old Goes to Nursery School: A Case Study of Separation Anxiety.* Washington, D.C.: National Association for the Education of Young Children, 1964.

Macoby, E. E., and J. C. Masters. Attachment and dependency. In P. Mussen, ed., *Carmichael's Manual of Child Psychology.* New York: Wiley, 1970.

Plank, E. *Working with Children in Hospitals,* 2d ed. Cleveland: The Press of Case Western Reserve University, 1971.

Schwarz, J. C., and R. Wynn. The effects of mothers' presence and previsits on children's emotional reaction to starting nursery school. *Child Development,* 1971, *42*:871–882.

Selmon, R. Taking on other's perspective: Role-taking development in early childhood. *Child Development,* 1971, *42*:1721–1734.

Speers, R. W., and others. Recapitulation of separation-individuation processes when the normal three-year-old enters nursery school. In J. McDevitt and C. Settlage, eds., *Recapitulation—individuation: Essays in Honor of Margaret Mahler.* New York: International Universities Press, 1971.

Thomas, A., and S. Chess. *Temperament and Development.* New York: Bruner/Mazel, 1977.

Yarrow, L. Separation from parents during early childhood. In M. L. Hoffman and L. W. Hoffman, eds., *Review of Child Development Research,* vol. 1. New York: Russell Sage, 1964.

Chapter 10 HELPING CHILDREN IN ROUTINE SITUATIONS

Food for the Preschool Child 13 Months to 6 Years. Washington, D.C.: Department of Health, Education, and Welfare, Children's Bureau SRS, 1969.

Hirsch, E. *Transition Periods, Stumbling Blocks of Education.* New York: Early Childhood Education Council of New York City, 1971.

Lansky, V. *Feed Me I'm Yours.* Wayzata, Minn.: Meadowbrook Press, 1975.

Mugge, D. J. Taking the routine out of routines. *Young Children,* 1976, *31*:209–217.

Murphy, L. B., and E. M. Leeper. *Away from Bedlam.* Washington, D.C.: Superintendent of Documents, DEW Publication Number (OCD), 73-1029.

Murphy, L. B., and E. M. Leeper, *Preparing for Change.* Washington, D.C.: Superintendent of Documents, DEW Publication Number (OCD) 72-1028.

Raman, S. P. Role of nutrition in the actualization of the potentialities of the child. *Young Children,* 1975, *31*:24–32.

Report of the Committee on Infectious Disease. Evanston, Ill.: American Academy of Pediatrics, 1977.

Reinisch, E. H., and R. E. Minear. *Health of the Preschool Child.* New York: Wiley, 1978.

Weinraub, M., and M. Lewis. The determinants of children's responses to separation. *Monographs of the Society for Research in Child Development,* 1977, *42,* 4 (172).

Chapter 11 THE ROLE OF THE TEACHER

Ashton-Warner, S. *Teacher.* New York: Simon & Schuster, 1963.

Baumrind, D. Socialization and instrumental competence in young children. *Young Children,* 1970, *26*:104–119.

Bowman, B. Teacher training: Where and how. In B. Spodeck, ed., *Teacher-Education, of the Teacher, by the Teacher, for the Child.* Washington, D.C.: National Association for the Education of Young Children, 1974.

Braun, J., and M. G. Lasher. *Preparing Teachers To Work with Disturbed Preschoolers.* Cambridge, Mass.: Nimrod Press, 1970.

Castillo, M., and J. Cruz. Special competencies for the teachers of preschool Chicano children. *Young Children,* 1974, *29*:341–347.

Frazier, A., ed. *Early Childhood Education Today.* Washington, D.C.: Association for Supervision and Curriculum Development, 1968.

Gordon, I., ed. *Early Childhood Education.* Seventy first Yearbook of the National Society for the Study of Education. Chicago: University of Chicago Press, 1972.

Gordon, I. J. Parenting, teaching and child development. *Young Children,* 1976, *31*:173–183.

Gracey, H. L. Learning the student role: Kinder-garten as academic boot camp. In D. W. Wrong and G. L. Gracey, eds., *Readings in Introductory Sociology.* New York: Macmillan, 1967.

Hartman, K. How do I teach in a future shocked world? *Young Children,* 1977, *32*:32–36.

Hirsch, E. Accountability: A danger to humanistic education? *Young Children,* 1975, *31*:57–64.

Rafael, B., and S. Marinoff. Using video tape for teacher training. *Young Children,* 1973, *28*:217–219.

Seaver, J. V., C. A. Cartwright, C. B. Ward, and C. A. Heasley. *Careers with Young Children: Making Your Decision.* Washington, D.C.: National Association for the Education of Young Children, 1979.

Spodek, B., ed. *Teacher Education.* Washington, D.C.: National Association for the Education of Young Children, 1974.

Spodek, B. *Teaching in the Early Years,* 2d ed. Englewood Cliffs, N.J.: Prentice-Hall, 1978.

Spodek, B., and H. Walberg, eds., *Early Childhood Education, Issues and Insights.* Berkeley, Calif.: McCutchan, 1977.

Ward, E. H., and others. The child development associate consortium's assessment system. *Young Children,* 1976, *31*:244–254.

Chapter 12 FEELINGS OF SECURITY AND CONFIDENCE

About Birth, Family Crises. 1978.

Cohn, E. S. *Our Brother's Keeper: The Indian in White America.* Mountain View, Calif.: World Publishing, 1969.

Comer, J. P. *Beyond Black and White.* New York: Quandrangle, 1972.

Comer, J. P., and A. F. Poussaint, *Black Child Care, How To Bring Up a Healthy Black Child in America: A Guide to Emotional and Psychological Development.* New York: Simon & Schuster, 1975.

Engstrom, G., ed. *Play: The Child Strives toward Self-Realization.* Washington, D.C.: National Association for the Education of Young Children, 1971.

Goodman, M. E. *Race Awareness in Young Children.* New York: Macmillan, 1964.

Granger, R. C., and J. C. Young, eds. *De-mythologizing the Inner-City Child.* Washington, D.C.: National Association for the Education of Young Children, 1976.

Seminar on infants: Some considerations for optimal infant care. Pittsburgh: Arsenal Family and Children's Center, University of Pittsburgh, 1975.

Solnit, A. J. Changing psychological perspectives about children and their families. *Children Today,* 1976 (5):5–9; 43.

Sroufe, A. *Knowing and Enjoying Your Baby.* Englewood Cliffs, N.J.: Prentice-Hall, 1977.

White, R. N. Ego and reality in psychoanalytic theory. *Psychological Issues Monograph.* New York: International Universities Press, 1963.

Yamamoto, K., ed. *The Child and His Image.* Boston: Houghton Mifflin, 1972.

Chapter 13 FEELINGS OF HOSTILITY AND AGGRESSIVENESS

Arnstein, H. *The Roots of Love.* Indianapolis: Bobbs-Merrill, 1975.

Cairns, R. B. Fighting and punishment from a developmental perspective. In J. K. Cole and

D. D. Jensen, eds., *Nebraska Symposium on Motivation,* vol. 20. Lincoln: University of Nebraska Press, 1973.

Deur, J. L., and R. D. Parke. Effects of inconsistent punishment on aggression in children. *Developmental Psychology,* 1970, *2*:403–411.

Feshbach, S. Aggression. In P. H. Mussen, ed., *Carmichael's Manual of Child Psychology,* vol. 2. New York: Wiley, 1970.

Feshbach, S., and R. D. Singer. *Television and Aggression.* San Francisco: Jossey-Bass, 1971.

Furman, E. Helping children cope with death. *Young Children,* 1978, *33* (4):25–32.

Goodenough, F. L. *Anger in Young Children.* Minneapolis: University of Minnesota Press, 1931.

Gould, R. *Child Studies through Fantasy.* New York: Quadrangle, 1972.

Schowalter, J. When dinosaurs return: Children's fascination with dinosaurs. *Children Today,* 1979, *8*:2–5.

Smith, P. K., and M. Green. Aggressive behavior in English nurseries and play groups: Sex differences and response of adults. *Child Development,* 1975, *46*:211–214.

Chapter 14 DRAMATIC PLAY—AVENUE FOR INSIGHT

Cohen, D. Is TV a pied piper? *Young Children,* 1974, *30*:4–14.

Fowler, W. On the value of both play and structure in early education. *Young Children,* 1971, *27*:24–35.

Lesser, H. *Television and the Preschool Child.* New York: Academic Press, 1977.

Lowenfeld, M. *Play in Childhood.* New York: Wiley, 1968.

McLellan, J. *The Question of Play.* Oxford, England: Pergamon, 1972.

Millar, S. *The Psychology of Play.* Baltimore: Pelican, 1968.

Mukerji, R., M. Akers, M. Campbell, and E. Liddle. *Television Guidelines for Early Childhood Education.* Bloomington, Ill.: National Instructional TV, 1969.

Osborn, D. K., and J. D. Osborn. Television violence revisited. *Childhood Education,* 1977, *53*:309–311.

Ruben, K. Play behaviors of young children. *Young Children,* 1977, *32* (6):16–23.

Singer, J. *The Child's World of Make Believe.* New Haven, Conn.: Yale University Press, 1973.

Williams, M. *Children's Television: The Economics of Exploitation.* New Haven, Conn.: Yale University Press, 1973.

Chapter 15 THE PROCESS OF LEARNING IN EARLY CHILDHOOD

Bailey, N. Development of mental abilities. In P. Mussen, ed., *Carmichael's Manual of Child Psychology,* vol. 1. New York: Wiley, 1970.

Biber, B., E. Shapiro, D. Wickens. *Promoting Cognitive Growth: A Developmental-Interaction Point of View.* Washington, D.C.: National Association for the Education of Young Children, 1971.

Case, R. Gearing the demands of instruction to the developmental capacities of the learner. *Review of Educational Research,* 1975, *45*:59–89.

Davis, A. *Social-Class Influences upon Learning.* Cambridge: Harvard University Press, 1962.

Donaldson, M. *Children's Minds.* New York: Norton, 1978.

Estavan, F. Teaching the very young: Procedures for developing inquiry skills. In R. H. Anderson and H. G. Shane, eds., *As the Twig Is Bent: Readings in Early Childhood Education.* Boston: Houghton Mifflin, 1971.

Franklin, M. B. Non-verbal representation in young children: A cognitive perspective. *Young Children,* 1973, *29*:33–55.

Gallagher, J. J. Productive thinking. In M. Hoffman and L. Hoffman, eds., *Review of Child Development Research,* vol. 1. New York: Russell Sage, 1964.

Goodnow, J. J. Rules, repertoires, rituals and tricks of the trade: Social and information aspects to cognitive and representational development. In S. Farnham-Diggory, ed., *Information Processing in Children.* New York: Academic Press, 1972.

Hawkins, E. P. *The Logic of Action—Young Children at Work.* New York: Pantheon, 1974.

Hertzig, M. E., H. G. Birch, A. Thomas, and O. A. Mendez. Class and ethnic differences in the responsiveness of preschool children to cognitive demands. *Monographs of the Society for Research in Child Development,* 1968, *33* (1):117.

Inhelder, B., H. Sinclair, and M. Bovet. *Learning and the Development of Cognition.* Cambridge: Harvard University Press, 1974.

Kail, R. *The Development of Memory in Children.* San Francisco: Freeman, 1979.

Kunkle, E., and G. Engstrom. *The Infant.* Milwaukee: University of Wisconsin Press, 1970.

Piaget, J. *The Grasp of Consciousness, Action and Concept in the Young Child.* Cambridge: Harvard University Press, 1976. (Originally published, 1974.)

Piaget, J. *Success and Understanding.* Cambridge: Harvard University Press, 1978. (Originally published, 1974.)

Pick, A. D., D. G. Frankel, and V. L. Hess. Children's attention: The development of selectivity. In E. M. Hetherington, ed., *Review of Child Development Research,* vol. 5. Chicago: University of Chicago Press, 1975.

Sigel, I. E. The distancing hypothesis: A causal hypothesis on the acquisition of representational thought. In M. Jones, ed., *The Effects of Early Experience.* Miami, Fla: The University of Miami Press, 1970.

Sinclair, H. The transition from sensory-motor to symbolic activity. *Interchange,* 1970, *1*:119–126.

Spitzer, D. R. *Concept Formation and Learning in Early Childhood.* Columbus, Ohio: Merrill, 1977.

Stevenson, H. W. *Children's Learning.* Englewood Cliffs, N.J.: Prentice-Hall, 1972.

Stevenson, H. W., G. A. Hale, R. E. Klein, and L. K. Miller. Interrelations and correlates in children's learning and problem solving. *Monographs of the Society for Research in Child Development,* 1968, *33* (7):123.

Stone, J. L., H. T. Smith, and L. B. Murphy. *The Competent Infant: Research and Commentary.* New York: Basic Books, 1973.

Streissguth, A., and H. Bee. Mother-child interaction and cognitive development in children. In W. W. Hartup, ed., *The Young Child: Reviews of Research.* Washington, D.C.: National Association for the Education of Young Children, 1972.

Suchman, J. R. The child and the inquiry process. In H. H. Passow and R. R. Leeper, eds., *Intellectual Development: Another Look.* Washington, D.C.: Association for Supervision and Curriculum Development, 1964.

White, S. H., and A. Siegel. Cognitive development: The new inquiry. *Young Children,* 1976, *31*:425–436.

Chapter 16 Play as a Mode of Learning

Berger, J. H. The multifaceted levels of play in preschool children. *Child Welfare,* 1979, *58*:327–332.

Bruner, J. S., A. Jolly, K. Sylva, eds. *Play: Its Role in Development and Evolution.* New York: Basic Books, 1976.

Fein, G. A transformational analysis of pretending. *Developmental Psychology,* 1975, *11*:291–296.

Garvey, C. *Play: The Developing Child.* Cambridge: Harvard University Press, 1977.

Gross, D. Play and thinking. *Play: Children's Business.* Washington, D.C.: Association for Childhood Education International, 1963.

Guillaume, P. *Imitation in Children.* Chicago: University of Chicago Press, 1971. (Originally published, 1926.)

Herron, R. E., and B. Sutton-Smith, eds. *Child's Play.* New York: Wiley, 1971.

Piers, M., ed. *Play and Development.* New York: Norton, 1972.

Sigel, I., and B. McBone. Cognitive competence and level of symbolization among five year old children. In J. Hellmuth, ed., *The Disadvantaged Child.* Seattle: Special Child Publications, 1967.

Speers, R. W. *Variations in Separation—Individuation and Implications for Play Ability and Learning as Studies in the Three Year Old in Nursery School.* Pittsburgh: Arsenal Family and Children's Center, University of Pittsburgh, 1968.

Stern, V. *The Role of Play in Cognitive Development.* New York: Bank Street College of Education, 1973.

Sutton-Smith, B. Play as novelty training. In J. D. Andrews, ed., *One Child Indivisible.* Washington, D.C.: National Association for the Education of Young Children, 1975.

Chapter 17 Curriculum Areas: Mathematics and Science

Mathematics

Bingham-Newman, A. M., and R. M. Saunders. Take a new look at your classroom with Piaget as a guide. *Young Children,* 1977, *32* (4):62–72.

Gelman, R., and C. R. Gallistel. *The Child's Understanding of Number.* Cambridge: Harvard University Press, 1978.

Lovell, K. *The Growth of Understanding in Mathematics: Kindergarten through Grade Three.* New York: Holt, Rinehart and Winston, 1971.

Nuffield Mathematics Series. *Beginnings; I Do and I Understood; Pictorial Representations.* New York: Wiley, 1968.

Payne, J. N., ed. *Mathematics in Early Childhood.* Thirty-seventh yearbook. Reston, Va.: National Council of Teachers of Mathematics, 1976.

Piaget, J. *The Child's Conception of Time.* New York: Ballantine, 1971. (Originally published, 1927.)

Piaget, J. *The Child's Conception of Number.* New York: Norton, 1965. (Originally published, 1941.)

Piaget, J., B. Inhelder, and A. Szeminska. *The Child's Conception of Geometry.* New York: Basic Books, 1960.

Sigel, I. E. The development of classificatory skills in young children: A training program. *Young Children,* 1971, *26*:170–184.

Zimilies, H. The development of conservation and differentiation of number. *Monographs of the Society for Research in Child Development,* 1966, *31* (6):108.

Science

Abbot, R. T. *Seashells of the World, A Guide to Better-Known Species.* New York: Golden, 1962.

Borrov, P. J., and R. E. White. *A Field Guide to Insects of America North of Mexico.* Boston: Houghton Mifflin, 1970.

Buck, M. W. *How They Grow.* Nashville: Abingdon, 1972.

Carmichael, V. *Science Experiences for Young Children.* Sierra Madre, Calif.: Southern California Association for the Education of Young Children, 1972.

Davis, B. *Learning Science through Cooking.* New York: Sterling, 1964.

DeSchweinitz, K. *Growing Up: The Story of How We Become Alive, Are Born and Grow Up.* New York: Macmillan, 1965.

Goldberg, L. *Children and Science.* New York: Scribner, 1970.

Harlan, J. D. *Science Experiences for the Early Childhood Years.* Columbus, Ohio: Merrill, 1976.

Hochman, V. *Trips in Early Education.* New York: Bank Street College of Education, 1957.

Hochman, V., and M. Greenwald. *Science Experiences in Early Childhood Education.* New York: Bank Street College of Education,

Karplus, R., and H. Thier. *A New Look at Elementary School Science.* Skokie, Ill.: Rand McNally, 1967.

Koocher, G. Why isn't the gerbil moving anymore?: Discussion of death in the classroom and at home. *Children Today,* 1975, *4* (1):18–21; 36.

Levi, H. W., and L. Levi. *A Guide to Spiders.* New York: Golden, 1968.

Mitchell, R. T. *Butterflies and Moths.* New York: Golden, 1964.

Nickelsburg, J. Learning about Nature. *Children Today,* 1975, *4* (5):9–11; 35–36.

Peterson, R. T. *A Field Guide to Birds: Eastern Land and Water Birds,* 3d ed. Boston: Houghton Mifflin, 1947.

Piaget, J. *The Child's Conception of Physical Causality.* Paterson, N.J.: Littlefield Adams, 1960. (Originally published, 1930.)

Reid, G. K. *Pond Life.* New York: Golden, 1967.

Rowe, M. B. *Teaching Science as Continuous Inquiry.* New York: McGraw-Hill, 1973.

Weir, M. K., and P. J. Eggleston. Water play for preschoolers. *Young Children,* 1975, *31*:5–11.

Zim. H. S. *Birds: A Guide to the Most Familiar American Birds.* New York: Golden, 1956.

Zim, H. S. *Reptiles and Amphibians.* New York: Golden, 1956.

Zim, H. S., and C. Cottam. *Insects: A Guide to Familiar American Insects.* New York: Golden, 1956.

Zim, H. S., and D. F. Hoffmeister. *Mammals: A Guide to Familiar American Species.* New York: Golden, 1955.

Zim, H. S., and A. C. Martin. *Flowers: A Guide to Familiar American Wildflowers.* New York: Golden, 1950.

Chapter 18   CURRICULUM AREAS: LANGUAGE ARTS AND SOCIAL STUDIES

Language Arts

Anglin, J. M. *The Growth of Word Meaning.* Cambridge, Mass.: M.I.T. Press, 1970.

Bellugi, V., and R. Brown, eds. *The Acquisition of Language.* Chicago: University of Chicago Press, 1975.

Brown, R. *A First Language, the Early Stages.* Cambridge: Harvard University Press, 1973.

Cazden, C. B. *Child Language and Education.* New York: Holt, Rinehart and Winston, 1972.

Cazden, C. B., V. P. John, and D. Hymes, eds.

Functions of Language in the Classroom. New York: Teachers College, 1972.

Dale, P. *Language Development, Structure and Function,* 2d ed. Hinsdale, Ill.: Dryden, 1976.

Dimitrovsky, L. and M. Almy. Early conservation as a predictor of later reading. *Journal of Psychology,* 1975, *90*:11–18.

Durkin, D. *Children Who Read Early.* New York: Teachers College, 1966.

Galen, H. Cooking in the curricula. *Young Children,* 1977, *32*:59–69.

Granger, R. C. The nonstandard speaking child: Myths past and present. *Young Children,* 1976, *31*:478–485.

Labov, W. The logic of nonstandard English. In F. F. Williams, ed., *Language and Poverty.* Chicago: Markham, 1970.

Lincoln, R. D. Reading to young children. *Children Today,* 1974, *3*:28–30.

Lowes, R. Do we teach reading in the kindergarten? *Young Children,* 1975, *30*:328–331.

Mattick, I. The teacher's role in helping young children develop language competence. *Young Children,* 1972, *28*:133–142.

Nedler, S. E. Explorations in teaching English as a second language. *Young Children,* 1975, *30*:480–485.

Pflaum, S. W. *The Development of Language and Reading in the Young Child.* Columbus, Ohio: Merrill, 1974.

Rhea, P. Invented spelling in kindergarten. *Young Children,* 1976, *31*:195–200.

Sandberg, J. H., and J. D. Pohlmon. Reading on the child's terms. *Young Children,* 1976, *31*:106–112.

Schickedanz, J. Please read that story again. *Young Children,* 1978, *33* (5):48–55.

Sherman, J. L. Storytelling with young children. *Young Children,* 1979, *34* (1):20–27.

Siks, G. B. *Drama with Children.* New York: Harper & Row, 1977.

Siks, G., and H. B. Dunnington, eds. *Children's Threatre and Creative Dramatics.* Seattle: University of Washington Press, 1967.

Spache, G. P., and E. B. Spache. *Reading in the Elementary School,* 3d ed. Boston: Allyn and Bacon, 1973.

Waller, G. T. *Think First, Read Later: Piagetian Prerequisites for Reading.* Newark, Del.: International Reading Association, 1977.

Wassermann, S. Key vocabulary: Impact on beginning reading. *Young Children,* 1978, *33* (4):33–38.

Winsor, C., ed. *Dimensions of Language Experiences.* New York: Agathon, 1975.

Social Studies

Bogdanoff, R. F., and E. T. Dolch. Old games for young children: A link to our heritage. *Young Children,* 1979, *34* (1):37–45.

Edge, N. *Kindergarten Cooks.* Port Angelus, Washington: Pen Print, 1977.

Flavell, J. H., and others. *The Development of Role-Taking and Communication Skills in Children.* New York: Wiley, 1968.

Foster, F. P., ed. *Adventures in cooking.* Westfield, N.J.: New Jersey Association for the Education of Young Children, 1971.

Greenleaf, P. T. *Liberating Young Children from Sex Roles: Experiences in Day Care Centers, Play Groups and Free Schools.* Sommerville, Mass.: New England Free Press, 1972.

Isaacs, S. The nursery school as a community. In J. Rosenblith and W. Allinsmith, eds., *The Causes of Behavior: Readings in Child Development and Educational Psychology.* Boston: Allyn and Bacon, 1962.

Kohlberg, L. Stage and sequence: The developmental approach to socialization. In D. Goslin, ed., *Handbook of Socialization.* Skokie, Ill.: Rand McNally, 1968.

Kositsky, V. What in the world is cooking in class today? Multiethnic recipes for young children. *Young Children,* 1977, *33* (1):23–31.

Lewis, M., and L. A. Rosenblum, eds. *Friendships and Peer Relations.* New York: Wiley, 1975.

Mead, M. Can socialization of children lead to greater diversity? *Young Children,* 1973, *28*:322–332.

Menig-Peterson, C. L. The modification of communicative behavior in preschool-aged children as a function of the listener's perspective. *Child Development,* 1975, *46*:1015–1018.

Mitchell, L. S. *Young Geographers.* New York: Agathon, 1971. (Originally published, 1934.)

Moore, S. G. Considerateness and helpfulness in young children. *Young Children,* 1977, *32* (4):73–76.

O'Connor, M. Role taking and social orientation in young children. *Journal of Psychology,* 1976, *94*:135–137.

Piaget, J. *The Child's Conception of the World.* Paterson, N.J.: Littlefield Adams, 1969. (Originally published, 1929.)

Piaget, J., and B. Inhelder. *The Child's Conception of Space.* New York: Norton, 1967. (Originally published, 1948.)

Ross, S. and C. Seefeldt. Young children in traffic: How they can cope. *Young Children,* 1978, *33* (4):68–73.

Rubin, K. H. The relations between social participation and role taking skills in young children. *Psychological Reports,* 1976, *39*:823–826.

Sprung, B. *Non-sexist Education for Young Children: A Practical Guide.* New York: Citation, 1975.

Urberg, K. A., and E. M. Docherty. The development of role taking skills in young children. *Developmental Psychology,* 1976, *12*:198–203.

Webb, R. A., ed. *Social Development in Childhood, Daycare Programs and Research.* Baltimore: Johns Hopkins University Press, 1977.

Wilson, K. E., and C. U. Shoutz. Perceptual role taking ability and dependency behavior in preschool children. *Merrill-Palmer Quarterly,* 1977, *23*:207–211.

Chapter 19 CURRICULUM AREAS: ART, MUSIC, AND MOVEMENT

Art

Biber, B. *Premature Structuring as a Deterrent to Creativity.* New York: Bank Street College of Education, 1963.

Brittain, W. L. *Creativity, Art, and the Young Child.* New York: Macmillan, 1979.

D'Amico, V. *Experiments in Creative Art Teaching.* Garden City, N.Y.: Doubleday, 1960.

D'Amico, V., F. Wilson, and M. Maser. *Art for the Family.* New York: Simon & Schuster, 1954.

Diamondstein, G. *Exploring the Arts with Children.* New York: Macmillan, 1974.

Golumb, C. Children's representations of the human figure: The effects of models, media, and instructions. *Genetic Psychology Monographs,* 1973, *87*:197–251.

Goodnow, J. *Children's Drawings.* Cambridge: Harvard University Press, 1977.

Lark-Horovitz, B., H. Lewis, and M. Luca. *Understanding Children's Art for Better Teaching.* Columbus, Ohio: Merrill, 1973.

Lasky, L. R. Personalizing teaching: Action research in action. *Young Children,* 1978, *33* (3):58–64.

Lindstrom, M. *Children's Art.* Berkeley: University of California Press, 1959.

Pile, N. F. *Art Experiences for Young Children.* New York: Macmillan, 1973.

Sigel, I. E., and P. Olmstead. The development of classification and representational competence. In A. J. Biemiller, ed., *Problems in Teaching Young Children.* Toronto: Ontario Institute for Studies in Education, 1970.

Smith, N. R. Creativity in the paintings of children and artists. In C. B. Winsor, ed., *Creative Experiences: Aspects and Interplay.* New York: Bank Street College of Education, 1975.

Music

Aronoff, F. W. *Music and Young Children.* New York: Holt, Rinehart and Winston, 1969.

Bailey, E. *Discovering Music with Children.* New York: Philosophical Library, 1958.

Boardman, E. L. An investigation of the effect of preschool training on the development of vocal accuracy in young children. *Council for Research in Music Education, Bulletin 11,* 1967: 46–49.

Drexler, E. N. A study of the development of the ability to carry a melody at the preschool level. *Child Development,* 1938, *9*:319–332.

Fletcher, H. J. *Finger Play, Poems and Stories.* New York: Macmillan, 1958.

Fowke, E. *Sally Go Round the Sun.* Garden City, N.Y.: Doubleday, 1969.

Glazer, T. *Eye Winker, Tom Tinker, Chin Chopper: Fifty Musical Fingerplays.* Garden City, N.Y.: Doubleday, 1973.

Grayson, M. F. *Let's Do Fingerplays.* Washington, D.C.: Robert B. Luce, 1962.

Greenberg, M. *Your Children Need Music.* Englewood Cliffs, N.J.: Prentice-Hall, 1979.

Jenkins, E. *The Ella Jenkins' Song Book for Children.* New York: Oak, 1969.

Jones, E. *What Is Music for Young Children?* Washington, D.C.: National Association for the Education of Young Children, 1969.

Landeck, B. *More Songs To Grow On.* New York: Morrow, 1954.

Landeck, B. *Songs To Grow On.* New York: Morrow, 1950.

Langstaff, N., and J. Langstaff. *Jim along Josie.* New York: Harcourt, 1970.

McDonald, D. T. *Music in Our Lives: The Early Years.* Washington, D.C.: National Association for the Education of Young Children, 1979.

McDonald, D. T., and H. H. Ramsey. Awakening the artist: Music for young children. *Young Children,* 1978, *33* (2):26–32.

Music for Young Children's Living. Washington, D.C.: Association for Childhood Education, International, 1955.

Nye, V. *Music for Young Children.* Dubuque, Iowa: William C. Brown, 1975.

Pugmire, M. C. *Experiences in Music for Young Children.* Albany, N.Y.: Delmar, 1977.

Seegar, R. C. *American Folk Songs for Children.* Garden City, N.Y.: Doubleday, 1948.

Sendack, M., and C. King. *Really Rosie.* New York: Harper & Row, 1975.

Smith, R. B. *Music in the Child's Education.* New York: Ronald, 1970.

Winn, M. *What Shall We Do and Allee Galloo.* New York: Harper & Row, 1970.

Yolen, J., B. Green, and P. Parnall. *The Fireside Songbook of Birds and Beasts.* New York: Simon & Schuster, 1972.

Movement

Baker, K. R. *Let's Play Outdoors.* Washington, D.C.: National Association for the Education of Young Children, 1966.

Engstrom, G., ed. *The Significance of the Young Child's Motor Development.* Washington, D.C.: National Association for the Education of Young Children, 1971.

Gerhardt, L. *Moving and Knowing: The Young Child Orients Himself in Space.* Englewood Cliffs, N.J.: Prentice-Hall, 1973.

Julius, A. K. Focus on movement: Practice and theory. *Young Children,* 1978, *34* (1):19–26.

Maynard, O. *Children and Dance and Music.* New York: Scribners, 1968.

Russel, J. *Creative Dance in the Primary School.* London: Macdonald and Evans, 1965.

Stecher, M. B., and H. McElheny. *Music and Movement Improvisation, Threshold Early Learning Library,* vol. 4. New York: Macmillan, 1972.

Stinson, S. W. Movement as creative interaction with the child. *Young Children,* 1977, *32* (6):49–53.

Chapter 20 TEACHERS AND PARENTS WORK TOGETHER

Auerback, A. *Parents Learn through Discussion: Principles and Practices of Parent Group Education.* New York: Wiley, 1968.

Auerback, S., and L. Freedman. *Choosing Child Care: A Guide for Parents.* San Francisco: Parents and Child Care Resources, 1976.

Benedek, T. Parenthood as a developmental phase. *Journal of the American Psychoanalytic Association,* 1959, 7:389–417.

Bigner, J. J. *Parent-Child Relations.* New York: Macmillan, 1979.

Caplan, F., ed. *The Parenting Advisor.* Garden City, N.Y.: Anchor Press, 1977.

Chess, S., A. Thomas, and H. G. Birch. *Your Child Is a Person.* New York: Viking, 1965.

Curtis, J. *A Parents' Guide to Nursery Schools.* New York: Random House, 1971.

Emmerich, W. The parental role: A functional-cognitive approach. *Monographs of the Society for Research in Child Development,* 1969, *34* (8):132.

Ginott, H. G. *Between Parent and Child: New Solutions to Old Problems.* New York: Avon, 1969.

Goldman, R., and D. W. Champagne. Kibbutz Zafone, Northern Israel: Some speculations on parent-school-child interactions. *Children Today,* 1975, *4* (2):27–29.

Gordon, I., and W. Brievagel, *Building Effective Home-School Relationships.* Englewood Cliffs, N.J.: Prentice-Hall, 1974.

Grollman, E. A. *Explaining Divorce to Children.* Boston: Beacon Press, 1969.

Grollman, E. A. *Explaining Death to Children.* Boston: Beacon Press, 1967.

Harns, T. O., and D. Cryer. Parent Newsletter: A New Format. *Young Children,* 1978, *33* (5):28–32.

Honig, A. *Parent Involvement in Early Childhood Education,* rev. ed. Washington, D.C.: National Association for the Education of Young Children, 1979.

Issacs, S. *Troubles of Children and Parents.* New York: Schocken Books, 1973. (Originally published, 1948.)

It's Time To Stand Up for Your Children. Washington, D.C.: Children's Defense Fund, 1979.

Kastenbaum, R., and R. B. Arsenberg. *Psychology of Death.* New York: Springer, 1972.

Katz, L. G., and E. H. Ward. *Ethical Behavior in Early Childhood Education.* Washington, D.C.: National Association for the Education of Young Children, 1978.

Lamb, M. *The Role of the Father in Child Development.* New York: Wiley, 1976.

Lane, M. B. *Education for Parenting.* Washington, D.C.: National Association for the Education of Young Children, 1975.

Lynn, D. B. *The Father: His Role in Child Development.* Belmont, Calif.: Wadsworth, 1974.

Naylor, A. K. Work with parents, team collaboration, and problem solving (in day care). In J. F. Gorman, ed., *Social and Health Needs in Childhood and Adolescence.* Berkeley, Calif.: School of Public Health, University of California, 1972.

Newman, S. *Guidelines to Parent-Teacher Coopera-*

tion in Early Childhood Education. New York: Book-Lab, 1971.

Parenting. Washington, D.C.: Association for Childhood Education, International, 1974.

Pickarts, E., and J. Fargo. *Parent Education: Toward Parental Competence.* New York: Appleton, 1971.

Rutherford, R. B., and E. Edgar. *Teachers and Parents: A Guide to Interaction and Cooperation.* Boston: Allyn and Bacon, 1979.

Spock, B. *Bringing Up Children in a Difficult Time.* New York: Norton, 1974.

Stevens, J., and M. Mathews, eds. *Mother/Child.*

Father/Child Relationships. Washington, D.C.: National Association for Education of Young Children, 1978.

Strauss, B., and F. Strauss. *New Ways to Better Meetings.* New York: Viking, 1955.

Wenig, M., and M. L. Brown. School Effort + Parent/Teacher Communication. *Young Children,* 1975, *30*:373–376.

Wolf, A. Parent education: Reminiscence and comment. In A. J. Solnit and S. Provence, eds., *Modern Perspectives in Child Development.* New York: International Universities Press, 1963.

Chapter 21 ACCEPTING OUR COMMON RESPONSIBILITIES

Bergstrom, J. M., and G. Morgan. *Issues in the Design of a Delivery System for Daycare and Child Development Services to Children and Their Families.* Washington, D.C.: Day Care and Child Development Council of America, 1975.

Clarke-Stewart, A. *Child Care in the Family: A Review of Research and Some Propositions for Policy.* New York: Academic Press, 1977.

Coles, R. *Still Hungry in America.* Cleveland, Ohio: New American Library, 1969.

Evans, E. D. *Contemporary Influences in Early Childhood Education,* 2d ed. New York: Holt, Rinehart and Winston, 1975.

Fraiberg, S. *Every Child's Birthright: In Defense of Mothering.* New York: Basic Books, 1977.

Goodlad, J. T., M. F. Klein, J. M. Novotney. *Early Schooling in the United States.* New York: McGraw-Hill, 1973.

Hymes, J. *Early Childhood Education, The Year in Review.* Carmel, Calif.: Hacienda, 1975–78.

Kammerman, S. B. *Developing a Family Impact Statement.* New York: Foundation for Child Development, 1976.

Kenniston, K., and The Carnegie Council on Children. *All Our Children: The American Family Under Pressure.* New York: Harcourt, 1977.

Levine, J. A. *Who Will Raise the Children? New Options for Fathers (and Mothers).* New York: Lippincott, 1976.

Mearing, J. S., and associates. *Working for Children: Ethical Issues beyond Professional Guidelines.* San Francisco: Jossey-Bass, 1978.

Neimeyer, J., ed. *The Role of the Family in Child Development: Implications for State Policies and Programs.* Denver: Education Commission of the States, 1976.

Robertson, J. *Hospitals and Children: A Parent's-Eye View.* New York: International Universities Press, 1962.

Robinson, N. M., H. B. Robinson, M. A. Darling, and G. Holm. *A World of Children: Daycare and Preschool Institutions.* Monterey, Calif.: Wadsworth, 1979.

Schmitt, B. D., ed. *The Child Protection Team Handbook.* New York: Garland, 1978.

U.S. Department of Labor, Women's Bureau. *Who Are the Working Mothers?* Leaflet 37 (Rev.). Washington, D.C.: U.S. Government Printing Office, 1970.

Zimiles, H. Early childhood education: A selective overview of current issues and trends. *Teachers College Record,* 1978, *79*:509–527.

INDEX